Understanding Life Now

Nina van Gorkom, Sarah Procter Abbott

2022

Published in June 2022 by:
Zolag
www.zolag.co.uk

ISBN 9781897633427

Front cover created by Shirley Trimmer
Front cover tree design by Sarah Knight

Contents

Editor's Foreward xix

Preface xxi

I Zoom Jottings 1

1 August 2020 **3**

1.1 Zoom jottings 1 3
Conditions 3
1.2 Zoom jottings 2 4
The Best Medicine 4
1.3 Zoom jottings 3 6
Taking Refuge 6
1.4 Zoom jottings 4 7
The Examination 7
1.5 Zoom jottings 5 8
Āsavas 8
1.6 Zoom jottings 6 9
What is Vinaya? 9
1.7 Zoom jottings 7 11
The Truths 11
1.8 Zoom jottings 8 12
Understanding has to Develop 12
1.9 Zoom jottings 9 14
What is Practice? 14
1.10 Zoom jottings 10 15
The Meaning of Reality 15

1.11 Zoom jottings 11 17
Can Anyone Practice? 17
1.12 Zoom jottings 12 19
Can Anyone do Anything? 19
1.13 Zoom jottings 13 20
Is there any Short-cut? 20
1.14 Zoom jottings 14 22
Why Study Pāli? 22
1.15 Zoom jottings 15 23
4 Right Understandings and 4 Right Efforts 23
1.16 Zoom jottings 16 25
What is there Now? 25
1.17 Zoom jottings 17 27
Enlightened to What? 27
1.18 Zoom jottings 18 28
Depending on Conditions 28

2 September 2020 **31**
2.1 Zoom jottings 19 31
Just do Your Best! 31
2.2 Zoom jottings 20 32
Virtue and Abandoning (Pahāna) 32
2.3 Zoom jottings 21 34
Once in Nowhere 34
2.4 Zoom jottings 22 35
The Empty World 35
2.5 Zoom jottings 23 36
Letting go of Desire for Understanding 36
2.6 Zoom jottings 24 38
Sammā Saṇkappa (Right Thinking) 38

3 October 2020 **41**
3.1 Zoom jottings 25 41
The World of Nimitta (Signs) 41
3.2 Zoom jottings 26 42
Just Once in Saṃsāra 42
3.3 Zoom jottings 27 44

The Dear Self 44
3.4 Zoom jottings 28 45
Considering the True Words 45
3.5 Zoom jottings 29 47
The Proof of Understanding 47
3.6 Zoom jottings 30 48
Wrong Practice and Rituals 48
3.7 Zoom jottings 31 50
Study the Truth Respectfully 50
3.8 Zoom jottings 32 51
Soul 51
3.9 Zoom jottings 33 53
What is Now? 53
3.10 Zoom jottings 34 54
The Chief of Experiencing 54
3.11 Zoom jottings 35 55
Dhātu (Element) 55

4 November 2020 **57**
4.1 Zoom jottings 36 57
The Value of Patience 57
4.2 Zoom jottings 37 59
Anattā & Suññāta 59
4.3 Zoom jottings 38 60
Where is the World? 60
4.4 Zoom jottings 39 61
The Raft 61
4.5 Zoom jottings 40 63
The Magic Show 63
4.6 Zoom jottings 41 64
Why Bother? 64
4.7 Zoom jottings 42 66
The Bhikkhu's Life 66
4.8 Zoom jottings 43 68
Giving to a Bhikkhu or a Beggar 68
4.9 Zoom jottings 44 70
Hearing Again and Again 70

4.10 Zoom jottings 45 72
Preparation for Understanding 72
4.11 Zoom jottings 46 74
All Gone! 74
4.12 Zoom jottings 47 75
Once in Saṃsāra! 75

5 December 2020 **77**
5.1 Zoom jottings 48 77
Nutriment (Āhāra) 77

6 January 2021 **81**
6.1 Zoom jottings 49 81
Sīla (1) 81

7 February 2021 **85**
7.1 Zoom jottings 50 85
Sīla (2) 85
7.2 Zoom jottings 51 87
Ānāpānasati 87
7.3 Zoom jottings 52 88
Kusala (wholesome) or Akusala (unwholesome) Cittas now? 88

8 March 2021 **91**
8.1 Zoom jottings 53 91
Ummagga, the "popping up" of Paññā 91
8.2 Zoom jottings 54 93
Bhava (existing) and Bhāva (nature) 93
8.3 Zoom jottings 55 95
Groups of Rūpas 95

9 April 2021 **99**
9.1 Zoom jottings 56 99
Sacca Pāramī (the perfection of truthfulness) 99
9.2 Zoom jottings 57 100
Meditation 100
9.3 Zoom jottings 58 102
Dreaming about how "I can do!" 102

9.4 Zoom jottings 59 . . . 103
Seeing in the Dark . . . 103
9.5 Zoom jottings 60 . . . 104
Loss of a Dear Sister . . . 104
9.6 Zoom jottings 61 . . . 106
Ordaining . . . 107
9.7 Zoom jottings 62 . . . 109
The Worldly Conditions . . . 109
9.8 Zoom jottings 63 . . . 111
Surgery . . . 111

II Meetings on line **113**

10 April 2020 **115**
10.1 Meeting on line, 1 . . . 115
Whatever is conditioned . . . 115
10.2 Meeting on line, 2 . . . 117
Paññā verifies the truth . . . 117
10.3 Meeting on line, 3 . . . 118
Living alone . . . 118
10.4 Meeting on line II, 1 . . . 119
Consider the present moment . . . 119
10.5 Meeting on line, II, 2 . . . 121
What is knowing Abhidhamma? . . . 121
10.6 Meeting on line, II, 3 . . . 123
Everything arises by conditions . . . 123
10.7 Meeting on line, II, 4 . . . 124
What are accumulations? . . . 124
10.8 Meeting on line, III, 1 . . . 126
Thinking of "stories" . . . 126
10.9 Meeting on line III, 2 . . . 128
We cannot hurry up . . . 128
10.10Meeting on line III, 3 . . . 129
Desire is all around . . . 129
10.11Meeting on line III, 4 . . . 131
One reality at a time . . . 131

11 May 2020 **133**
11.1 Meeting on line, III, 5 133
The four foundations of mindfulness 133
11.2 Meeting on line III, 6 136
Taking refuge 136
11.3 Meeting on line IV, 1 138
Dhamma is now 138
11.4 Meeting on line, IV, 2 140
Intoxicants and latent tendencies 140
11.5 Meeting on line, IV, 3 143
Perversity of citta 143
11.6 Meeting on line V, 1 145
Where are you now? 145
11.7 Meeting on line V, 2 146
The importance of understanding citta 146
11.8 Meeting on line, V,3 148
No one makes it (reality) arise 148
11.9 Meeting on line, VI, 1 150
Thinking about concepts and wrong view 150
11.10Meeting on line, VI, 2 151
Sacca ñāna 151
11.11Meeting on line VI, 3 154
The second noble Truth 154
11.12Meeting on line, VI, 4 156
Following the rules in the Vinaya 156
11.13Meeting on line, VII, 1 159
Understanding one characteristic 159
11.14Meeting on line VII, 2 161
Doubt 161
11.15Meeting on line, VII, 111 163
The order of the suttas 163

12 June 2020 **167**
12.1 Meeting on line IX, 1 167
Intention to kill 167
12.2 Meeting on line IX, 2 169
Being a vegetarian 169

12.3 Meeting on line IX, 3 171
What is life at this moment? 171
12.4 Meeting on line, 10, 1 174
Nimitta 174
12.5 Meeting on line X, 2 175
Truthfulness (sacca) 175
12.6 Meeting on line 10, 3 177
Everything depends on conditions 177
12.7 Meeting on line, XI, 1 178
Conventional truth 178

13 July 2020 **181**
13.1 Meeting on line XI, 2 181
Unprompted and prompted 181
13.2 Meeting on line XI, 3 183
Meanings of nimitta 183

III Saturday discussions **187**

14 July 2020 **189**
14.1 Saturday Discussion, 2 189
What is the meaning of suññāta? 189
14.2 Saturday discussion, II, 2 190
Living for what? 190
14.3 Saturday discussion, II, 3 191
Even trying to understand is lobha 191
14.4 Saturday discussion II, 4 192
Life is just: going to die each moment 192
14.5 Saturday discussion, III, 1 193
The truth is covered up, every day 193
14.6 Saturday discussion, III, 3 194
Shall we just talk about what appears now? 194
14.7 Saturday discussion III, 4 195
The perfection of truthfulness 195
14.8 Saturday discussion, IV, 1 196
Where is meditation? 196

14.9 Saturday discussion, IV, 2 198
Understanding is so precious 198

15 August 2020 201
15.1 Saturday discussion, V, 1 201
Confidence that there is no one now 201
15.2 Saturday Discussion V, 3 202
Study carefully 202
15.3 Saturday discussion V,4 204
Understand whatever appears now, naturally 204
15.4 Saturday discussion, V, 5 205
A long way to "let go" 205
15.5 Saturday discussion VI, 1 207
The pariññās 207
15.6 Saturday discussion VI, 2 208
Sacca, truthfulness 208
15.7 Saturday discussion VI, 3 210
Understanding illuminates 210
15.8 Saturday discussion VI, 4 211
Awareness of just one reality 211
15.9 Saturday discussion VI, 5 213
There is no one 213
15.10 Saturday discussion, VII, 2 214
Be truthful to the truth 214
15.11 Saturday discussion, VII, 3, 4 216
Doubt about what appears 216
Direct awareness of what? 217
15.12 Saturday discussion VII, 6 218
Clinging to the idea of "something" 218
15.13 Saturday discussion, VIII, 1 220
Understanding arises suddenly 220
15.14 Saturday discussion VIII, 2 222
Citta is pandara or clear 222
15.15 Saturday discussion, VIII, 3 223
We cannot make anything arise 223
15.16 Saturday discussion VIII, 4 224
What is the mind? 224

15.17 Saturday discussion VIII, 5 . . . 226
Paññā develops among akusala . . . 226
15.18 Saturday discussion IX, 1 . . . 227
Every citta is clear . . . 227

16 September 2020 **231**
16.1 Saturday discussion, IX, 2 . . . 231
Confidence . . . 231
16.2 Saturday discussion, IX, 3 . . . 233
The four Great Elements . . . 233
16.3 Saturday Discussion IX, 4 . . . 235
The innermost is citta . . . 235
16.4 Saturday discussion, IX, 5 . . . 237
We are like in a dream . . . 237
16.5 Saturday discussion X, 1 . . . 239
Reality appears well . . . 239
16.6 Saturday discussion X, 2 . . . 241
Not a refuge of any kind . . . 241
16.7 Saturday discussion, X, 3 . . . 242
Nobody can make seeing arise . . . 242
16.8 Saturday discussion X, 4 . . . 244
The understanding of conditions . . . 244
16.9 Saturday discussion X, 5 . . . 246
The Magician . . . 246
16.10 Saturday discussion, XI, 1 . . . 247
No expectation, no choice . . . 247
16.11 Saturday discussion XI, 2 . . . 249
What is outside? . . . 249
16.12 Saturday discussion XI, 3 . . . 251
The perfections . . . 251
16.13 Saturday discussion XI, 4 . . . 252
Saṅkhāra khandha, no one at all . . . 252
16.14 Saturday discussion XI, 5 . . . 254
Sincerity to that very moment . . . 254
16.15 Saturday discussion XI, 6 . . . 256
Where is the latent tendency? . . . 256
16.16 Saturday discussion XII, 1 . . . 258

What is enlightenment? 258
16.17 Saturday discussion, XII, 2 260
The Bodhisatta 260
16.18 Saturday discussion, XII, 3 262
What does khandha mean? 262
16.19 Saturday discussion, XII, 4 265
Is there your arm or leg? 265
16.20 Saturday discussion XII, 5 266
Without understanding it cannot be direct awareness . . 266
16.21 Saturday discussion, XII, 6 268
Saññā with diṭṭhi 268
16.22 Saturday discussion, XIII, 3 270
The truth appears only to paññā 270
16.23 Saturday discussion, XIII, 4 271
Atta saññā (wrong remembrance of self) 271

17 October 2020 **273**
17.1 Saturday discussion XIII, 5 273
Strong saññā (tira saññā) 273
17.2 Saturday discussion XIV, 1 274
The understanding of gocara 274
17.3 Saturday discussion, XIV, 2 276
Arakkha gocara is not self 276
17.4 Saturday discussion, XIV, 3 278
The five khandhas as no one 278
17.5 Saturday discussion XIV, 4 279
Appearing well 279
17.6 Saturday discussion XIV, 5 280
Understanding of anattā becomes firmer 280
17.7 Saturday discussion, XIV, 6 282
Ten perfections 282
17.8 Saturday dsicussion XV, 1 283
Ten instances of talk 283
17.9 Saturday discussion XV, 2 285
Food for paññā 285
17.10 Saturday discussion XV, 3 286
A trap of lobha 286

17.11 Saturday discussion XVI, 2 289
The four āsavas 289
17.12 Saturday discussion XVI, 3 290
Understand the truth of it, little by little 290
17.13 Saturday discussion XVI, 4 291
Each word of the Buddha can be understood 291
17.14 Saturday discussion, XVI, 5 292
Clinging to being 292
17.15 Saturday discussion XVI, 6 294
All are saṅkhārakkhandha 294

18 November 2020 **297**
18.1 Saturday discussion XVII, 1 297
What is dhamma? 297
18.2 Saturday discussion, XVII, 2 299
Upanissaya gocara is not an ordinary object 299
18.3 Saturday discussion XVII, 3 300
Attā, something 300
18.4 Saturday discussion XVII, 4 302
The function of the brain 302
18.5 Saturday discussion XVII, 5 304
The world of nimitta 304
18.6 Saturday discussion XVII, 6. 305
Not moving away 306
18.7 Saturday discussion, XVIII, 2 307
Fantasy 307
18.8 Saturday discussion, XVIII, 3 309
The ocean 309
18.9 Saturday discussion, XVIII, 4 311
Viriya 311
18.10 Saturday discussion, XVIII, 5 313
Viriya and saddhā 313
18.11 Saturday discussion, XVIII, 6 314
The bonds yoke one to existence 314
18.12 Saturday discussion, XIX, 1 316
There is "something" all the time 316
18.13 Saturday discussion XIX, 3 318

Lobha is there all the time, to hinder 318
18.14 Saturday discussion XIX. 4 319
Is there now dukkha? 319
18.15 Saturday discussion, XIX, 5 321
Impermanence is dukkha 321
18.16 Saturday discussion XX, 1 323
One moment of experiencing an object 323
18.17 Saturday discussion XX, 2 325
Understanding will let go clinging 325
18.18 Saturday discussion XX, 3 326
All pāramīs (come) from understanding 326
18.19 Saturday discussion, XX,4 327
Dhammāyatana 327
18.20 Saturday discussion, XX, 5 328
Ārammaṇa 328
18.21 Saturday discussion, XXI, 1 329
What is touched now? 329

19 December 2020 **331**
19.1 Saturday discussion XXI, 2 331
Patience develops 331
19.2 Saturday discussion XXI, 4 333
The eye-door covers up the mind-door 333
19.3 Saturday discussion XXI, 5 334
Jhāna is dukkha 334
19.4 Saturday discussion XXII, 1 336
Four nāma-khandhas are taken for self 336
19.5 Saturday discussion, XXII, 2 338
No being in this world 338
19.6 Saturday discussion, XXII, 3 340
No self to be lost 340
19.7 Saturday discussion, XXII, 4 341
Three kinds of bodhisatta 341
19.8 Saturday discussion XXIII, 2 343
Truthfulnes 343
19.9 Saturday discussion, XXIII, 3 345
The truth of reality conditions more mettā 345

19.10 Saturday discussion XXIII 4 346
Paññā is difficult 346
19.11 Saturday discussion, XXIII, 5 347
Remorse about something that happened 347
19.12 Saturday discussion XXIV, 1 349
Worldly beings are like mad people 349
19.13 Saturday discussion, XXIV, 2 350
Different levels of sati 350
19.14 Saturday discussion XXIV, 3 351
This moment is Abhidhamma 351
19.15 Saturday discussion, XXIV, 4 353
Anattāness is there, every moment 353
19.16 Saturday discussion XXV, 1 355
The less idea of "I", the easier life is 355
19.17 Saturday discussion, XXV, 2 356
Dhamma is to understand, not just to listen 356
19.18 Saturday discussion XXV, 3 358
Being without akusala is the best 358
19.19 Saturday discussion XXV, 4 359
Satipaṭṭhāna 359
19.20 Saturday discussion, XXV, 5 360
Begin and begin again and again 360

20 January 2021 **363**
20.1 Saturday discussion XXVI, 1 363
Nothing to something to nothing 363
20.2 Saturday discussion, XXVI, 2 365
What is seen? 365
20.3 Saturday discussion, XXVI, 3 367
Dhamma means: no thing 367
20.4 Saturday discussion, XXVI,5 369
Lastingness 369
20.5 Saturday discussion XXVI, 6 370
Being tired 370
20.6 Saturday discussion XXVII, 1 371
Wholesomeness 371
20.7 Saturday discussion XXVII, 2 373

Saṅkhāra dhammas, conditioned dhammas 373
20.8 Saturday discussion XXVII, 3 374
What did the Buddha enlighten? 374
20.9 Saturday discussion XXVII, 4 376
How to live our life? 376
20.10Saturday discussion, XXVII, 5 377
The right beginning 377
20.11Saturday discussion XXVII, 6 377
Nimitta and anubyancana 377
20.12Saturday discussion, XXVIII, 1 379
Always "I" who sees, hears, thinks 379
20.13Saturday discussion XXVIII, 2 380
Continuity, santati 380
20.14Saturday discussion XXVIII, 3 382
The role of chanda 382
20.15Saturday discussion, XXVIII, 4 383
Thīna and middha 383
20.16Saturday discussion XXVIII, 5 384
What is seen is only that which is seen 384
20.17Saturday discussion, XXIX, 2 385
The truth is very subtle 385
20.18Saturday discussion, XXIX, 3 386
What is visible object? 386
20.19Saturday discussion, XXX, 1 387
Nekkhamma, renunciation 387

21 February 2021 **389**
21.1 Saturday discussion XXX, 2 389
Decisive support-condition 389
21.2 Saturday discussion, XXX, 3 390
Life is conditioned right now 390
21.3 Saturday discussion XXX, 4 391
Live to understand the truth 391
21.4 Saturday discussion XXXI, 1 392
What is ageing? 392
21.5 Saturday discussion XXXI,2 393
When will death come? 393

21.6 Saturday discussion . . . 394
Bahu-sutta, heard a lot . . . 394
21.7 Saturday discussion XXX, 6 . . . 395
Hearing more in the future? . . . 395
21.8 Saturday discussion XXX, 7 . . . 396
Dhammas are very subtle . . . 396
21.9 Saturday discussion, XXX, 7a . . . 397
Reality is there to be understood . . . 397
21.10 Saturday discussion XXX, 8 . . . 398
No arms and legs . . . 398
21.11 Saturday discussion, XXX, 9 . . . 400
All our thoughts are concepts . . . 400
21.12 Saturday discussion, XXXI, 2 . . . 401
Everything is gone now . . . 401
21.13 Saturday discussion XXXI, 5 . . . 402
Sīlabbata parāmāsa, wrong practice . . . 402
21.14 Saturday discussion XXXI, 7 . . . 403
Each moment is unexpected . . . 403
21.15 Saturday discussion, XXXI, 8 . . . 403
What is dukkha ariya sacca? . . . 403

22 March 2021 **405**
22.1 Saturday discussion, XXXII, 2 . . . 405
Understanding is not anyone . . . 405
22.2 Saturday discussion XXXII, 3 . . . 406
Conventional truth, sammutti sacca . . . 406
22.3 Saturday discussion, XXXII, 4 . . . 407
Who can control life? . . . 407
22.4 Saturday discussion XXXII, 5 . . . 409
Pariyatti, paṭipatti and paṭivedha . . . 409
22.5 Saturday discussion XXXII, 6 . . . 410
Realities "pop up" . . . 410
22.6 Saturday discussion, XXXIII, 1 . . . 411
The meaning of popping up . . . 411
22.7 Saturday discussion XXXIII, 2 . . . 413
What is the meaning of a good friend? . . . 413
22.8 Saturday discussion XXXIV, 1 . . . 414

The Buddha's virtues 414
22.9 Saturday discussion XXXIV, 2 415
Nāma rūpa pariccheda ñāna 415
22.10 Saturday discussion, XXXIV, 3 416
Different levels of anusaya (latent tendency) 416
22.11 Saturday Discussion XXXIV, 4 417
The best miracle 417
22.12 Saturday discussion XXXIV, 5 418
Nāma, as no one at all 418
22.13 Saturday discussion XXXV, 1 419
Appears well 419
22.14 Saturday discussion XXXV, 2 420
Do you know the Buddha? 420
22.15 Saturday discussion, XXXV, 3 422
Hiri, shame of akusala 422
22.16 Saturday discussion, XXXV, 4 423
Shame of akusala 423
22.17 Saturday discussion, XXXV, 5 425
Touching fire 425
22.18 Saturday discussion, XXXVI, 1 426
Nimitta (sign of a reality) 426
22.19 Saturday discussion, XXXVI, 2 427
Nimitta and concept 427
22.20 Saturday discussion XXXVI, 3 428
Can there be anyone moving? 428

23 April 2021 **431**
23.1 Saturday discussion XXXVI, 4 431
The danger of saṃsāra 431
23.2 Saturday discussion, XXXVI, 5 432
Kalapas 432
23.3 Saturday talk, XXXVII, 1 434
Against the stream of common thought 434
23.4 Saturday discussion XXXVII, 2 435
The uselessness of dhamma 435
23.5 Saturday discussion XXXVII, 3 436
Life is very short 436

23.6 Saturday discussion XXXVII, 4 437
Not "I" who is aware 437
23.7 Saturday discussion XXXVII, 4 438
Clinging to what is next? 438
23.8 Saturday discussion XXXVIII, 1 440
Begin again, begin again 440
23.9 Saturday discussion, XXXVIII, 2 441
The greatest kind of wholesomeness 441
23.10Saturday discussion, XXXVIII, 3 442
Atta is something 442
23.11Saturday discussion XXXVIII, 4 444
Sacca ñāna and pariyatti 444
23.12Saturday discussion XXXVIII, 5 445
Paññā is not sharp enough 445
23.13Saturday discussion XXXVIII, 6 446
Wise considering 446
23.14Saturday discussion XXXIX, 1 447
Can there be my arms, my legs? 447
23.15Saturday discussion XXXIX, 2 448
Is what is heard true? 448
23.16Saturday discussion, XXXIX, 3 449
Against the stream of common thought 449
23.17Saturday discussion XXXXI, 4 450
What are the realties? 450
23.18Saturday discussion XXXIX, 5 452
Life and death 452

24 Pāli Glossary 455

25 Books by Nina van Gorkom 469

Editor's Foreward

The aim of this book is to help the reader understand life in a way that has not been understood before.

In the natural sciences, we have different subjects: physics, chemistry, biology. These look at life, the world, through different 'lenses'.

So it is with Buddhism that we look at life, the world, through a different 'lens'. The 'lens' of the present moment.

This 'lens' does not depend on belief or hearsay because the present moment is so real. Seeing is real, it is now, hearing is real, it is now, thinking is real, it is now. However, just as in the sciences, this subject is 'deep, difficult and subtle' and so we need very careful consideration of the Buddha's word in order to not go wrong. Therefore, we need discussion and lots of it.

The book consists of 276 jottings posted onto Dhamma Study Group (dsg@groups.io), an internet group discussion list. The jottings themselves have been taken from Zoom discussions with the Dhamma Study and support Foundation, Thailand held over a period of 9 months. The original discussions are around 2 hours long and have mostly been recorded and are freely available on YouTube (dhammahometv). I also have a YouTube channel where there are shorter discussions of around 5-10 minutes, mostly taken from these discussions.

I have structured the jottings in chapters according to month for each author. This can help the reader research more on each topic from either dsg or YouTube. I have also added the subtitles to Nina van Gorkom's jottings.

The book is suitable for the beginner, but with a caveat. It is difficult and takes great patience over a long period of time to appreciate. It is an impressive piece of work but only for those who have persevered with its meaning.

I would like to thank Acharn Sujin Boriharnwanaket, Nina van Gorkom, Sarah and Jonothan Abbott and the Dhamma and Support Foundation who have helped me glimpse the depth and subtlety of this great teaching.

With much gratitude and appreciation, I share this work with a wider audience.

Alan Weller

Preface

When our trips to Vietnam, Taiwan, Thailand to share and study the Dhamma were cancelled due to Covid 19, we started to run Zoom discussions at the request of many friends. We were delighted that Ajahn Sujin was able to join these zoom discussions and to take the lead. They have been extremely beneficial to many people around the world.

The following jottings I've made and quotes Nina has given are based on these Zoom talks.

They are all about the truth of life at the present moment as taught by the Buddha. They are for anyone with an interest in learning more about what is most precious in life: the understanding of what is real now as opposed to what we assume to be real.

The beginning of the Path is the understanding of life now, little by little. The Teachings of the Buddha are unique in revealing that each conditioned reality in life is not only impermanent and unsatisfactory but also anattā, not self.

Sarah

Part I

Zoom Jottings

1
August 2020

1.1 Zoom jottings 1

Sarah Procter Abbott
08/04/20 #164078

Conditions

Friends

A friend, Jeff, had made a comment about giving more to people we meet.

Ajahn Sujin stressed that giving or not giving is by conditions, no matter what, not by anyone's control.

Understanding this is the only way that there will be less clinging, less attachment. If we try to change what is experienced the idea of "I" is there again.

Don't regret! Don't think about the past or future!
All conditioned dhammas are gone instantly or have not yet come!

> "Let not a person revive the past
> Or on the future build his hopes;
> For the past has been left behind
> And the future has not been reached.
> Instead with insight let him see
> Each presently arisen state."
>
> *Majjhima Nikāya 131 A Single Excellent Night (translated by Bhikkhu Ñāṇamoli & Bhikkhu Bodhi)*

Sarah

1.2 Zoom jottings 2

Sarah Procter Abbott
08/06/20 #164095

The Best Medicine

Friends

I had minor surgery yesterday and now the day at the hospital seems like a dream. It's all gone. Apparently during the surgery I was in some pain and asked the doctor to stop the operation at one point but afterwards I had no recollection of it. It's just like a nightmare which is forgotten when one wakes up or like experiences in former lives which we don't remember at all.

In one of the sessions Ajahn was referring to how good or bad situations don't belong to us. Whatever fortune or misfortune, happiness or unhappiness arises, it's just there for a moment. The world is just for a moment now and then gone completely.

When there is more understanding of the momentariness of dhammas (realities) in life as anattā (not self) there is freedom from the bondage of taking these worldly conditions (happiness and unhappiness, fame and insignificance, praise and blame, gain and loss) for something significant.

All day there is the taking of what is impermanent for permanent, what is not self for self, what is foul for beautiful and what is unsatisfactory for satisfactory. These are the perversions of thinking, memory and views, the vipallāsas as we read in the Vipallāsa Sutta:

> "Perceiving permanence in the impermanent, perceiving pleasure in what is suffering, perceiving a self in what is non-self, and perceiving attractiveness in what is unattractive, beings resort to wrong views, their minds deranged, their perception twisted.
>
> Such people are bound by the yoke of Mara, and do not reach security from bondage. Beings continue in saṃsāra, going to birth and death.
>
> But when the Buddhas arise in the world, sending forth a brilliant light, they reveal this Dhamma that leads to the stilling of suffering.
>
> Having heard it, wise people have regained their sanity. They have seen the impermanent as impermanent and what is suffering as suffering.
>
> They have seen what is non-self as non-self and the unattractive as unattractive. By the acquisition of right view, they have overcome all suffering."
>
> *Aṅguttara Nikāya 4:49 (9) Inversions (Translated by Bhikkhu Bodhi)*

In reality there is no hospital, no surgery, no good or bad situation. There are just dhammas arising by their particular conditions and falling away instantly.

Understanding the truth as taught by the Buddha about the present moment is really the best medicine at any time.

Sarah

1.3 Zoom jottings 3

Sarah Procter Abbott
08/07/20 #164109

Taking Refuge

Friends

Taking refuge means understanding the words of the Buddha, understanding that there is no self. No one can condition right understanding. A moment of understanding is taking refuge. The more understanding of the meaning of his words, the greater the refuge.

The refuge has to always be now. Don't mind which reality is experienced. Whatever arises is gone instantly. There can only ever be the understanding of what is experienced at this very moment.

A Vietnamese friend asked a question about the rule of behaviour for monks with regard to walking with eyes downcast. Like other rules to be followed, this can either be with attachment or with understanding of the right path. Just following conventional ideas about walking with downcast eyes with attachment doesn't lead to any understanding. The same applies to other rules if there is just the following of them without understanding the purpose of the Teachings. The purpose is always for the development of awareness and understanding of what appears now.

We read in the Visuddhimagga about "guarding" with awareness:

> "What is (proper) resort as guarding? Here 'A bhikkhu, having entered inside a house, having gone into a street, goes with downcast eyes, seeing the length of a plough yoke, restrained, not looking at an elephant, not looking at a horse, a carriage, a pedestrian, a woman, a man, not looking up, not looking down, not staring this way and that' (Nidd I 474). This is called (proper) resort as guarding."

Visuddhimagga 1 50 (Translated by Bhikkhu Ñāṇamoli)

When there is "guarding", sati (awareness) and understanding arise and at such moments there is no attachment to what is seen. Naturally there will be less paying attention to the details. Usually we think a lot about what is seen and build up many stories about people and things, forgetting that it is only visible object which is seen and only seeing consciousness which sees for an instant and then they are gone forever. In truth there are no elephants or horses and no people at all no matter where we look.

Sarah

1.4 Zoom jottings 4

Sarah Procter Abbott
08/07/20 #164112

The Examination

Friends

Ajahn Sujin stressed that whatever part of the Tipiṭaka it is, each word points to this moment.

Paññā (right understanding) knows what is meant by developing understanding. When a dhamma (reality) appears, nothing else appears. It knows that which experiences and that which is experienced.

Whatever arises does so by conditions. It seems normal and obvious, but the truth is very subtle.

We may be afraid of danger but whether there is danger or not, whatever the circumstances of life, there must be seeing, hearing and so on. In the deepest sense, each conditioned reality is dangerous because it arises and falls away and can be the object of clinging:

> "Friend Koṭṭhita, a virtuous bhikkhu should carefully attend to the five aggregates subject to clinging as impermanent, as suffering, as a disease, as a tumour, as a dart, as misery, as

an affliction, as alien, as disintegrating, as empty, as non-self."

Saṃyutta Nikāya 22:122 (10) Virtuous (Translated by Bhikkhu Bodhi)

Daily life is the examination. The Dhamma is not in the book! There has to be the understanding of the realities in daily life as "not me" or "mine". There has to be the understanding of the characteristic of what appears now instead of thinking about how much or how little understanding has been developed. Whatever appears and is known is according to the accumulation of understanding with no expectation of what will come next.

A friend had a birthday. The birthday is each day, each moment!

Sarah

1.5 Zoom jottings 5

Sarah Procter Abbott
08/08/20 #164122

Āsavas

Friends

There was a discussion about how in truth there is no "me" and how there are just the realities in life, those which can experience and those which can only be experienced.

Lukas: I'm not interested in dhamma.
Ajahn Sujin: Always "I".

The second ariya sacca (Noble Truth) is lobha (attachment).

Ajahn Sujin continued to talk about the 4 āsavas, (the subtle taints or defilements which ooze out instantly after seeing, hearing and so on. Three of these are kinds of lobha, the clinging to sense objects (kāmāsava), the clinging to becoming (bhāvāsava) and the clinging with wrong view (diṭṭhāsava). The other one is ignorance (avijjāsava).

Āsava refers to that which "flows out" like pus which oozes from an abscess or intoxicants which have been fermented for a long time. The taints are called āsavas because they are similar to pus oozing out and to fermented intoxicants.

> The āsavas are exuding: "from unguarded sense-doors like water from cracks in a pot, in the sense of constant trickling".
>
> *Visuddhimagga XXII 56 (Ñāṇamoli translation)*

The light of understanding refers to what can be understood at this moment as not self. When it begins to develop and there is no desire or attachment as usual, it doesn't forget this moment. It understands that whatever arises is anattā, not in anyone's control.

When there is wanting all the time, like "wanting to come back to study or have good qualities", it leads to the wrong way. It is not understanding dhammas as not self and there is attachment to the cycle of birth and death all the time.

Now, the exam is at this moment of seeing and hearing, each reality arising and falling one at a time. Life goes on by conditions.

Sarah

1.6 Zoom jottings 6

Sarah Procter Abbott
08/09/20 #164128

What is Vinaya?

Friends

A Vietnamese friend asked a question about the Vinaya and the following of rules. He said he had had discussions on this topic and he gave details about various situations and the conduct of the monks. He asked how to have more wise reflections when studying the Vinaya. He also mentioned some people find it a boring topic too.

All the rules are for the purpose of the development of satipaṭṭhāna, the development of awareness with right understanding of the Path. When paññā (right understanding) arises it knows what is meant by developing understanding of what appears. At such moments nothing else appears but the reality which is the world, the reality which experiences an object (nāma) or the reality which cannot experience anything (rūpa). Whatever part of the Tipiṭaka we read, it points to this moment, not to situations.

> "I say, friend, that by travelling one cannot know, see, or reach that end of the world where one is not born, does not grow old and die, does not pass away and get reborn. Yet I say that without having reached the end of the world there is no making an end of suffering. It is in this fathom-long body endowed with perception and mind that I proclaim (1) the world, (2) the origin of the world, (3) the cessation of the world, and (4) the way leading to the cessation of the world.
>
> The end of the world can never be reached by means of travelling [across the world]; yet without reaching the world's end there is no release from suffering.
>
> Hence the wise one, the world-knower,
> who has reached the world's end and lived the spiritual life,
> having known the world's end, at peace,
> does not desire this world or another."
>
> *Aṅguttara Nikāya 4:45 (5) Rohitassa 1 (Translated by Bhikkhu Bodhi)*

What is Vinaya? "Vineti" (the verb in Pāli) means it leads away from akusala (unwholesome states). It leads out of saṃsāra (the cycle of life) through the removal of defilements. So the Vinaya refers to the understanding which leads out of saṃsāra.

Sarah

1.7 Zoom jottings 7

Sarah Procter Abbott
08/10/20 #164133

The Truths

Friends

Nina raised the subject or wrong view. Ajahn stressed that it has to be understood as a reality. If it's not the object of understanding when it appears, it's only thinking about it.

A dhamma (reality) is not in Holland, not in Thailand, not in any place at all. It's just a reality. It's the wrong view that takes it as a self or thing or place. Only paññā (right understanding) can eradicate the idea of self as something permanent. Paññā is not self either. Whatever arises is a dhamma (reality), not self.

Sacca ñāna is the firm intellectual understanding of the Four Noble Truths beginning with the 1st Noble Truth of Dukkha (unsatisfactoriness). Dukkha is that reality which arises and falls away. The 2nd, 3rd and 4th Noble Truths can not be known if the 1st Truth is not understood. What is the truth at this moment? This moment is the 1st Truth, dukkha. The 2nd Truth is that lobha (attachment) is the cause of dukkha. It is more difficult to understand the truth of it. Any truth, any reality appearing, is to be known now otherwise there will never be even the understanding of the 1st Truth.

As we read in the 1st sermon spoken by the Buddha in the Dhammacakkappavattana Sutta:

> "This noble truth of suffering is to be fully understood."
> "This noble truth of the origin of suffering is to be abandoned."

> "This noble truth of the cessation of suffering is to be realized."
> "This noble truth of the way leading to the cessation of suffering is to be developed."

Saṃyutta Nikāya 56:11 Setting in Motion the Wheel of the Dhamma (Translated by Bhikkhu Bodhi)

> "The truth of suffering is to be compared with a disease, the truth of the origin of suffering with the cause of the disease, the truth of extinction of suffering with the cure of the disease, the truth of the path with the medicine."

Visuddhimagga XVI 87 (Translated by Bhikkhu Ñāṇamoli)

What is the purpose of listening? Each word brings about the understanding as taught by the Buddha. Paññā understands the truth as the truth. Because of attachment there's no understanding of what arises and falls away. Instead there is attachment to what has already gone or not yet come almost all the time. This is why the 2nd truth doesn't appear yet. The 4 āsavas (taints or very subtle defilements) of kāmāsava (clinging to sense objects), bhāvāsava (clinging to existing), avijjāsava (ignorance) and diṭṭhāsava (wrong view) arise after seeing and hearing all day long, quite unknown.

Sarah

1.8 Zoom jottings 8

Sarah Procter Abbott
08/11/20 #164150

Understanding has to Develop

Friends

There has been further discussion about the āsavas (taints). These are kāmāsava (clinging to sense objects), bhāvāsava (clinging to existing), avijjāsava (ignorance) and diṭṭhāsava (wrong view). The reason that the Buddha taught about these āsavas is to show how ignorance and attachment "ooze" out even in the sense door processes, long before there is any idea of anyone or anything. So even now as we read and study dhamma, there is no knowing at all about these very subtle defilements.

The understanding of anattā (not self) of all realities has to develop from intellectual right understanding to satipaṭṭhāna to vipassanā ñāna. Vipassanā ñānas refer to different levels of insight when the realities appear very clearly in succession. After the vipassanā ñānas the pariññās (understanding as realisations) apply what has been understood by the vipassanā ñānas, that which hasn't been understood clearly before. What has been realised clearly is "applied" to other objects of understanding.

In the beginning, when intellectual right understanding develops, the understanding of realities is not enough to condition direct understanding of what appears. Even when it is direct understanding, satipaṭṭhāna, the moments of understanding of dhammas as anattā are not sufficient and not clear enough to overcome doubts and wrong view.

Gradually, through the growth of right understanding there's more and more understanding that sati (awareness) is not "my awareness" and paññā (understanding) is not "my understanding. It depends on paññā to see what hinders the knowing of dhammas as realities. This hindrance is attachment and especially attachment with wrong understanding, clinging to the idea that "I can be aware" or "I can follow the path". The 2nd Noble Truth of lobha (attachment) as the cause of dukkha and life in saṃsāra cannot be known in the beginning.

With regard to the 3rd Noble Truth, dukkha nirodha (the cessation of dukkha), if there is no understanding of the 1st Truth of dukkha, how can there be the understanding of the ending of all conditioned realities, the end of dukkha? If there is no understanding of the danger of what arises and falls away there cannot be the understanding of the 3rd Truth. For this understanding there must be the understanding of the arising and falling away of dhammas by conditions. If there are no conditions, nothing arises.

"Of all those things that arise from a cause,
The Tathagata has explained the cause;
And how they cease to be has also been explained,
This is the doctrine of the Great Recluse."

"Yē dhammā hetuppabhavā
tesam hetum Tathāgato āha,
tesanca yo nirodho
evam vādī Mahāsamano tī"

Peṭakopadesa 1 (Translated by Bhikkhu Nyanaponika)

Sarah

1.9 Zoom jottings 9

Sarah Procter Abbott
08/14/20 #164182

What is Practice?

Friends

Each word of the Buddha is precious. It's now!
A friend asked about practice in a Chinese discussion.

Ajahn Sujin: What does it mean?
Answer: A standardised procedure to get something, about doing something.
AS: What is doing and what is it for?
Answer: to have more wisdom
AS: So it's "I want to get something". Is seeing "doing"? Is there anyone to do anything? When there's no understanding, what is doing?

I talked about bhāvanā, the development of understanding. It's not following a practice or anyone doing anything. It begins with understanding one word at a time. This is the beginning of understanding of paññā (right understanding) which conditions the development of all kusala (wholesome) states.

> "Bhikkhus, just as the dawn is the forerunner and precursor of the sunrise, so right view is the forerunner and precursor of wholesome qualities."
>
> *Aṅguttara Nikāya 10:121 (9) Forerunner (Translated by Bhikkhu Bodhi)*

The difference between ignorance and right understanding can be understood now. Pariyatti (intellectual right understanding) is learning to understand reality now. It must be the understanding of not self, firmer and firmer. So if someone says a self exists, this firm understanding knows it's not true.

From birth to death, there is nothing but the arising of realities, but it's unknown. If there is no understanding, there is just ignorance from birth to death for aeons and aeons, non-stop!

Sarah

1.10 Zoom jottings 10

Sarah Procter Abbott
08/15/20 #164191

The Meaning of Reality

Friends

It's essential to know the purpose of listening and considering. If it's not for understanding of whatever appears now then it's bound to be for oneself. We discussed this topic in a Chinese session.

Ajahn Sujin: What appears now?

Answer: Reflecting on what you're saying, my foot on the floor, observing hardness.

AS: Different realities or just one? Is there wanting to observe, wanting to be aware? This is just a story about realities, not the nature of reality as anattā.

Sound is just that which appears. Understand a reality as it is, not my voice or the sound of music, just sound. Gradually this is the way to eliminate the idea of something or someone, no one there at all. For example, when the sound "nāma" is heard, there's no understanding yet, but it must be different from another sound, "rūpa". The idea of "I" is there all the time because what appears is not distinguished from other realities. At the moment the sound appears, it's not the same as the meaning of the word. It doesn't appear well because there's no understanding of the sound as just sound.

There has to be understanding of the meaning of dhamma (reality). Without understanding each dhamma as it is, it won't be known that there is nothing else at all. There has to be the understanding of how the story of sound is different from the moment when sound appears.

To be truthful, is there any understanding of sound yet? There is usually ignorance of sound that is heard, there is the idea of "my" sound or the sound of music. In truth it's just sound which falls away instantly.

Life is like this from moment to moment. Each reality has its characteristic by conditions and is uncontrollable, never to return again. This is the beginning of understanding life and the world and what is meant by "dhamma". No one is there, no one is in the room, there are just different realities. When there is no understanding there is the idea of something all the time, the idea of the sound of this and that.

> "Suppose, bhikkhus, there was a king or a royal minister who had never before heard the sound of a lute. He might hear the sound of a lute and say: 'Good man, what is making this sound—so tantalizing, so lovely, so intoxicating, so entrancing, so enthralling?' They would say to him: 'Sire, it is a lute that is making this sound—so tantalizing, so lovely, so intoxicating, so entrancing, so enthralling.' He would reply: 'Go, man, bring me that lute.'

They would bring him the lute and tell him: 'Sire, this is that lute, the sound of which was so tantalizing, so lovely, so intoxicating, so entrancing, so enthralling.' The king would say: 'I've had enough with this lute, man. Bring me just that sound.' The men would reply: 'This lute, sire, consists of numerous components, of a great many components, and it gives off a sound when it is played upon with its numerous components; that is, in dependence on the parchment sounding board, the belly, the arm, the head, the strings, the plectrum, and the appropriate effort of the musician. So it is, sire, that this lute consisting of numerous components, of a great many components, gives off a sound when it is played upon with its numerous components.'

The king would split the lute into ten or a hundred pieces, then he would reduce these to splinters. Having reduced them to splinters, he would burn them in a fire and reduce them to ashes, and he would winnow the ashes in a strong wind or let them be carried away by the swift current of a river. Then he would say: 'A poor thing, indeed sir, is this so-called lute, as well as anything else called a lute. How the multitude are utterly heedless about it, utterly taken in by it!' "

Saṃyutta Nikāya 35:246 (9) The Simile of the Lute (Translated by Bhikkhu Bodhi)

In truth there never was, is or will be a lute. There is just sound that is heard and just thinking about all kinds of ideas about what is heard now.

Sarah

1.11 Zoom jottings 11

Sarah Procter Abbott
08/17/20 #164202

Can Anyone Practice?

Friends

The discussion about practice and anattā continued in a Chinese discussion,

Ajahn Sujin stressed that to understand the meaning of reality as not self, there must be the understanding of each reality. Hearing, memory, feeling, like and dislike are all suññāta and anattā. Without proper conditions they cannot arise. This is why they are anattā, uncontrollable.

Sound is not my voice and seeing is not my seeing. We need to begin to consider the words of the Buddha respectfully because it's not easy to directly understand the truth of realities.

We use many words without understanding them, such as awareness. Seeing is seeing now, not a moment ago. Without listening and considering carefully there cannot be the clear understanding of what the Buddha taught.

What is nāma now at this moment of seeing? What about understanding now? It has to be one's own understanding, not the other's. Is it direct understanding now?

"I hear", "I think", is it right? When there's no clear understanding, it cannot eradicate the idea of self. Hearing about pariyatti (intellectual right understanding) is only the story of what arises.

Can anyone practice?

> "Bhikkhus, the eye is non-self. What is non-self should be seen as it really is with correct wisdom thus: 'This is not mine, this I am not, this is not my self.'
>
> The ear is non-self... The nose is non-self... The tongue is non-self... The body is non-self... The mind is non-self. What is non-self should be seen as it really is with correct wisdom thus: 'This is not mine, this I am not, this is not my self.'
>
> "Seeing thus... He understands: '... there is no more for this state of being.' "

Saṃyutta Nikāya 35:3 (3) The Internal as Non-self (translated by Bhikkhu Bodhi)

Sarah

1.12 Zoom jottings 12

Sarah Procter Abbott
08/19/20 #164225

Can Anyone do Anything?

Friends

Ariya Kamma asked during a Chinese discussion whether we should stay in a good mood or "adjust kamma and cultivate kusala kamma". She asked how to avoid cittas which are "frustrated and inferior" and can condition disease. According to the book, one should avoid inferior states. If there is no practice, how is this possible?

Ajahn Sujin asked her if anyone can do anything or whether there are only realities. What is there now? Is there "I" now or just seeing which arises to see? Without citta, the body cannot move or do anything.

Is life "my life" or what is life now? Practice, what is it? What's the purpose of practising?

Ariya Kamma answered the purpose is to cultivate the habit to 'stay awake'. Someone else mentioned to 'manage akusala to kusala'.

What is the difference between practising and understanding? At the moment of understanding, it's clear that no one is practising. Right understanding has to be developed from moment to moment, but not by an imaginary Self. We talked further about bhāvanā (mental development), sati (awareness), paññā (understanding) and how they are not self. We also discussed awareness and awakening. When there is seeing, is there any awakening? When seeing arises, it arises with seven cetasikas (mental factors), no one can make more arise. When there's an idea of changing the reality now, it's not understanding anattā.

Only when there is firmer confidence can there be the understanding of different realities. Without careful study there's always the idea of "I want to understand". When there's more understanding about the cittas before and after seeing, gradually there's more understanding of no self. Who could make or determine what cittas arise in an eye-door process? Seeing is only a moment of experiencing no matter it's the ant's or the elephant's seeing. What is is seen is not a floor, a table or any thing at all. It's just the visible object which appears now.

> "Bhikkhus, form is non-self. For if, bhikkhus, form were self, this form would not lead to affliction, and it would be possible to have it of form: 'Let my form be thus; let my form not be thus.' But because form is non-self, form leads to affliction, and it is not possible to have it of form: 'Let my form be thus; let my form not be thus.'
>
> Feeling is non-self... Perception is non-self... Volitional formations are non-self... Consciousness is non-self. For if, bhikkhus, consciousness were self, this consciousness would not lead to affliction, and it would be possible to have it of consciousness: 'Let my consciousness be thus; let my consciousness not be thus.' But because consciousness is non-self, consciousness leads to affliction, and it is not possible to have it of consciousness: 'Let my consciousness be thus; let my consciousness not be thus.' "
>
> *Saṃyutta Nikāya 22:59 The Characteristic of Non-Self (translated by Bhikkhu Bodhi)*

Sarah

1.13 Zoom jottings 13

Sarah Procter Abbott
08/21/20 #164244

Is there any Short-cut?

Friends

We had a discussion about the First Noble Truth (ariya sacca) in a Chinese session.

This is the truth about dhammas (realities). Whatever arises is conditioned. It's dukkha (unsatisfactory). Is dukkha known to paññā? Is it the absolute truth now or just an idea? Ignorance cannot tell.

Paṭipatti doesn't mean practice at all. If there is no clear understanding of reality now, one at a time, it's impossible to understand the arising and falling away of a reality. Paṭipatti is that which reaches the particular object to be known, the direct understanding.

Ariya Kamma asked about the objects of samatha bhāvana.

Ajahn Sujin: Can samatha bhāvana understand reality now?

AK: Yes.

AS: As self.

AK: As a short-cut.

AS: Then there must have been Sammā Sambuddha before the Buddha's Teachings!

> " 'What do you think, bhikkhu, is the eye permanent or impermanent?'–'Impermanent, venerable sir'... 'Is the ear ... the nose ... the tongue ... the body ... the mind ... mind-consciousness ... mind-contact ... whatever feeling arises with mind-contact as condition–whether pleasant or painful or neither-painful-nor-pleasant, permanent or impermanent?' – 'Impermanent, venerable sir.'–'Is what is impermanent suffering or happiness?'–'Suffering, venerable sir.'–'Is what is impermanent, suffering, and subject to change fit to be regarded thus: "This is mine, this I am, this is my self?" '–'No, venerable sir.' "

Saṃyutta Nikāya 35:75 (2) Sick (translated by Bhikkhu Bodhi)

Sarah

1.14 Zoom jottings 14

Sarah Procter Abbott
08/21/20 #164245

Why Study Pāli?

Friends

Maeve asked a question about the development of the Path and accumulations in an English discussion.

Ajahn Sujin explained that the development of paññā (right understanding) understands accumulations now from moment to moment. There are always conditions for ignorance and akusala (unwholesome states) such as attachment now, but not always conditions for paññā. When there is more paññā, there are more pāramī (perfections) to understand the truth.

Maeve asked another question about the use of Pāli terms and language.

AS: What's the purpose of studying in Pāli? Can you understand Pāli better than your own language? Even in the Buddha's time could the person who spoke Pāli understand seeing consciousness? Any word which can bring about understanding of reality now is the right word. For example, seeing or cakkhu viññāna - which conditions more understanding?

As understanding grows it understands more about the depth of ignorance and attachment. Even though we are talking about dhamma, there is not understanding of the depth of dhamma. For example, we're talking about seeing but does it appear now?

Is attachment understood now?

> "Puṇṇa, there are forms cognizable by the eye that are desirable, lovely, agreeable, pleasing, sensually enticing, tantalizing. If a bhikkhu seeks delight in them, welcomes them,

> and remains holding to them, delight arises in him. With the arising of delight, Puṇṇa, there is the arising of suffering, I say. There are, Puṇṇa, sounds cognizable by the ear... mental phenomena cognizable by the mind that are desirable, lovely, agreeable, pleasing, sensually enticing, tantalizing. If a bhikkhu seeks delight in them, welcomes them, and remains holding to them, delight arises in him. With the arising of delight, Puṇṇa, there is the arising of suffering, I say."
>
> *Saṃyutta Nikāya 35:88 (5) Puṇṇa (translated by Bhikkhu Bodhi)*

Sarah

1.15 Zoom jottings 15

Sarah Procter Abbott
08/22/20 #164262

4 Right Understandings and 4 Right Efforts

Friends

In a Vietnamese discussion there was mention of the 4 sampajaññas (understandings) and also the 4 padhānas (right efforts), so I'll elaborate for anyone who had difficulty following the discussion.

Sampajañña is paññā (understanding). Sati-sampajañña refers to awareness and understanding, as referred to in the development of satipaṭṭhāna.

In brief these are:

a) **sātakkha sampajañña** - sātakkha means what is the purpose or what is beneficial. The understanding of what is beneficial or good from knowing what is the purpose of the right understanding of realities.

b) sappāya sampajañña - sappāya means what is suitable. Understanding what is suitable for the path.

c) gocara sampajañña - gocara means object (ārammaṇa) or field of experience. Here it refers to the object for right understanding, such as visible object which appears now.

d) asammoha sampajañña - asammoha is the opposite of ignorance. It refers to understanding of reality now without ignorance.

There was a question about the 4 right efforts (sammā padhāna) which are sammā vāyāma of the 8 fold Path.

1. the effort to avoid (saṃvara-padhāna)
2. the effort to overcome (pahāna-padhāna)
3. the effort to develop (bhāvanā-padhāna)
4. the effort to maintain (anurakkhaṇa-padhāna)

No self is involved from beginning to end. Viriya cetasika arises by conditions and when it arises with right understanding it is right effort.

Saṃvara-padhāna refers to the effort to avoid unwholesome states. Now at moments of wise consideration, there is such restraining from what is unprofitable or unwholesome states not yet arisen.

Pahāna-padhāna refers to the effort overcome unwholesome states. At moments of understanding, there is abandoning of unwholesome states that have arisen.

Bhāvanā-padhāna refers to the effort to develop wholesome states not yet arisen. At moments of understanding with right effort, there is the arising of profitable states not yet arisen.

Anurakkhaṇa-padhāna refers to the effort to maintain the wholesome states. The profitable states that have arisen are maintained and developed.

> "Bhikkhus, there are these four right strivings. What four? (1) Here, a bhikkhu generates desire for the non-arising of unarisen bad unwholesome states; he makes an effort, arouses

energy, applies his mind, and strives. (2) He generates desire for the abandoning of arisen bad unwholesome states; he makes an effort, arouses energy, applies his mind, and strives. (3) He generates desire for the arising of unarisen wholesome states; he makes an effort, arouses energy, applies his mind, and strives. (4) He generates desire for the persistence of arisen wholesome states, for their non-decline, increase, expansion, and fulfilment by development; he makes an effort, arouses energy, applies his mind, and strives. These are the four right strivings."

Aṅguttara Nikāya 4:13 (3) Striving (Translated by Bhikkhu Bodhi)

It may seem that such terms are in the book, but they are referring to the realities now which are conditioned at moments of right understanding.

Sarah

1.16 Zoom jottings 16

Sarah Procter Abbott
08/23/20 #164276

What is there Now?

Friends

Ngoc Dang asked a question in a Vietnamese discussion about pariyatti, reading, listening, hearing and practice, paṭipatti. Should we notice or practice?

It was pointed out that pariyatti (intellectual right) understanding from reading, listening and considering what is true begins with very little right consideration and understanding to more and more understanding. From the beginning it's not "me" or "you" who understands, but understanding arising by conditions. It leads to paṭipatti (direct) understanding and eventually to paṭivedha understanding or direct realisation, vipassanā ñāna up to enlightenment.

No matter what level of understanding it is, it must be the understanding of what appears now. This may be sound or hearing or thinking of whatever reality appears now. Usually because of ignorance it's taken for some thing or some one all the time.

Pariyatti is not just a word that we're interested to talk about, it's understanding now! Without the Teachings we don't know what is what. We just want to understand the word but don't know what it's about. When we hear the words, there can be the beginning of understanding what is there now. From not knowing anything, there is the beginning of understanding of what appears at this moment.

Another listener mentioned that inside she feels very nervous and always thinks about "I" or "you" or "he" or "she". Also, when there is anger, she tries to be aware and follow the words of the Buddha.

Ajahn Sujin: Forget about the words of the Buddha and consider what the truth is there now. There are moments of anger, seeing, thinking and so on. Can it be "I" or someone or some thing?

The way to develop understanding is to understand at this moment. What is there now? What is real now? There's no way to do anything.

Someone else asked how she can accumulate paññā?

AS: Does paññā want anything? Wanting, wishing, craving all the time. Each word should be understood as letting go! Letting go of what? Let go of craving. Whenever there is the idea of "how can I", it indicates no understanding of dhamma.

Hearing and considering leads to firmer confidence. No one can make it happen. Without khanti (patience), sacca (truthfulness), adiṭṭhāna (determination) and viriya (effort) pāramī, it's impossible to understand reality now.

Sarah

1.17 Zoom jottings 17

Sarah Procter Abbott
08/27/20 #164315

Enlightened to What?

Friends

Thao asked about meditation and the Buddha's enlightenment in a Vietnamese discussion. He asked about samatha and the intention to sit still to calm the mind.

Ajahn Sujin: Who is meditating? Can anyone meditate? Can anyone calm the mind?

T: I can do that. I will set the mind. I can clear the mind. When the Buddha understood the truth, he was sitting under the tree meditating. There is clarity of mind from sitting, relaxing.

AS: Let's consider one word at a time. He was enlightened to what? He understood the truth of what? He was enlightened to the truth of seeing, hearing, everything. So what did he say about seeing which he had been enlightened to? Is the mind dirty or clean? Some people try to make it clear or clean by some method, but it's so very dirty with ignorance.

There was a discussion about pariyatti leading to the direct understanding, satipaṭṭhāna. Bhāvanā is the development of understanding. Vipassanā is the clear understanding of realities as they are. Right understanding has to be very firm to condition the direct understanding of a reality now.

Hearing and wise considering leads to the end of ignorance and the end of all kilesa (defilements). Before hearing the Teachings, everything is "me", "I", but after hearing the Teachings that there are just realities which are gone, never to return. There is the development of the understanding of the Truth, but not yet the direct understanding. Just listen!

> "Bhikkhus, without directly knowing and fully understanding the all, without developing dispassion towards it and abandoning it, one is incapable of destroying suffering.
>
> And what, bhikkhus, is the all...?
>
> The eye and forms and eye-consciousness and things to be cognized by eye-consciousness. The ear and sounds and ear-consciousness and things to be cognized by ear-consciousness...
> The mind and mental phenomena and mind-consciousness and things to be cognized by mind-consciousness.
>
> This, bhikkhus, is the all without directly knowing and fully understanding which, without developing dispassion towards which and abandoning which, one is incapable of destroying suffering.
>
> But, bhikkhus, by directly knowing and fully understanding the all, by developing dispassion towards it and abandoning it, one is capable of destroying suffering."
>
> *Saṃyutta Nikāya 35:27 Full Understanding (2) (Translated by Bhikkhu Bodhi)*

Sarah

1.18 Zoom jottings 18

Sarah Procter Abbott
08/28/20 #164328

Depending on Conditions

Friends

Whatever arises depends on paccaya, conditions. We discussed this topic further in a Vietnamese session. Without the understanding of the various dhammas as being conditioned, there can never be the second stage of insight, the paccaya pariggaha ñāna, (the clear understanding of the conditioned nature of dhammas). There is no one at all, just kusala, akusala, vipāka (result), kiriya (inoperative) cittas and rūpas arising by various conditions.

Each word of the Buddha will lead to the understanding of what appears now, little by little. There should be no selection or expectation of what will arise, no choosing at all. The future hasn't come and the past has gone. The Buddha didn't say "Do that"! It's impossible. When it's taught by anyone to do or to try to do anything, it's not the word of the Enlightened One.

The Teachings are so subtle and profound. If this were not so, there would not be the vipassanā ñānas, the clear insights of different degrees of paṭivedha understanding.

Right understanding is the "forerunner" like the dawn. Without right understanding there can never be any development of the Path.

> "Bhikkhus, this is the forerunner and precursor of the rising of the sun, that is, the dawn. So too, bhikkhus, for a bhikkhu this is the forerunner and precursor of the breakthrough to the Four Noble Truths as the really are, that is, right view. It is to be expected that a bhikkhu with right view will understand as it really is: 'This is suffering'...'This is the way leading to the cessation of suffering.' "
>
> *Saṃyutta Nikāya 56:37 (7) The Sun (1) (Translated by Bhikkhu Bodhi)*

Sarah

2
September 2020

2.1 Zoom jottings 19

Sarah Procter Abbott
09/04/20 #164384

Just do Your Best!

Friends

In an English discussion, a friend mentioned her mother was dying in hospital and she was dependent on a breathing tube. Her mother wants her children to remove it. She wonders whether this is killing.

Ajahn Sujin reminded her that when someone dies it depends on kamma. The tube may be removed but she may continue to live or may die before it's removed. It depends on one's intention. One just does the best for one's mother at the time.

Everyone is going to die, but we don't know when. The death moment can arise anytime, even now! The best thing is to understand realities as not self, no one at all, to gradually eliminate the idea of self. When there's the idea of I, I know a lot, I know a little, there's no way to understand reality now. However, when there's understanding of reality now, death or anything can be understood as dhamma. The right intellectual understanding develops on and on to be the condition for direct understanding, not just to understand words. It's the only way to understand that each word represents reality as not self.

Jeff also mentioned world conflicts and we discussed about the worlds at each moment, through the 6 doorways. Whatever arises and falls away now is a world.

> "Then a certain bhikkhu approached the Blessed One... and said to him: "Venerable sir, it is said, 'the world, the world.' In what way, venerable sir, is it said 'the world'?"
>
> 'It is disintegrating, bhikkhu, therefore it is called the world. And what is disintegrating? The eye, bhikkhu, is disintegrating, forms are disintegrating, eye-consciousness is disintegrating, eye-contact is disintegrating, and whatever feeling arises with eye-contact as condition... that too is disintegrating. The ear is disintegrating... The mind is disintegrating... Whatever feeling arises with mind-contact as condition... that too is disintegrating. It is disintegrating, bhikkhu, therefore it is called the world.' "
>
> *Saṃyutta Nikāya 35:82 The World (Translated by Bhikkhu Bodhi)*

Sarah

2.2 Zoom jottings 20

Sarah Procter Abbott
09/08/20 #164425

Virtue and Abandoning (Pahāna)

Friends

A friend asked us in a Vietnamese discussion about virtue, abandoning (pahāna) and non-transgression. I referred to some of the different kinds of abandoning (pahāna) as given in the texts. These are:

1. Tadaṅga pahāna refers to the partial elimination of self view and vitikammma kilesa (strong defilements) through the vipassanā ñānas (insights). Ordinary kusala can be tadaṅga (temporary elimination of akusala), but it's not pahāna unless it is vipassanā ñāna which begins to abandon kilesa. Each vipassana ñāna is therefore tadaṅga pahāna.

2. Vikkambhana pahāna refers to different levels of samādhi, specifically to jhāna which temporarily suppresses and overcomes pariyuṭṭhāna (subtle) kilesa.

3. Samuccheda pahāna refers to the function of the four magga cittas to eradicate anusaya (latent tendency) kilesa at various stages when realizing Nibbāna. Samuccheda is the "cutting off".

4. Paṭippassaddhi pahāna refers to the path knowledge when any of the four magga cittas arise. The knowledge of Nibbāna is realized.

5. Nissaraṇa pahāna refers to Nibbāna itself.

Now when there is any understanding of realities, it is the beginning of the path leading to abandoning of defilements, the beginning of "abandoning" of kilesa (defilements).

> "And what are the things to be abandoned neither by body nor by speech but by having repeatedly seen with wisdom? Greed is to be abandoned neither by body nor by speech but by having repeatedly seen with wisdom. Hatred... Delusion... Anger... Hostility... Denigration... Insolence... Miserliness is to be abandoned neither by body nor by speech but by having repeatedly seen with wisdom."
>
> *Aṅguttara Nikāya, 10:23 (3) Body (Translated by Bhikkhu Bodhi)*

2.3 Zoom jottings 21

Sarah Procter Abbott
09/08/20 #164426

Once in Nowhere

Friends

"Where are we?" Ajahn Sujin asked everyone in a Vietnamese discussion. Nowhere at all! Where is seeing, just seeing? It's only the idea of somewhere. This is the way to understand about nothing, nowhere at all. Once in nowhere! Apart from the absolute truth, there is nothing else. If one thinks otherwise, there's always the idea of I am sitting somewhere, not understanding that each reality has gone completely.

The best thing is to understand what is at this moment, no "I" at all, nothing. Only such understanding can lead to the end of saṃsāra (the cycle of births and deaths). When there is no precise understanding, there cannot be the idea of no self. There has to be understanding which develops gradually. Is there the beginning of understanding at this moment? Otherwise there is always the idea of I know, I understand, I learn and I listen, when actually there is no "I" at all from the very beginning.

So where are you now? Each reality arises once in saṃsāra only.

There was a question about going forth and the meaning of nekkhamma (renunciation). No matter where you are, whenever there is no understanding there is no getting away from or renunciation of the wrong idea of self. The clinging is to sense objects and whatever is taken for self. Now if right understanding arises, it is moving away from wrong understanding little by little. It's not easy at all to take away clinging to the idea of self and things.

> "There are, Migajāla, sounds cognizable by the ear... odours cognizable by the nose... tastes cognizable by the tongue... tactile objects cognizable by the body... mental phenomena cognizable by the mind that are desirable, lovely, agreeable, pleasing, sensually enticing, tantalizing. If a bhikkhu

> seeks delight in them... he is called one dwelling with a partner.
>
> Migajala, even though a bhikkhu who dwells thus resorts to forests and groves, to remote lodgings where there are few sounds and little noise, desolate, hidden from people, appropriate for seclusion, he is still called one dwelling with a partner. For what reason? Because craving is his partner, and he has not abandoned it; therefore he is called one dwelling with a partner."
>
> *Saṃyutta Nikāya 35:61 Migajāla (1) (Translated by Bhikkhu Bodhi)*

Sarah

2.4 Zoom jottings 22

Sarah Procter Abbott
09/09/20 #164432

The Empty World

Friends

In the Vietnamese discussion, we discussed how we think we're living in the world but we're not there because there are only conditioned realities arising and falling away. Only paññā can understand the difference between the imaginary world and the world of realities arising and falling away. When reality appears, there is nothing, no person at all. Without understanding there is always something or someone.

In fact the world is empty, empty of anything or anyone.

> "Then the Venerable Ānanda approached the Blessed One... and said to him: Venerable sir, it is said, 'Empty is the world, empty is the world.' In what way, venerable sir, is it said, 'Empty is the world'?

> 'It is, Ānanda, because it is empty of self and of what belongs to self that it is said, 'Empty is the world.' And what is empty of self and of what belongs to self? The eye, Ānanda, is empty of self and of what belongs to self. Forms are empty of self and of what belongs to self. Eye-consciousness is empty of self and of what belongs to self. Eye-contact is empty of self and of what belongs to self... Whatever feeling arises with mind-contact as condition—whether pleasant or painful or neither-painful-nor-pleasant—that too is empty of self and of what belongs to self.
>
> It is, Ānanda, because it is empty of self and of what belongs to self that it is said, 'Empty is the world.' "
>
> *Saṃyutta Nikāya 35:85 (2) (Translated by Bhikkhu Bodhi)*

There is nothing to do at all, just listen to the right words of the Buddha until there is confidence in what appears now as it is. The flux of the arising and falling away of each reality covers up the truth there's nothing at all, just the rapidity of the arising and falling of realities, changing all the time. So life goes along by conditions quite unknown until there is understanding of what it is.

It's so useless to cling because there is no one at all and the object of clinging has already fallen away.

Sarah

2.5 Zoom jottings 23

Sarah Procter Abbott
09/25/20 #164613

Letting go of Desire for Understanding

Friends

There was a question about attaining vipassanā (clear insight) in the Vietnamese discussion. It was stressed that there must be the understanding of reality now. The understanding has to develop on and on.

Is there enough intellectual understanding to become just a little detached from that which hears now? If there is not enough intellectual understanding it cannot condition satipaṭṭhāna, the direct understanding and awareness which has to arise by conditions. Now it is "I" who thinks about hearing and about attaining vipassanā. This is because there's not enough understanding that in truth now there's just a moment of experiencing sound and then it's gone.

It takes time to understand that it's always a dhamma, a reality, which experiences an object, no matter what.

Instead of thinking about vipassanā, what about understanding more and more about what appears now? This is the way to become detached from wanting to understand. Know that everything in life is right now, non-stop. Nothing can be taken for "I" or something permanent at all.

There has to be the letting go of the wanting or desire to understand what appears. Hearing, considering and understanding develop little by little. If it's not this way it's sīlabbataparāmāsa, wrong practice.

> "Suppose, bhikkhus there was a hen with eight, ten, or twelve eggs that she had not covered, incubated, and nurtured properly. Even though such a wish as this might arise in her: 'Oh, that my chicks might pierce their shells with the points of their claws and beaks and hatch safely!' yet the chicks are incapable of piercing their shells with the points of their claws and beaks and hatching safely. For what reason? Because that hen with eight, ten, or twelve eggs had not covered, incubated, and nurtured them properly.
>
> So too, bhikkhus, when a bhikkhu does not dwell devoted to development, even though such a wish as this might arise in him: 'Oh, that my mind might be liberated from the taints by non-clinging!' yet his mind is not liberated from the taints by non-clinging. For what reason? It should be said: because of non-development what? Because of not developing. . . the Noble Eightfold Path."

Saṃyutta Nikāya 22:101 The Ship (Translated by Bhikkhu Bodhi)

2.6 Zoom jottings 24

Sarah Procter Abbott
09/25/20 #164614

Sammā Saṇkappa (Right Thinking)

Friends

There was a question from Duong Tuan in a Vietnamese discussion about sammā saṇkappa, right thinking.

We are discussing vitakka cetasika. At moments of seeing and hearing, no vitakka arises. After these cittas, vitakka is like the "foot of the world" and is needed to experience the object. It "touches" or leads to the object. In the sense door processes the following cittas experience the same object as seeing or hearing because of vitakka leading them to experience that visible object or sound.

When it's right vitakka, sammā saṇkappa, it arises with the citta with paññā, right understanding. If vitakka doesn't touch the object and sati isn't aware of it, paññā cannot arise. Sammā saṇkappa (right thinking) and sammā diṭṭhi (right understanding) make up the understanding part of the 8-fold path. Right vitakka therefore develops to be sammā saṇkappa

All realities are anattā. Learning to consider the truth and hear the truth is right thinking.

We live in the world of nimitta (signs on account of different realities arising and falling away in such rapid succession). All the nimitta are taken for some thing or some one. However, the words of right thinking are that all dhammas are anattā, arising and falling away just for an instant. They are so brief and fleeting like bubbles.

We read again and again about the transience and corelessness of dhammas.

> "When the several truths, aspects of dependent origination, methods, and characteristics have become evident to him thus, then formations appear to him as perpetually renewed: 'So these states, it seems, having previously unarisen, arise,

> and being arisen, they cease'. And they are not only perpetually renewed, but they are also short-lived like dew-drops at sunrise (A.iv,137), like a bubble on water (A. iv,137), like a line drawn on water (A.iv,137)), like a mustard seed on an awl's point (Nd.143), like a lightning flash. (Nd.143)"
>
> *Visuddhimagga XX 104 (Translated by Bhikkhu Ñānamoli)*

Sarah

3
October 2020

3.1 Zoom jottings 25

Sarah Procter Abbott
10/01/20 #164692

The World of Nimitta (Signs)

Friends

Nina asked a question about nimitta in an English discussion.

Ajahn asked her what is seen now. Is it visible object or people now? What is seen conditions different shapes and forms so that what appears is something with many details. That is nimitta.

One reality cannot appear, so from birth to death it's the world of nimitta which appears. Reality is not known at all before the Buddha's enlightenment. Each reality appears as nimitta because of the rapidity of the arising and falling away of each one.

What is experienced now is nothing, but there is always the idea of something. Everything is nothing. Everything is nimitta. It's only the image of that which has been conditioned. There is the wrong idea of something permanent and there is clinging to nimitta but it's only the nimitta, no one, no thing. What is left from the flux of rūpa, saññā and other realities are just nimittas but each reality has completely gone. There is no one. We refer to the nimitta anubyañjana (signs and details) as trees, branches and so on but they are not the actual realities which have arisen and fallen away.

> "And what, bhikkhus, is the Dhamma exposition on the theme of burning? It would be better, bhikkhus, for the eye faculty to be lacerated by a red-hot iron pin burning, blazing, and glowing, than for one to grasp the sign (nimitta) through the features (anubyañjana) in a form cognizable by the eye."
>
> Commentary note: "One grasps the sign through the features' (anubyajanaso nimittaggāho) thinking: 'The hands are beautiful, so too the feet, etc.' "
>
> *Saṃyutta Nikāya 35:235 The Exposition on Burning (Translated by Bhikkhu Bodhi)*

Sarah

3.2 Zoom jottings 26

Sarah Procter Abbott
10/01/20 #164693

Just Once in Saṃsāra

Friends

Lukas raised some questions about awareness in an English discussion. Ajahn Sujin reminded him not to mind about the awareness but to understand what appears now. "Don't try to detect whether it's that which understands or not. Life is just in a moment of experiencing." She also reminded him to be firm about dhammas as anattā. "Just live naturally, as usual, otherwise lobha is there unknown."

Lukas said he day-dreams all the time.

Ajahn Sujin asked about understanding.

L: Only a bit, not all the time.

AS: Is there understanding of the word or the reality now?

L: It's easy to think about the word. There needs to be sati (awareness) to help understand, otherwise it's only intellectual.

AS: So you understand the word "awareness" but you have doubt whether there is awareness.

L: My point is that I don't have any motivation.

AS: Are you interested in knowing what awareness is or whether there is awareness?

L: I'm worried that if there is not awareness there will be a bad rebirth.

AS: What about seeing now? Should everything be the object of understanding? There is no choice, no selection. There is reality no matter what. If there is no understanding, there is no awareness of a reality, one at a time. What is known now? Or do you just want to know awareness, to have awareness?

L: I know what you mean.

AS: No I, there is only a moment of experiencing. Sabbe dhammā anattā. (All realitiies are not self). There is no one, no self, no me. Without awareness there is no understanding. We should not crave or want to have understanding because it's not self, not me, not under my control. There are just different realities appearing by different conditions. This (understanding) will lead to more understanding and confidence of realities as anattā, no wishing or hoping to know this or that because there is no one at all, just different realities. Right awareness of the eightfold path is not just understanding words that condition understanding. That's the wrong idea.

What is real now? There is a new one and another new one and it appears just once in saṃsāra. No one can do anything at all. The seeing now - who makes it arise? The (idea of) self just wants to understand this or that but the only way is to become detached, little by little, detached from taking everything for a permanent reality. It's much shorter (than one imagines) but because of nimitta it appears as something.

> "Bhikkhus, all is burning. And what, bhikkhus, is the all that is burning? The eye is burning, forms are burning, eye-consciousness is burning, eye-contact is burning, and whatever feeling arises with eye-contact as condition—whether pleasant or painful or neither-painful-nor-pleasant—that too is burning. Burning with what? Burning with the fire of lust, with the fire of hatred, with the fire of delusion; burning with birth, ageing, and death; with sorrow, lamentation, pain, displeasure, and despair, I say.
>
> The ear is burning... The mind is burning... and whatever feeling arises with mind-contact as condition—whether pleasant or painful or neither-painful-nor-pleasant—that too is burning. Burning with what? Burning with the fire of lust, with the fire of hatred, with the fire of delusion; burning with birth, ageing, and death; with sorrow, lamentation, pain, displeasure, and despair, I say."
>
> *Saṃyutta Nikāya 35:28 (6) Burning (Translated by Bhikkhu Bodhi)*

Sarah

3.3 Zoom jottings 27

Sarah Procter Abbott
10/02/20 #164718

The Dear Self

Friends

Lukas mentioned he lacked the motivation to practice and had no goal. Ajahn Sujin responded by saying this was the idea of self. Usually there is pre-occupation, the obsession with the self most of the day.

> "Having explored all quarters with the mind, one would simply not attain that dearer than the self in any place; thus is the self dear separately to others - therefore one desiring self should not harm another."

Udāna 5:1 "Dear" (Translated by Peter Masefield)

The proof of the Teachings is the understanding of whatever appears now.

There was some discussion about the meaning of paṭipatti. It refers to the reaching (patti) of the particular (paṭi) object (with understanding), paṭipatti. It is not the following of a practice or method.

It's easy to say that everything is anattā but what about "there's no I", "all dhammas are not me" in your own language? Not "me", not anything at all. Understanding leads closer and closer to what appears, to the truth now. Whatever arises and falls away in the world is just a reality.

Life is just in a moment, from moment to moment. It's not me! When it seems to be more than a moment, it's me! There are conditions for dhammas to go on and on. This is understanding dhamma. Without dhammas, there's no world at all. What is taken for the sun or moon or anything are dhammas which arise and fall away all the time.

Sarah

3.4 Zoom jottings 28

Sarah Procter Abbott
10/02/20 #164719

Considering the True Words

Friends

An Le asked a question in an English discussion about the development of understanding and the danger of ignorance.

At a moment of understanding there is no mohā (Ignorance), but when there is no understanding, mohā is there. When there is understanding it is true and sincere.

All dhammas are anattā (not self). What about sincerity? It all depends on understanding from considering the true words, from hearing more and more so that understanding will be firmer and more confident in the truth.

> "At Savatthı. Bhikkhus, before my enlightenment, while I was still a bodhisatta, not yet fully enlightened, it occurred to me: 'What is the gratification, what is the danger, what is the escape in the case of form? What is the gratification, what is the danger, what is the escape in the case of feeling... perception... volitional formations... consciousness?'
>
> Then, bhikkhus, it occurred to me: 'The pleasure and joy that arise in dependence on form: this is the gratification in form. That form is impermanent, suffering, and subject to change: this is the danger in form. The removal and abandonment of desire and lust for form: this is the escape from form.'
>
> 'The pleasure and joy that arise in dependence on feeling... in dependence on perception... in dependence on volitional formations ... in dependence on consciousness: this is the gratification in consciousness. That consciousness is impermanent, suffering, and subject to change: this is the danger in consciousness. The removal and abandonment of desire and lust for consciousness: this is the escape from consciousness.' "
>
> *Saṃyutta Nikāya 26:5 Gratification (Translated by Bhikkhu Bodhi)*

3.5 Zoom jottings 29

Sarah Procter Abbott
10/04/20 #164738

The Proof of Understanding

Friends

In a Vietnamese discussion, Nga Hoa raised the topic of sīla for monks and purifying the mind as taught in the Visuddhimagga. She mentioned that wearing brown robes was a reminder about being a monk, so that the mind would not wander as usual. The topic of sīlabbataparāmāsa (clinging to rituals with wrong view) was also raised.

Ajahn Sujin asked everyone if there can there be understanding of what a monk is if there is no understanding of the truth. She said not to mind about what is in the Visuddhimagga or Tipiṭaka because the truth is all about now. There must be patience to understand the truth at this moment.

What is appearing now is not known so there cannot be understanding of what a Bhikkhu is or what is sīlabbataparāmāsa. No one knows the truth so the idea or what is read is wrongly taken for something like sīlabbataparāmāsa, (wrong practice and rituals) instead of understanding the words of the Buddha about now!

If this moment is known as it is, is seeing a monk? Is sīlabbataparāmāsa a monk? If there's no understanding of what appears it's useless to talk about other things because they don't bring any understanding about the present reality appearing now.

The point is not just reading about different dhammas but understanding what appears now as not self, not anything. If there is doubt about sīlabbataparāmāsa it means there's no understanding of this moment.

It was also stressed that the proof of understanding is whether there is such understanding of reality now and whether it's understood that no one one can make such realities arise. Otherwise we're just talking about that which appears without understanding at all.

> "A peaceful bhikkhu: peaceful through the stilling of lust, the stilling of hatred, the stilling of delusion, the stilling of anger, hostility, denigration, insolence, envy, miserliness, hypocrisy, deceitfulness, obstinacy, vehemence, conceit, arrogance, vanity, and heedlessness; of all defilements, all misconduct, all disturbances, all fevers, all afflictions, all unwholesome volitional activities."
>
> *Suttanipāta 4:3 Niddesa I 50, Commentary to The Octad on the Hostile, (Translated by Bhikkhu Bodhi)*

Sarah

3.6 Zoom jottings 30

Sarah Procter Abbott
10/14/20 #164879

Wrong Practice and Rituals

Friends

In the Vietnamese discussion we considered more about understanding at this moment. This followed the earlier questions about sīlabbataparāmāsa (wrong practice). Nga Hoa asked about understanding whilst reading books, going to the beach or swimming.

Ajahn Sujin asked her whether there can be understanding of what appears now as it is. When there's understanding, there's no sīlabbataparāmāsa.

It's important to just listen to the truth about life now and consider carefully whether it's true or not. When there's no understanding, who can understand the truth? When it's not this way, it's all sīlabbataparāmāsa. One tries and it's the story of "I" at such times.

If there's no avijjā (Ignorance), there's no akusala (unwholesomeness), no misunderstanding about what appears now, no idea of a thing at all. The right understanding is the opposite of attānūdiṭṭhi (the wrong understanding of self and things). It's the wrong understanding which leads to sīlabbataparāmāsa. No matter how many different wrong views there are, they all come from sakkāya diṭṭhi (self view) and attānūdiṭṭhi as base.

> "As to the various views that arise in the world, householder, 'The world is eternal' or 'The world is not eternal'; or 'The world is finite' or 'The world is infinite'; or 'The soul and the body are the same' or 'The soul is one thing, the body is another'; or 'The Tathāgata exists after death,' or 'The Tathāgata does not exist after death,' or 'The Tathāgata both exists and does not exist after death,' or 'The Tathāgata neither exists nor does not exist after death' these as well as the sixty-two speculative views mentioned in the Brahmajāla: when there is identity view (sakkāya diṭṭhi) these views come to be; when there is no identity view, these views do not come to be."
>
> "But, venerable sir, how does identity view come to be?" "Here, householder, the uninstructed worldling, who has no regard for the noble ones and is unskilled and undisciplined in their Dhamma, who has no regard for the good persons and is unskilled and undisciplined in their Dhamma, regards form as self, or self as possessing form, or form as in self, or self as in form. He regards feeling as self... perception as self... volitional formations as self... consciousness as self, or self as possessing consciousness, or consciousness as in self, or self as in consciousness. It is in such a way that identity view comes to be."

Saṃyutta Nikāya 41:3 Isidatta (2) (Translated by Bhikkhu Bodhi)

Long asked a question about the computer screen we're looking at. We discussed more about the āsavas, the taints or very subtle kinds of attachment, ignorance and wrong view which "ooze out" even in the sense door processes. Usually there's always "I" or something there all the time, even before what is seen is known as a computer or table.

Sarah

3.7 Zoom jottings 31

Sarah Procter Abbott
10/15/20 #164891

Study the Truth Respectfully

Friends

Sakkaccabhāvanā means to study the truth respectfully. Such respect for the truth develops in a moment when there is more understanding, little by little. This topic was discussed in the Vietnamese session. As long as there are no conditions for understanding there has to be truthfulness that there is none at all. It means there are no conditions for sati (awareness) of anattā (non-self) now.

Gradually there will be more and more confidence in realities as being anattā. The development of understanding is the only way to gradually eliminate the idea of self. Otherwise there is sīlabbataparāmāsa (wrong practice). Right understanding understands the difference between the right and the wrong paths, otherwise it's not the right path. It's very subtle and takes a long time to eradicate the idea of self and things. The understanding has to be keener and keener, sharper and sharper. When there is no sammā diṭṭhi (right understanding) we live in darkness.

There is no rule about place or time but there can be understanding of seeing now, that reality which just experiences.

We can read about sakkaccabhāvanā in the commentary in the Cariyapiṭaka. These four kinds of bhāvanā referred to:

1. Sabbasambhāra-bhāvanā : developing all kinds of kusala
2. Nirantara-bhāvanā : continuous developing of kusala
3. Cīrakāla-bhāvanā : endless developing of kusala
4. Sakkacca-bhāvanā : developing with respect of kusala

In the Cariyapiṭaka commentary it mentions how 1) sabbasambhāra-bhāvanā is the complete development of all the Perfections, (2) nirantara-bhāvanā is the development of the Perfections throughout countless asankhyeyya (epochs or great aeons) and aeons without a break of even a single existence, (3) cīrakāla-bhāvanā is the endless development of the Perfections for a long duration of asankheyya and aeons; and (iv) sakkacca-bhāvanā is development of Perfections with respectfulness and truthfulness.

Sarah

3.8 Zoom jottings 32

Sarah Procter Abbott
10/16/20 #164898

Soul

Friends

Da-Zhuang asked what the difference is between "citta" and "soul".

Ajahn Sujin: The best thing is to understand what is now. Begin to understand what is clear now. Is there anything now?

DZ: Many things like seeing, visible object, hearing and sound.

AS: All around, but no understanding, is that right? For example, seeing now, but no understanding of seeing which sees now. Can the tree see? Can the table see? Seeing is that which experiences and knows the object seen only. The object appears because of seeing. Is seeing real? Does it arise? If it doesn't arise, can there be that which is seen?

We discussed how there are two different realities, one which arises to experience an object and one which doesn't experience anything. There is seeing and hearing all through life from birth to death. If there were no seeing or hearing could we say there is "I" now? What we call life are just different kinds of experience from moment to moment. If there was no experiencing, there would be no life at all now. Life is whatever appears at each moment. Each one is conditioned, not arising at anyone's will.

Only at the moment of seeing is there seeing. Only at the moment of hearing is there hearing and sound experienced, never to return, only arising once in saṃsāra (the cycle of birth and death). So life is that which can experience and that which cannot experience. In life there are different moments of experience until the end of life, but that's not the end of realities arising.

Citta is that which experiences whatever appears. In the absolute truth, there is no one at all, just conditioned realities arising from moment to moment, life to life. What is left is only shape and form, taken for a permanent thing because of the rapidity of the arising and falling away. What are taken for people and things are just different realities arising and falling away.

> "Theravadin - Is the concept of soul (puggala) derived from the corporeal qualities (rūpas)?
>
> Puggalavadin - Yes.
>
> T: But has a soul also any or all of these qualities?
>
> P: Nay, that cannot truly be said....
>
> T: Or is the concept of soul derived from feeling, from perception, from mental coefficients, from consciousness?
>
> P: Yes (to each aggregate in succession).
>
> T: Is any mental aggregate impermanent, conditioned? Does it happen through a cause? Is it liable to perish, to pass away, to become passionless, to cease, to change?
>
> P: Yes.
>
> T: But has soul also any of these qualities?
>
> P: Nay, that cannot truly be said..."
>
> *Kathāvatthu (Points of Controversy) 1, 111 "Derivatives" (Translated by Schwe Zau Aung & Mrs Rhys Davids)*

Sarah

3.9 Zoom jottings 33

Sarah Procter Abbott
10/25/20 #165020

What is Now?

Friends

Ajahn Sujin asked Da-Zhuang where he was and he replied that there is no one, so no one to be anywhere.

AS: Yes, but in ordinary language where are you? Without paramattha dhammas (absolute realities) can there be concepts?

DZ: No

AS: We answer "I'm in Bangkok or I'm in Taipei" but how much understanding is there when we speak?

DZ: We try to keep awareness in conventional...

AS: Can we do?

DZ: No 'I'. By listening...

AS: So no one at all can do. For example, seeing now. How can there be the highly developed understanding to understand the arising and falling away, to understand nothing at all which arises and falls? What is in the book is all about cittas and cetasikas and functions but has the understanding of one reality at a time come yet?

It's easy to say "concept", like "tree is concept" but who knows seeing just sees now? Otherwise it's only thinking. One has to be truthful to what is seen now because now it's the memory of nimitta, a concept of reality, the idea of something there.

DZ: For liberation, do we all go through understanding the arising and falling of realities? It seems supernatural.

AS: But what is now? Can there be understanding now? It's not supernatural but very natural, only a reality. This is the truth. One reality which experiences now, conditioned just to see, nothing else. It arises just to experience. No one can do anything, no one can stop it. So study dhamma from whatever appears. This is the best thing. No matter whether we talk about seeing, if there's no understanding now of seeing now, it's useless.

> Through hankering for the future,
> Through sorrowing over the past,
> Fools dry up and wither away
> Like a green reed cut down.
>
> *Saṃyutta Nikāya 1:10 Forest (Translated by Bhikkhu Bodhi)*

Sarah

3.10 Zoom jottings 34

Sarah Procter Abbott
10/25/20 #165021

The Chief of Experiencing

Friends

In the Chinese discussion, there was a discussion about the conditions for seeing to arise at this moment.

It was stressed that there must be the eye-sense and there must be that which impinges on it. Kamma conditions the experience of a pleasant or unpleasant object. All these dhammas are conditioned, arising and falling away, always bringing the idea of some thing because there is no understanding. Just one moment of seeing is so short and cannot be directly experienced. If there were no reality, there could not be the idea of I see or some thing existing.

Citta is the chief or leader in experiencing. It just experiences what is there only. If we just talk about the definition it's not like understanding what appears now, such as the reality of seeing consciousness which experiences.

Is seeing a cat's, a bird's, a crocodile's or that of a fish? No, it's only that which arises to see. In the absolute truth it cannot be taken for anything. Seeing is seeing. It's anattā (not self), suññāta (empty, having fallen away).

The world is that which arises and falls away, never to return. It's only the world of fantasy and dreaming, when there are the ideas of things and people. What is true is reality arising and falling away from moment to moment. Paramattha dhamma is the absolute reality which is not self, not a thing, no matter in what world or realm it arises.

Sarah

3.11 Zoom jottings 35

Sarah Procter Abbott
10/30/20 #165074

Dhātu (Element)

Friends

The Chinese discussion about different realities continued. There were questions about ear-sense and eye-sense. It seems there are eyes and ears there all the time, just like it seems we are sitting or we are listening and thinking. There are just dhammas falling away all the time. What appears now?

It was stressed that it's useless to know a lot from books and many words but not understand anything about what appears now. There should not be any hurry to understand from the books at all, but understanding what appears now is pariyatti (intellectual right understanding). Listening to anything (or reading anything) which doesn't bring understanding at this moment is not the teaching of the Buddha. It's so very subtle. It must be understanding of that which is appearing as not self.

This is the way that gradually there will be the relief from the burden of the idea of "I" from life to life. Gradually as the development of right understanding increases there will be less and less wrong idea of self.

There has to be "no I" from the very beginning when there is a little more understanding.

Whatever arises is dhātu, an element which has a characteristic which cannot be changed at all. It bears its own characteristic. There are elements which are nāma dhātu and those which are rūpa dhātu. They cannot be any different. That's why reality or dhātu is the absolute reality. No one can do anything. The chief of experiencing, the chief nāma dhātu is citta. It cannot arise alone. It needs cetasikas such as phassa which contacts the object. The chief cannot do anything, it just experiences the object, like the king. The cetasikas condition the citta to be different, to be wholesome or unwholesome, for example.

> "Just as in saying, 'the king has arrived.' it is clear that he does not come alone without his attendants, but comes attended by his retinue, so this consciousness should be understood to have arisen with more than fifty moral (mental) phenomena. But it may be said that consciousness has arisen in the sense of a forerunner."
>
> *Atthasālinī (The Expositor) 1, Part 11, Ch 1 (Translated by Pe Maung Tin)*

Sarah

4

November 2020

4.1 Zoom jottings 36

Sarah Procter Abbott
11/01/20 #165090

The Value of Patience

Friends

Ajahn Sujin reminded us that whatever reality arises, it is only once in saṃsāra (the cycle of births and deaths). There is never an "I", just different realities arising and falling away. All gone!

Nina commented that paññā (right understanding) arises so seldom.

AS: That's the idea of self, always thinking about "I". Nothing can be done, only understanding. If there is no understanding at this moment, how can there be other moments of understanding?

Nina mentioned there's not enough, pariyatti (intellectual right understanding).

AS: The question is "I" again. How long? How from? It's not a matter of thinking. What appears now is conditioned. Before paññā, it's ignorance.

Later it was stressed that if anyone tries not to think about self, it's there. Whatever one does in a day is for oneself. No "I" is quite a relief, letting go of the wrong understanding. Suññāta means no thing at all.

There was also mention of cira kāla bhāvanā and sakacca bhāvanā. These refer to how long it takes before there can be understanding of what the Buddha taught and the understanding respectfully of each word as being true.

All dhammas are anattā. Understanding the value of patience brings about all kinds of kusala (wholesome states) and good results. Paññā sees there's no need to doubt, no need to try at all. There are just saṅkhāra dhammas. If this isn't understood one just listens for oneself for "I who knows" or "I who wishes to know". Each word can bring the understanding of "no me", "no self". If there's no understanding and awareness now, whatever appears is gone with ignorance again.

> "Patience (khanti pāramī) is the unimpeded weapon of the good in the development of noble qualities, for it dispels anger, the opposite of all such qualities, without residue. It is the adornment of those capable of vanquishing the foe; the strength of recluses and brahmins; a stream of water extinguishing the fire of anger; the basis for acquiring a good reputation; a mantra for quelling the poisonous speech of evil people; the supreme source of constancy in those established in restraint. Patience is an ocean on account of its depth; a shore bounding the great ocean of hatred; a panel closing off the door to the plane of misery; a staircase ascending to the worlds of gods and Brahmās; the ground for the habitation of

all noble qualities; the supreme purification of body, speech, and mind."

Cariyapiṭaka Commentary, A Treatise on the Pāramīs, (translated by Bhikkhu Bodhi)

Sarah

4.2 Zoom jottings 37

Sarah Procter Abbott
11/05/20 #165124

Anattā & Suññāta

Friends

There was a discussion about how each reality is anattā and suññāta. There is nothing permanent, nothing that can be found in saṃsāra. Whatever arose has gone completely. There is no "I", no thing, nowhere. It's a relief when there is the understanding that there's no "I", to be free from lobha and the idea of self existing, even a little. Suññāta refers to the reality which falls away instantly and has completely gone. There can be listening with understanding of whatever truth can be penetrated until it's direct understanding, satipaṭṭhāna and vipassanā ñāna (insight).

There was a question about nimitta. Something is seen, that is the nimitta of what is seen. All realities appear by way of nimitta, the sign or mark of reality. There are nimittas of all conditioned realities.

We live in the world of nimitta and fantasies all the time because there is no understanding of the truth of the arising and falling away of realities. It looks like something with shape and form, so we say we see flowers and a table but there must be the absolute reality which only appears by way of nimitta. It's made known by concepts, such as "flowers" and "table". The concepts make known what appears and the reality doesn't appear as it is.

> "Bhikkhus, forms are impermanent. What is impermanent is suffering. What is suffering is non-self. What is non-self should be seen as it really is with correct wisdom thus: 'This is not mine, this I am not, this is not my self.'
>
> Sounds... Odours... Tastes... Tactile objects... Mental phenomena are impermanent. What is impermanent is suffering. What is suffering is non-self. What is non-self should be seen as it really is with correct wisdom thus: 'This is not mine, this I am not, this is not my self."
>
> *Saṃyutta Nikāya 35:4 The External as Impermanent (Translated by Bhikkhu Bodhi)*

Sarah

4.3 Zoom jottings 38

Sarah Procter Abbott
11/05/20 #165125

Where is the World?

Friends

There were some questions raised about problems in different situations in daily life. How should they be solved? Ajahn Sujin stressed that trying to solve the problems of the world by ways other than the development of the path taught by the Buddha doesn't work at all. This is because there is no understanding of the truth.

The Buddha referred to three kinds of loka (world). There is the world that is taken for beings (satta loka), the world taken for the universe of stars, sun, moon, geographic world and so on (okāsa loka) and the world of conditioned, absolute realities (saṅkhāra loka).

The world in the absolute sense are the realities which arise and fall in split seconds, continuously, all the time, unknown. So the true meaning of the world is that which arises and falls away.

When we think of the world with people and places this is only thinking about what has been experienced through different sense doors. It seems that the whole world is there with many different people and things but in truth the world lasts just for one moment. The citta arises and experiences an object and then falls away instantly.

> "Life, person, pleasure, pain - just these alone
> Join in one conscious moment that flicks by.
> Ceased aggregates of those dead or alive
> Are all alike, gone never to return.
> No [world is] born if [consciousness is] not
> Produced; when that is present, then it lives;
> When consciousness dissolves, the world is dead:
> The highest sense this concept will allow" (Nd.1,42).
>
> *Visuddhimagga V11, 39 (Translated by Bhikkhu Ñānamoli)*

All questions can be answered by understanding what appears now. Where is the world now?

Sarah

4.4 Zoom jottings 39

Sarah Procter Abbott
11/08/20 #165166

The Raft

Friends

A Vietnamese friend asked about the analogy of the raft used to cross the water. He said this showed that even the right Dhamma has to be let go of. He asked how it should it be understood.

Ajahn Sujin asked what appears now to be understood as it is? If it's not now, what can be understood? Is there anything to be understood?

Hearing now, who makes it arise? Can it stay longer? It falls away instantly as not self. This is not just at the moment of death, but all the time. Whatever arises falls away instantly. It's nowhere.

In other words, that which falls away instantly is dukkha, unsatisfactory. It's not worth clinging to at all. This is what the raft simile is referring to.

> "I teach, bhikkhus, even the abandoning of desire and attachment to such peaceful and sublime states as serenity and insight, how much more so to that low, vulgar, contemptible, coarse, and impure thing that this foolish Ariṭṭha sees as harmless when he says that there is no obstruction in desire and lust for the five cords of sensual pleasure."
>
> *Majjhima Nikāya 22 Commentary, The Simile of the Raft (Translated by Bhikkhu Bodhi)*

Phong asked about the twenty kinds of sakkāya diṭṭhi (wrong view of self).

Ajahn asked whether there is the idea of I'm seeing or I'm sitting now. At the moment of taking something for "I", like seeing or hearing, is it true or is it just a reality which arises and falls away? Without understanding, there's always the idea of "I see". The wrong idea takes what appears as "I", "I like", "I am".

Phong asked about the difference between "my hand" and "a person's hand". Ajahn asked if the other's hand was his hand. In reality, it's attānudiṭṭhi (wrong idea of something or someone) when the other hand is taken for something, What is touched is hardness, but there's the idea of a hand as something permanent. It's the wrong understanding which brings more miccha diṭṭhi.

Right understanding at just that moment is letting go just a very little of such wrong understanding.

Sarah

4.5 Zoom jottings 40

Sarah Procter Abbott
11/08/20 #165167

The Magic Show

Friends

There was a discussion about the characteristic of hardness which is touched. Hardness is the characteristic of paṭhavī dhātu one of the four primary rūpas. A friend asked a question about having paññā (right understanding) immediately to understand what is heard about hardness or whether it is just thinking about concepts.

If one tries to think about hardness or tries to be aware or understand it, it's diṭṭhi, wrong understanding. Forget about how much or little paññā there is. What appears now? Is there seeing now of the particular rūpa, visible object? It impinges on eye-sense by conditions for seeing to arise. That's all.

We live in the world of Māyā, the magic show or fantasy like in a movie, from beginning to end. It's the same as life from birth to death.

> "Consciousness is like a magical illusion (māyā) in the sense that it is insubstantial and cannot be grasped. Consciousness is even more transient and fleeting than a magical illusion. For it gives the impression that a person comes and goes, stands and sits, with the same mind, but the mind is different in each of these activities. Consciousness deceives the multitude like a magical illusion."
>
> *Saṃyutta Nikāya 22:95 Commentary, A Lump of Foam (Translated by Bhikkhu Bodhi)*

Tinh asked about intellectual understanding as we cannot penetrate reality as it is. Ajahn Sujin replied that as long as there is the idea of "I", it's impossible to let go of anything because of the ignorance of the arising and falling away of realities. There is nimitta of reality and then the concept of everything as some thing. If no reality arises, is there a world? Without reality, there's no idea of grass, bird, worm. There is just nothing, something, nothing all the time.

The question "where am I?" really means where is seeing, where is hearing, where is thinking? They are all gone, nowhere at all. We don't need to look for anything. Whatever arises does so by conditions.

Sarah

4.6 Zoom jottings 41

Sarah Procter Abbott

Why Bother?

Friends

Friends from Taiwan and China raised questions in a Chinese discussion:

Yuan: If there's no I, then why bother about kusala and akusala (wholesome and unwholesome consciousness)?

Ajahn Sujin: Everything is dhamma. There cannot be "I". Hardness is not anyone. It cannot be changed. Is kusala real? Is akusala real?

Y: Yes, real.

AS: So where is it now? Is it real at that moment? What is real now? Is there you now?

Yuan repeats her question about kusala and akusala and avoiding the latter.

AS: There is thinking about kusala but is there kusala now to be known?

Y: Kusala is mettā (loving kindness).

AS: What is kusala? What is dhamma?

Hui Yueh: That which can be directly experienced.
AS: Why is it real? Consider each word carefully.
Da-Zhuan: It's the object of the six doors.
AS: That's too far. What is real now?
Hui Yueh: Realities arising and falling which can be known.
AS: That's the story of dhamma arising and falling.
Hui Yueh: Sound.

We had further discussion about sounds. Hardness of different kinds and degrees of hardness and softness condition different sounds. They cannot arise without the hardness. There must be the impact, like when you put something on the table, there is the impact which conditions the sound.

The world can be broken into tiny elements. Only one can be known at a time. Each one arises and falls. Like the world of magic, we live in the world of nimitta, the world of mirages. Only one reality appears.

> "Suppose, bhikkhus, that in the last month of the hot season, at high noon, a shimmering mirage appears. A man with good sight would inspect it, ponder it, and carefully investigate it, and it would appear to him to be void, hollow, insubstantial. For what substance could there be in a mirage? So too, bhikkhus, whatever kind of perception there is, whether past, future, or present, internal or external, gross or subtle, inferior or superior, far or near: a bhikkhu inspects it, ponders it, and carefully investigates it, and it would appear to him to be void, hollow, insubstantial. For what substance could there be in perception?"

> *Saṃyutta Nikāya 22:95 A Lump of Foam(Translated by Bhikkhu Bodhi)*

Citta (consciousness) can only be known by the nimitta of citta. The citta itself arises and falls so rapidly. It seems that many, many things appear but only a rūpa impinges on the eyeball. All dhammas are anattā, nothing is permanent. This is the difference between not knowing anything and paññā which can understand all dhammas are anattā.

Study the truth of one reality at a time.

Sarah

4.7 Zoom jottings 42

Sarah Procter Abbott
11/12/20 #165198

The Bhikkhu's Life

Friends

A question was asked in a Vietnamese discussion about the difference in value in donating to a beggar or to a bhikkhu (monk). In the course of the discussion it was stressed how one shouldn't give money to a bhikkhu (or anything else which is not according to the rules for a monk) because it destroys the Teachings and the bhikkhu's life and future lives too. One should just give the requisites what are useful for him to live and study the Teachings.

The following sutta which stresses how acts such as accepting money by a bhikkhu and not living according to the Vinaya can lead to rebirth in hell.

> "I inform you, bhikkhus, I declare to you that for an immoral man... it would be far better if a strong man were to wrap a tough horsehair rope around both his shins and tighten it so that it cuts through his outer skin, inner skin, flesh, sinews, and bone, until it reaches the marrow. For what reason? Because on that account he might undergo death or deadly pain, but for that reason he would not, with the breakup of the body, after death, be reborn in the plane of misery, in a bad destination, in the lower world, in hell. But when that immoral man... accepts the homage of affluent khattiyas, brahmins, or householders, this leads to his harm and suffering for a long time. With the breakup of the

body, after death, he is reborn in the plane of misery, in a bad destination, in the lower world, in hell."

"What do you think, bhikkhus? Which is better, for a strong man to force open one's mouth with a hot iron spike—burning, blazing, and glowing—and insert a hot copper ball—burning, blazing, and glowing—which burns one's lips, mouth, tongue, throat, and stomach, [132] and comes out from below taking along one's entrails, or for one to consume almsfood given out of faith by affluent khattiyas, brahmins, or householders?"

"It would be far better, Bhante, for one to consume almsfood given out of faith by affluent khattiyas, brahmins, or householders. It would be painful if a strong man were to force open one's mouth with a hot iron spike—burning, blazing, and glowing— and insert a hot copper ball... which burns one's lips... and comes out from below taking along one's entrails."

"I inform you, bhikkhus, I declare to you that for an immoral man... it would be far better if a strong man were to force open his mouth with a hot iron spike—burning, blazing, and glowing—and insert a hot copper ball... which burns one's lips... and comes out from below, taking along his entrails.

For what reason? Because on that account he might undergo death or deadly pain, but for that reason he would not, with the breakup of the body, after death, be reborn in the plane of misery, in a bad destination, in the lower world, in hell. But when that immoral man... consumes almsfood given out of faith by affluent khattiyas, brahmins, or householders, this leads to his harm and suffering for a long time. With the breakup of the body, after death, he is reborn in the plane of misery, in a bad destination, in the lower world, in hell."

More examples are given.

"This is what the Blessed One said. Now while

> this exposition was being spoken, sixty bhikkhus vomited hot blood. Sixty bhikkhus gave up the training and returned to the lower life, saying: 'It is difficult to do, Blessed One, very difficult to do.' And the minds of sixty bhikkhus were liberated from the taints by non-clinging."
>
> *Aṅguttara Nikāya, 7.72 (8) Fire (Translated by Bhikkhu Bodhi)*

Sarah

4.8 Zoom jottings 43

Sarah Procter Abbott
11/13/20 #165207

Giving to a Bhikkhu or a Beggar

Friends

Qu: Why is there a difference between donating to a bhikkhu and a beggar?

A Vietnamese friend raised this question. Tiny Tam helped answer Ajahn Sujin's questions on her behalf:

AS: Who is the bhikkhu?
TT: The one who has gone forth away from the household life.
AS: Why and what for?
TT: To seek a way to eliminate...
AS: How?
TT By understanding the truth.
AS: How?
TT: By understanding what is appearing now.
AS: How to understand that?

TT: From listening and considering.

AS: Can the lay person listen and understand?

TT: Yes.

AS: There are so many meanings of "bhikkhu". One who sees the danger of saṃsāra vatta (the rounds of birth and death), not just understanding now.

TT: The question was about donating to a bhikkhu.

AS: To chant or for what? According to the Vinaya can a bhikkhu receive money?

TT: No.

AS: So why do you give money to a bhikkhu? Is giving money to a bhikkhu a way to show respect to the Buddha?

TT: No.

AS: So do not destroy the body of the Buddha because no one can see his great virtues and wisdom. His body is the Dhamma otherwise no one can see him at all.

At the moment of giving money to the Buddha you destroy his life and bhikkhuhood because the bhikkhu has left house, family and so on to live as the Buddha lived to follow the Teachings, to have less attachment and kilesa (defilements). It is not sacca (truthful) if he cannot live that life. Would you like to ruin the Teachings in the Suttanta and Vinaya for monks and lay people?

People can develop understanding and become enlightened as lay people. Only when becoming an arahat they must leave the lay life. So the monk is just like the sign for the arahat, wearing yellow robes with no more kilesa (defilements).

When you see someone in trouble, friend or beggar, it's fine to help, but a monk is a monk and he cannot ask for anything from others except that which is allowed in the Vinaya. Understand the life of the bhikkhu and give just what is useful for him to live and study the Teachings. Lay people can have whatever they like. So giving money to a monk is to destroy him.

Ajahn Sujin referred again to the Aggikkhandhopama Sutta (Fire Sutta).

As the Buddha says it's so very dangerous for an immoral bhikkhu not following the Vinaya, to consume the food given by supporters, worse than having hot coal or copper balls burning one's mouth:

> "I inform you, bhikkhus, I declare to you that for an immoral man... it would be far better if a strong man were to force open his mouth with a hot iron spike—burning, blazing, and glowing—and insert a hot copper ball... which burns one's lips... and comes out from below, taking along his entrails.
>
> For what reason? Because on that account he might undergo death or deadly pain, but for that reason he would not, with the breakup of the body, after death, be reborn in the plane of misery, in a bad destination, in the lower world, in hell. But when that immoral man... consumes almsfood given out of faith by affluent khattiyas, brahmins, or householders, this leads to his harm and suffering for a long time. With the breakup of the body, after death, he is reborn in the plane of misery, in a bad destination, in the lower world, in hell."

Aṅguttara Nikāya 7:72 (8) Fire (Translated by Bhikkhu Bodhi)

Sarah

4.9 Zoom jottings 44

Sarah Procter Abbott
11/15/20 #165223

Hearing Again and Again

Friends

There was a discussion about the importance of hearing again and again about the present dhammas (realities) in order to understand no self. The understanding gradually wears away ignorance. It doesn't mean one should hurry to understand because that's bound to be with more attachment to "me". Instead understanding itself develops to understand the truth little by little. No one can do anything.

There can be learning about the truth at this moment. That which is seen is no one, no thing. Afterwards there is remembering what is seen as some thing, but it's only thinking. It's a relief when there is understanding because it's not "me", seeing is just seeing! The purpose of such understanding is just for dhammas to appear as they are. Otherwise they are not understood life after life.

The truth is the truth. When there is true understanding of the realities of life one will not to be inclined to try other things which lead away from the right path. Lobha (attachment) is always searching for other solutions.

That which is seen cannot be anything yet, no thing, no person. Where are you? Where is that which is seen? All gone. There is nothing which can be kept by anyone. Without phassa (contact), there can be no seeing, no world, no thing at all. What is seen now is just that which appears for such a brief instant.

Nina: It's hard to take it all in.

Ajahn Sujin: You do not see lobha (attachment) yet. It goes everywhere with you. "I cannot" or "I can" is atta (self belief).

The Buddha pointed out that lobha is the teacher and also the student who follows:

> "Bhikkhus, this holy life is lived without students and without a teacher. A bhikkhu who has no students and no teacher dwells happily, in comfort.
>
> And how, bhikkhus, does a bhikkhu who has students and a teacher dwell in suffering, not in comfort? Here, bhikkhus, when a bhikkhu has seen a form with the eye, there arise in him evil unwholesome states, memories and intentions connected with the fetters. They dwell within him. Since those evil unwholesome states dwell within him, he is called 'one who has students.' They assail him. Since

evil unwholesome states assail him, he is called 'one who has a teacher.'

Further, when a bhikkhu has heard a sound with the ear... cognized a mental phenomenon with the mind... he is called 'one who has a teacher.'

It is in this way that a bhikkhu who has students and a teacher dwells in suffering, not in comfort."

Saṃyutta Nikāya 35:151 A Student (Translated by Bhikkhu Bodhi)

Sarah

4.10 Zoom jottings 45

Sarah Procter Abbott
11/15/20 #165224

Preparation for Understanding

Friends

Maeve asked a question about the preparation for pariyatti (intellectual) understanding.

Ajahn Sujin stressed that the "I" is still there until paññā arises and understands the anattāness of everything. Whatever dhamma (reality) arises, it's anattā. "Preparation" is clinging to the idea of self, wanting to have more understanding. Saṅkhāra khandha are the cetasikas (mental factors) other than vedanā (feeling) and saññā (memory) arising by conditions.

All conditioned realities are saṅkhāra dhammas. This is to be understood, no one can prepare anything.

Saṅkhāra dhammas prepare from moment to moment. In particular, understand the meaning of "saṅkhāra khandha". It means no one can do anything. There's no need for the idea of "I will try to understand" or "I will prepare to understand" because there is no "me". Pariyatti understanding is the condition for paṭipatti understanding (direct understanding), from the understanding of "no one".

For example, we live in the world of rūpas (the realities which cannot experience anything). Ignorance doesn't understand them and takes them for some "thing" which is liked instantly. We find them so important, that's why they are the first khandha. There is clinging to rūpas, such as what is seen and heard, all day.

> "How, householder, is one afflicted in body and afflicted in mind? Here, householder, the uninstructed worldling, who is not a seer of the noble ones and is unskilled and undisciplined in their Dhamma, who is not a seer of superior persons and is unskilled and undisciplined in their Dhamma, regards form as self, or self as possessing form, or form as in self, or self as in form. He lives obsessed by the notions: 'I am form, form is mine.' As he lives obsessed by these notions, that form of his changes and alters. With the change and alteration of form, there arise in him sorrow, lamentation, pain, displeasure, and despair."
>
> The same is said for the other khandhas.
>
> "And how, householder, is one afflicted in body but not afflicted in mind? Here, householder, the instructed noble disciple, who is a seer of the noble ones and is skilled and disciplined in their Dhamma, who is a seer of superior persons and is skilled and disciplined in their Dhamma, does not regard form as self, or self as possessing form, or form as in self, or self as in form. He does not live obsessed by the notions: 'I am form, form is mine.' As he lives unobsessed by these notions, that form of his changes and alters. With the change and alteration of form, there do not arise in him sorrow, lamentation, pain, displeasure, and despair."
>
> Again the same is said for the other khandhas.

Saṃyutta Nikāya 22:1 Nakulapīta (Translated by Bhikkhu Bodhi)

Sarah

4.11 Zoom jottings 46

Sarah Procter Abbott
11/17/20 #165255

All Gone!

Friends

The discussion continued from the question of preparation for understanding and remembering what has been said.

If there is not the understanding of whatever reality appears there cannot be the eradication of self (atta belief) of that reality. It's a relief when there is understanding of what appears, a relief from not understanding anything at all. Lobha (attachment) is the second Noble Truth. There has to be understanding of lobha of no matter what degree as not self. Why think about what's gone and that which hasn't come, wasting time instead of just understanding what is a reality now, not self.

There's no need to try and keep in mind all the words. It depends on conditions what is remembered. All dhammas are anattā, just different realities appearing as nimitta (signs). Whether there is understanding or no understanding, there are just dhammas arising and falling away. Whatever arises does so by conditions. Don't mind about what will be next because there is only this moment. With understanding the idea of "I will" is gone. It's so useless to think about that which has gone.

There was a question about "gone completely" and suññāta. Suññāta means that what arose has gone completely never to arise again. There are always useless thoughts about that which has gone. When we understand by saṅkhāra khandha (referring to the 50 cetasikas), attachment is to sense objects or ideas which have all gone instantly. Whatever arises is so very, very short and it's so very useless to think about that which is no more, worrying and not liking it or clinging to it again and again. "All gone", this is the key. This life will finish and death will come. There will not be this person any more and in truth there is not this person at all now. There is just that which appears now.

"At Sāvatthī. 'Bhikkhus, form is impermanent, both of the past and the future, not to speak of the present. Seeing thus, bhikkhus, the instructed noble disciple is indifferent towards form of the past; he does not seek delight in form of the future; and he is practising for revulsion towards form of the present, for its fading away and cessation.

Feeling is impermanent... Perception is impermanent... - Volitional formations are impermanent... Consciousness is impermanent, both of the past and the future, not to speak of the present. Seeing thus, bhikkhus, the instructed noble disciple is indifferent towards consciousness of the past; he does not seek delight in consciousness of the future; and he is practising (paṭipanno) for revulsion towards consciousness of the present, for its fading away and cessation.' "

Saṃyutta Nikāya 22:9 Impermanent in the Three Times (Translated by Bhikkhu Bodhi)

Sarah

4.12 Zoom jottings 47

Sarah Procter Abbott
11/22/20 #165308

Once in Saṃsāra!

Friends

Whatever arises is by conditions. Angulimāla couldn't have known what would arise next or that he would be fully enlightened. There is life and death at this moment. Who knows what will be the next moment. It may be death, the end of this life, the end of this person. What arises after this death is birth again, nothing to be afraid of. Meanwhile the best thing in this life is to understand what is there, what appears now.

Touching, seeing, hearing are all gone. It's the way of paññā (right understanding) to let go of ignorance and clinging to that which is no more. It's such a relief to understand there's no "I", no place, no world as we think of it. The arising and falling away of any reality is just once in saṃsāra, the cycle of births and deaths. As understanding develops and the vipassanā ñānas arise, there is the understanding of the danger of whatever reality is conditioned. What has already fallen away is empty, nothing. Nothing is there at all, the whole world is gone. This has to be understood more and more clearly, but it cannot be understood clearly by pariyatti (intellectual understanding) and paṭipatti (direct understanding) before vipassanā ñānas are realised.

Someone mentioned that visible object doesn't seem to have fallen away. Ajahn Sujin stressed that in order to eradicate lobha, this has to be known.

> "Friend Koṭṭhita, a virtuous bhikkhu should carefully attend to the five aggregates subject to clinging as impermanent, as suffering, as a disease, as a tumour, as a dart, as misery, as an affliction, as alien, as disintegrating, as empty, as non-self."

In the sutta, Sāriputta continues to explain that the ariyan (enlightened) disciples should continue to attend to and understand exactly the same realities as impermanent and so on. This is even true for the arahant:

> "Friend, Koṭṭhita, a bhikkhu who is an arahant should carefully attend to these five aggregates subject to clinging as impermanent, as suffering, as a disease, as a tumour, as a dart, as misery, as an affliction, as alien, as disintegrating, as empty, as non-self. For the arahant, friend, there is nothing further that has to be done and no repetition of what he has already done. However, when these things are developed and cultivated, they lead to a pleasant dwelling in this very life and to mindfulness and clear comprehension."

Saṃyutta Nikāya 22:122 Virtuous (Translated by Bhikkhu Bodhi)

Sarah

5

December 2020

5.1 Zoom jottings 48

Sarah Procter Abbott
12/03/20 #165465

Nutriment (Āhāra)

Friends

Three kinds of nutriment are nāmas (mental dhammas) and one kind is rūpa (physical dhamma).

With regard to the physical āhāra (the edible nutriment), even when we don't eat it still performs its function conditioning the next rūpas. Without it, the body cannot be maintained. When there is no more internal āhāra nutriment, the body needs to eat again.

Trees and plants don't need āhāra paccaya. Only the body needs physical āhāra for life to continue.

Tam Tanh asked about oxygen and air. Ajahn asked if she'd like to discuss these or the absolute truth now.

The second āhāra paccaya is phassa āhāra (contact nutriment, the cetasika). Without phassa, other nāmas (i.e. the citta and cetasikas) cannot experience anything, It is āhāra (nutriment) for all nāmas conditioned by it. At each moment, each reality is conditioned by many other realities. This is the way to understand each dhamma, each reality, is anattā (no self).

The third āhāra paccaya is cetanā āhāra (intention nutriment or "will to do", the cetasika). Without cetanā arising at each moment, there cannot be other kinds of experiencing by the citta and cetasikas. It coordinates their arising at each moment. It is the "will to do", such as the will to live on and on. Whatever follows is because of this "will to do". No one can get out of saṃsāra vata (the rounds of becoming) until paññā (right understanding) is ready to let go, having understood the uselessness of dhammas just arising and falling away each life such as seeing, hearing, pleasant and unpleasant feelings and thinking.

To understand conditions is to understand no self, no thing at all.

The fourth āhāra paccaya is citta āhāra (consciousness nutriment). Citta is the chief in experiencing. Without citta, there is no experience at all.

The four āhāras are just different conditions, showing there is no one at all. There's no point in just reading the meaning and explanation but there has to be the understanding of the reality that the words represent. There is phassa now, for example, but it cannot be known because even the understanding of nāma, that which experiences is not known yet. Study to understand that which is appearing now! There will be āhāra (nutriment) for cittas and life to go on forever when there is no right understanding developed.

When there is understanding of what is in the book, there's no need to remember the words because the meaning is not forgotten. There is sacca pāramī, the moment of understanding the truth, letting go of the idea of self little by little. People think that sacca is the Four Noble Truths, but it's now. As understanding develops there is sacca of each stage. Without sacca there cannot be the experience of the Four Noble Truths at all.

> "And what is nutriment, what is the origin of nutriment, what is the cessation of nutriment, what is the way leading to the cessation of nutriment? There are four kinds of nutriment for the maintenance of beings that already have come to be and for the support of those seeking new existence. What four? They are: physical food as nutriment, gross or subtle; contact as the second; mental volition as the third; and consciousness as the fourth. With the arising of craving there is the arising of nutriment. With the cessation of craving there is the cessation of nutriment. The way leading to the cessation of nutriment is just this Noble Eightfold Path; that is, right view, right intention, right speech, right action, right livelihood, right effort, right mindfulness, and right concentration."
>
> *Majjhima Nikāya 9 The Discourse on Right View (Translated by Bhikkhu Ñāṇamoli and Bhikkhu Bodhi)*

Sarah

6
January 2021

6.1 Zoom jottings 49

Sarah Procter Abbott
Jan 5 #165943

Sīla (1)

Friends

Giao had asked about the 5 precepts and practising the precepts in a Vietnamese discussion.

Ajahn Sujin stressed that each word of the Teachings helps to condition understanding of no self. Before hearing the Teachings there is always the idea of oneself from life to life. Each word should be studied carefully.

We keep thinking about sīla and behaviour and so on but what about dhamma? So cultivate understanding of each word about what appears now as "no I" at all. For example, we may think about sīla, but it's not known as dhamma, a reality.

There are so many words and many moments have passed with the idea of self. Dhamma is now and here and then gone. What arises and falls is not known to be by conditions.

What is sīla now and what is it not? That which can experience an object is citta and cetasikas together. When they arise, they behave differently at each moment. Sīla is the behaviour of that which can experience an object. It has to be kusala, akusala or avyākata behaviour at each moment. (Avyākata dhamma refers to those dhammas which are not kusala or akusala. In this case it refers to the kiriya cittas arising in the javana process of the arahat).

AS: What sīla is there now?

G: Kusala sīla.

AS: At what moment?

G: At the moment of understanding.

AS: Only. So valuable because without this moment there cannot be more understanding building up by saṅkhāra khandha (the accumulation of all cetasikas other than vedanā and saññā) which is not me, not "I".

Why cannot there be understanding of the exact moment of kusala or akusala?

G: Not understanding

AS: Each reality arises and falls so fast. So intellectual understanding cannot say which is which until satipaṭṭhāna is there. Be truthful to the truth. Is intellectual understanding firm enough yet or not? It needs sacca pāramī. (The perfection of truthfulness).

> "When a man possesses ten qualities, carpenter, I describe him as accomplished in what is wholesome, perfected in what is wholesome, attained to the supreme attainment, an ascetic invincible. [But first of all] I say, it must be understood thus:

'These are unwholesome habits (akusala sīla),' and thus: 'Unwholesome habits originate from this,' and thus: 'Unwholesome habits cease without remainder here.' and thus: 'One practising in this way is practising the way to the cessation of unwholesome habits.' "

"And I say, it must be understood thus: 'These are wholesome habits (kusalā sīlā)', and thus: 'Wholesome habits originate from this,' and thus: 'Wholesome habits cease without remainder here,' and thus: 'One practising in this way is practising the way to the cessation of wholesome habits.' "

Further on in the sutta, the Buddha says:

"And where do these wholesome habits cease without remainder? Their cessation is stated: here a bhikkhu is virtuous, but he does not identify with his virtue, and he understands as it actually is that deliverance of mind and deliverance by wisdom where these wholesome habits cease without remainder."

Majjhima Nikāya 78 Samaṇamaṇḍikā Sutta (Translated by Bhikkhu Ñāṇamoli and Bhikkhu Bodhi)

Sarah

7
February 2021

7.1 Zoom jottings 50

Sarah Procter Abbott
Feb 25 #166757

Sīla (2)

Friends

> We discussed more about virati sīla in the Vietnamese discussion. There are three kinds of abstinences or virati-cetasikas. They are:

Abstinence from wrong speech, vaci-duccarita virati

Abstinence from wrong action, kāya-duccarita virati

Abstinence from wrong livelihood, ājīva-duccarita virati.

All three virati only arise with kusala cittas when there is the opportunity to speak wrongly, to take wrong action such as harming another or for unwholesome speech or action in the course of one's livelihood. Only one can arise at a time in daily life.

When kusala (wholesome) cittas just think about not killing or not speaking harshly, it's not virati, abstaining. When time comes and there is the opportunity, who knows whether kusala or akusala cittas will arise, whether there will be virati or not virati at that time? If kusala cittas with virati arise, one doesn't kill.

If one just abstains from harming the other or speaking harshly without kusala cittas, there is no virati. However when there is abstaining at such a time with kindness it is virati. The abstention at that moment may be with or without understanding.

The important point is that the kusala or akusala cittas are not self. When there's the idea that "I can do" or "I don't do" or "I'm so bad", the idea of self is there which cannot eradicate the wrong idea. Whatever arises is "not me". It's gone, it's not self and it only arises by conditions.

Sīla including virati sīla can only become firm through the development of right understanding of realities as anattā.

Only when wrong view has been eradicated and there is no more idea of a self observing or abstaining from akusala can it be said that there will be no more transgression of the five precepts. There will then be no more killing for example, even when one's life is in danger.

So the higher morality, adhi sīla, is only developed with the right understanding of realities as not self.

> "When that Path has once arisen, not even the thought, 'we will kill a creature', arises in the ariyans."
>
> *Aṭṭhasālinī part 3, Ch 6, Courses of Moral Action (104) (Translated by Pe Maung Tin)*

Sarah

7.2 Zoom jottings 51

Sarah Procter Abbott
Feb 25 #166758

Ānāpānasati

Friends

Da-Zhuang asked about ānāpānasati, being aware of breath, during a Chinese discussion.

Ajahn asked him what his purpose was. Does he just want to have ānāpānasati? Is ānāpāna (breath) not just an ordinary dhamma? Is it different from what is hot or cold now? What is now appearing?

In other words, we think of it as something special, but the rūpas referred to as breath are just passing, ordinary dhammas like any other rūpas. What is important is what is appearing now, not looking for something different, like a subtle rūpa.

Ajahn asked him whether it appears now like seeing or hearing? Understanding develops by conditions, not by one's will. The Teachings are for detachment, letting go.

What is the truth of ānāpāna (breath)? If it's real, it must have its own characteristic different from other realities. Is it that which is hard and soft? Usually what we touch is very, very solid but is this rūpa not as solid as what is touched now? It's very deep or subtle to understand because it does not show up like ordinary hardness or softness when it touches body-sense.

Whatever appears as the object of understanding is not self, like now. There is no attention to hardness appearing, no idea of how little is experienced and is gone. The breath is just like that. When there is understanding there is detachment, letting go, no control. When time comes there is the understanding of the reality.

Who knows what will be the object of understanding? All dhammas are anattā. There has to be the letting go of this or that object, no wish for this or that. There can be breath as object unexpectedly but it's just like other earth element (pathavī dhātu) rūpas, no different at all.

If anyone tries to understand or wants to have it, lobha (attachment) is there unknown.

When there is understanding of no self, there is no wish to have such and such a reality as object. It depends on conditions what will be the object of understanding. There are always realities, cittas, cetasikas and rūpas. Which one would you like to be aware of? It's you, at such times of wishing, not understanding at all. Paññā (understanding) knows it's the accumulation of attachment and that what appears does so by conditions.

When ānāpāna is experienced, is it different from what is touched now? Without understanding of anattā it's impossible to let go of the idea of self trying. The letting go has to be little by little otherwise lobha (attachment) leads to what one considers to be the desirable object all the time.

Sarah

7.3 Zoom jottings 52

Sarah Procter Abbott
Feb 25 #166759

Kusala (wholesome) or Akusala (unwholesome) Cittas now?

Friends

There was a discussion about kusala (wholesome) cittas with Yuan in a Chinese discussion. Ajahn Sujin asked her what kusala is and whether there is kusala now?

Yuan replied there was kusala now, pīti, joy for learning.

Ajahn said it was thinking, not understanding. At the moment of seeing, there's no kusala. After seeing, is there kusala? Yuan said she thought there was. Again Ajahn replied that this was thinking, not knowing.

When there's no dāna, sīla or bhāvanā, there must be akusala (unwholesome mental states) unknown. There are many more moments of akusala in a day than kusala.

Khanti pāramī (the perfection of patience) with right understanding has to develop for a long time until there can be understanding of one reality at a time, patiently, truthfully and with confidence in the truth. It's not for "me", just for understanding the absolute truth. When there is awareness of what appears, it doesn't matter what the object is. It's just dhamma that has gone!

Khanti must be developed with paññā to show that there is no one, no thing. The patience is a bodhipakkiya dhamma (factor of enlightenment) which develops at this moment with the understanding of no self. There must also be the wholesome interest (chanda cetasika) in understanding the truth.

> "Patience (khanti pāramī) has the characteristic of acceptance; its function is to endure the desirable and undesirable; its manifestation is tolerance or non-opposition; seeing things as they really are is its proximate cause."
>
> *Cariyapiṭaka Commentary, A Treatise on the Pāramīs, (translated by Bhikkhu Bodhi)*

Sarah

8

March 2021

8.1 Zoom jottings 53

Sarah Procter Abbott
Mar 15 #166955

Ummagga, the "popping up" of Paññā

Friends

I introduced the Ummagga Sutta. Ummagga is paññā at the level of vipassanā ñāna which "pops up". It must be paṭivedha (direct realisation) understanding to really "let go" of clinging to the 5 khandhas for understanding to develop. The point is to let go, not to understand the word, but the meaning.

We don't know how many kalapas of rūpas impinge on the eye-sense, but there must be one which impinges for seeing to arise. Paññā can "pop up" to understand what appears directly.

We discussed how in the rūpa brahma realms, visible object is still seen and sound is still heard but there is no smelling, tasting or experiencing through the body-sense. There is still seeing and hearing is because it's useful to see and hear to understand the Buddha's Teachings. There is no clinging any more in the case of the anāgāmī (having attained the 3rd stage of enlightenment) to sense objects, such as visible object and sound, but there can still be clinging to seeing and hearing. Clinging to bhava (life, existing) can still be to seeing, hearing, thinking and living at a very slight level.

There was also a discussion about the meaning of buddhanussati (wise reflection on the qualities of the Buddha). Only when understanding is developed can there be wise reflection on the Buddha's qualities at anytime without any preparation or special act, but by conditions.

There can be reflection now on the virtues of the one who taught the truth. When there is a moment of understanding, there is the beginning of seeing the truth, getting closer and closer to the Buddha. Likewise, without the understanding of dhammas, there cannot be any dhammānussati, wise reflection on the Dhamma. It's the wise thinking about the truth of reality from considering carefully. Thus it is dhammānussati that leads to satipaṭthāna but it's not satipaṭṭhāna itself.

Only an ariyan (enlightened) disciple can attain upacāra samādhi (access concentration)) with buddhānussati, dhammānussati or saṅghānussati because of the degree of right understanding required. All wrong views must have been eradicated. In the Ummagga Sutta we read about the importance of understanding:

> "I have taught many teachings, bhikkhu: discourses, mixed prose and verse, expositions, verses, inspired utterances, quotations, birth stories, amazing accounts, and questions-and-answers. If, after learning the meaning and Dhamma of even a four-line verse, one practices in accordance with the Dhamma, that is enough for one to be called 'a learned expert on the Dhamma.' "

The "learned expert" is the one with "ummagga", understanding of the degree of vipassanā ñāna who clearly understands one world, one reality appearing, at a time, that which arises falls away immediately. The understanding "pops up" unexpectedly to realise the truth. This is the opposite of when attachment keeps talking about the story of the Dhamma, not understanding the reality.

After the first vipassanā ñāna, there must be ñāta pariññā (understanding of what has been known) which gets used to that which has been clearly known as not self. What has been understood has to be applied to other realities arising in daily life until there is the direct, clear understanding of paccaya (conditions) of what appears without words. This is udayabaya ñāna (the stage of insight) when it's clear that what arises is by conditions.

> "Here, bhikkhu, a bhikkhu has heard: 'This is suffering,' and he sees the meaning of this, having pierced through it with wisdom. He has heard: 'This is the origin of suffering,' and he sees the meaning of this, having pierced through it with wisdom. He has heard: 'This is the cessation of suffering,' and he sees the meaning of this, having pierced through it with wisdom. He has heard: 'This is the way leading to the cessation of suffering,' and he sees the meaning of this, having pierced through it with wisdom. It is in this way that one is learned, of penetrative wisdom."
>
> *Aṅguttara Nikāya, 4:186 (6) Ummagga Sutta (Translated by Bhikkhu Bodhi)*

Sarah

8.2 Zoom jottings 54

Sarah Procter Abbott
Mar 15 #166962

Bhava (existing) and Bhāva (nature)

Friends

Bhava and bhāva are two different terms. Each reality has its bhāva (nature or essence). For example it may have its bhāva to be soft or hard. The bhāva cannot be changed. The bhāva of kamma is cetanā (intention). Sabhāva dhammas refer to those realities with bhāva (a characteristic) which can be known.

Strong clinging conditions bhava (existing or becoming) as we read in paticca samuppāda. Bhava in this context is of 2 kinds, kamma bhava and upapatti bhava. Kamma bhava conditions upapatti bhava (becoming).

Bhāvāsava which has been accumulated is the fine clinging to life or existing. It is common to each life. This kind of clinging arises in the very first mind process in life before there is any sense door experience or story yet. It's "the core of life in saṃsāra". There can be clinging to life with or without wrong view.

The anāgāmī is reborn in the brahma realm because of no more kāmāsava, but still there is bhāvāsava. There is still clinging to life and different experiences even thought there is no more clinging to sense objects, For the arahat, all āsavas are completely eradicated so the arahat is referred to as kināsava (without āsavas or anusayas, latent tendencies of akusala, of any kind).

> "It was said: 'With clinging as condition there is existence.' How that is so, Ānanda, should be understood in this way: If there were absolutely and utterly no clinging of any kind anywhere - that is no clinging to sense pleasures, clinging to views, clinging to precepts and observances, or clinging to the doctrine of self - then, in the complete absence of clinging, would existence be discerned?'
>
> 'Certainly not, venerable sir.'
>
> 'Therefore, Ānanda, this is the cause, source, origin, and condition for existence, namely, clinging.' "
>
> *Dīgha Nikāya 15 The Great Discourse on Causation (Translated by Bhikkhu Bodhi.)*

Sarah

8.3 Zoom jottings 55

Sarah Procter Abbott
Mar 16 #166981

Groups of Rūpas

Friends

Harji, Sukin's son, asked me about which rūpas condition each other and I gave these details in brief. I suggested we need to consider the various conditions carefully. (All the details can be found in the Paṭṭhāna, the Book of Abhidhamma.) Here is a little more detail.

1. By aññamaññā paccaya (mutuality condition) the citta and cetasikas arising together mutually condition each other.

This is also true for the 4 great elements, the earth, air, fire and water elements. They mutually condition each other but not the other rūpas.

Also by this condition, just at the moment of birth, the birth consciousness (paṭisandhi citta) and the heart-base (hadāya vatthu) mutually condition each other. At this moment only the heart-base arises at the same moment as the citta which it is a support for. (There are two other groups of rūpas which arise at the same first moment, but they do not condition the citta.)

2. By nissaya paccaya (support condition) again the citta and accompanying cetasikas condition each other by way of being a support.

The 4 great elements also mutually support each other.

By nissaya paccaya cittas and cetasikas support the cittaja rūpas. The cittaja rūpas are the rūpas conditioned by citta. When they are conditioned by citta they arise at the first moment of citta, so they arise together with the citta and are conditioned by the citta. For example, when speaking, the rūpas are conditioned by citta but they don't mutually condition the citta as a support.

This is also true in the case of the 4 great elements which condition the upādā (derived) rūpas by way of supporting them, but the upādā rūpas do not support the 4 great elements or other upādā rūpas in this way.

Again the paṭisandhi citta and hadāya vatthu condition each other by nissaya paccaya. They are a support for each other.

Finally, the eye-base conditions the eye-consciousness when it arises. The eye base has to have already arisen. The same applies to the other sense bases conditioning hearing, smelling, tasting and body-consciousness.

3. By sahājāta paccaya (conascence condition) again the citta and associated cetasikas arising together condition each other by conascence.

The 4 great elements also condition each other by conascence and so do the paṭisandhi citta and hadāya vatthu.

By this condition the paṭisandhi citta also conditions the other two groups of rūpas arising with it at birth. These are the body-sense group of rūpas and the masculinity/femininity group. These groups of rūpas do not, however, condition the paṭisandhi citta.

Again the citta and cetasikas arising together are sahājāta paccaya for the cittaja rūpas arising at the same moment. They arise at the uppada khana (arising moment) of citta. A citta has 3 moments, the arising moment (uppāda khaṇa), presence moment (tiṭṭhi khaṇa) and falling moment (bhaṅga khaṇa).

The rūpas are not sahājāta paccaya for the citta and cetasikas.

Finally the 4 great elements condition the upādā (derived) rūpas by this condition but the upādā rūpas do not condition the 4 great elements or each other in this way. It seems the odour conditions the taste in this way, for example, but it's because there are countless experiences of taste and odour with thinking in between which makes it seem like this.

The detail shows the intricacy of the nature of conditionality and how it's impossible for there to be any self that can control or condition the arising of any reality in life.

> "This dependent arising, Ānanda, is deep and it appears deep. Because of not understanding and not penetrating the Dhamma, Ānanda, this generation has become like a tangled skein, like a knotted ball of thread, like matted rushes and reeds, and does not pass beyond saṃsāra with its plane of misery, unfortunate destinations, and lower realms."

Dīgha Nikāya 15 The Great Discourse on Causation (Translated by Bhikkhu Bodhi)

Sarah

9

April 2021

9.1 Zoom jottings 56

Sarah Procter Abbott
Apr 3 #167143

Sacca Pāramī (the perfection of truthfulness)

Friends

In a Chinese discussion, Lily mentioned unwholesome reactions when discussing various situations. Usually there isn't enough wise consideration. Ajahn asked her before hearing the Buddha's Teachings whether there was any wise consideration about what is now, the present moment.

Do you own anything now? There is wasting time all the time with ignorance when there is no understanding of what appears now.

Without the development of the pāramīs (perfections), it's impossible to understand the truth. Understand whatever is there by conditions as not self. When there is firm confidence there is adiṭṭhāna (resolution) pāramī, along with viriya (effort) pāramī and sacca (truthfulness) pāramī.

Is anyone brave enough to let go the idea of self now? Only sacca pāramī. Not yet! It develops by itself naturally with right understanding, understanding the truth of whatever appears now.

> "Whatever tastes there are on earth,
> truth is the sweetest of those tastes;
> firm in truth, ascetics and brahmins
> cross to the beyond of birth and death."
> *(Ja V 491)*

> "Of these tastes, truth is the sweetest, the sweetest or the most excellent, the best, supreme; for such tastes as those of roots nourish the body and bring defiled pleasure; but the taste of truth - truth as abstinence and truthful speech - nourishes the mind with serenity and insight and brings undefiled pleasure; the taste of liberation is sweet because it is permeated by the taste of the supreme truth; and the taste of the meaning and taste of the Dhamma are sweet because they occur in dependence on the meaning and the Dhamma that are the means for achieving that [taste of liberation]."
>
> *Suttanipāta 1:10 Commentary to Ālavaka Sutta (Translated by Bhikkhu Bodhi)*

Sarah

9.2 Zoom jottings 57

Sarah Procter Abbott
Apr 3 #167144

Meditation

Friends

A friend mentioned she no longer goes to meditation centres. Ajahn stressed that it depends on paññā (right understanding) which has been accumulated to let go of the wrong understanding. Much more subtle understanding has to develop to understand what appears now. There is no one at all. There has to be the understanding there is no "you", no person in reality. Understand the sacca (truth). No one can understand by themselves. These are precious moments of listening and discussing the sacca.

Lukas mentioned meditation as taught in the Visuddhimagga including awareness of the body and bodily feelings. Ajahn asked him what meditation is and whether there is mediation now. We need to consider the Buddha's words carefully. Whatever can be understood now is better than going somewhere to meditate. She asked if it is "I" that tries to understand and be aware. There can be reading with or without understanding. When it's without understanding, one just remembers the words from different pages.

Lukas mentioned the 40 objects of samatha (calmness). Ajahn asked him if there is no understanding of what appears now, can we talk about samatha?

> "The Blessed One, Brahmin, did not praise every type of meditation, nor did he condemn every type of meditation. What kind of meditation did the Blessed One not praise? Here, Brahmin, someone abides with his mind obsessed by sensual lust, a prey to sensual lust, and he does not understand as it actually is the escape from arisen sensual lust.
>
> While he harbours sensual lust within, he meditates, premeditates, out-meditates, and mis-meditates (jhāyanti pajjhāyanti nijjhāyanti apajjhāyanti). He abides with his mind obsessed by ill will, a prey to ill will... with his mind obsessed by sloth and torpor, a prey to sloth and torpor... with his mind obsessed by restlessness and remorse, a prey to restlessness and remorse... with his mind obsessed by doubt within, a prey to doubt, and he does not understand as it actually

is the escape from arisen doubt. While he harbours doubt within, he meditates, premeditates, out-meditates, and mis-meditates. The Blessed One did not praise that kind of meditation."

Majjhima Nikāya 108 With Gopaka Moggalāna (Translated by Bhikkhu Ñānamoli and Bhikkhu Bodhi)

Sarah

9.3 Zoom jottings 58

Sarah Procter Abbott
Apr 4 #167165

Dreaming about how "I can do!"

Friends

If there is no understanding now, there cannot be understanding at other moments. There is just dreaming about "How can I do something" all the time, forgetting that there is no "I" from the very beginning. There has to be the right attitude to let go of that wrong understanding which cannot be let go of by ignorance. Paññā performs its function very secretly and gradually! Learn about dhammas to understand what appears now.

When there are conditions no one can stop the appearing of dhamma more and more. From the beginning there has to be the understanding of nāma (the reality which can experience) such as seeing as well as the rūpa (which cannot experience) such as visible object.

Khun Dim mentioned it will take a long time. Ajahn stressed the importance of khanti (patience), viriya (strength or effort) and adiṭṭhāna (determination) which has to be so resolute to let go of the idea of "I will do something". Only paññā assisted by these and the various pāramī (perfections) can do this. When there is understanding that it is "not me", there is no disturbance at that moment.

Vakkali spoke to the Buddha:

> "For a long time, venerable sire, I have wanted to come and see the Blessed one, but I haven't been fit enough to do so."
>
> "Enough, Vakkali! Why do you want to see this foul body? One who sees the Dhamma sees me; one who sees me sees the Dhamma. For in seeing the Dhamma, Vakkali, one sees me; and in seeing me, one sees the Dhamma."
>
> *Saṃyutta Nikāya 22:87 (5) Vakkali (Translated by Bhikkhu Bodhi)*

Sarah

9.4 Zoom jottings 59

Sarah Procter Abbott
Apr 4 #167166

Seeing in the Dark

Friends

Thang Huong had a question about seeing in a dark room.

Whether seeing in the dark or not, there's only the story of that which is not known as dhamma. There is not understanding the truth of the world, that which is experiencing and that which is experienced. There is just wanting to know what is there. Is there enough understanding of what experiences? If not, there is doubt about what is experienced. If there is just thinking about what is experienced, there is no understanding of the experiencing.

If there is no eye-base, there is no seeing in the light or the dark. No matter what is seen, light or dark, it is only that which is experienced. In the dark, only black colour appears, not other colours, but no matter what, it's just that which appears. That dhamma which experiences sees any colour or the dark. No matter what is said it's different from what is there. Close your eyes and there must be the object which is seen.

There's no "I" to understand what we are talking about. There will be less doubt about the object when there is more understanding of seeing. There is just the object experienced, nothing, no thing in it. There must be more precise understanding of the difference between the experiencing and that which is experienced.

> "Therefore, Bāhiya, you should train yourself that with respect to the seen there will be merely the seen, that with respect to the heard, there will be merely the heard, that with respect to the sensed, there will be merely the sensed, that with respect to the cognised, there will be merely the cognised - so should you, Bāhiya, train yourself."

Udāna 10 With Bāhiya (Translated by Peter Masefield)

Sarah

9.5 Zoom jottings 60

Sarah Procter Abbott
Apr 12 #167280

Loss of a Dear Sister

Friends

Ann's younger sister had suddenly died a few days ago after many difficulties in life.

We discussed a common Thai expression which is used to indicate "kamma is up" or kamma has brought its result.

Death is so very common, like this moment. In ignorance we have the idea that someone has died and it brings great sorrow. Only the understanding of the Dhamma can lead to wise reflection of the truth without the usual unwholesome thoughts.

Whoever dies, no matter when, it's the common condition, just like this moment. Without this understanding there must be a lot of attachment and grief. Actually, there's no one at all now or when death comes.

The point is to let go, little by little. Even when we cry, there are feelings and other realities appearing, but no one, just the sad feeling or other reality conditioned to arise and then gone, just like death at each moment.

We like to sleep and not to experience anything. It's time to rest. Death is just like that. The bhavaṅga (life continuum) cittas follow the new paṭisandhi (birth) citta. There are more experiences in the new life but it's the end of everything in this life. In the new life nothing is known about this life, all the memories of it are gone. It's just like falling asleep.

When you cry, there is thinking about many stories about your sister or this special person but there is not your sister or this person any more. There is a completely new personality who knows nothing about us. It's the way of cittas and cetasikas arising and falling away only. There is no more connection, no more relationship, but there is thinking about my sister, my house, my arm for a moment again and again. There is clinging all the time. That's the way it is.

It's so miraculous to understand reality now as not self! Without understanding it is taken as something or someone from life to life, endlessly. With less ignorance and more understanding it's quite different, less and less akusala (unwholesomeness) such as sadness. The great danger is ignorance, not understanding and attachment, trying and doing with the idea of Self. With paññā (understanding) the feeling is quite different to other moments. These are precious moments in life. It's only paññā which can understand realities as not self and can let go of wrong view and ignorance. When it becomes sharper, the reality appears well. It arises beyond expectation and this is the meaning of anattā. Whatever arises does so unexpectedly and by conditions.

When paññā arises, there is no thought or regret about the past or future.

No regret!

Each life is like this one with no understanding, just ideas of me, my sister or beloved one in ignorance. This is how life keeps going in saṃsāra because of no understanding. Whatever arises is taken for something or someone or for "I" who owns something. We keep thinking of the world as "me", "my sister", "my family" and so on. As long as there is "I", there is "my sister". It's just thinking. She doesn't know you any-more.

Seeing just sees right now but there's always the idea that "I experience". There has to be the understanding that gets closer and closer to the reality which experiences to let go the idea of "I". There is no one. There is no sister, no family member even now. There are just the arising and falling away of cittas, cetasikas and rūpas.

No regret!

> "The young and old, the foolish and the wise, all are stopped short by the power of death, all finally end in death. Of those overcome by death and passing to another world, a father cannot hold back his son, nor relatives a relation. See! While the relatives are looking on and weeping, one by one each mortal is led away like an ox to slaughter.
>
> In this manner the world is afflicted by death and decay. But the wise do not grieve, having realized the nature of the world. You do not know the path by which they came or departed. Not seeing either end you lament in vain. If any benefit is gained by lamenting, the wise would do it. Only a fool would harm himself. Yet through weeping and sorrowing the mind does not become calm, but still more suffering is produced, the body is harmed and one becomes lean and pale, one merely hurts oneself. One cannot protect a departed one (peta) by that means. To grieve is in vain."
>
> *Suttanipāta 3:8 The Arrow (Translated by John Ireland)*

Sarah

9.6 Zoom jottings 61

Sarah Procter Abbott
Apr 15 #167337

Ordaining

Friends

Hui Yueh mentioned in a Chinese discussion that we may talk about "not trying" because there is no Self, but "what about becoming a monk or nun?", she asked.

Ajahn Sujin: What for?
HY: The purpose is for ending dukkha or suffering.
AS: Is there dukkha now?
HY: Yes, there is dukkha, so there is the intention to stop it.
AS: Intention cannot stop it. Only paññā (right understanding) can understand it little by little.

Hui Yueh suggested that if one ordains there can be the correcting of the understanding along the way.

AS: If there is no understanding of the Teachings about realities now, what's the use of becoming ordained?

All the Teachings are about paññā (understanding) and the accumulation of the pāramīs (perfections which develop with paññā) just to understand the truth about what appears now, no matter one is ordained or not. To develop understanding is always the point, not to leave home or do anything without understanding. So before becoming a monk, one should know what it's for. It should be for the eradication of all defilements, to live as an arahat (fully enlightened).

Even though we're not monks, we can follow what monks do in a day by way of good behaviour that is useful and good for everyone. The one who becomes a monk should see the danger of even very slight akusala (unwholesomeness), such as when clinging to food, to what is seen or heard. We can all read the Vinaya. Even slight akusala conditions madness and is dangerous. Lay people can follow as many rules as they like. The way to eradicate kilesa (defilements) is not to become ordained but to understand the truth of different realities.

What is better? To understand what is taught in the Vinaya, Suttas and Abhidhamma as not self or just wanting to be ordained and not understanding the danger of ignorance and other akusala? Just understand one's own accumulations of akusala even now. Is the wanting to become ordained because of attachment rather than the right understanding of what appears now? Without truthfulness we go wrong. Clinging, taṇhā, is the 2nd Noble Truth, the cause of dukkha. There is clinging when there is "wanting to do". There has to be the understanding of the accumulation of one's nature of clinging.

The true monk's life is far away from the attachment of the lay life. If one is untruthful about the real purpose in the beginning when ordaining, it leads to being more and more untruthful. If there is not the understanding of the truth, no matter one is a monk or a lay person, one is not part of the Sangha that one takes refuge in.

Anyone who is a monk should understand the great benefit, otherwise what's the difference? Being a monk means there is paññā which can see the virtues taught by the Buddha and there are the accumulations to eliminate all akusala. It's very different from the lay life. This is why lay people should show respect to monks.

There was a discussion about bad monks. Bad monks are like robbers, as the Buddha said. It's very dangerous to live as a monk without the understanding of the Teachings.

> "One living as a dissembler is the defiler of the path: Having taken on the dress of the disciplined, he acts in such a way that people think of him thus: 'he is a forest dweller, one who lives at the foot of a tree, a rag-robe wearer, one who lives by alms round, with few desires, content.' Displaying such dissembling conduct, which appears proper and polished, this person should be understood as 'a defiler of the path' because he defiles the world-transcending path for himself and defiles the path to a good destination for others."
>
> *Suttanipāta, 1:5 Commentary to Cunda Sutta (Translated by Bhikkhu Bodhi)*

The true purpose of the Teachings is for the understanding now that there is no one, no self. There are just conditioned realities from life to life. The monk's life is for the one who can renounce home, family, everything because they are not suitable for him. It is for the one that can live the life of an arahat. The monk cannot enjoy ordinary things like lay-people. Even at the lily-pond, smelling the fragrance is not suitable for a monk. "Bhikkhus" refers to the one who understands.

> "A bhikkhu: One is a bhikkhu by having broken seven qualities: the view of the personal entity, doubt, seizing upon good behaviour and observances, lust, hatred, delusion, and conceit."
>
> *Suttanipāta 4:3 Niddesa 1 50, Commentary to The Octad on the Hostile (Translated by Bhikkhu Bodhi)*

Sarah

9.7 Zoom jottings 62

Sarah Procter Abbott
Apr 16 #167350

The Worldly Conditions

Friends

There was a discussion about patience (khanti). Without understanding, can there be the development of patience no matter whether it's a good or bad situation? It's not me or mine. Whatever fortune, misfortune, happiness or unhappiness there is, it's just there for a moment. The world is just a moment. Patience (or other wholesomeness) is not for anyone, it's just for the moment it arises and then it falls away instantly. When there is understanding, it's the moment of letting go.

Sukin asked a question about the pāramī (perfections).

AS: What is pāramī for?

Sukin: For enlightenment.

AS: It's to understand the truth, sacca, as no one. So there must be right understanding, there must be viriya (courage) for understanding. There must be more and more understanding of no self, otherwise one is enslaved by lobha (attachment) whatever one hears about.

When there is nekkamma (renunciation) pāramī there is the getting away little by little from attachment to the sense doors as usual. The development of all these pāramīs takes a very long time with more and more understanding required.

When one doesn't think of the result, it's better than thinking "I understand" or "I need to understand more".

The Buddha spoke about the worldly conditions that change all the time: gain and loss, disrepute and fame, blame and praise, pleasure and pain. One minute we're blamed and the next praised, depending on conditions that are beyond control. These worldly conditions are the ups and downs of life. The more understanding and patience, the less susceptible we will be to the worldly conditions

This sutta exhorts the development of right understanding of whatever appears at the present moment, without selection of any kind and without concern about the result or how much or little understanding there may be.

> "Gain and loss, disrepute and fame,
> blame and praise, pleasure and pain:
> these conditions that people meet
> are impermanent, transient, and subject to change.
>
> A wise and mindful person knows them and sees that they are subject to change. Desirable conditions don't excite his mind nor is he repelled by undesirable conditions.
>
> He has dispelled attraction and repulsion;
> they are gone and no longer present.
> Having known the dustless, sorrowless state,
> he understands rightly and has transcended existence."
>
> *Aṅguttara Nikāya 8:5 (5) World (1) (Translated by Bhikkhu Bodhi)*

9.8 Zoom jottings 63

Sarah Procter Abbott
Apr 16 #167351

Surgery

Friends

It was the day after my foot surgery. Whatever the worldly conditions of happiness, suffering, fame, insignificance, praise, blame, gain or loss, none of it is "me". The world of the reality appearing is just for a moment, no matter through one of the sense doors or through the mind door.

In truth there's no me, no foot, no surgery, just different dhammas (realities) arising and falling away. Whatever arises is anattā, not in anyone's control, arising unexpectedly. The fantasy, the dreams about various situations are all gone instantly with the moments of thinking. Nothing is left at all after the reality has fallen away completely. It's like this from moment to moment.

There should be no expectation of any result when helping others otherwise it's "I who knows" or "I who wants the others to know". Anattā is covered up all the time.

Share and help those who can see the value of the most precious thing in life, the understanding of each reality, the understanding that each moment is conditioned.

Everyone is going to die and dies each moment now.

> "Insignificant, bhikkhus, is the loss of relatives. The worst thing to lose is wisdom."
>
> "Insignificant, bhikkhus, is the increase of relatives. The best thing in which to increase is wisdom. Therefore, bhikkhus, you should train yourselves thus: 'We will increase in wisdom.' It is in such a way that you should train yourselves."
>
> "Insignificant, bhikkhus, is the loss of wealth. The worst thing to lose is wisdom."

> "Insignificant, bhikkhus, is the increase of wealth. The best thing in which to increase is wisdom. Therefore, bhikkhus, you should train yourselves thus: 'We will increase in wisdom.' It is in such a way that you should train yourselves."
>
> "Insignificant, bhikkhus, is the loss of fame. The worst thing to lose is wisdom."
>
> "Insignificant, bhikkhus, is the increase of fame. The best thing in which to increase is wisdom. Therefore, bhikkhus, you should train yourselves thus: 'We will increase in wisdom.' It is in such a way that you should train yourselves."
>
> *Aṅguttara Nikāya 1:76 (6) - 81 (11) (Translated by Bhikkhu Bodhi)*

Sarah

Part II

Meetings on line

10
April 2020

10.1 Meeting on line, 1

Nina
Apr 12 #162464

Whatever is conditioned

Dear friends,

Because of all the emotions, I forgot to turn on my recorder. I was excited seeing you all. My Dutch friends were so interested so I might as well write a report, using my quick notes. I put my own thoughts between brackets.

Again, I express my thankfulness to Sarah and Jonothan who organised the meeting, it must have been a lot of work behind the scene.

Sarah referred to me our discussion on dsg about superstition, thinking of a dear one who passed away and looks after us on high. It is only thinking and speculating about a story. Also this thinking is just a dhamma and gone already. Whatever the stories in life we are involved in, let us not forget the reality of the present moment. Seeing now, hearing now, only conditioned dhammas. Whatever question is asked, it can always be brought back to the present moment.

Sarah: Whatever is conditioned cannot be any other way.

Nina: A good reminder, also in relation to Corona. We have to be careful, but it helps to have less fear when realizing that it cannot be any other way.

Jeff: Seeing and hearing, different realities. A problem: having accumulated thinking with worry.

Nina: I did not catch the answer, but if I understood rightly your remark, also that is only, only a conditioned dhamma. Perhaps then we attach less importance to that. (Nice to see you live after reading your posts.)

Minh: Speaking about no control. He understood well that pariyatti is not yet direct understanding.

Ann: Emphasizing patience in the development of right understanding.

Sarah: Trying to be aware of rūpa or feeling, that is impatience. Lack of confidence, thinking that it can be done.

Sundara: Reading suttas can so easily be done with wrong understanding. The meaning is so subtle.

Sarah: There are conventional ideas about patience. It can be unwholesome patience.

Sundara: We do not realize when. There is conceit, when thinking of what others are doing. Only by understanding dhamma we can know the meaning of the suttas. There can be confidence in the subtlety of the teachings. It is more elusive than we would think.

Nina

10.2 Meeting on line, 2

Nina
Apr 12 #162465

Paññā verifies the truth

Dear friends,

Huong: Hearing now, seeing now, nothing can be changed.
Sarah: No matter the circumstances.
Nina: Good reminder: Corona now, but reality is reality, we shouldn't forget this. No matter the circumstances.
Jonothan: Paññā verifies the truth, that is the function of paññā. Conventional understanding is different from verification in the ultimate sense, which is a matter of paññā. This takes a long time.
Nina: Here patience comes in, the development of paññā cannot be hastened
Sarah: Seeing now. Confidence develops together with understanding. When understanding is not firm there are doubts. In the ultimate sense there is no supermarket, no missing toilet rolls.
As to the satipaṭṭhāna sutta: we should ask ourselves: what is seen now? Is it a table? Just what is visible should be known.
Jonothan: Is there any verification now? For conventional verification no understanding of dhamma is required. there is the idea of: I see now, I hear now. The best verification is a moment of awareness and insight that has a characteristic of reality as object. Visible object is just the object of seeing-consciousness.
Sarah: What is dhamma now? There is sound now, can it be verified that it is just sound? A moment of understanding is the beginning of verification. It is not a conventional idea of: I can hear the voice of the speaker.
Jonothan: It is a beginning level of wisdom. Repeated listening is necessary.
Nina: Very good reminder: again and again.

Nina

10.3 Meeting on line, 3

Nina
Apr 12 #162466

Living alone

Dear friends,

Sarah: living alone: just a moment of seeing. (N: I am reflecting on this when not seeing a living soul for a few days. Citta is always alone. We are born alone, die alone.)

Question: Santirana-citta at rebirth is not accompanied by pleasant feeling (as may be the case when it performs the function of investigating in a process). Why?

Sarah explained: It is a very weak vipāka (result of kamma). In the case of a stronger vipāka in the sense sphere, the vipākacittas are with two or three roots and then they can be accompanied by pleasant feeling, and in that case the function of rebirth is not performed by santiranacitta.

Question (from Vietnam): Shall I go or not go to the supermarket?

Sarah: Each moment is conditioned. It's anattā. It's just a dhamma that thinks because of past memory, thinking it is "I" who goes to the supermarket, no supermarket, there are no toilet rolls.

Discussion with little Nam and his brother about seeing and hearing with ignorance. (Nam showed great interest)

Jonothan to Nam: There is not anything to do, understanding can develop gradually. There is seeing and the object of seeing, and these are different objects of understanding. It is difficult to understand at first. Consider more and there will be more understanding.

Sarah asked Nam: What is heard how? Can you hear a voice?

Nam: Just sound.

Sarah: And then we can think of the meaning of words. Usually after hearing there is attachment instantly. Attachment after seeing, hearing, etc., all day. If there wouldn't be a discussion about it you would not know.

Nina: As I said, a child can understand deep dhamma, age does not matter.

Nina

10.4 Meeting on line II, 1

Nina
Apr 21 #162621

Consider the present moment

Dear friends,

Nina: When we do not consider the present moment, this leads to wrong interpretation of the Tipiṭaka. The teachings are not theoretical, for example, the precepts. One may think: I want to keep the precepts. What are citta, cetasika and rūpa now? It is not the words, not what is in the books. The Buddha asked: is seeing impermanent? He did not mean impermanence in general, but at this moment. I am grateful to hear about this more and more, because we keep on forgetting it.

Jonathan: What is appearing at present, rather than in the book should be known.

Sarah: Life before and after the corona virus: there are lock downs etc. This is just conventional thinking. In the absolute sense there is no difference. There is delirious thinking (thinking with unwholesomeness) now: about the virus, what will happen, how many cases are there. Realities are exactly the same as before the corona virus. Seeing and thinking followed by the fantasy world with long stories.

Sarah said about studying the Dependent Origination: If there is no understanding about seeing now, it is not useful to study the details of the Dependent Origination. There is an idea of "I can practise, I can follow". The discussion has to come back to now.

Jonathan: Understand the present moment rather than think of stories.

Nina: This is so helpful. We keep on thinking of Corona with anxiety, of being contaminated, but there are only citta, cetasika and rūpa, and these change each moment.

Alan speaks about the importance of intellectual understanding: Without a lot of intellectual understanding there will be the idea of "me" doing something. There should be a balance between learning details and knowing the present moment.

Jonathan: Some of the realities the Buddha speaks about will be appearing, some will not. Seeing experiences visible object, but not all realities appear.

Sarah: No need to use the word pariyatti (intellectual understanding) but consider what life is at this moment. There can be wise reflection. At this moment there is not direct understanding of seeing, but there can be a beginning of wise reflection that there is just this moment of seeing that sees and then it is gone. Not an "I" that can see or hear. If one would not hear about it, it would not be known. But having heard about it there can be wise reflection. Life carries on as usual. We take precautions, avoid gatherings etc. But there can be understanding at any moment.

Alan: What is the purpose of Abhidhamma? It is very detailed, consisting of seven books and commentaries.

Sarah: No matter the Suttas, the Vinaya, or the Abhidhamma, the purpose is to understand life now, realities as not self, as anattā. If we just hear: seeing sees visible object, it is not enough. The understanding has to develop deeper to eradicate the idea of self. This is the purpose of the details. Seeing is the result of kamma and then the wholesome or unwholesome cittas follow. These are "cause", different from results, such as seeing. We learn more details for the purpose of understanding. No "I" who does anything, or who experiences anything.

Details are important, for the purpose of not "I", not self. It does not matter we call it Abhidhamma, Sutta, pariyatti or anything. Just details for the understanding of life now, directly realized by the Buddha.

Alan: We understand, in order to correct misunderstandings. There is a lot of misinterpretation of the teachings, of wrong practice. This is an advantage of knowing details too.

Nina

10.5 Meeting on line, II, 2

Nina
Apr 22 #162630

What is knowing Abhidhamma?

Dear friends,

Sarah: What is knowing Abhidhamma?

Alan: There is the inclination to try, to select an object, to go to a special place. Then you can refer to the Abhidhamma, stating that you begin with detachment. You can show details, show that this is wrong practice.

Sarah: I do not think that this is knowing Abhidhamma. To me, seeing now, hearing now, attachment, aversion, reality now, each one is Abhidhamma. Knowing Abhidhamma means understanding this moment. A theoretical discussion is not knowing Abhidhamma at this moment

Nina: People think only of the book, but it is really about this moment. It is good to talk about seeing and hearing all the time. We are seeing and hearing now, but we forget that it is not in the book. It is this moment. We talk about this moment; "this moment", it can be very vague when we say this. It is good to discuss this more. I find questions from beginners and children very helpful.

Betty: This moment is already gone. How can there be awareness of this moment? Usually there is reflection after the moment has passed.

Sarah: That is why we talk about different levels of understanding. In the beginning it is not direct understanding of seeing or visible object. There has to be wise consideration of the nature of seeing. Seeing has gone, but as understanding develops it gets closer to directly understand the reality.

Jonathan: It is conditioned to understand, not because we are trying to understand or to focus on what is appearing at the present moment. The function of understanding is to understand what is presently there. There are certain conditions for the arising of understanding.

Betty: Understanding always arises after the moment a reality presents itself.

Nina: It does not matter that it is already gone. Very closely afterwards the characteristic can still appear. It is important to know that seeing is not thinking about people and all the things we notice. If there is not wise reflection about the difference, paññā (understanding) can never develop. It all depends on paññā to condition right awareness. It is better not to think too much about it, such as "how can I?", "I have to try and how is it possible?"

Sarah: That is the trap of attachment: "How can I understand exactly the moment when reality arises."

Jonathan (to Alan): Is there a need to deal with Abhidhamma separately from the suttas?

Alan: Without a basic understanding of Abhidhamma one cannot understand the suttas. How can you understand realities without the Abhidhamma. We get from the Abhidhamma what the very beginning of satipaṭṭhāna is and what the object (of satipaṭṭhāna) is. What is real and what is a concept. That understanding is very difficult to get from the suttas alone.

Jonathan: It is there. In the Sutta all different dhatus (elements) are to be understood. The elements, the khandhas, dhamma in different classifications are to be understood. We could not read Abhidhamma and Sutta by ourselves. We need others who have the same interest and can help us to understand what it is all about.

Nina

10.6 Meeting on line, II, 3

Nina
Apr 23 #162640

Everything arises by conditions

Dear friends,

Acharn Sujin speaking about reality right now:
Without hearing the teachings it is impossible.
Alan: How many details we need to know?
Acharn: There are seeing and visible object, no "I" who can have them at will. Sati-sampajañña (sati and paññā) and satipaṭṭhāna do not arise yet because there are no conditions for their arising. Right understanding knows that this is not satipaṭṭhāna. When times comes satipaṭṭhāna arises by conditions, it arises by conditions. Everything arises by conditions. All cetasikas (mental factors), manasikāra (attention) included, are now developing by themselves, not by anyone. The other cetasikas that arise with paññā develop, now. No one is there.

Hearing, pariyatti (intellectual understanding), paṭipatti (direct understanding), pativedha (direct realization) are not anyone. (One should be) aware of anything, no selection. It (can) appear just as it is. Visible object, no thing in it.

Everything is appearing as some "thing", not as it is. It is not easy to understand, but this is the way. At the very beginning, from hearing, considering, before it can be understood. So it is not "I". Right understanding can be developed little by little, so very little. Just one moment of understanding is accumulated, by conditions.

Sarah: Alan, you talked about finding a balance, should we study more details? That is the idea of "I". It is just thinking by conditions, each moment is conditioned.

Sarah to Michael (a newcomer): We are talking about what life is at this moment. We think that life is different because of the corona virus. But any time there is just seeing, hearing, smelling, tasting, touching and thinking. We used to think that I can see, such as many faces on the screen. Seeing just sees what is visible, not I who sees. Without the development of understanding it can never be known. Does this make sense to you?

Michael: Yes, it is very digestible.

Sarah: What is touched at this moment?

Michael: I am aware of my own ignorance.

Sarah: It has to come back to this moment, that is all we know. We think we see people and the ocean, and then there is thinking. Seeing sees just what is visible. There is hearing now, just the sound is heard. That is the world at this moment. The world is not corona virus. The world is just a moment of seeing, hearing, smelling, tasting, touching and thinking.

There are many moments of thinking. We think that we can touch a computer. Where is the computer? Just in our imagination. Hardness or softness is touched. The Buddha's teaching is just about life at this moment, no matter we call it Abhidhamma or sutta, with Pāli, English or Vietnamese words. This is basic of all the teachings.

Trin: Understanding of the intellectual level can condition understanding of moments now, seeing, hearing, as not self. The Abhidhamma helps us to understand that there is nobody there, just dhammas. Patience to listen, patience to understand.

Nina

10.7 Meeting on line, II, 4

Nina
Apr 23 #162641

What are accumulations?

Dear friends,

Jonathan: To come back to how many details we have to know. There is no answer to this. It varies from one individual to another.

Maeve: Ignorance is conditioned, we do not want to have it. It is real, it can be useful. It tells us about the lack of understanding. I appreciate this more and more.

Sarah: The more understanding there is, the more ignorance becomes apparent. Before studying the teachings there was no idea of any ignorance.

Jonathan: We are concerned about our level of understanding. It is not a question of having more understanding; awareness arises only by conditions. Interest in the teachings, in having a discussion, this is conditioned to arise.

Azita: What are accumulations?

Sarah: Attachment now is accumulated from the past, and it will condition more attachment in the future. There is the accumulation of all wholesome and unwholesome mental factors. After seeing, wholesome and unwholesome mental states arise. When they arise they condition the same. Understanding now, wise reflection now conditions more understanding and wise reflection in the future, by accumulation.

Azita: While walking in the bush I focus on different flowers. Focussing on a certain plant, is that by accumulation?

Sarah: Attachment to and interest in flowers is accumulated. When we are swimming, some people like stories of fish or the sunrise. It depends on interest and attachment what is accumulated.

Azita: When we see how different we are it may help kindness and tolerance.

Sarah: They do not belong to a person, they are just different realities that are conditioned.

Alan: Does accumulation condition seeing and hearing? We see now. That is: we are interested in that.

Sarah: Many conditions are involved: kamma, visible object, eyesense condition seeing. At the moment of seeing there is no attachment. Immediately after seeing, interest and attachment arise by conditions even in a sense-door process. They do not belong to anyone.

Jonothan: The object that is seen is not conditioned by accumulated tendency, but the reaction to it is.

Alan: We are hearing sound while listening to Dhamma. But listening to that sound is by accumulations. There are many conditions to support the hearing of the sound. It has to be conditioned by interest as well.

Sarah: Past kamma conditions the experiencing of sound and there are many other conditions. Ignorance is also an indirect condition for each reality that arises now.

Jonathan: speaking in conventional sense: as to joining in a Dhamma discussion, one's interest has been accumulated and is a condition.

Jonathan repeats Sun's question on wholesome and unwholesome saññā (remembrance). The mental factors (cetasikas) can also be wholesome or unwholesome. How can one know saññā, how can one know whether it is wholesome or unwholesome?

Sarah: Usually saññā does not commonly appear. A moment of wise reflection on Dhamma is only possible because of memory. That memory is different from memory with attachment or anger. saññā is conditioned by all the other mental factors that arise with it.

Nina: The citta arises and falls away so fast, it is impossible to catch that moment. We should not try, that is of no use. It is good to know that all is conditioned, anattā. Only paññā, when it is more developed, can distinguish between what is wholesome and unwholesome. We should not try to find out.

Alan: Is it right to say: understanding of realities now is conditioned by saññā?

Sarah: Without saññā there could not be any thinking, or memory of the meaning of words.

Alan: What conditions right awareness at that very moment? Is it the memory of the intellectual understanding? Saññā has a part to play in a moment of insight.

Sarah: Right saññā is often given as a proximate cause of awareness.

Nina

10.8 Meeting on line, III, 1

Nina
Apr 27 #162745

Thinking of "stories"

Dear friends,

Nina: The time before and after Corona we talked about is a good example that shows the difference between thinking of "stories" and understanding realities. Seeing and hearing arise, no matter what the circumstances are, they are realities. Hearing is always hearing (before or after Corona). It is good to be reminded. When we are absorbed in stories we keep on forgetting realities.

All of your remarks were very useful. Maeve said that ignorance is useful, when you realize how much ignorance there is. Before we studied the teachings, we did not realize this. Trin reminded us that patience is so important. We like to understand everything immediately, but this is not possible. All of your remarks are useful, reminding us of reality. I am looking forward to them. Alan had questions about the usefulness of knowing details. After seeing there is straight away the arising of the intoxicants (very subtle defilements). We did not realize that after seeing now, hearing now already ignorance or wrong view arise. They may be very subtle, we do not notice them. It is very good to know our amount of ignorance.

Lukas: Besides realities there is also conventional life, such as dāna. We are giving to someone on the street who is hungry.

Nina: It all depends on the citta (consciousness) at that moment. It is not wholesome when we like to gain something or we want approval. Citta is complicated and very detailed. The Buddha explained all the subtle points and details of citta. The more we study, the more it is helpful for daily life, also for conventional life. We often forget that, we are totally absorbed in stories.

Jonathan: There are different levels of kusala (wholesomeness). Dāna is one kind of wholesomeness, depending on consciousness, not the outward act.

Sundara: Understanding supports all levels of wholesomeness, be it dāna or sīla.

Sarah: Without understanding, how do we know what is dāna? For Jonothan's birthday I made a gift. There are so many different moments involved: kindness, attachment, hoping that he will be happy. Without understanding we take all such moments for wholesome, for being my kindness, my giving.

Nina

10.9 Meeting on line III, 2

Nina
Apr 28 #162765

We cannot hurry up

Dear friends,

Trin: If you want to explain Dhamma, there is dāna, higher dhamma, kindness, these are also conditioned. It is not so simple. Sometimes you give for "self", there is a lot of attachment.

Lukas: I stopped studying the Abhidhamma.

Trin: When there is a little moment of kindness, there is no self there.

Sarah: Each moment is conditioned. If you go out in the street and you see someone who is hungry, each moment is conditioned. Whether you make or don't make an offering, each moment of thinking is conditioned. Like now, who knows who will answer your question or make a comment? What is dhamma now? Is there seeing now, kindness now? When you think of a person who is hungry in the street, there is just thinking of a story.

Maeve: Once dhamma is planted, does it flourish?

Jonathan: It depends on conditions.

Maeve: What encourages it to flourish?

Jonathan: There can be interest in different ways. One may be academically inclined or one may be poor and uneducated.

Sarah: Only when understanding is really firm can it condition direct understanding of realities. In the beginning it is not firm, one follows other interests. One needs discussion, one forgets life at this moment. One thinks about a lot of stories such as 'what will I do when I meet a beggar on the street?' One needs reminders and to keep reflecting and considering about the purpose of study. There is no self at this moment.

Maeve: One listens, sometimes with confidence, sometimes not. Hearing the Dhamma discussed is a great way.

Sarah: In the discussions one has one's own ideas questioned. When one listens just on one's own, one believes that one has understood. When one is questioned one realizes that it is not understood. Questioning is helpful.

Sundara: One needs to be incredibly patient and this itself is conditioned. Listen carefully, consider carefully, and then there can be more conditions for understanding. We cannot hurry up the Dhamma. We cannot make understanding grow as we like.

Nina

10.10 Meeting on line III, 3

Nina
Apr 29 #162787

Desire is all around

Dear friends,

Acharn: How can one know that there is right understanding? Daily life is the examination of how much understanding of dhamma there is. Dhamma is not in the book, it is now. Seeing right now is dhamma. The accumulation of right understanding can have conditions to arise, there should be no expectation. We read a lot but the understanding of realities is different from book knowledge. Now from book knowledge we understand theoretically that there is no one. How can this moment be no self, no one? It depends on conditions. Those who have attained enlightenment understand the arising and falling away (of realities), not "I" at all. To what extent can the understanding of daily life be known as not me, at this moment of seeing, instead of thinking of cetasikas? From hearing there can be the considering of what appears. It can condition the understanding of no self. The development of understanding has to be very gradual, and it has to be truthful, sacca pāramī (the perfection of truthfulness). How much understanding is there of the characteristic of no self, right now? There should be no regret while thinking how much or how little understanding there is. It is the understanding which is conditioned. Begin to understand that which experiences and that which cannot experience.

Lukas: I did not study dhamma for a long time. How can I come back to study?

Acharn: It is always I. Do not forget the second noble Truth which is lobha. It is there after seeing, hearing, smelling, tasting, touching and thinking. There are the āsavas (intoxicants, very subtle defilements) of clinging to sense objects, to existence, of wrong view and of ignorance. Seeing experiences, we do not have to name it seeing. Visible object appears to seeing, it is conditioned and then gone. The accumulation of understanding stemming from hearing again and again conditions a moment of understanding. In the beginning it is just thinking, not clear understanding of the reality that experiences all the time. So long as conditions are not enough yet it is impossible to really penetrate the truth of it.

It is not desire, it is the understanding that has to be this moment, it is gone all the time. The desire is all around. The understanding that it is anattā cannot be controlled. It can become less, just very, very little. Citta and cetasika are now, by conditions, uncontrollable.

Intellectual understanding conditions not being forgetful of what is now appearing, by conditions, uncontrollable, no self. Such as wanting to come back to study; this has been accumulated from life to life, so that it can be known as that which leads us to the wrong way. It is attached to the cycle of birth and death, to nāma and rūpa now.

Right understanding can begin to understand it as it is. It becomes less and less, just a little.

Nina

10.11 Meeting on line III, 4

Nina
Apr 30 #162795

One reality at a time

Dear friends,

Jeff (reacting to Acharn's explanations): It is clear to me. When giving food to someone who is hungry, it may be with attachment (lobha) or with kindness. One may give with the idea of "I am a good person." Or with kindness, you do not care if someone notices (your giving).

Acharn: It is by conditions whether or not you give. The study of the teachings is a like a reminder. Learn to understand conditions. That is most difficult. The Buddha's Path leads to less clinging. Whatever one gets is with lobha. At the moment of not giving it is not "me". If one tries to change there is "I" again, all the time. Paññā understands kusala and akusala. Nothing can be controlled. Giving or not giving is not me. Do not regret or think of the future. The past has gone, it is not the object of understanding. The future has not come yet. Now, it can be understood what experiences and what cannot experience. Only these two kind of realities, arising by conditions. The past is not remembered in the next life and even in this life can the past not come back to be object of understanding. The object has to be just right then. One cannot force the arising of satipaṭṭhāna, but paññā can understand when there is satipaṭṭhāna and when not.

Satipaṭṭhāna is the development of understanding. It is just a reality which is different from other realities. It arises with sobhaṇa (beautiful) citta. The point of listening and understanding is: no "I".

We do not mind how long it takes, 20 years or many lives. It depends on the understanding. It has to be the understanding of no self.

There is lobha all day, it is hidden all the time. Only paññā can see it. It is the condition for the cycle of birth and death.

Dhamma is not self. Only paññā can penetrate the truth. Intellectual understanding will lead to paññā that understands just one characteristic of reality at a time. One will know the difference between understanding from hearing and understanding of one reality at a time. The latent tendency of doubt is only eradicated by the path-consciousness of the sotāpanna (at the first stage of enlightenment). Paññā will see the difference between self and no self, between wrong understanding and right understanding.

Huong: A question about āyatana as meeting place.

Acharn: Is there seeing right now?

Huong: Yes.

Acharn: What is there at the moment of seeing?

Huong: Visible object.

Acharn: Without visible object can there be seeing?

Huong: No.

Acharn: So, āyatana means meeting point. At the moment of seeing there are many realities. They are there already. What are there at this moment: āyatana. We learn: not me. No one can control.

Sarah: Seeing is āyatana, visible object is āyatana. What other realities are there at this moment? There has to be eye-sense and also cetasikas (mental factors). All together, each one is āyatana. It is now, seeing now, memory and contact. All are coming together or associating.

Sundara: Appreciates that Acharn brought the question to the present moment. That is a valuable reminder.

Sarah: There is no point in talking about āyatana, unless we talk about this moment.

Nina

11

May 2020

11.1 Meeting on line, III, 5

Nina
May 1 #162799

The four foundations of mindfulness

Dear friends,

Azita asks about the four foundations of mindfulness. Is investigation of states (dhammas) the fourth foundation?

Nina: All realities that are included or not included (here I had to correct myself) in the first three foundations of mindfulness are the fourth foundation of mindfulness, mindfulness of dhammas. Here they are dealt with under different aspects, such as the khandhas (aggregates). We do not have to think of those four foundations. They are real at this moment, and we may forget this. People make it more complicated than it is.

The four applications of mindfulness is one of the two conditions for sati and paññā (sati-sampajañnna). The other condition is firm remembrance of what we heard and learnt. All that is real at this moment.

Jonathan: They are foundations, because they are the objects of mindfulness. The fourth one is translated as mindfulness of dhammas, not investigation of dhammas (that is another aspect).

Lukas: Acharn has a nice voice.

Sarah: Even while listening to Dhamma there can be attachment.

Alan: A question about the Middle Way and this moment.

Sarah: Understanding seeing now, hearing now, attachment now, that is the Middle Way. It is the right Path, understanding of that reality as not self.

Alan: Why is it called the Middle Way?

Sarah: There is no wrong view. Understanding of that reality as not self.

Jonathan: No indulgence nor asceticism.

Alan: It is another way of saying: any moment of life, such as when listening to music.

Sarah: Intellectual understanding of dhamma now leads to satipaṭṭhāna: direct understanding of reality now.

Alan: Often there is an idea of situation, such as going shopping or being in the forest. It makes no difference as to understanding realities. Hardness is hardness when you are in the street or in the forest. Thinking in terms of situation is not the Middle Way.

Sarah: When Lukas asked: "How can I come back to the Dhamma", there was the idea of self. Even-so when asking, "How can I get more understanding, shall I go to the forest, to the meditation centre." Because there is not the understanding of seeing now. If there is no understanding of reality now, it cannot lead to the Middle Way. It has to be this moment.

Sun: With Vietnamese friends we discussed about the Vinaya. It is very detailed about situations and about the conduct of the monk, such as looking ahead not further than the length of a plough, not looking around. How to have more wise reflection about all this? What is wise reflection when studying the Vinaya?

Sarah: Walking along with eyes downcast is just a physical action one is following. There is "I" again, one can do this with attachment. It has to be with understanding of reality at this moment. It has to be kusala citta with understanding.

Nina: The Vinaya is useful also for laypeople. There are so many occasions for attachment. It is not a question of following rules but knowing citta. Decorating one's dwelling is not allowed (for the monk). It is good to know that there is attachment when decorating our house. There is no need to force ourselves not to do so, but (know) there is citta with attachment. All these different examples are very useful, also for laypeople.

Sarah: People think it is just a matter of following rules. It has to be with understanding of dhammas as anattā.

Questioner, a remark: The Buddha taught the second noble Truth, attachment. It is important to understand this. It is a reminder not to run after objects and create more problems.

Nina: It is all about the Middle Way. That is the Middle Way. Not forcing, but understanding.

Sundara: It is a reminder, all these different dhammas. When walking with downcast eyes, there can be mindfulness in conventional sense, knowing what one is doing. This can be a condition for sati and paññā instead of more attachment.

Jonathan: Wise consideration refers to wholesome consciousness. There is no answer to the question whether there is wholesomeness while doing this or that. Kusala citta can be dāna, sīla, or restraint from unwholesome conduct.

Nina: I appreciate Acharn's constant reminder that the development of understanding has to be natural in daily life. One should not try to change one's life style.

Alan: Understanding realities in the present moment, is that taking refuge in the teachings?

Sarah: If there is no understanding of life now, can there be a beginning of the Middle Way? If one just goes to the temple and kneels down without any understanding there cannot be any beginning.

Alan: Taking refuge, you go to safety by listening and considering the teachings.

Sarah: Only the understanding that leads to the end of the cycle of birth and death can be a refuge. The more understanding there is, the more appreciation of the Buddha's teaching of realities.

Nina

11.2 Meeting on line III, 6

Nina
May 2 #162810

Taking refuge

Dear friends,

Nguyen (ten year old child): a question about offering a gift and thinking of the benefit, and about the fact that there is also a moment of attachment.

Sarah: We talked about the perfections (wholesome qualities the Bodhisatta accumulated from life to life) that develop together with understanding. If there is no understanding of seeing as not self, of kindness, of generosity as not self, there cannot be the development of the perfections. Kindness has to develop with understanding. Without understanding it cannot be a perfection.

Jonathan: In any situation there can be wholesome and unwholesome states intermingled. Only the wholesome ones can be a perfection when they are with some level of understanding.

Sarah to Nguyen: Is there any perfection now? That is homework for you, you can think about it. I hope Nam (older brother) can help explain the answer. Nam really appreciates this discussion, helping us to understand Dhamma and what is happening right now.

You are a very good older brother to him.

Acharn, about taking refuge: Before hearing the Buddha, who knows (this moment) now as not self? That is why we take refuge. Without hearing there cannot be understanding. At the moment of understanding the words of the Buddha, even one word, one takes refuge in the Buddha and in the Dhamma. No one (else) can condition right understanding.

There is a beginning of understanding of what has not been understood before, until all realities appear as not self. No one else can help us to have understanding of whatever appears. That is why one takes refuge, more and more, to understand the Buddha's words.

Alan: We take refuge from what? From realities which are suffering?

Acharn: Consider his words carefully. He just points to this very moment. Each moment is gone. No one can understand it by himself.

Alan: The ultimate refuge is Nibbāna.

Acharn: This is unknown for uncountable lives.

Alan: We are attached to what arises, but Nibbāna does not arise, and it cannot be the object of attachment.

Acharn: One is attached to everything, except lokuttara dhammas (supramundane dhammas: the cittas that experience Nibbāna and Nibbāna). There is attachment that hinders to understand what arises, because of the intoxicants (āsavas, very subtle defilements). After a few moments of seeing, hearing, etc. the āsavas arise. They are unknown, because they are very subtle. There is attachment when thinking: "I want to know this, how to know that". Even thinking right then is not self.

Alan: While experiencing Nibbāna, attachment is eliminated.

Acharn: Can you experience Nibbāna? What level of paññā can experience Nibbāna?

Alan: A high level.

Acharn: a level of insight (vipassanā ñāna). No idea about it when satipaṭṭhāna is not developed yet. The second noble Truth (lobha, attachment) should be object of paññā. Only paññā can experience all four noble Truths. When there is an idea of "I do", it is wrong.

Understanding from moment to moment is to eliminate ignorance and doubt. It is about now, all the time. Are you taking refuge?

Alan: To some extent, for sure, because I am listening and considering.

Acharn: At the moment of understanding there is no self, no doubt about taking refuge.

Sarah: Alan also asked about the Middle Way and I said it was the moments of understanding now, not anything else.

Acharn: Is there any way now? The Middle Way is different from other ways. Without understanding, nothing can be the Middle Way. The Middle Way means: no attachment, no aversion. When one thinks: "I would like to understand" there is attachment and that is not the Middle Way.

Alberto: The refuge is understanding realities little by little.

Nina

11.3 Meeting on line IV, 1

Nina
May 4 #162848

Dhamma is now

Dear friends,

Nina: Last time we received reminders all the time: Understanding this moment, taking refuge, and as Acharn said: Dhamma is now. My niece phoned me and asked whether in this group the mood is not depressed because of Corona. I said: on the contrary, it is very animated, while speaking about seeing now, hearing now. And as Alan said: hardness is hardness, no matter what the situation is. We think in terms of situation, such as, I am in my dusty house or in the forest. It makes no difference.

Long sent me an Email, asking what the difference is between the Middle Way and taking refuge. It all pertains to this moment. When we take refuge, the object is not a concept, it is understanding reality at this moment. It is not about situations, like we are greeting each other and laughing. They are all nāma and rūpa. We are so forgetful and it is good to discuss more. There is the reality that experiences and the reality that does not experience. People may wonder why we should discuss these two kinds of reality.

Acharn: When there is no understanding we cannot take refuge. From the very beginning there should be understanding of whatever appears now. Realities appear but there is no understanding. If there is no understanding it is impossible to follow the Middle Way. The way of ignorance and attachment cannot lead to understanding. Right thinking (samma-sankappa) accompanies right view (sammā-diṭṭhi). Understanding is the chief, and virati (abstention from unwholesomeness) is also needed.

Sarah: We were friendly, chatting and greeting each other, in a natural way. We were not going to a special place; the development of understanding has to be natural from the start.

Acharn: It is natural, no one can condition the arising of a reality, it has already arisen and fallen away. It has to be developed little by little. There should not be any expectation, no wish. It can appear well. There is no ignorance that hides the truth.

Sarah: As to the phone call with Nina's niece, there are different moments, some with enthusiasm, some moments are sad, some happy. Just different realities, no self. Nothing lasts.

Acharn: The idea of self is very strong, it can condition akusala, like moments of being depressed. It is gone. No self but different realities, conditioned. There is no "I" who tries to understand.

Sarah: One should not try to change what is conditioned, just understand.

Sarah, to Simin and Carmen(from Holland): The development of understanding is very natural, not trying to do something. How does this sound to you?

Simin: It is not so easy to stay aware, to be aware of conditions. Fear, Corona, so many conditions make it difficult to stay with understanding. Understanding is very important.

Sarah (to Acharn): She has studied Abhidhamma and agrees that understanding now is very important, but she says it is very difficult to stay aware because different things come up by conditions, like the corona virus.

Acharn: If there cannot be the understanding of whatsoever appears now, realities that arise are the same, like seeing or hearing. Very soon after they have arisen there are the intoxicants (āsavas) of clinging to sense objects, clinging to existence, of wrong view and ignorance. They arise and fall away so fast, they cannot be known.

Sarah: Staying aware is not the natural way. It is not the right way to try to do something thinking that there should be awareness now when there is depression or attachment. It is not a matter of staying aware but understanding what is conditioned. Otherwise "I" am doing something or following a practice.

Acharn: Where are you now? Alone or with many people?

Simin: I am now in Holland.

Acharn: That is exactly the same. Seeing is seeing, no matter you are in Holland or wherever. When realities appear, there is no place. Thinking of a place is taking you away from understanding reality right now, Seeing is seeing, wherever you are. There is the reality that experiences and the reality that does not experience.

When there is strong confidence (in the teachings) there is no place. There are conditions for whatever arises now. Ignorance arises wherever one is, depending on conditions. Understanding can arise, little by little. What falls away does not return. It takes a long time to know the truth. What appears now is very, very subtle, no one can understand it immediately. Learn to understand it when it is there. When it is not there how can there be understanding of it? It is just that, no one. It takes more than one life, more than hundred lives, to really penetrate the truth of it. The idea of self is very deeply rooted as intoxicant (āsava), as latent tendency or as other types of akusala.

Nina

11.4 Meeting on line, IV, 2

Nina
May 5 #162854

Intoxicants and latent tendencies

Dear friends,

Sarah wants to explain the terms intoxicant (āsava) and latent tendency(anusaya) for the benefit of newcomers. When you look at a lotus flower or at friends, there is attachment instantly. But there are also very subtle kinds of attachment and these are intoxicants. Immediately after seeing or hearing ignorance arises. When looking at the computer there is seeing and then very subtle kinds of ignorance. Or one may be wishing to see, wishing to be, very subtle kinds of wrong view of self. These are moments of intoxicants, āsavas.

As to latent tendency, anusaya, depression suddenly arises, out of the blue. Or attachment. A tendency for those unwholesome states lies dormant but it is ready to condition their arising. That is why we listen to Dhamma, the condition for understanding can arise any time, like now.

Sukin: The Middle Way is a moment of right understanding. Is there a difference between the Middle Way and taking refuge? What reality is the taking of refuge?

Acharn: Can ignorance take refuge? The understanding knows that there are different realities performing their functions. When seeing appears nothing can appear together with seeing. But different realities seem to appear together, they appear as "something" all the time. Now is the moment of testing the truth that is known from hearing: is there wholesomeness or not?

Sarah: Understanding the reality of life at this moment as not self is the Middle Way. This leads to taking refuge in the qualities of the Buddha. Without understanding this would just be the following of a kind of ritual.

Jonathan: Different aspects refer to the development of understanding, such as a sense of urgency (saṃvega).

Sukin: How easy it is to go wrong, such as when thinking of the difference between understanding and taking refuge.

Jonathan: There are many different aspects to understanding. Realities are classified in different ways, as khandhas, as elements. One should always come back to the actual reality at the present moment. These are different ways of helping us to have a better understanding.

Minh had a question about right considering.

Acharn: Who or what is considering right now?

Sarah: Is it self or dhamma that considers?

The idea of self is so deeply rooted. It seems that I can hear, I can consider. There are just moments of hearing and thinking of what is heard. Just different dhammas. It depends on conditions what kind of thinking arises and considers wisely or unwisely.

Nina: I appreciate it so much that Acharn always goes back to dhamma now. She asked (Lukas): Is it not an idea of self who wants to return to Dhamma? Just as Lukas, we all have moments that we are wondering about something. Acharn reminds us all the time that this is a reality, not self. It is good to be reminded again and again because we forget.

I think that "I" consider the Dhamma, while wondering whether this is a reality that experiences or that does not experience. How to find out, how to consider this. All the time it is still a subtle idea of self. If the Buddha had not taught about non-self we would not know it at all. It is good to know.

Jonathan: When we are happy or sad, there are happy feeling or unhappy feeling and these are dhammas arising by conditions. It is consciousness (citta) that considers.

Sarah: There is a trap all the time when we say that we keep on reminding ourselves. There is a subtle idea of following a practice or trying to do something. It is not just understanding this moment.

Minh: Can you give an example of wise considering?

Jonathan: A wholesome consciousness that reflects on the Dhamma that is heard. Not a situation.

Maeve: I appreciate the reminders. We think that there is wise considering, but it is not so. It is enough to know what experiences and what does not experience anything.

Nina

11.5 Meeting on line, IV, 3

Nina
May 6 #162877

Perversity of citta

Dear friends,

Sukin speaks about the threefold classification of paññā as suta-mayapaññā, paññā based on hearing, cinta-mayapaññā, paññā based on thinking, bhāvanā -mayapañña, paññā based on development.

Sukin: I hear from Acharn that only understanding of what appears matters. Otherwise we become forgetful. We are depressed or we worry because we are lost in concepts. We need to hear and then there can be understanding. Hearing and considering happens even now. It has to be on and on, a lot.

Sarah: Hearing conditions to consider more carefully. We should not try to remember, but reflecting can be natural. Hearing can be a condition any time, unexpectedly.

Alan: We listen, hear and think, and does this conform to reality? We hear that hardness is just hardness. We can verify this, not just by thinking. It has to be tested against reality now. We hear that all conditioned realities are uncontrollable. This has to be tested. We have a pleasant feeling, not by choice but by conditions. The Buddha said that attachment conditions aversion. The truth of what he taught, all of it shows up. There are many words to explain anattā, not self, such as uncontrollable, unexpectedly. We should not just know the words, but the reality: not somebody, not something.

Ann: Conditioned by past accumulations there will be listening. The more one listens, the more one understands.

Trin: Acharn said that if one just hears the Dhamma and not considers but just believes, one will forget (what one heard). There will not be understanding. Considering will condition more understanding, little by little and then it can condition further understanding.

Alberto: Considering is not just thinking about the teachings. It is more subtle than just thinking which is always with "me" and "I".

Sarah: It is not just repeating words and memorizing. That is just to be forgotten, as Trin said. It has to be understanding.

Azita: What is citta vipallāsa, perversity of citta?

Sarah: Thinking with any kind of unwholesomeness is citta vipallāsa. (The same for saññā vipallāsa. Diṭṭhi vipallāsa is with wrong view).

Robert spoke about meditation centres where people believe that they see all their defilements.

Sukin: There should not just be hearing the words of the teachings but also understanding at that very moment.

Jonathan: One should not try and see the unwholesome mental states.

Metta: Most important is the right consideration. Reality arises and falls away, by conditions. There is no self, only realities that arise and fall away by conditions.

Sarah: We cannot emphasize that enough.

Hoi An group: While considering is the citta kusala or akusala?

Cuan: Which cetasika is considering?

Sarah: What is the main cetasika while considering?

Cuan: Sometimes wondering, sometimes understanding. I am not sure it is kusala or akusala.

Sarah: The main mental factor(while considering) is vitakka, thinking. It depends what object it touches at that moment. Even now, while reflecting on Dhamma it can be kusala or akusala. It is conditioned by memory (saññā). If one had not heard about the different words and ideas there could not be considering about them. All these kinds of thinking, wise or unwise, are accumulated. Reflecting now conditions more in this way in the future.

Ann: There is manasikāra that is yoniso manasikāra, wise attention.

Jonathan: Manasikāra arises with every citta.

Sarah: They all arise together.

Nina

11.6 Meeting on line V, 1

Nina
May 10 #162956

Where are you now?

Dear friends,

I appreciate it that Acharn asks us questions to make us consider reality. She asked Simin: Where are you now? She answered: In Holland. When we think of a place we are not considering reality. We think: I am here, I, I, I. The realities are seeing, hearing or thinking, no person. This is an excellent reminder. So often we think: *We* are here. In reality there are consciousness, citta, mental factor, cetasika, and physical phenomena, rūpa. These are really true, but we forget. All the other thoughts are conventional realities.

Acharn: What is meant by the development of understanding? When a reality appears nothing else can appear together with it. Developing understanding by conditions is a long way. No one can do anything, this is most difficult. Each word of the Buddha, in the Vinaya, Sutta and Abhidhamma points to this moment.

Question: Is considering (the truth) directing citta towards the object?

Sarah: As soon as the idea of directing arises there is an idea of "I can do". That is not understanding naturally what appears.

Nguyen (ten years old): Acharn says 'Can anyone stop seeing'? When I Close my eyes there is no seeing. I can control it.

Acharn: When there is no intention can the eye be closed by itself? The intention is not self. Can one open or close the eyes without intention? Is intention you? Intention (or volition, cetanā) arises with each moment of citta. It can be wholesome (kusala), unwholesome (akusala), result (vipāka) or inoperative (kiriya).

Sarah: Can you decide what to hear? If there are no conditions there is no hearing. Can you decide now to be angry or happy? They just depend on different conditions.

Nina

11.7 Meeting on line V, 2

Nina
May 11 #162974

The importance of understanding citta

Dear friends,

Alan: What is the importance of knowing the difference between nāma (mental phenomena) and rūpa (physical phenomena)? We can have some understanding of cetasikas (mental factors), such as anger, happiness and sadness. But it is very difficult to understand citta. What is the importance of understanding citta as opposed to rūpa?

Acharn: Can you understand indifferent feeling?

Alan: No.

Acharn: Citta is the chief of experiencing. The object that is experienced can appear in daily life. There is wrong understanding all the time, it takes the object for "something". When anger arises it appears as something, it is "me". What is doubt? It is still "me". By conditions. People pay attention to the object that is experienced and the experience itself is hidden. There is doubt and ignorance about the five khandhas.

Alan: We are occupied with the object, we do not know the nature of the reality which thinks.

Sarah: Trying to understand, to catch saññā (remembrance) and other realities is not understanding. When there is wanting it is a trap.

If there is no understanding of the distinction between seeing and what is seen, there is definitely the idea of "I see, I hear" and of "something" that is seen. Begin to understand those realities as not self, not "I see". If we think that it is easier to understand cetasika than to understand citta, it is just thinking, not understanding what appears now.

Acharn: I am here in my room.

Sarah (laughter): We think we are in our room, just thinking. I am somewhere, in the world of concepts.

Alan: If there is no thinking, there is no room, I can understand this intellectually. When there is awareness of hardness, there is just hardness, not a room. When there is thinking that I am somewhere, there is no understanding of reality, there is the world of concepts.

Acharn: When there is just that which experiences, there is no room, no where. Otherwise there is always the idea of "I am sitting here." The experience does not appear well. When it appears well, it appears just to the level of paññā (that has been attained) there is nothing else with that reality (there is only that reality).

Alan: Just one reality, no place, no person. When it arises it can only arise by conditions.

Acharn: There is just the right condition for that reality at that moment.

Alan: In spite of the fact that attachment arises each split second, understanding works its way while we listen. So, there are conditions.

Acharn: When the āsavas (intoxicants, very subtle defilements) arise it is so clear that nothing can be done. Seeing arises, then receiving-consciousness, investigating-consciousness, determining-consciousness and then the intoxicants arise already. There is attachment to sense-objects, wrong view, clinging to existence or ignorance. Ignorance is already there. We should not underestimate the Buddha's words. The development of understanding takes time, because it is so very deep and subtle. To understand this moment: there is the reality that experiences, and what appears is the object of the reality that experiences; it is gone very rapidly. It is beyond expectation how fast it is. When our eyes are closed, nothing can appear as house or window any more. What impinges on the eye-sense appears very shortly and then the intoxicants follow instantly. It takes a long time to let go of the idea of self who can do something. What appears is only what can impinge on the eye-sense, and it is already gone. It can be the object of right understanding, that is what is meant by ariya sacca dhamma (dhamma of the noble Truth). The noble Truth can be experienced by highly developed paññā. Begin from now on. Paññā develops every moment of hearing and understanding. Nina

11.8 Meeting on line, V,3

Nina
May 12 #162990

No one makes it (reality) arise

Dear friends,

Alan: What eradicates attachment? Nobody can control the arising of attachment.

Acharn: There can be the understanding that no one can make it arise. When there is more understanding there will be more confidence. There is only citta that experiences, it is the chief of experiencing. Different cittas arise all the time. There are ignorance and clinging, taking it (the object that is experienced) for "something", from life to life, even now. The words of the Buddha are that no one makes it (reality) arise. Seeing sees, that's all, thinking, thinking, that's all. No one knows the arising and falling away, until hearing the teachings of the Buddha. Thinking is not seeing. Wanting is not detachment. There are conditions for the arising of each reality.

Just a moment of seeing is conditioned by what impinges on the eye-sense and by the object that impinges on it. There are citta (consciousness), cetasika (mental factors arising with citta) and rūpa(physical phenomena). We understand each moment as very temporary, appearing and disappearing. No one knew about this, until the Buddha enlightened the truth. Each word can condition understanding that could not arise by itself. There can be right considering to understand that this is so true.

Right understanding is very weak in the beginning. One can see how slowly it develops. The understanding from hearing and considering just begins very, very little.

Carmen: tells about her conversations with others about effort. The Buddha says that we have to make an effort, but that is also conditioned.

Acharn: How can I? What is there instead of thinking, "how can I"? Without the reality which thinks can there be the idea of "I think"? Thinking is not seeing, it can experience different objects. There are two kinds of realities: one reality that cannot experience anything, such as sound, smell, heat or cold, and one reality that experiences. Seeing is conditioned; it cannot arise without eye-sense; and also kamma (past action) is a condition. Actually what appears is not under anyone's control. Where is "I"? The arising and falling away is not realized and, thus, this brings about the idea of something permanent.

Sarah: What is conditioned is not self. There are just different dhammas at this moment.

Carmen: Buddha is teaching to get us out of saṃsāra (the cycle of birth and death). Others told me that I can exert effort. They called me fatalistic.

Sarah: As to the idea of getting myself out of saṃsāra, it is "me". It is not the understanding of realities. Even doubt is conditioned, it falls away instantly.

Sundara: The conditionality of dhammas is very different from fatalism. These two matters are easily confused. When there is a strong idea of "I", it is easy to misunderstand the Dhamma.

Jonathan wants to ask Carmen how she understands fatalism.

Carmen: As to getting out of saṃsāra, one cannot make it happen more quickly. As to fatalism, one does not have any influence (how things happen).

Jonathan: They were accusing you of being fatalistic, because you said that you cannot make things happen more quickly by directed effort. Effort is conditioned. It is for the purpose of more wholesomeness and more understanding.

Alan: By the understanding of conditions we are going into the right direction. We are mostly making an effort with the idea of self. We are progressing by understanding more about conditionality. When there is fatalism there will be no progress.

Sukin: The understanding of the present moment is the understanding that this is the Path.

Alan: It is moving out of saṃsāra.

Nina

11.9 Meeting on line, VI, 1

Nina
May 17 #163049

Thinking about concepts and wrong view

Dear friends,

Thinking about concepts and wrong view:

Acharn asked Carmen: 'Where are you now?' and she answered, 'in Holland'. Acharn then explained: when there is awareness of nāma (mental phenomena) and rūpa (physical phenomena) there is no place. There are only the reality that experiences and the reality that does not experience. Jonothan reminded me that this does not mean that there is always wrong view when thinking of concepts. We can cling to self without wrong view.

The sotāpanna (who has attained the first stage of enlightenment) has no wrong view but he can still cling to an idea of self. There are three ways of clinging to a self: one without wrong view, one with wrong view and clinging with conceit. We all have clinging to self without wrong view, but it is not so easy to understand that. We have an idea of "it is me". Only paññā can know this. It is a good reminder that when we are living in the world of concepts there is not always wrong view. I am very grateful for all reminders.

Acharn: Can there be the understanding of wrong view as just a reality? Otherwise we only think about it. So long as wrong view is not the object of right understanding when it appears, there is only thinking about it. When there is wrong view, right understanding understand it as just a reality. If it does not arise how can there be the understanding as not you, as a reality?

Understand what is now. It cannot appear to ignorance and attachment. It can appear to right understanding that begins to understand what appears by conditions.

Sarah: In another group we were discussing the difference between pariyatti (intellectual understanding) and paṭipatti (direct understanding). We discussed thinking of the "story" of realities. For example we know that sound is experienced by hearing, that it is rūpa, not self. The story is not the same as direct understanding when it appears now.

Sound can be experienced as just a dhamma, not the sound of a voice, of rain, of traffic. There is sound at this moment. It is the same with wrong view. There can be a long story about it, such as, that it does not arise when there is conceit. This is different from direct understanding of it, the direct understanding of the characteristic of wrong view when it appears. When a reality appears it can be known directly. Otherwise we are always repeating the story about it.

We should always come back to now, to what appears now.

Nina

11.10 Meeting on line, VI, 2

Nina
May 18 #163062

Sacca ñāna

Dear friends,

Mai Son: I have a question about the third Noble Truth, Nibbāna, on the level of sacca ñāna, correct intellectual understanding. Sacca ñāna is not the "story" about reality.

Acharn: What is ñāna (understanding)? Each word should be understood clearly. What is sacca ñāna?

Mai Son: Sacca is truth and ñāna is the understanding of the truth. It is understanding reality right now. Understanding what appears now. Nibbāna is not yet understood.

Acharn: Is there thinking or understanding?

Mai Son: Thinking is considering.

Acharn: What is sacca? Sacca is the truth. Is there any truth now, to be known from the very beginning? When it is very firm it can be sacca ñāna; it never changes. The ñāna which understands sacca, the truth, clearer and clearer.

(N: it is the first of the three phases: sacca ñāna, kicca ñāna, which is direct understanding developed through satipaṭṭhāna and kata ñāna, the clear realisation of the truth.)

What is the truth, sacca, to be known? Not me, but paññā understands it as it is. Sacca is truth, the truth of what? Is there any truth now? Sacca ñāna of the first noble Truth, dukkha ariya sacca.

Mai Son: It is not yet known now.

Acharn: So it is not sacca ñāna. Before knowing the third noble Truth, there should be understanding of the others one by one. What is the first noble Truth?

Mai Son: Dukkha now, the reality that arises and disappears now.

Acharn: Is there any understanding of the truth of that which appears? What is the truth? Otherwise there is not even understanding of the first Truth. If there is no understanding of the first Truth, how can there be understanding of the second, the third and the fourth Truth?

What is the first noble Truth?

Mai Son: Dukkha now.

Acharn: Understanding is not just hearing and remembering. It is useless without understanding what is now appearing.

This moment is the first Truth. The second Truth is more difficult to understand. It is not just understanding the word, but understanding the truth of it.

Understanding is understanding, not just hearing and thinking. It is understanding reality now.

Is dukkha ariya sacca (the noble Truth of dukkha) real? What moment does not have dukkha?

Mai Son: We do not know dukkha, we think it is me, it is permanent. The characteristic of dukkha does not appear now.

Acharn: Sacca is the truth. Is there anything real or true? Ariya sacca (the noble truth) is realised by the highly developed paññā. This is the paññā that directly experiences the truth of whatever appears.

Why do we listen? What for? What is the purpose? We have to consider carefully the truth of each of the Buddha's words. What is dukkha now?

Mai Son: The arising and disappearing of realities. Nothing lasts, there is no self.

Acharn: Why is it dukkha?

Mai Son: It is not under anyone's control. It arises by conditions, and it is beyond our power.

Acharn: What is not dukkha in this life?

Mai Son: Seeing is dukkha, everything is dukkha.

Acharn: Is what is pleasurable dukkha?

Mai Son: It arises and disappears.

Acharn: Why is Nibbāna not dukkha? Is Nibbāna understanding?

Mai Son: Nibbāna can be understood by paññā of the level of the ariyans (enlightened ones), not right now.

Acharn: What is the difference between Nibbāna and anything else? Nibbāna is not understanding, not seeing or thinking.

Mai Son: Nibbāna is unconditioned, it is not saṅkhāra dhamma (conditioned dhamma).

Acharn: Can it be dukkha?

Mai Son: No, it cannot.

Acharn: Why not?

Mai Son: It is not dependent on conditions.

Acharn: Does Nibbāna arise?

Mai Son: No.

Acharn: What arises and falls away is dukkha. Is there Nibbāna now, in this life?

Mai Son: No, not yet.

Acharn: Whatever in this life appears, is it dukkha? Everything that arises and falls away, is it dukkha? So life is dukkha. Is right understanding dukkha? Does paññā arise?

Mai Son: Yes.

Acharn: Is it dukkha? What is not dukkha? That should be directly understood, not just by thinking. Is it different from now? This is the sacca ñāna of the four noble Truths. It should be clear understanding of whatever is now. It is not talking about words.

Right understanding has to begin, it has to become stronger and stronger, firmer and firmer until there is no doubt. That is the meaning of sacca ñāna of the four noble Truths, on the level of pariyatti (intellectual understanding).

Sarah: The understanding of sacca ñāna on the level of pariyatti is very firm understanding of the noble Truths. It is not the direct understanding, but firm intellectual understanding of what dukkha is now, for example.

Nina

11.11 Meeting on line VI, 3

Nina
May 19 #163068

The second noble Truth

Dear friends,

Betty: Can Acharn explain about the second noble Truth?

(N: The cause of dukkha which is attachment)

Acharn: Is there attachment to everything? Is it known now?
Betty: No.
Acharn: We have to understand the characteristic of the first Truth before seeing the cause which is there to condition life. At this moment there is just intellectual understanding of attachment which is there almost all the time. The āsavas (intoxicants) arise: clinging to sense objects, to existence, to views and ignorance. Three moments after seeing (or after the other sense-cognitions), there are intoxicants: attachment and the idea of "I". We need the Buddha's teachings to understand this. It is not easy, it goes on so fast, one reality to another reality. There must be the understanding of reality, of dhamma. Later on, after a long time (of development) they can appear to sati and paññā.

At the first vipassanā ñāna the arising and falling away of realities is not yet realized. There is the understanding of the truth that there is no one there: only what experiences and what is experienced. No place is experienced. That is the meaning of reality: no one can make it arise, no one can change its characteristic or the way it has arisen and fallen away. There is no doubt, each characteristic appears as it is.

The second Truth does not appear yet. Paññā can know the difference between very strong and very weak lobha. Not by thinking, but by right mindfulness and paññā of the level of satipaṭṭhāna.

Now we are just talking about realities and there is ignorance of what is arising and falling away. Attachment to what appears cannot be easily known, until paññā develops. The object which is anattā cannot be selected, nor can the time of understanding. Understanding develops from intellectual understanding to satipaṭṭhāna. But a few moments that arise in the beginning are not enough, even one life is not enough (to develop paññā). No one can condition higher understanding. The knowledge of the arising and falling away of realities can let go of attachment to a following reality. When there is no attachment to the next reality then whatever appears becomes clearer.

Sundara: Can Acharn talk about the third noble Truth?

Acharn: If there is no understanding of dukkha how can there be the end of clinging? There is thinking about the arising and falling away of realities. If there is no direct experience of the arising and falling away one does not see the danger of this. There is so much to learn before there is understanding that there is no "me".

As to seeing the danger, there is no desire or attachment to see again, to be born again. Would you like to see something or experience something? Before there can be understanding of Nibbāna, there must be understanding of what arises and falls away. There should be understanding of the conditions for the arising of nāma and rūpa. Nothing arises without conditions. There will be more understanding by keeping on listening to the Dhamma.

Sundara expresses his appreciation and he will listen again to Acharn's explanations. He said: looking at Dhamma from different angles is always helpful.

Nina

11.12 Meeting on line, VI, 4

Nina
May 20 #163080

Following the rules in the Vinaya

Dear friends,

Mai Son: I like to understand the true meaning of following the rules in the Vinaya for the monk.

Acharn: What is Vinaya?

Mai Son: There are many aspects of considering the Vinaya. Some people understand Vinaya as rules of conduct, some people understand it as (learning about) akusala qualities.

Acharn: What is the benefit of understanding Vinaya?

Mai Son: It helps us to understand what is kusala and what akusala, and to understand the quality of citta.

Sarah: The purpose of Vinaya is not just to follow rules. One could do that with ignorance and without understanding of the teachings. The purpose is the relinquishment of akusala in order to develop the Path, leading the life of the arahat; not without the development of satipaṭṭhāna.

Sundara: Vinaya is derived from vineti, meaning leading out. The Vinaya leads away from akusala, out of saṃsāra, the cycle of birth and death. There are different levels of akusala, some of which are very subtle.

Sarah: It has to do with this moment, understanding of akusala now. If this is not the case there is no training (sikkha).

Alberto: Speaks about breaking the rules intentionally and the subtlety of the study of realities.

Sundara: We read that the monk is not to stand with arms akimbo, this is unbecoming. This reminds him of dosa (aversion) he may be having.

Nina: There are many exceptions to the rules such as in the case of sickness or beig mentally disturbed. This shows the Buddha's great compassion. He thought of all those situations with the wish to help people.

Trin: Alan Driver was a monk before but he disrobed later on. He was telling Nina, while in India, that he wanted to live like Upāli. He wanted to keep the Vinaya perfectly but could not find any place with perfect Vinaya. He understood so well that the Vinaya has to go together with satipaṭṭhāna, the understanding of realities right now.

Sarah: In the beginning Alan thought that living as a monk was a favourable condition for having more time to be spend with study and reading. Then he realized that this was not the right way. It does no matter how busy one is in daily life, occupied with worldly chores, taking care of family. Seeing is seeing, hearing is hearing and there can be understanding and awareness at any moment. Understanding matters, not the amount of time for book study, including the study of Pāli.

There can be understanding of this very moment.

Tam: For the monk there is the disciplinary code, the restraint of Patimokkha, and restraint of the senses (indriya samvara sīla). Sati and paññā are needed for sīla, understanding should not be lacking.

Sarah: It is wrong understanding to think that there should be sīla first so that later on there will be understanding. Understanding should be there from the beginning. The restraint of Pātimokkha has to be with understanding.

Now, while we look at our friends, there can be attachment or understanding. Anything we read in the "Visuddhimagga", in whatever section, is about satipaṭṭhāna.

Mai Son read in Visuddhimagga, Ch 14, § 16-18 about three ways of classifying understanding. Three ways of skilfulness. He wanted to know whether this is related to the Vinaya. (N: In this whole section understanding is classified in many different ways.)

Mai Son said: I should do or should not do seems related to "I".

Sarah: We can talk about skilful in a conventional sense. The Visuddhimagga talks about satipaṭṭhāna and the direct understanding of realities.

Metta: In the Vinaya the monk may try to follow the rules, but there may not be understanding. But the Vinaya is Dhamma, leading out of defilements.

Sarah: If it is not leading out of defilements and out of the cycle it is useless. If it is not leading away from the idea of self and there is the idea of "I can do, I can follow", it is useless. The observance of Pātimokkha without understanding dhamma as anattā cannot lead away from defilements and there is the accumulation of more and more defilements.

Sarah refers to the four kinds of sati-sampajañña (mentioned in the commentary to the satipaṭṭhāna sutta): what is suitable, what is the purpose, what is the object of understanding and non-delusion as to the object. Listening to the Dhamma is very suitable, but if we set a rule that we must listen that is not the understanding of suitability. There has to be the understanding of reality.

As to the object, each object can be the object of satipaṭṭhāna, such as visible object or sound now. As to the purpose, it is not following particular rules.

Trin: When one is counting rules, when the monk thinks that he can keep so many rules, there is an idea of self.

Sarah: There is clinging, not following with understanding.

Ann: spoke about confession by a monk when there is the breach of a rule. It can be with understanding.

Jonothan: When there is the breach of a rule and no confession, it can lead to bad results, regardless of a level of understanding.

Sarah: Alan Driver disrobed. As a monk he kept the rules very well, and as a layperson life was very difficult for him. Acharn's comment was that this was more natural, better than forcing oneself. Understanding can develop naturally, it has to know those accumulations. If they are not known as they are, understanding is blocked.

Trin: When a fault is committed and one understands it as it is there is truthfulness.

Sarah: There is the perfection of truthfulness (sacca pāramī).

Tam was reading the passage of the Visuddhimagga about the three different kinds of paññā Mai Son mentioned. There is a reference to the four right efforts.(N: unarisen akusala dhammas do not arise and arisen akusala dhammas are abandoned; unarisen kusala dhammas arise and arisen kusala dhammas advance in growth.)

Sarah: The four right efforts develop along with right understanding.

Nina

11.13 Meeting on line, VII, 1

Nina
May 26 #163171

Understanding one characteristic

Dear friends,

Last time there were many helpful points and good reminders. Someone wanted to become a monk so that he would have more free time for study and reading. This is the wrong purpose of monkhood. Also some laypeople think that they want to be away from daily life, from all the daily chores and from taking care of family members. They go on long retreats in order to have more free time for awareness. This is the wrong way, it is clinging to an idea of self who wants to have more awareness. The development of understanding has to be very natural, in daily life.

The conversation between Mai Son and Acharn was also full of reminders to understand the present moment. Acharn asked Mai Son what the first noble Truth is. He did not say: dukkha, but he said: dukkha now. He understood very well that the present reality has to be understood. Acharn emphasized that memorizing and thinking is useless without understanding this very moment. We heard this before, but when you hear it many times it becomes more meaningful.

It is the same when hearing repeatedly about the intoxicants (āsavas), the very subtle defilements that arise almost immediately after seeing, hearing and the other sense-cognitions. They are unknown, and we have to hear this many times before it makes more sense.

Acharn explained about the understanding of the arising and falling away of realities, which can be realised at a higher stage of insight. There is letting go if one does not cling to the next reality. But attachment hinders the "letting go". I am wondering what the next reality is one clings to, is it in the same process?

Sarah: Acharn explained that only when there is direct understanding of the arising and falling away of realities, understanding sees how useless it is to cling to the next reality that has not come yet and has then already gone. We can talk about the danger of seeing and hearing, but it is thinking, even when there is the understanding of seeing or hearing. There is not yet the direct understanding of their arising and falling away.

Acharn: There is clinging all the time and without understanding it, it hinders and covers up the truth of the falling away of the previous reality. Then it is impossible to let go of clinging. All the teachings of the Buddha are about letting go little by little, of hearing, of the idea of self that is unknown. As soon as seeing has fallen away, after three moments of consciousness, the intoxicant, āsava, is there, unknown. At this moment, seeing, hearing, everything arises and falls away, but it is unknown. It does not appear well.

The beginning is the understanding of one characteristic. There is hardness, but there is no clear understanding of it, it does not appear to sati. It arises and falls away, and it is covered up by other realities. Seeing and hearing keep on falling away, how can anything appear well? Seeing is only seeing, now, it experiences visible object. Its arising and falling away do not appear yet. Pariyatti is not firm enough to condition a few moments with direct understanding. Direct understanding is different from pariyatti.

Paññā begins to understand the characteristic of sati as not self. There is no wishing or expecting for the arising of anything. Understanding develops, to understand the moment of conditioned reality. This is the only way.

Even now, we talk about realities but they do not appear well, because it is not direct sati, only sati at the level of intellectual understanding. All the way understanding will lead to more detachment, detachment from taking anything for self. Attachment is a hindrance to knowing the reality which follows. Realities do not appear well so that there could be letting go of the idea of self. Just like now, paññā knows of what level it is. Or there may be doubt or attachment. We live in darkness, but sati conditions a moment of reality appearing well, little by little. Paññā is not clear yet, it is very slight and develops on and on.

There will be more understanding of sati at the level of pariyatti and of sati at the level of paṭipatti. It depends on the conditions for its arising, when time comes. This is the way to eradicate the wish and craving for sati. The development has to be in daily life. Now all conditioned realities are arising and falling away, beyond any expectation.

Jonathan: Anything that is real at the present moment arises and falls away by conditions, but it is not known to us. There is no way of knowing what reality is going to arise.

Sarah: The more understanding develops the less clinging is there to what is coming, to the next moment. This is because of understanding it naturally, not because of any wish to have less clinging. What is the point of clinging to what is unknown and has not come yet?

Nina

11.14 Meeting on line VII, 2

Nina
May 27 #163205

Doubt

Dear friends,

Azita: Doubts about the arising and falling away of realities and finds it too difficult to understand, why bother?

Acharn: Is there doubt now? Even now there may be doubt about (the difference between) seeing and that which is seen. There are so many realities but not even one appears as it is, right now. Because there is not paṭipatti (direct understanding) yet.

Jonathan: You may have no doubt but a lack of confidence.

Sarah: When doubt arises it is just another dhamma, not my doubt. There can be understanding of its characteristic at that moment.

Mai had a question about the Yuganaddha Sutta (In Tandem, AN IV. 170.) Some people develop jhāna first and then insight, some insight first and then jhāna, some develop jhāna and insight yoked together and some develop insight alone.

Sarah explained that this is a description of people with different accumulations, these are not different paths. She said: "People are different but, whatever their accumulations, there can be understanding of what appears now."

Acharn: Each word of the Buddha pertains to the anattāness of all dhammas, and this is the answer (to all questions).

Sarah: When people read suttas they think of a set of instructions rather than understanding that there is a description of dhammas that are anattā and depending on different accumulations.

Acharn: What about you? Is there samatha now, is it conditioned? Can it arise any time at will? Can anyone have it, by sitting, doing something, thinking that it is samatha?

Sarah: We are talking about calmness, a cetasika (mental factor). If there is no understanding it is impossible to develop it. It is a matter of understanding of what life is now. It is not a matter of choosing: I will take this path or that path. There is one Path: understanding life at this moment. If one wants to have a quick result there is no calm.

Maeve was wondering what the distinction is between the development of paññā and the accumulation of paññā.

Acharn: Kusala and akusala are accumulated. Understanding arises and is then gone, but it is accumulated. Citta has the function of accumulating kusala and akusala. No one is doing anything. There are always attachment and ignorance as conditions for the arising of akusala, but there are not always conditions for paññā. Paññā will lead to more wholesome moments, such as the perfections (pāramīs).

Maeve asked whether the study of Pāli is helpful for the development of understanding.

Sarah: The teachings are not in the book, the language, the Pāli terms. They are all for the sake of understanding this moment, it is not a matter of collecting words.

Nina

11.15 Meeting on line, VII, 111

Nina
May 28 #163219

The order of the suttas

Dear friends,

Alan: before the Buddha's teaching was known samatha was developed. But after hearing his teaching, what is the point of developing samatha? Is it a matter of accumulation?

Sarah: Calm is a cetasika arising with each kusala citta. Calm develops with insight, it develops with understanding naturally. Then there is no interest in developing another type of calm, such as jhāna. The Path is just about developing understanding of this moment.

Jonathan: The distinction between kusala and akusala is usually not known, such as true mettā and attachment. When Samatha is developed that distinction becomes clearer.

Sarah: When one focuses on breath, there is no understanding at all. There is an idea of "I can focus". There is no development of calm, no kusala at all.

Alan: As to letting go, it is a conditioned moment, nobody can let go.

Sarah: When understanding is developed there will gradually be less the idea of "I can do." The highly developed insight that understands directly the arising and falling away of realities is really letting go. There is letting go of what arose before and of what has not arisen yet. It is useless to cling to what has gone like seeing.

Alan: The first noble Truth (understanding dukkha) leads to the second noble Truth(the cause of dukkha, clinging).

Sarah: If there is no understanding of how unsatisfactory realities are, there cannot be understanding of the cause: continuous clinging to what is unsatisfactory.

Alan: How do the rules (for the monk) help to understand reality now?

Nina: The rules deal with all the subtle kinds of akusala that occur. When we hear about this we can also think of the defilements in our own daily life. Defilements are not self, they arise because of accumulations. The more we understand that they are not self, the more paññā can grow. No self is what the Buddha stressed all the time. Whatever happens is all by conditions.

Sarah: It is not the rules that lead to understanding. We hear about the precepts like abstaining from stealing. If we just follow the rules we may do this because we are afraid to get into trouble. It is understanding which sees the harm of akusala. Seeing the difficulty of life bound up with akusala may lead to living the monk's life naturally. Understanding can lead to following the monk's life.

Trin: Why did the Buddha teach about the four accumulations (Yuganaddha sutta, about developing first jhāna and then insight, etc.)? The Buddha shows that there are different accumulations to be understood. It is understanding all the way. Just as Assaji taught Sāriputta: whatever dhamma arises, it does so by conditions.

Sarah: There is only one Path, no matter what the accumulations are.

Mai: had a question about tranquillity as a vehicle.

Trin: Even tranquillity can be understood as not self.

Sarah: We read in the suttas about making an effort, or great determination. This is just an explanation of different dhammas which are anattā. The more there is understanding of dhammas like seeing now, hearing, kusala or akusala now, the more confidence there is that all are anattā. No matter what one reads, no one can make anything happen. No one can make an effort, or have calm arise.

Jonathan: When one reads about the description of right effort, one gets a wrong idea. Effort is just a cetasika.

Trin: In the beginning of the satipaṭṭhāna sutta it is said that understanding of realities that arise is the only way. Even calm can be the object of understanding. There is no choosing.

Sarah: He teaches about the one Way, the one Path, no matter what accumulations there are.

Sundara: Acharn said about the intoxicants (āsavas), that they arise so quickly, are so subtle, working all the time. It is very fortunate that she can help us to understand this.

Nina: By ourselves we would never know about the intoxicants, which are so subtle and arise so quickly. It is very helpful to hear about that again and again, because we forget.

Alan and Sundara discussed about the order of the first three suttas the Buddha uttered after his enlightenment. "Setting in motion the Wheel of Dhamma", about the four noble Truths was the first sutta. The Buddha said that the truth he attained was deep, subtle, hard to understand. He would preach to people with little dust in their eyes. The second sutta was the "Anattā lakkhaṇa Sutta" and the third one was the "Fire Sutta"(Adittha sutta, S N IV, 19. The All is on fire with the blaze of lust, of ill-will and of ignorance).

As to the "Anatta Lakkhaṇa Sutta", Sarah remarked: each reality arises and falls away by conditions. No one can choose anything. Even when it is not directly said, it is implied in this sutta.

Nina

12
June 2020

12.1 Meeting on line IX, 1

Nina
Jun 7 #163381

Intention to kill

Dear friends,

There was a debate about killing, such as in the case of a dog given anti-worm medicine. One may know the outcome of this act, but there may not be the intention to kill. Two different things were discerned: the intention and the likely outcome. Sundara spoke about the removal of a life support that keeps a person alive.

Sarah: Did the daughter who removed this want to make the mother feel comfortable? What is the intention, to kill? It is much more subtle.

Sundara had his doubts when it is the case of a human being.

Jonathan: Each act of kamma patha involves intention.

There was a discussion about euthanasia, following a parent's wish. Jonathan said the child does not want to cause the parent's death.

Sarah: Acharn said it just depends on the person's intention at that moment.

Sundara: Even a person asks that his life is to be taken, it does not mean you have to.

Jonathan: We just talk about the dhammas involved, not what you are going to do, there is a lot of emotion involved. The question is what are the requirements involved to be kamma patha. What is the intention, and this is not the same as knowing the likely consequence.

Sarah: It is not always apparent from the outside what the intention is.

Azita: It is not sure the person will die when the tube is removed. Is it one's intention to kill or to remove the tube.

Ann wanted to know more about pariññā, and the following stage of vipassanā ñāna (insight knowledge, which develops in stages).

Sarah: It is the direct applying of insight in daily life. It is a different level of understanding based on that insight, from that direct experience. Acharn used a simile: if you never have been to Japan you can just talk about it and this is different from actually having been there.

There are different stages of insight. It depends on accumulations whether there is a long time between different stages of insight, a lot of applying, or very little applying. No rule at all.

Jonathan: after attaining a particular level of ñāna, there may be many moments of awareness and insight of different degrees. Some weak, some stronger. They carry one further towards the next stage. Others don't, they just accumulate; they are just moments of awareness and insight, not making (further) progress.

Nina

12.2 Meeting on line IX, 2

Nina
Jun 11 #163434

Being a vegetarian

Dear friends,

Alan: About being a vegetarian. It seems my thinking, what I want, what it seems to me. One thinks: when one is a Buddhist one should be a vegetarian. Thinking is taken for self.

Sarah: It comes back to intention at this moment. Thinking about being a vegetarian is like thinking of a situation. One believes that less cattle will be killed. It is a long story and a lot of clinging to self-righteousness. To know what is real comes back to citta now, to intention at this moment. I take up a chicken at the supermarket and I have no intention to kill or harm.

Alan: Thinking can be understood as an uncontrollable reality that arises and falls away. "I am making a decision", even that is wrong thinking.

A General orders a battle and the result may be many deaths. Killing may not be his intention at that moment.

Sarah: Acharn gave the example of dropping a bomb. One does not know what the consequences may be. One may just be following an order and have no intention to kill. When we think in terms of a situations, there can never be understanding of realities or understanding what the intention is at any moment.

Sundara refers to the Amagandha Sutta (Sutta Nipata II, 2, Carrion), where it is said that fish and meat are not carrion (foul) but defilements are carrion. We read that the Buddha (and a former Buddha) at fish and meat. Sundara mentioned that Acharn had said that eating is not killing.

Alan: The second factor of the eightfold Path is sometimes translated as right intention. Is it right intention or right thinking? Thinking does not have to be thinking in words.

Sarah: Even thinking can be misleading.

Alan: Intention may suggest that you can have mindfulness by intention. Then one is going into the wrong direction.

Sundara: Words can be misleading. Most important is the understanding of the Dhamma. When there is understanding of the reality of the present moment, it does not matter what words are used.

Sarah: Acharn mentions Right Thinking (sammā saṇkappa, vitakka cetasika) as the cetasika that is touching the object (N: It touches the object so that right understanding can understand it). But then people think of physical touch.

Alan: Mind-door is one of the six doorways, it is not just thinking.

Sarah: Mind-door is the last bhavaṅga-citta before the mind-door adverting-consciousness arises and the object is experienced through the mind-door. Without it the mind-door adverting-consciousness cannot experience the object through that doorway. It is a kiriyacitta arising at the heart-base, not at a sense-base. It experiences both realities and concepts.

Jonathan: When someone translates samma-sankappa as right intention, he is not thinking of cetanā (volition).(N: It is difficult to find a suitable translation. Ven. Bodhi found this an option.)

Question: Why can cetanā not be a Path factor?

Sarah: Cetanā, volition, arises with each citta and the development of the Path does not depend on it. It is not one of the factors leading to enlightenment.

Right concentration is a Path factor. It is the proximate cause of paññā, it develops together with paññā. Cetanā is not a proximate cause of paññā.

Sundara: We are fortunate to be able to listen to Acharn. Ven. Bodhi is a brilliant translator and he has a good knowledge of Pāli. But Acharn reminded him that a reality is appearing.

Many do not understand the difference between concept and reality, which is very fundamental. Otherwise understanding is very hazy.

Maeve tries to find the connection between every day experience and understanding Dhamma.

Sarah: Back to life now, at this moment. The cetasika vitakka arises with almost every citta. It touches the object so that citta and the other cetasikas can experience it. It depends on vitakka which object is experienced.

Sundara on dictionaries: They can be misleading and only help on the conventional level.

Nina

12.3 Meeting on line IX, 3

Nina
Jun 12 #163452

What is life at this moment?

Dear friends,

Dialogue with Chin, Roxanne's husband.

Sarah: What is life at this moment?

Chin: Life is energy.

Sarah: Is there seeing now? At each moment there is a different consciousness. Seeing, hearing, thinking, each moment arises by different conditions. At the moment of seeing or hearing now, who or what sees or hears?

Chin: It is me.

Sarah: What is Chin that sees?

Chin: Seeing is communication. There is communication.

Sarah: If we know already: "I see Roxanne", why do we need the Buddha's teaching to know this? What is special about the Buddha's teaching?

Chin: It is leading to the end of suffering.

Sarah: We need more understanding of life at this moment. Is there first seeing of what is visible and then thinking of the idea of Roxanne?

Hearing of what is heard and then thinking of the meaning? Thinking of different words and ideas? Only sound is heard, only visible object is seen. There is thinking "I see Roxanne". The visible object that is seen is seen for a moment, and then it is gone. It is not satisfactory, not worth clinging to. It is just visible object.

Chin: What can we do to come to the right conditions for understanding more quickly? Will and intention?

Jonathan: The explanation of the way things are in reality has to be heard in order to have understanding. You heard explanations by Sundara and Sarah. Sarah was helping you to understand what is seen, what is heard at the present moment. When you think about what is heard there is conceptualization. The truth is so deep and subtle, it cannot be comprehended at a single hearing. It depends on conditions. We use the expression "conditioned reality" to explain this. We can know what are the necessary factors for understanding to develop, such as contact with others who also have an interest, and sharing our knowledge.

Chin: How to attain enlightenment more quickly?

Jonathan: We cannot decide what we are going to hear. Even we can say in general that the Buddha's explanation of things can be a condition. We cannot determine when enlightenment is going to happen. It is no point to think that more discussion means faster development of understanding. There is no rule.

Sarah: The Buddha's teaching is about the understanding of different realities now, such as seeing, hearing, attachment. Each one is not self. It is not: "I am seeing, hearing or thinking." It is not Roxanne who is seen. There are just different moments (of reality). This is the way to understand what suffering, unsatisfactoriness, is. Each of the realities, like seeing now, is not in anyone's control. No one can choose what will be seen or heard, like now. That is why it is unsatisfactory. It cannot be the way we want. No one can have pleasant experiences all the time. No one can choose to see what he wants. Seeing arises by conditions and falls away instantly. Hearing arises by conditions and falls away instantly. None of these belong to Chin, Roxanne or Sarah.

Sundara: You think: "I see Roxanne", anybody can understand that. Sarah tried to help you to understand the difference between concept and reality, or the distinction about what is seen and our idea about what is seen."I see somebody" is thinking of a story. Concept and reality are different.

Jonathan: Understanding is not a matter of choice. What you are going to see or hear is that a matter of choice? Things happen by conditions, not by choice. We do not really understand conditions that make things happen. We have no control or choice. We cannot choose whether we get sick or not. We do the best to stay healthy. You could choose to join the discussion today but not be able to get a connection (on internet). There is no guarantee that what we will do will bring result.

Chin: Why put a mask on (as protection against Corona).

Jonathan: We do not say: don't do anything. We do the best we can, but the outcome is always uncertain.

Sarah: It seems that I can control or decide, such as putting a mask on. Just a moment that sees what is visible, a moment of hearing sound, a moment of attachment, no one can control these or make a decision about these. Who can control what sound will be heard next. There are just the realities that can experience and that cannot experience, which are not self.

This is the subtlety of the Buddha's teachings, about the understanding of the reality of life at this moment. While looking at Roxanne, is there mettā ot attachment? Can you choose to have only pleasant feeling, no unpleasant feeling when hearing someone's voice?

Chin: If you are mindful, you can take things positively instead of negatively.

Sarah: Depending on conditions at that moment and on accumulations. Some people have accumulated a lot of kindness. Each moment of thinking now depends on accumulations.

Jonathan: We are not saying: no control in conventional sense. We decide to get dressed or take a shower.

We talk about what is happening at the level of momentary consciousness. From moment to moment there is no direction or control. What is seen is result of past kamma, we have no influence over that.

Trin: The more we listen, the more we appreciate the benefit of the teachings.

Chin: So long as we are not attached to the outcome.

Sarah: If there is a moment of attachment, it is conditioned.

Maeve: What can you do to develop understanding. People like to know what the formula is. Acharn always says that the question of "how" is motivated by attachment. Jonothan spoke about the subtlety of the Dhamma. It takes a very long time to know how learning takes place and how understanding develops. It takes long to let go of that "model", of what we are used to. It is a long process of letting go of our ways of understanding, of attachment to understanding that arises again and again. You are not alone!

Nina

12.4 Meeting on line, 10, 1

Nina
Jun 23 #163600

Nimitta

Dear friends,

Nina: The first subject today was nimitta. Realities arise and fall away very rapidly and what can be experienced is only the sign or nimitta of a reality.

Sarah: explained that we can repeat the word nimitta but what about the understanding just now of what appears. She explained that we just think about the term nimitta and not understand the reality now that experiences and the reality that does not experience. We cling to the meaning of the term. This leads to more doubt and it is the wrong Path.

Alan asked: How does the understanding of nimitta help the understanding of the present moment?

Sarah explained: If we do not know about nimitta there will be confusion. How can we be aware of seeing that has fallen away. In the beginning we just talk about the reality of seeing, of hearing without understanding nimitta. There is doubt about it, how seeing can be known, how hearing can be known. Knowing about nimitta helps to explain how reality is experienced.

Jonathan: Attachment that is an unwholesome mental factor cannot arise at the same time as awareness, and yet it can be object of awareness. Awareness takes as object the nimitta of the reality that has just fallen away.

Nina: Realities fall away so fast. When we are thinking about a reality it has fallen away, it is nothing, never to return. It helps us to see that it is non-self.

Sarah: It is the characteristic of reality that can be understood, no matter one calls it nimitta or not.

Tam Chan, a question about following others in a group. They think that one should all wear an outfit of the same colour. She was told to just listen and not give her own opinion.

Sarah: There are different habits because of different accumulations. Whatever we do is conditioned. Even thinking: I will wear a different colour, or: speaking or not speaking, it is all conditioned. Understand what is conditioned at this moment.

Jonathan: It shows the conditioned nature of thinking. Should we do this or that concerns situations. Therefore there is no particular answer to this.

Sarah: Each way of thinking is conditioned. There can be understanding of reality at any time.

Nina

12.5 Meeting on line X, 2

Nina
Jun 24 #163607

Truthfulness (sacca)

Dear friends,

There was discussion about truthfulness (sacca).

Sarah spoke about truthfulness with regard to citta at this moment.: "What is seen: pictures of friends on the computer screen or what is visible at this moment?"

Sukin: Usually self is leading the way. There can be understanding of that, and that is truthful.

Nina: We should know what we do not know. The level of understanding is still pariyatti (intellectual understanding). We should consider realities more, we did not consider enough. Confidence is very important. The Buddha would not teach what cannot be understood. Many lives of development of understanding are needed, the situation is not hopeless.

With Jeff, a discussion about mettā and the way he helps groups of prisoners. He spoke about having mettā for oneself.

Sarah explained that mettā is towards others, not towards oneself.

Jeff spoke about helping others in a conventional sense. The inmates have a very low opinion about themselves and they can learn to be kind to themselves in conventional sense.

Jonathan explained that in Dhamma terms this would not be mettā. Being less caught up in their situation would help them.

Sarah: All those bad experiences are all gone. "We all get lost in dramas of the past. Life is just at this moment. That is meant by truthfulness. It is not my thinking we find so important. We are stuck in the story. We should know the distinction between reality and situation. Understand seeing now, hearing now."

Maeve: The more your own understanding develops, the more are you able to help others.

There was a discussion with Roxanne about the ideas of her husband Chin. He had been a monk and he had a conventional idea of self improvement. The truth of non-self is difficult for Chin.

Jonathan: There is another way of explaining. Pointing out the conditioned nature of whatever appears. It is conditioned by factors that are beyond control.

Sarah: Can anyone decide what is seen at this moment? No control helps to understand anattā.

Nina

12.6 Meeting on line 10, 3

Nina
Jun 25 #163617

Everything depends on conditions

Dear friends,

Tan Chan: Everything depends on conditions, just develop understanding.

Sarah: We have to understand what that "everything" is. Seeing now, no situation like "shall I speak out or not". Just different moments of citta, cetasika and rūpa.

There can be understanding that seeing is conditioned by visible object that impinges on the eye-sense. If we just think of conventional situations we will never understand realities and what is meant by conditions. The understanding gets closer to the truth of life. We should know the difference between absolute truth and what is true in conventional sense. In a conventional sense we can say that we go out and prepare a meal. In that way conditions will not be understood. In the absolute sense there are just a moment of seeing, hearing and other sense impressions, all day long, each one conditioned.

Discussion is useful, otherwise we are stuck with our own ideas, with understanding in conventional sense.

Nina: Understanding of nimitta again. A second meaning. It is not the understanding of what appears right now.

Jonathan: Learning all the meanings of a given term is more an academic exercise.

Another meaning of nimitta is: mark in the function of saññā (remembrance). Saññā marks the object and in terms of that mark there is nimitta. It is a completely different meaning of what we were talking about before, the nimitta of the presently arisen dhamma.

Nina

12.7 Meeting on line, XI, 1

Nina
Jun 30 #163718

Conventional truth

Dear friends,

Alan: In reality there is no place.

Sarah: Memory conditions that kind of thinking. Carmen lives in the Netherlands, but I cannot see the Netherlands, nor taste it. At the moment of seeing, where are the Netherlands?

Jonathan: Conventional truth is a consensus. Absolute truth is the way things are. It is not what we read in the book.

Alan: Conventional truth can also be wrong.

Sarah: Wrong thinking conventionally can be with wholesome or with unwholesome consciousness. When we say thinking of science is unwholesome and thinking of Dhamma is wholesome there is no understanding of reality now. There are so many different cittas (types of consciousness). Each citta arises and falls away so rapidly.

Jonathan: It does not depend on the subject matter of thinking (whether citta is kusala, wholesome, or akusala, unwholesome).

Alan: Knowing kusala and akusala is an advanced stage of insight.

Sarah: If there is no right understanding of nāma (mental phenomena) and rūpa (physical phenomena), it is all taken for my kusala and my akusala.

Jonathan: It is not a matter of insight. Also those who did not learn the teachings can know, to a degree, the difference between kusala and akusala. There can be kusala of the level of calm.

About the perfections, Tan Thanh: If I jump into the river to save someone who is drowning is that the perfection of generosity?

Sukin: The perfections are dhammas that lead to the other shore (out of the cycle of birth and death). Understanding is the only way. (N: good deeds should be accompanied by paññā that does no take kusala for self so that they are perfections.)

Tan: Shall I jump into the river or not?

Jonathan: Can you have paññā by choice?

Tan: You give yourself up to help someone.

Jonathan: This does not mean that he has eradicated the idea of self. To have kusala and help another person does not require understanding of the Buddha's teaching. It always depends on the mental state of the individual. No one can tell what mental state someone else has by looking at a person doing something.

Nina

13

July 2020

13.1 Meeting on line XI, 2

Nina
Jul 1 #163726

Unprompted and prompted

Dear friends,

Maeve asks about the difference between unprompted and prompted consciousness (asaṅkhārika and sasaṅkhārika) in the case of kusala citta and akusala citta.

Sarah: Sometimes kindness is strong and no prompting is needed, sometimes it is weaker and it needs encouragement. There are just different degrees. We usually translate unprompted and prompted consciousness as strong or weak.

Carmen: When I go to the temple there is a lot of akusala, more than at home. Is it better not to go?

Sarah: Each moment of thinking, each act is conditioned. We never know. Who knows what will happen. Like in the case of being enslaved to alcohol. Whatever resolution one takes, it is just for a moment. We do not know what will happen next. Instead of thinking: "shall I do this or that", it is more precious to understand how each reality is conditioned.

Sarah to Karina (whom is new, a friend of Azita): Is it useful to understand more what life is at this moment?

Karina: Azita always places me in the present moment.

Jonathan: Even when we think of the past or the future it is the present moment. We cannot avoid thinking of the past or the future, but understanding the quality of thinking if important. We each have different accumulated tendencies that condition us to react in a certain way. Accumulated tendencies cannot be changed. We need to accept them the way they are. The goal is more understanding.

Sarah: What is the present moment now? What is myself that is in the present moment? "I see, I think, I am here." What is this "I"? Can it be seen, heard or just thought about now? If there is no thinking about "I" there is not the idea that there is "my seeing".

This is the heart of the Buddha's teachings: different realities that experience like seeing, and realities that are experienced. Can you really find an "I"?

Azita: Is there always a mind-door process following a sense-door process?

Sarah: Also when a sense-door process is cut off sooner it cannot be followed by another sense-door process.

Nina: Pariyatti, intellectual understanding is not just study, but it always pertains to the present moment. There is already a beginning of a level of awareness.

Sarah: We have to come back to the present moment, otherwise we speculate about different situations. The intellectual understanding has to be about what is appearing now. There can be talking about details, but what about citta now?

Nina: Like seeing, this is immediately followed by thinking of what is seen. We are confused by thinking of what is seen.

Jonathan: Even on the intellectual level a good understanding is needed of awareness and what can be the object of awareness.

Nina: What is the present moment?

Jonathan: Different conditioned realities. All day long there are seeing, visible object, hearing, sound or thinking. Those are not difficult to find, but they do not appear as they are. Having heard the description of them can be a condition for reflecting. Any moment of intellectual understanding is appreciating something that one has heard. Any moment of new understanding is a confirmation of something one has heard many times before and considered.

Nina

13.2 Meeting on line XI, 3

Nina
Jul 2 #163736

Meanings of nimitta

Dear friends,

Jonathan: Nimitta is usually translated as sign. It is an after image of a dhamma that arises and falls away.

(Here I repeat now a post Jonothan sent about nimitta):

For the purpose of our discussions here, the most significant meaning of 'nimitta' is that of the image left by the rapid arising and falling away of a given conditioned dhamma.

However, consider the following other contexts:

1. Nimitta as the mark made by saññā when it marks the object

   As we know, saññā *marks* the object. The Pāli term for the mark made by saññā is 'nimitta'.

2. Nimitta as in the expressions 'nimitta and anubyañjana'(sign and the details).

   In MN 27 'The Shorter Discourse on the Simile of the Elephant's Footprint' (Bodhi translation, MLDB p269) we read:

   15. "On seeing a form with the eye, he does not grasp at its signs and features. Since, if he left the eye faculty unguarded, evil unwholesome states of covetousness and grief might invade him, he practises the way of its restraint, he guards the eye faculty, he undertakes the restraint of the eye faculty.

   (Here, 'signs and features' is a translation of the Pāli 'nimitta and anubyañjana'.)

   A footnote to this passage reads as follows:

   "This formula is analysed at Vsm I, 53–59. Briefly, - the signs (nimitta) are the most distinctive qualities of the object which, when grasped at unmindfully, can kindle defiled thoughts; - the features (anubyañjana) are the details that may subsequently catch the attention when the first perceptual contact has not been followed up by restraint."

   If this is a correct summary of the Vism passage (and that needs to be checked), then 'nimitta' here is a reference to something other than the image given off by the rapid rising and falling away of a conditioned dhamma.

3. Nimitta as the sign of the kammathana in samatha development

   E.g., uggaha nimitta ('learning sign') and papibhāga-nimitta ('counterpart sign')

   There is also nimitta in the expression 'saṅkhāra nimitta' ('sign of formations') in Vism. This may be close in meaning to the 'nimitta' that is most discussed here. The commentary explains 'sign of formations' as referring to 'the appearance of formations like graspable entities, which is due to compactness of mass, etc., and to individualization of function'.

Different contexts, different meanings.

Maeve: Acharn seems to be discouraging preoccupation with details. What is the balance, what is enough?

Jonathan: Everyone has different accumulations as to interest in details. What is a balance for one is not for another. It is important to know where one's level of understanding is. What is most useful: hear, consider and discuss what is arising at the present moment, rather than thinking of details.

Maeve: reality is completely different from what we think it is.

Jonathan: When hearing a voice there is already thinking of what is experienced. This is not the experience of sound. Those are different realities: the moment of hearing sound and thinking about a voice. This can be the basis of a better understanding of the present moment.

Ann: Too many details takes you away from the present moment.

Sarah: There is attachment when trying to understand dhamma with an idea of self. What about now? Do not look for the grey area, for what cannot be known. One does not see that there is an idea of self when trying to work out the story.

Alberto: There is already lots of work to do with understanding seeing and visible object (the basic level).

Jeff: When I heard about the study of nimitta it reminded me about details in the study of the "Dhatu Katha"(one of the books of the Abhidhamma).

Sarah: Acharn reminded us that there is a lot of detail that cannot be understood. She does not mind when anything is not clear and not understood. We cannot understand in the same way as the Buddha and his great disciples. At the end of this life it is all forgotten. We have to come back to what can be understood now. That is how pariyatti (intellectual understanding) develops.

Nina

Part III

Saturday discussions

14
July 2020

14.1 Saturday Discussion, 2

Nina
Jul 7 #163818

What is the meaning of suññāta?

Dear friends,

What is the truth of visible object? It cannot be a chair or the table. Only that which impinges on the eye-sense. What is life? What is appearing now.

Sukin: Everything is there, the table is there from yesterday to today. What is the meaning of suññāta?

Acharn: Suññāta is another word for anattā, meaning: completely gone. Each reality is anattā and suññāta. Nothing can be taken for permanent. It is no more. It cannot be changed and this is life, only in a moment.

All day there is an object that is seen, but seeing itself is not understood. Seeing does not appear as no one, no thing, as the reality that has no shape or form. The development of direct awareness is needed. When paññā is very weak there is doubt, but paññā can understand this as just a reality. Each reality has to be known before the idea of self is completely eradicated in daily life.

Nina

14.2 Saturday discussion, II, 2

Nina
Jul 13 #163873

Living for what?

Dear friends,

What appears now? Can it be anyone? Is it what arises and experiences to see? Life is not only seeing. Where is seeing right now? It is completely gone.

The room is still the room, the table is still the table. The moment of touching hardness just experiences hardness and then it is gone. It is no more. The hardness that is touched cannot return.

Everyone is going to die, this moment or soon, soon, soon. Everyone is going to the moment of not being this person any more. It will be the end of this person. There are conditions from aeons and aeons to be this person. From this life there are conditions to be another person. There will be seeing, hearing, smelling, tasting, touching, thinking and then they are gone.

It is a relief, because it is not me. Seeing just sees, no matter where, when and what, and then it is gone. There is no hurry to develop understanding. The understanding itself develops and it does so only at that very moment of understanding. It is the most valuable moment because it understands the truth, little by little; clearer and clearer and clearer, stage by stage. It realises that each word of the Buddha is the absolute truth. One sees the value of knowing what life is. Living for what? Just for Dhamma to appear as it is. For paññā to know what is what, rather than not knowing, from life to life.

Nina

14.3 Saturday discussion, II, 3

Nina
Jul 14 #163880

Even trying to understand is lobha

Dear friends,

Sarah: One is trying to solve the problems of the world, but nothing works. Only understanding of realities will work.

Acharn: One is following attachment, lobha. Lobha is hidden.

Sarah: Even trying to understand is lobha. That is why we have to listen again and again. Otherwise it is impossible to understand the truth.

Acharn: Where are you, where is seeing? No world, nothing stays. There is just the world appearing and disappearing, from life to life. When there is no contact, phassa, can there be seeing? It cannot be understood by just hearing the words, but study and understand what is there now.

It is quite a relief, one cannot do anything at all. That is the meaning of letting go. Trying to do something is attachment. Letting go of the idea of self who is seeing, or letting go of what is seen as "something". It has to be from one moment of understanding to the next moment of understanding. Each moment of understanding is very valuable.

Nina: I have to sigh, it is difficult to consider.

Acharn: You do not see lobha yet.

Nina: No, it is very difficult to see lobha.

Acharn: The Buddha, after his enlightenment, said that the Dhamma is very subtle. It is very, very difficult to understand lobha, but it can be known, little by little. One can understand that atta, self, is different from anattā, non-self. I can or I cannot is self, atta. Ignorance or understanding, it is not me.

Sarah: There is no hurry to understand or catch all the details. Thinking "I need to follow all" is not letting understanding develop naturally.

Acharn: It is more difficult than anyone can imagine because it has to develop with no one, no self.

Nina

14.4 Saturday discussion II, 4

Nina
Jul 16 #163891

Life is just: going to die each moment

Dear friends,

Life is just: going to die each moment. Every one is going to die. This person is no more, he cannot come back or return. Who knows what will be the next moment. Death and birth are very close, they are just two (successive) moments. These are very fast, no need to be afraid. The best thing in life is understanding of whatever appears. Is there touching, seeing? They are all gone. This is the way of paññā, to let go of wrong understanding and of clinging to what is there no more.

It is quit a relief that there is no one, no self. This moment is not last moment; it is completely gone, completely different. Can there be the idea of being, of something, of the world, as before? At enlightenment the idea of self is completely eradicated.

Everything is as it is, there is understanding or no understanding. Enlightenment is not thinking or pondering, but the direct experience of the absolute truth, of the four noble Truths.

Sarah: Living naturally without that big burden of "I can do".

Acharn: Suññāta and anattā. One has realized the truth of non-self, but not the arising and falling away of realities. One sees the danger of the arising and falling away, otherwise there cannot be vipassanā ñāna. The whole world is gone, there is nothing there.

Sarah: Suññāta refers in particular to that aspect of anattā which is the arising and falling away. Vipassanā ñāna is the direct understanding of the falling away of realities.

Acharn: One really understands that whatever is there it is only by conditions. No one can change it. No matter it is strong attachment, strong aversion, strong conceit, paññā can understand them as not me, no one, only a characteristic that is conditioned to arise. If there is no lobha, it is quite a relief.

Nina

14.5 Saturday discussion, III, 1

Nina
Jul 20 #163926

The truth is covered up, every day

Dear friends,

We cling to everything. It is not enough to only know that. What is the object of clinging, just one at a time? When we say that we cling to the table, to people, it is not understanding of what is the object of clinging. There is clinging to what appears while there is seeing; it does not appear as it is yet. There is clinging to what is not known. When there is the idea of something there, it is wrong understanding. The moment of more understanding of reality as it is, is the moment of letting go. When the object of clinging appears as it is, it appears as nothing.

Everyone is going to die, there is not I forever. Even when hardness appears, there is no attention to reality as not self. The truth is covered up, every day. It is the world of suññāta, nothing. The meaning of suññāta is: completely gone, never to return. In the beginning there can be the understanding of anattā, before experiencing the arising and falling away of realities.(N: the first stage of insight is knowing the difference between nāma and rūpa. Only at the third and fourth stage the arising and falling away of realities is known. The meaning of suññāta is completely fallen away.) Even now anattā does not appear as anatta; paññā develops stage by stage.

Nina

14.6 Saturday discussion, III, 3

Nina
Jul 21 #163942

Shall we just talk about what appears now?

Dear friends,

When we think that there is something there, it is wrong. There are ignorance and clinging. Hardness is hardness and it is gone completely. But it appears as "something". One believes that one sees Sarah and Jonothan, but what is there? No you. We never thought about what is no more, arisen and fallen away. Understanding the arising and falling away of realities is not the first stage of insight. (The first stage is knowing the difference between nāma and rūpa.)

Jonathan: Does understanding of individual realities like seeing, hearing, thinking, etc. help to understand "no me, no self"?

Acharn: What is seen is not Jonothan, no table. Only that which impinges on the eye-base can be seen. It is so very tiny. It cannot condition the appearance of the arising and falling away of what is there, there are many levels of understanding. It has to develop from pariyatti (intellectual understanding) that is firm until it is sacca ñāna (of the level of pariyatti) . There should be no expectation to have it, then it would not be conditioned by (the understanding of) anattā. One takes it for sati with an idea of "I can do, I can know".

We just talk about realities, but what is reality now?

Jonathan: When we speak about not self, people think: the computer is not self.

Acharn: What is a self?

Jonathan: Just an idea.

Acharn: Whatever appears seems to be something. There is no understanding that it is conditioned.

Sukin: The self is always around the corner. There is a little understanding and then the self comes in again.

Acharn: One can understand the difference between intellectual understanding and direct understanding and be truthful.

Sacca pāramī, the perfection of truthfulness, is the moment of understanding truthfulness, together with viriya (energy), khanti (patience) and adiṭṭhāna (determination).

The perfections are necessary, otherwise it is impossible to understand the truth.

Nina

14.7 Saturday discussion III, 4

Nina
Jul 24 #163967

The perfection of truthfulness

Dear friends,

Sukin: We have to listen to many aspects of dhamma before we understand the truth of not me.

Acharn: There are many realities by conditions and this is life. No one, no self. It takes a long time until there is no expectation to have it.

Each reality has its own characteristic and nobody can change it. There is sacca ñāna at level of pariyatti, of paṭipatti and of pativedha.

Sacca pāramī (the perfection of truthfulness) has to develop on and on with understanding, until it is pativedha (realization of the truth). Different levels.

When one tries very hard it is not sacca pāramī, understanding of the truth of no me, no self.

What can eradicate sīlabbata parāmāsa (wrong practice)? Only the magga-citta of the sotāpanna (arising at the first stage of enlightenment). Wrong practice can be just a slight deviation of the eightfold Path. Paññā knows and can let it go.

Who can imagine that the whole world is lost (at the moment of insight knowledge, when there is no world). Paññā must be very keen when only one reality appears.

Understanding of the truth now is sacca pāramī. If there is no understanding of this moment, is there sacca (truth)? The "I" is there.

Each moment of understanding is pāramī. "No I" is sacca pāramī. Trying very hard to understand cannot be sacca pāramī, because actually there is no "I". But when understanding is firm there is no "I" at all.

Nina

14.8 Saturday discussion, IV, 1

Nina
Jul 27 #163988

Where is meditation?

Dear friends,

Sarah to Lukas: on meditation, focussing on bodily feelings.

Acharn: Where is meditation? The purpose of the Buddha's teachings is just understanding, not reading, remembering or translating. What is awareness? Is it there or not? No one can know what awareness is without understanding. What is there now, is it known?

Sarah: Even awareness of the level of Samatha has to be developed with understanding. Otherwise one just focusses on an object without understanding. There is just the development of attachment.

Acharn: When we understand dhamma, we understand anattā. Dhamma cannot be taken for permanent, self or things. Each reality (of life) is conditioned, otherwise it cannot arise. There are so many different realities, arising and falling away, but no one knows. They appear as something, as nimitta, all the time. One takes them as permanent and that is the idea of atta, self. "I" see all day, there is no understanding.

One thinks that one can meditate, but what for, to understand what? What appears is not understood, not even to the degree of pariyatti (intellectual understanding). The teachings are for letting go of that which cannot be taken for anything. Even the simple question of "where are you now?", cannot be answered. Right understanding of different degrees brings about different answers.

When one thinks "I am meditating", the "I" is so strong. What is "I" and where is "I"? Gone completely. Can ignorance understand lobha? There is no "I" from the very beginning. Each word of the teachings shows that there is no "I".

Understanding the Buddha's teachings is letting go. Everyone is going to die, for sure. In the evening or tomorrow, no one knows. So, what is the best thing in life? Not wrong understanding of the idea of self, but right understanding (supported) by the perfections. There have to be the perfections, pāramīs, of patience, truthfulness, energy, determination. One begins to understand that there is no self. How long does it take? It depends on conditions. How can (the truth) appear as the Buddha had realized it at his enlightenment? It seems as if it is impossible. Understanding is covered up by ignorance, from moment to moment to moment.

There are three stages of understanding each of the four noble Truths, thus, there are twelve stages. (N: The noble Truth of dukkha has to be understood at the level of pariyatti, of paṭipatti, direct understanding, and pativedha, realization. Even-so for the noble Truth of the cause of dukkha, of the ceasing of dukkha and of the Path leading to the ceasing of dukkha.)

How can this condition abhisamaya, enlightenment? It can be, but only by conditions, by right understanding, not by "I". The understanding of anattā does not mean just following words, that is not enough. Not by a self, only by dhamma that is conditioned and arises unexpectedly. This is the only way to gradually eliminate the idea of self.

Nina

14.9 Saturday discussion, IV, 2

Nina
Jul 28 #164002

Understanding is so precious

Dear friends,

Hardness appears but there is no attention to it from morning to night. It is a reality that arises because of conditions. When one wants to experience something there is lobha, attachment, and it is there with "you", with the idea of self. One should not force oneself (to have understanding), but one should see the precious moment of understanding. It needs consideration. Seeing is not hearing, thinking or liking. After hearing the teachings paññā experiences what was not experienced before, namely, anattāness. One can feel relieved from being enslaved to lobha which is there all the time. There can be letting go, stage by stage, very little at a time.

One learns Dhamma just to understand what appears now. By truthfulness it can be known how much understanding there is, or none at all, or not yet, or just a beginning. Sāriputta had no idea that he would become enlightened after hearing the words from Assaji (about the cause of the arising of dhammas and their ceasing).

At the first stage of insight there is no doubt that what experiences is nāma. There have to be the perfections, pāramīs, of patience, truthfulness, energy and determination to let go the strong idea of "I will do, I will try, I will know." Only paññā can do that because it understands the truth.

We should not just say: "paññā, paññā", but we should know what paññā is and what it understands. We should follow the Buddha's teachings by understanding, not just by repeating, reciting or trying to know with an idea of self. Only one reality is the object of right awareness with right understanding. When paññā is there it is no me, not self, there is only that reality appearing. There is no expectation how long or how short (it lasts).

Where am I? There is no where. Where is the seeing? No where. (N: This answers her question "where are you now?") It arises at the eye-base; the eye-base falls away and so does seeing.

Sarah: Even when we think that it will take a long time, it is not me that takes a long time. Paññā takes a long time because ignorance has been accumulated for so long.

Acharn: The very moment of understanding is so precious because it can condition other moments of understanding, little by little. What appears has to be known otherwise there is ignorance. Even now, the reality that experiences does not appear as it is. No understanding yet, until time comes. When there is more understanding the subtlety of reality appears. It takes much longer to develop than one can imagine.

Nina

15
August 2020

15.1 Saturday discussion, V, 1

Nina
Aug 2 #164062

Confidence that there is no one now

Dear friends,

Nina: Acharn said that if we cling to awareness of what appears now, such as seeing, it is not possible to understand the next moment. Do you mean by the next moment receiving-consciousness, sampaṭicchana-citta?

Acharn: Is there sampaṭicchana-citta now?

Nina: Yes, but it is not known.

Acharn: What can be known now?

Nina: Seeing, but not precisely. There is usually an idea of seeing. I was reminded that we talk a lot about seeing, that we repeat what we heard, instead of understanding the present moment.

Acharn: What should be the beginning of understanding dhamma as not self? All dhammas are (just) dhammas, no one, no self, no thing in it. The understanding of what appears now should be a little clearer. Otherwise it is not the understanding of realities and we keep on not understanding, not understanding. Listen to whatever we can hear now, to understand the truth, sacca, of it. Otherwise there is no letting go of self.

How can awareness arise? By anyone, by "I"? If there is no intellectual understanding there is no condition for the arising of right awareness and the understanding of what has been heard before; the understanding of what was hidden for aeons and aeons. It did not appear as it is, until hearing the teachings. There should be hearing until there are sufficient conditions for direct understanding naturally, unexpectedly, without desire or intention. This is the way to let go.

The perfections have to be developed not just one life. It takes aeons to develop the firm confidence that there is no one now. Reality cannot be changed into anything else. It is just conditioned to arise and then it is gone, never to be again. This is the only way to develop understanding little by little, until it is time not to be forgetful of: "now it is not me." Hearing, considering, like, dislike, hardness, softness, all appear when there are conditions and then they are gone, never to return.

Nina

15.2 Saturday Discussion V, 3

Nina
Aug 4 #164084

Study carefully

Dear friends,

Sarah: There can be a beginning to understand that dhammas are anattā. No one can do anything or select an object. No one can choose what appears next.

Nina: We do not have to be aware of a particular reality.

Sarah: That would be the idea of self, not understanding naturally whatever appears. Wrong practice can come in any time, even in a dhamma discussion. Whatever arises, arises by conditions.

Acharn: What is meant by not clinging?

Nina: Clinging is the opposite of letting go. If there is no clinging one does not try to be aware.

Acharn: Can you tell anyone: don't try to be aware and don't cling?

Nina: Trying to be aware is clinging already.

Acharn: There is no understanding. From hearing the teachings one will study carefully. From the very beginning one can understand the word dhamma: a reality, no one. It is true.

The truth of everything is: no self, uncontrollable, not me. In a day is there even a short moment of considering: it is not me? It may be just thinking. This means that the conditions are not sufficient. Even thinking about what is appearing now is very difficult. So, it is impossible to say: don't cling, don't try.

Be truthful to this moment. Paññā knows what is right and what is wrong.

Anything is conditioned, no matter what kind of thinking. No one can tell anyone: don't do this or that. Understand completely what is the truth. It takes a long time, but it does not matter. Understanding is the moment of letting go.

Nina: When I ask a question I realize that the idea of self is behind it. But this is knowing by thinking. It is not the realization that my question is motivated by clinging to the wish to know.

Acharn: Until one has attained the first stage of enlightenment, the stage of the sotāpanna, there is still the idea of self.

It is so common, but it can be understood that there is no perfect understanding, even at the level of intellectual understanding. The Buddha spoke about Sāriputta and Moggallana, but this does not mean that he did not realize the truth of nāma and rūpa. When the Buddha said: do good deeds, it is not a command. The value of what is right and what is wrong can be realized. Paññā understands the word of the

Buddha about the truth all the time, the truth that there is not self, not me. Even when doing good deeds it is not "I" who acts, it is the function of dhamma. By the understanding of dhamma there can be a letting go of self, little by little. There can be more conditions for understanding of what appears now. There is no choice, it has arisen by conditions. No one can change this moment, it is so natural. It depends on paññā how much understanding there is. When there is doubt, paññā knows it. When there is not enough paññā, it is me. It is just a matter of paññā to perform its function when it has developed to higher degrees.

Nina

15.3 Saturday discussion V,4

Nina
Aug 5 #164092

Understand whatever appears now, naturally

Dear friends,

Sarah: Nina, when you say: "I know that behind my question there is an idea of self, but this is only intellectual understanding", then it seems that there is wishing it to be deeper and higher. There is wishing instead of knowing that what understanding there is, is conditioned at that moment. When there is "I" wishing to have more understanding there is more clinging instead of just being contented with whatever is conditioned at that moment. It does not matter how little or how much understanding there is, but clinging hinders.

Nina: We see the usefulness of discussion, because then it appears what one does not understand yet.

Acharn: We are talking about now, but there is no understanding of what is now.

Nina: Often there is only talking about realities, that is a good reminder.

Acharn: We listen just to understand whatever appears now, naturally, by conditions. Realities cannot be changed or controlled. Can one select to know this or that moment? All five khandhas are objects of clinging, from birth. The point is just to understand and understanding is not "I". It is a reality, different from ignorance. At the moment of understanding there can be letting go of clinging, of taking realities for "I". Was there today any moment of thinking: "Not me"? Be truthful. The development of understanding will wear away the idea of self, at the moment of understanding.

When the development is not natural, the "I" is there. Without understanding how can there be patience to develop understanding? Happiness or unhappiness just appear for a moment. That is the world.

Sukin: When paññā increases do the perfections also increase?

Acharn: Without paññā there cannot be any perfection, pāramī.

Sukin: When we do anything for this or that (purpose), is it usually attachment?

Acharn: Certainly, until there is no "I" at all.

Nina

15.4 Saturday discussion, V, 5

Nina
Aug 7 #164115

A long way to "let go"

Dear friends,

How can seeing appear as it is? At that moment there is nothing else in the world, only that which arises and experiences. There are many different levels of paññā. Sabba pariññā has to be after vipassanā ñāna. (sabba means all. A moment of vipassanā ñāna is very short and what has been realized at the moment of vipassanā ñāna has to be applied to all realities of daily life that appear.) Otherwise we just talk about the words and think about what appears. The understanding of not "I" begins little by little. It has to develop by understanding all realities in life, anything that appears as sabba pariññā, before higher paññā can develop. This is detachment from wanting a result, from clinging to the idea of self, as permanent, from life to life. There is no "I" at all. Life is so short and everyone is going to die, we do not know when. The truth of each reality is beyond expectation. The word dhamma means everything that is real. It is true right now. We can talk about seeing, because there is seeing. Seeing is real, it is dhamma. It cannot be "I" at all. This is not yet direct understanding of seeing yet.

How can there be vipassanā ñāna which experiences each reality as a different one? The "whole" is "I": I see, I hear, I think. They are different realities at different moments arising by different conditions. There is no me, never more in saṃsāra, the cycle of birth and death. The understanding of what is now appearing should be understanding (stemming) from hearing. This is intellectual understanding.

How can there be the understanding of nāma and rūpa right now? It is vipassanā ñāna which sees clearly. Vipassanā ñāna is very short, very rapid. As rapid as each moment now. There is no doubt about the object of vipassanā ñāna when it is there. Paramis, the perfections, are needed all the way.

When there is hoping, there is attachment, lobha. Everything can be object of lobha. Whatever appears, paññā begins to understand the anattāness of realities, just from hearing, not from (direct) experience. The most difficult (to understand) is that it is by conditions, not by anyone. There are less conditions for paññā then for ignorance. Therefore, it takes a long way to "let go". Even understanding by way of thinking is not easy.

Sarah: Pariññā means to understand all. There are three pariññās arising in between the stages of insight, vipassanā ñānas: ñata pariññā is the understanding arising after the first stage of insight (knowing the difference between nāma and rūpa). Tirana pariññā, understanding of investigation, arises in between the second stage of insight and the fifth stage. Pahana pariññā, understanding of overcoming, begins at the fifth stage of insight, understanding of dissolution, bhanga ñāna. Sabba pariññā refers to all these pariññās.

Acharn: The moment of vipassanā ñāna is different from other moments (of paññā). Once it has arisen it is so clear. Saññā remembers the characteristic of anattā. But after that moment there are defilements and doubt (again). The first stage of insight is not enough. Paññā has to become keener and keener, stronger and stronger, to condition a higher level, stage by stage. How long it takes from one stage of insight to another, patience is needed. These are all anattā. The idea of self can be eradicated completely.

Nina

15.5 Saturday discussion VI, 1

Nina
Aug 10 #164145

The pariññās

Dear friends,

Nina: Resuming what Sarah had said about the pariññās, which is understanding of different levels arising in between the stages of insight.

Acharn: Realities arise and fall away, exactly the same as now. It depends on paññā how much understanding of that object there is. Only one nimitta of one reality can be known. (N: Realities arise and fall away very rapidly. For example seeing, there is seeing again and again and nobody could catch one moment of seeing, but the sign or nimitta of seeing can be experienced.)

Now while we are talking, visible object is appearing. But it does not appear well until paññā is more developed. Then just one characteristic appears and it begins to appear well.

Characteristics do not appear as clearly as at the moment of a stage of insight, vipassanā ñāna, it is not pariññā; it is only understanding from learning (pariyatti).

Sacca pāramī is the perfection of truthfulness. How much understanding is there of the object of seeing? Is it known as it is or not?

Sukin: When you say, it appears well, do you refer to paññā? Vipassanā ñāna is of a higher level than paṭipatti as I understand. (N: pariyatti, intellectual understanding, can, when it is firm enough, condition paṭipatti, direct understanding. When paññā is further developed there are conditions for pativedha, direct realization of the truth at the stages of insight and after that at enlightenment) Is sati also of a higher level?

Sarah: The level of pativedha is higher than satipaṭṭhāna of the level of paṭipatti. Pativedha is much clearer.

Nina: Is vipassanā ñāna already pativedha?

Acharn: Is a moment of paṭipatti different from now?

Nina: Now there is just a beginning of pariyatti, intellectual understanding.

Acharn: One can understand paṭipatti when it arises. It has to be different from understanding stemming from considering and intellectual understanding.

Sacca pāramī, the perfection of truthfulness. One has to be truthful to the truth. The truth the Buddha has enlightened is now. Citta arises, but if there is no paṭipatti there is no experience of the arising of any reality now. Each reality that is experienced has arisen but it is unknown.

Paññā begins to understand. There is sati at the moment of talking about dhamma and understanding is there, and it is different from talking without understanding of the words. It is there now. Intellectual understanding is different from only listening and considering. A moment of hearing and no understanding is different from hearing and understanding.

Nina

15.6 Saturday discussion VI, 2

Nina
Aug 11 #164158

Sacca, truthfulness

Dear friends,

Acharn: Sati that is directly aware is different from sati of the intellectual level. Without intellectual understanding how can direct awareness arise? It cannot arise by hoping, no one can do anything.

Sukin: Understanding helps to avoid wrong practice.

Acharn: We are talking about realities, not self. We have to be truthful: seeing is seeing, seeing is not thinking. Seeing just arises to see and falls away instantly, never to return.

Sukin: Sacca, truthfulness, prevents us from going the wrong way.

Sarah: When we think how little understanding we have, we have to remember that there is not my understanding at all. It is taken for my understanding and there is concern about the result. Sacca parami knows the wrong path. There is already the wrong path when there is the idea of my little understanding. Lobha comes in so quickly taking it for my understanding, and there is thinking: how can there be more understanding? That is not understanding of the reality that appears now. When there is understanding of seeing or hearing, there is no thought of how much understanding one has.

Sukin: We can also see the importance of the other perfections besides the perfection of truthfulness, sacca pāramī.

Sarah: Understanding is just for a moment. When we talk about vipassanā ñāna (stages of insight) and pativedha (direct realization of the truth), it is just the understanding of what appears now. It is just for a moment and then it is gone. It is not a matter of "I have this understanding". Do not think of how little I have, but have confidence in the development of understanding itself. Do not think about when, how much or how little. There is not my understanding that is in this or that way.

Alan: There will always be the desire for understanding. The idea of self is always with us, but it can be understood. That desire always comes, that is our nature, by conditions. It can be understood, it is the wrong path. The idea of self is behind everything we do.

Sarah: That is the perfection of truthfulness, sacca pāramī. Clinging can be understood. Clinging to result is a hindrance to the Path. Clinging to self is the wrong way.

Alan: The moment of vipassanā ñāna is very short. The idea of self will come in, immediately afterwards. But at the moment of vipassanā ñāna there is the clear understanding that there is nobody there.

Nina

15.7 Saturday discussion VI, 3

Nina
Aug 12 #164165

Understanding illuminates

Dear friends,

Alan: At the moment of insight knowledge, vipassanā ñāna, there is no one who experiences.

Sarah: Even at the level of intellectual understanding, or even at the moment of satipaṭṭhāna there is no one who understands. Only paññā understands, right from the beginning. Paññā begins to understand dhamma as anattā. Even now, when there is considering and intellectual understanding of visible object, what is seen, it is known as just a reality, there is not someone who is seen. That understanding has to develop deeper and deeper, so that it becomes clearer and firmer. Thus, right from the beginning there is no one who understands.

Alan: Understanding illuminates, like a light that is shining. If the object is hardness, it shows up as it is.

Sarah: The commentary speaks about paññā as lighting up in a dark room. Paññā illuminates the object that is experienced so that it is seen more and more clearly until the level of insight is reached. At that level paññā and sati are so firm and strong. Even now when paññā begins to develop, at the level of intellectual understanding and the level of direct understanding, it begins to illuminate the object.

Alan: When paññā develops it can understand conditions for realities. Realities arise and fall away very rapidly, and so, how can conditions be understood?

Sarah: Like now, there is seeing. How could it arise without conditions for its arising? Seeing arises unexpectedly, it is not in anyone's control. Even at the beginning when there is intellectual understanding, dhamma can be understood as anattā. There is a beginning of understanding of the conditioned nature of dhamma and that understanding becomes firmer and firmer.

Alan: Realities arise and are then completely gone. The taste experienced at breakfast is gone. But tomorrow there is a similar taste. There is a continuity of a similar characteristic. You have not changed much in the last week. Realities have completely gone, but we have the idea: it is the same or similar. How can there be this idea that it is the same?

Sarah: Because of the rapidity of the arising and falling away of realities. Citta plays tricks all the time. It seems that the same object is seen for five or ten minutes, or taste is experienced for some time. Actually it is just rūpa fallen away completely, never to return.

Alan: Rūpa has fallen away and it conditions a similar rūpa.

Sarah: The taste of your breakfast is conditioned, not by last week, but by temperature. The other rūpas that arise together with taste (in one group) condition it. That taste seems similar to the one last week. But taste has fallen away and cannot condition taste now.

Nina

15.8 Saturday discussion VI, 4

Nina
Aug 13 #164171

Awareness of just one reality

Dear friends,

Acharn: At the first stage of insight (paññā knows) the reality that experiences and the reality that does not experience. (Now) the citta and cetasikas do not appear as they are, they do not appear well. We talk about whatever is now. At what level of understanding can there be conditions for awareness of just one reality at a time? (When) they all come together there is the idea of something. From learning the truth of whatever appears now, (realities appear) just one by one. Seeing just arises and falls away, and this is the truth that can be directly experienced.

Everything comes from the truth of anattā. Even now while talking about realities.

Hearing again and again and again can condition awareness of just one reality. There is understanding of what is meant by just one reality, only one. It develops little by little. There is no expectation about what is direct awareness, and how does it come (about)? When many things appear together they do not appear well. But when only one reality appears, how short it is. It is a test for oneself how much understanding there is of that which appears. It is very little and very subtle.

From intellectual understanding and careful considering there must be conditions to let go of the idea of "I" who is seeing or hearing.

Alan: When we have the idea of a place or something like a cup, it indicates that there is no awareness of a reality, taking it for something.

Acharn: So what is there now?

Alan: Something.

Acharn: It does not appear well as it is. Know the difference between intellectual understanding and awareness.

Alan: The enlightened person knows the difference when there is clear understanding of a reality and when a concept is known. The unenlightened person gets mixed up. There is hardness when it is touched and then it is followed by thinking. When there is awareness a reality appears as it is. When it appears as something there is no right awareness of that reality.

Jonathan: Knowing a concept is not necessarily an indication of lack of understanding. Moments without awareness and understanding do not have to be moments of wrong view. Understanding is accumulated and not lost, it will condition a slightly different view of the world, of reality.

Nina

15.9 Saturday discussion VI, 5

Nina
Aug 14 #164187

There is no one

Dear friends,

Acharn: The idea of self is there, more and more. Understanding has to begin; there has to be considering and understanding from the very beginning. Actually, there is no self when there are no citta, cetasika and rūpa, no world. Whatever arises is there. When there is no understanding it is "something". Before its arising, where is it? There is nothing. It just arises to experience only. It sees only. Does it appear well? No, until a moment of higher understanding. Direct awareness is conditioned. It is like letting go (and this is) from hearing, considering, little by little, naturally. Even right now at a moment of understanding there is sati, but it is not directed to any object.

Alan: When there is the intellectual understanding of anattā, there must be sati.

Acharn: It is only intellectual understanding of citta, that now arises to experience. Without this understanding there is no condition to be aware of a reality now. There is no selection, no control if there are conditions for its arising. It all depends on conditions, whatever arises, even the moment of sammā-sati, right awareness. What about paññā? When it just begins only one object appears, even right now, but no understanding. When there are enough conditions there is not just thinking. How much paññā is there when it just begins to be aware? Sati does not show up, whatever appears. Paññā begins to be aware of a reality by anattāness. Is the understanding enough or not yet? It is very weak, but it is there. It is the beginning of the level of direct awareness but not as clear as vipassanā ñāna (insight knowledge). We can imagine what it means: appearance of just one object. We begin to understand just that one object without thinking. Thinking is conditioned to think.

Tam Thanh: When you ask: where are you, and my answer is: not on the table, is that correct?

Acharn: How can there be the understanding whether it is good enough? Only paññā knows. At the moment of understanding realities there is no one at all. Can the hardness be somewhere? In the room? It just arises and falls away.

Alan: This moment cannot be lost. When we do not understand it, it is lost and we waste our life.

Acharn: If nothing arises, where are you? It seems that realities are together, but when there is direct awareness of one characteristic it appears well.

Realities arise by conditions. The truth is always covered up. There is an idea to have only this object and no other objects.

Sarah: Begin again now, all understanding is gone.

Acharn: The "I" is there, there is clinging to everything that is not known. When hearing the word sati, it seems that we understand, but when it arises there is no doubt about direct awareness. Each day is like a test for understanding. We get closer to understanding the virtues of the Buddha. How can anyone have such understanding? It takes a long time to be truthful. There is no one, otherwise it is I who knows. Then the truth is covered up.

Nina

15.10 Saturday discussion, VII, 2

Nina
Aug 18 #164215

Be truthful to the truth

Dear friends,

Acharn: All have to be understood as anattā, otherwise there is no condition for direct awareness to arise. It is impossible, because there is a lot of ignorance and attachment. The understanding of no self is firm when it is sacca ñāna. At the moment of direct awareness it (understanding) shows itself as anattā. Any moment of paññā arises with the understanding of anattā.

Nina: You say that every moment is lobha (attachment). That is very hard to understand.

Acharn: If the Buddha did not tell us who can understand the āsavas (intoxicants). After three moments (after seeing which is vipākacitta, there are three more moments of citta before the javanacittas arise which are kusala cittas or akusala cittas) they (the intoxicants) are there, unknown. There is no understanding of what appears.

Nina: It is very useful that you remind us of the āsavas. They are so subtle and hardly known.

Acharn: Actually there is no me. We do not know the next moment. There is seeing and if there is no understanding of seeing as a conditioned reality there must be an idea of self and attachment to that. Nothing can eliminate wrong understanding but right understanding. There are just conditioned realities arising and falling away all the time, unknown, because they cannot be known by ignorance and attachment.

There is seeing which experiences and there is what cannot experience but which just impinges on the eye-base and is then gone. It takes time before ignorance is worn away little by little. Understand the perfection of truthfulness, sacca pāramī. Be truthful to the truth. Without conditions nothing can arise.

Vipassanā ñāna (insight wisdom) can eliminate lobha and ignorance from time to time. The first stage of insight cannot understand the arising and falling away (of realities), but it sees perfectly the difference between nāma and rūpa. Now there is seeing. There is not a high level of understanding. Its function is just to see. There is seeing and there is that which is seen, one by one. A moment of seeing is so short, it appears as nimitta (N: There are many moments of seeing arising and falling away very rapidly; no one can catch one moment, but the sign of it, nimitta, appears.) On can see how much ignorance there is, from moment to moment, all day long.

Nina

15.11 Saturday discussion, VII, 3, 4

Nina
Aug 19 #164229

Doubt about what appears

Dear friends,

Acharn: Now there is doubt about what appears and what experiences.

Nina: When nāma and rūpa are not distinguished from each other, does it mean that one takes them together? How is that, it means that one takes seeing and visible object together?

Acharn: From hearing, study and considering one knows that what is experienced cannot be that which sees. Do not forget what is heard: what experiences has no shape and form. At the moment of experiencing the characteristic of seeing it is known as that which experiences. You do not have to call it seeing. Just understand that characteristic. The reality which sees is this moment of seeing. This is the way to understand realities as no one, no me. Because there is that which experiences all day, from moment to moment, unknown. It appears as something all the time.

The perfections of energy, patience, truthfulness and determination are necessary.

Sarah: When realities are understood as dhamma, seeing is just that which experiences and visible object is the reality that is experienced. One is thinking about a story of seeing being something difficult (to understand). When one thinks "What is seen is something" and (that here is) thus no clear understanding of the distinction between nāma and rūpa, that is because there is no understanding of the realities themselves. This is meant by taking them together, a story about things and people.

Acharn spoke earlier about when there is time to be aware. When one believes that "I can do", it cannot be a condition for awareness, but it is taken for awareness. This is the wrong path, wrong understanding and wrong awareness. Focussing on seeing or on visible object, trying to catch realities is the wrong path and it cannot lead to direct awareness and direct understanding.

Lobha is unseen but it is there, even in a dhamma discussion. Trying to catch the word or the meaning is no condition for direct awareness.

Direct awareness of what?

(Alberto's transcription):

Acharn Sujin: Can there be direct awareness without direct understanding, together? That's why we try to think about direct awareness, but what about understanding? Without understanding it cannot be direct awareness, because: direct awareness of what? And what conditions it to understand directly that as it is: because right understanding is not enough! So it all depends on understanding. When there is little understanding why can't there be direct understanding, yet? Because understanding is not enough. So right understanding knows that: it doesn't matter at all the trying to have it, the wish to have it, because all depends on conditions, and the condition for right or direct awareness must be the intellectual understanding firm enough to be sacca-ñāna. Not changing to trying to understand, because that's not the way: it hinders, and that is lobha, and the idea of self is still there, very strong because the understanding is not enough. So all depends on understanding, stage by stage.

Even if hardness is appearing now, no moments of direct awareness yet, because understanding is not enough to understand. With more sacca-ñāna of that which has that characteristic as... we don't have to think about nimitta because that would never be the paññā which can experience just one, never, because realities arise and fall away in split seconds. So by way of understanding the vāra (round or series of cittas within a process) and the dvāra and the citta which arises, one by one, little by little, we understand that paññā cannot arise right after seeing, immediately, it's impossible, that's why realities even now or when or where appear as nimitta, but without the paramattha dhamma, without absolute realities there cannot be nimitta, but the nimitta indicates that at that moment there must be realities arising and falling away unknowingly all the time, so very rapidly. So only paññā can eliminate wrong understanding with attachment, little by little, otherwise there must be attachment to: "I just want to experience it as I have heard". As long as there is the idea of "I" it is wrong, attachment is there, wrong understanding is there.

So that is the very very fine and very very difficult way, only paññā from moment to moment can begin to understand how it is, how difficult: it's so subtle, but it can be understood stage by stage, as it is. No one can change the characteristic of hardness at all, even right now, but not enough understanding for direct awareness which knows that it's only there for just when it appears, and even while it does appear there must the arising and falling away of that reality, so very rapidly that can appear as hardness. And this understanding will gradually, very slowly eliminate the idea of self. Very firm in the beginning, enough to condition direct awareness unexpectedly, to understand the anattāness of all dhammas, even that one.

(end of Alberto's transcription)

Nina

15.12 Saturday discussion VII, 6

Nina
Aug 21 #164254

Clinging to the idea of "something"

Dear friends,

The cetasika saññā, remembrance, accompanies each citta. Acharn: No one knows it is there, even now there is saññā. Thinking thinks about what saññā marks and remembers. If we do not talk about the Buddha's teachings we do not know saññā as not self.

It takes time to develop understanding at the moment of awareness, on and on and on, by conditions. The fourth noble Truth is the Path and there is no doubt about the Path. Does the object appear well?

Nina: Not yet.

Acharn: Not as it is. From hearing and considering, the difference (will be known) between that what appears as "something" and that which arises and falls away. Hardness, not one moment, but several moments arise and fall away, that is why it does not appear well.

Even though there are many manodvaravajjana cittas (cittas arising in a mind-door process), it does not appear as mind-door (manodvāra).

Sarah: For those not familiar with Pāli I should explain about manodvāravajjana-citta It seems that seeing lasts and there is "something" that is seen all the time. One sense-door process (is followed by) many mind-door processes and this is covered up by the idea of "something" that is seen.

Nina: I am glad you say this. I was just wondering why so many mind-door processes are unknown. It seems that seeing lasts.

Sarah: Seeing "something". I can see Nina for a long time, but actually there is just one very brief moment of seeing what is visible, (followed by) other cittas in the eye-door process that do not see anything, then there are bhavaṅga-cittas (life-continuum) and many mind-door processes. The mind-door process cittas think of shape and form, the idea about

Nina: Because of attachment they cling to the story, cling to shape, to colour and form, all conditioned by saññā that marks and remembers. It seems that seeing lasts. Just as in the case of my (injured) foot, it seems that the painful experience is lasting a long time. There are so many mind-door processes, thinking of the form, the painful foot. There is just one moment of bodily experience and then many mind-door processes, not understanding for what they are, because of the idea of "something" experienced.

The perfection of renunciation, nekkhamma, develops with understanding, gradually, renouncing the clinging to the idea of "something". So very gradually, but it all has to be through the development of understanding.

Nina

15.13 Saturday discussion, VIII, 1

Nina
Aug 24 #164290

Understanding arises suddenly

Dear friends,

Nina: I find it helpful that Acharn often says that understanding arises suddenly, unexpectedly. We never know the next moment. We can make beautiful plans, but we do not know the outcome, this depends on conditions. We had a heatwave and I had no help and there was a lot of washing. Sarah had her foot injured. These are all situations. When we consider paramattha dhammas, absolute realities, we understand that we never know the next moment of seeing, of body-consciousness. It is helpful to consider this.

Acharn: What is the best thing at that very moment?

Nina: To be aware but that depends on conditions.

Acharn: They are all dhammas, but the truth of it does not appear. It does not appear as the object of a moment of experience.

Nina: We forget that and we are absorbed in the "story" we are thinking of.

Acharn: It is not self, nothing can be done at all. Just remember that all realities are conditioned and that they are there just for that moment and then gone. They are not permanent, and this is so very helpful. They cannot be taken for "I" or "something".

Just understanding is the best. Even just very little, it does not matter. It takes time for saṅkhāra khandha to develop little by little. (N: Saṅkhārakkhandha includes all cetasikas apart from remembrance and feeling. It includes all wholesome cetasikas such as sati, paññā, energy, confidence. These have a function in the development of paññā).

As to what is seen, there is nothing there. Whatever is appearing now is the truth. No one can change it or do anything, nothing is "I". Dhamma cannot be anything else, it has to be as it is, right now. But paññā is not enough to let go of clinging and of taking it for "something" all the time. But it is the truth to be known. As paññā does not grow sufficiently it is developing little by little, by saṅkhārakkhandha. No one, no self at any moment at all.

Just learn from the teachings of the Buddha that all dhammas are anattā. Not just the words, but it is right now. Understand that no one makes it (reality) arise, but that it is there. The arising and fallen away (of realities) is not known yet. What appears now is gone, all the time. There is momentary death (of realities, khanika marana): the truth that everything that is conditioned to arise has to fall away.

It is impossible to directly experience (the truth) just from understanding a few words of the teachings. But one should hear it again as a reminder and understand that the truth is the truth, no one, no self.

For example, right now there is hardness. Hardness cannot be tasted or smelt. When it is experienced it is hard. The truth is covered up by ignorance: one just takes it for "something" when it is there. Even when one does not yet know what is there, there is (already) clinging. Even in a sense-door process, a few moments after seeing, there are ignorance and attachment. Can this be known or experienced? It is now. Can it be experienced as no one? It takes time. How long have ignorance and attachment be there as "something". All gone, is that true?

Sarah: We spend a lot of time thinking of difficult situations such as no helper when there is a lot of washing, a heatwave. We completely forget that there is seeing now, hearing now, thinking now. The difficulty is not the washing or the (injured) foot, but the clinging and the aversion. It passes instantly, not my dosa (aversion) and my clinging. At the moment of seeing there is no difficulty, or at a moment of kindness, no difficulty. The difficulty is not the situation, but the moments of akusala (unwholesomeness) that arise and pass.

Nina: Your words are very consoling.

Jonathan: When talking about impermanence at the conventional level it is not the teaching of the Buddha. They are only reminders of the true nature of the present reality.

Nina

15.14 Saturday discussion VIII, 2

Nina
Aug 25 #164298

Citta is pandara or clear

Dear friends,

Ann: asked what the function is of citta in the javana process, thus when it is kusala citta or akusala citta.

Acharn: Do you have to call it kusala and akusala? If there is no understanding of citta as not self, there is only thinking about the words. How can one understand it is kusala or akusala without understanding the reality which experiences an object. Now there are realities, we just talk about realities, about the "story" about realities, while realities arise and fall away in split-seconds. It is real, it is now, but one does not understand the truth of it as not self. There is only the idea about kusala or akusala. It is only the word, but the characteristic which experiences is not realized. There is just thinking about words.

Ann: There is attachment, wanting to understand. Aversion and attachment are cetasikas.

Ann wanted to know what the function of citta is at the moments of javana.

Sarah: No matter we talk about seeing, kusala citta or akusala citta, citta is always the leader in experiencing (an object). Citta, the innermost, is always the leader. It has the function of experiencing the object. Citta itself is pandara or clear. (N: It can be accompanied by akusala cetasikas, but the function of citta is just experiencing an object. That is why it is by nature clear.) There was a discussion about outer āyatanas and inner āyatanas (N: āyatana is the coming together of different realities in the experience of an object). Sarah mentioned: The inner āyatanas are eye-sense, ear-sense nose-sense, tongue-sense, body-sense, and all cittas included in manāyatana (translated here also as mind). The outer āyatanas are visible objects, sounds, odours, tastes, tactile objects, and cetasikas and subtle rūpas all included in dhammāyatana (translated here as mental phenomena).

Acharn: At the moment of seeing, are there inner and outer rūpas? Can visible object be an inner rūpa?

Sarah: It just depends on conditions what object impinges (on a sense base) and what citta arises at any moment. There is not anyone doing anything. When there are conditions for hearing to arise, there are no conditions for tasting or touching.

Jonathan: Sense bases arise throughout life (N: produced by kamma) but there needs to be a supportive kamma to experience a particular object.

Sarah: Visible object may impinge, but there may not be conditions to experience that visible object. There have to be the coming together of inner and outer āyatanas.

Acharn: Can anyone make the eye-base arise? What appears has to arise by many conditions. What conditions it? Without conditions there cannot be any eye-base or ear-base... There is no "I". No self. By (the development of) understanding little by little, there are conditions for letting go the idea of self. If we think of inner and outer without understanding conditions, can that be true? Impossible... What is the use of clinging to what is all gone? There is the idea of self all the time because of ignorance. The self is thinking about no self.

Nina

15.15 Saturday discussion, VIII, 3

Nina
Aug 26 #164307

We cannot make anything arise

Dear friends,

Acharn: When there is understanding, in so far as it is possible for that level, it begins to develop, to understand the truth. It is better than to know how many thousands there are of vara (N: round or series of cittas within a process), but not understanding of the characteristic that appears as it is. There is "something" and "I" all the time. Life is so short, ignorance and attachment have been accumulated for a long time. It is best to understand (reality) as it is, not taking it for something permanent. One may think of the lifespan of rūpa and citta, but it is impossible to experience that. What is the use? Just know that nothing is permanent, (reality) just appears and disappears. (There are) seeing or hearing without there being understanding of the nature of no self, only that which experiences. Understanding has to be developed from a very low level to a very high level, by considering the truth which appears. There are so many layers of understanding. For example, attachment to seeing is not as much as attachment to the idea of me or self. There is less attachment when understanding the characteristic of anything as not self. That which is seen is there, together with hardness or softness, with the four primary rūpas (N: Visible object arises in a group or kalapa of rūpas, consisting of the four Great Elements and other rūpas). We cannot make anything arise, they are conditioned realities, conditioned by many conditions.

Nina

15.16 Saturday discussion VIII, 4

Nina
Aug 27 #164321

What is the mind?

Dear friends,

Azita: It is said that we take everything for mine, through the eyes, the ears, the nose, the tongue, the body-sense and the mind. Mind is vague for me.

Acharn: What is the mind?

Azita: Thinking...

Acharn asked whether there is citta before seeing and after seeing, and whether that is the mind?

Acharn: What we take for mind is what experiences an object. We are not used to the word experience. There is no idea of that which is seeing now; that which arises by conditions and experiences visible object. We take it as seeing, but it is a reality that experiences visible object. We know the word seeing, but we do not understand the nature of it. Each reality has its own characteristic, its own nature. When we talk about the nature of reality, no matter what is there, it is that which can experience or that which cannot experience. We begin to forget the word mind...

The mind is only the experiencing, the citta and cetasikas.

Sarah: Mind is just a translation of citta. "Mano" means any citta.

Maeve quoted Acharn, saying that the self thinks about no self. She was wondering whether it is ever possible to understand anattā.

Sarah asked whether she could make seeing arise, and whether there is any choice.

Acharn: It means anattā, no one there, (arisen) by conditions. You cannot think about what you have not seen before. When it is seen, it can be a condition for thinking about that which saññā (N: the cetasika remembrance arising with every citta) remembers...

So many things are unknown. There is seeing right now. What do you think about that? You hear about no self, no one, and you consider carefully whether it is true. One can know how little understanding there is of the truth. At the moment of seeing, is it you? Where is you?

Seeing sees, can we find the "you"? It is down deeply rooted in the mind, so that it is taken for "something"... Seeing arises and falls away by conditions. At the moment of hearing it is not there, so it is gone completely, but you still think of that which is seen, and there is no understanding of the reality which sees. That is the moment of taking that for self. Or the object is taken for "something", all the time. Until the enlightenment of the Buddha. He taught us what he had enlightened.

So we begin to understand the truth of whatever is there to be known.

Nina

15.17 Saturday discussion VIII, 5

Nina
Aug 28 #164335

Paññā develops among akusala

Dear friends,

Different moments of realities arise and fall away so very rapidly.

Acharn: That is why we learn to understand the very great wisdom of the Buddha, with higher understanding to let go all akusala, hatred, attachment.

Paññā develops among all those akusala. It is not strong enough to let go of the idea of self which is very deeply rooted. Ignorance (moha), attachment (lobha) and aversion (dosa) as the roots of all akusala are there, unknown. There is ignorance as long as there is no understanding of the characteristic that is now appearing. Because of hearing (the teachings) there is the beginning of thinking and considering carefully what is true and what is not true. It has to develop more and more and more, until the other higher level of understanding is there, by conditions, from understanding the truth of what is there. By considering wisely, otherwise it cannot arise again.

The truth (one has to consider) is whether there is something or self now. Can anyone find the self when it is not real, not true? The word of the Buddha is vaca sacca: vaca is word and sacca is truth (in Pāli). The truth of everything which is there by conditions, they are only different realities.

Thinking thinks of the object of thought, seeing experiences visible object, hearing experiences sound, only in a moment and then gone, never to return. Ignorance and attachment cling to that as permanent.

What appears arises and falls away in split-seconds, unknown. So long as that impinges on the eye it is there, it is real, but after that no more. That is the higher developed paññā which can directly experience the arising and falling away of a reality. A nimitta (sign) of a reality, not just one unit of it. How many things are there, how many arise? If there is no experiencing it cannot be known as it is, because of the rapidity of the arising and falling away of realities. (The understanding of) this will gradually eliminate attachment to the idea of self. It is so very strong, it is there from aeons until now.

We understand the word pāramī, perfection. Without the pāramīs it is impossible to understand that which is hidden all the time. All realities do not appear. Even though they arise, they do not appear. Like viriya, effort which does not arise with seeing, hearing and the other sense-cognitions, or with other ahetuka(rootless) cittas. But at the other moments it is there. Who knows it when it does not appear? But when it appears ignorance which does no understand realities conditions the idea of "it is I who tries". It is not you or anyone.

The development of understanding is this moment of understanding, little by little... This conditions direct awareness, unexpectedly. This shows the anattāness of each reality. When there is right understanding there is no expectation, (what arises is) only by conditions.

Jonathan: The understanding of realities as they are gradually eradicates the idea of self. We have to keep in mind that the eradication of self does not mean no people and things. They are concepts of the conventional world and necessary to have. We have to keep in mind the distinction between the wrong idea of self and (thinking of) concepts of people and things.

Nina

15.18 Saturday discussion IX, 1

Nina
Aug 31 #164361

Every citta is clear

Dear friends,

Acharn: Viriya, effort, does not appear as object yet. Is there still someone having viriya now? Only one reality can be the object, it depends on how much understanding there is. Pariyatti (intellectual understanding) should be firmer and firmer until it is so clear that nothing can be taken for self. It depends on conditions what will be the object of paññā at the moment of direct awareness. The actual reality, not just the word.

Sarah: I would like to bring up the word clear, pandara. You just mentioned that paññā understands clearly. Every citta is clear, pandara (N: Because its only function is knowing clearly an object). We often talk about confidence, saddhā, how it keeps citta clear.

Acharn: Does any object appear clearly enough now?

Sarah: No, only at the level of vipassanā ñāna (insight knowledge).

Acharn: Just listen to the words eye-sense, visible object, seeing. They do not appear clearly, but they are there. Without paññā they cannot be known as they are, they are "something", because they arise and fall away very rapidly. There has to be paññā which is not intellectual understanding (N: but direct understanding). But without pariyatti there is no condition for sati to arise with understanding of any reality right now.

We talked about hardness, does it appear?

Sarah: Only when understanding is very firm.

Acharn: There can be sati with understanding of the "story" (of realities), different from sati which is directly aware by conditions; it has to be by conditions. It conditions more confidence in anattā. In the beginning sati sampajañña (sati and paññā) is not as clear.

Sarah: Only when paññā knows clearly, there is saddhā, confidence, in the sense of discarding the hindrances and purifying the citta?

Acharn: We go a little too far. We have to consider from moment to moment. When there is direct awareness, for example of hardness, but no understanding, it is "my leg"; there is not understanding of the arising and falling away, no understanding of it as it is. There is intellectual understanding which knows the difference between intellectual understanding and direct understanding and awareness. The intellectual understanding develops so that it can condition direct awareness. That is different from intellectual sati (sati on the pariyatti level). Paññā begins to understand at what moment there is direct awareness and at what moment there is not. Paññā knows the truth very naturally; it is uncontrollable and dependent on conditions only. That is clearer than intellectual understanding but not as clear as vipassanā ñāna.

How can vipassanā ñāna arise? There should be no expectation, it depends on conditions. Like in the case of Sāriputta. How many moments of understanding were developed from life to life? Until there were conditions for such understanding, by hearing the words of Assaji.

Just develop understanding, no expectation. The word clear has more meanings. It seems that everything is so clear at the moment of seeing, with good eyesight, but no paññā. It cannot be so clear because there are other things around. (When there is vipassanā ñāna) there is only that (one object), by conditions. It is much clearer than the moments which are not vipassanā ñāna.

Shall we go on to saddhā? Is there saddhā now? It does not appear as the object of awareness. We can try to think of the characteristic of saddhā. When there are no lobha, dosa, or moha, when there is no akusala, citta is clear. There are many sobhaṇa (wholesome) cetasikas, but one (cetasika) that is clear. It makes the other cetasikas clear too.

Nina

16
September 2020

16.1 Saturday discussion, IX, 2

Nina
Sep 1 #164376

Confidence

Dear friends,

Nina: When I hear the word confidence, I am inclined to confuse it with lobha; I feel safe and secure. I know that this is wrong, it can only be sobhaṇa.

Acharn: What about it when you hear the word anattā? Is it true, is it real? Is it firm (confidence) or not yet?

Nina: Not firm.

Acharn: A little confidence or very strong?

Nina: Very little.

Acharn: So, you understand what is meant. We cannot use any word to represent the truth of reality so clear, impossible. Even if it is there, no word. But the characteristic is there to be experienced as it is, as not self. It has its own characteristic when it appears. Understanding is there which knows its characteristic; it shows up as it is, no one there at all.

Sarah: Acharn, you said earlier that confidence can condition understanding of a reality and that it is clear from akusala, that it purifies. Can we say saddhā, that which purifies, is a condition for that understanding?

Acharn: At the moment of understanding, it cannot be just understanding itself. It needs other realities to support it, as a condition to understand better and better. There must be sati too, if there I no sati there is no understanding. Sati is aware of a characteristic which is there. If there is no awareness, can paññā understand that characteristic?

Sati is not paññā, but it is needed, it has to go with paññā. When we say confidence, we do not mean just saddhā, but confidence in the truth. It means paññā that develops more, so the confidence is more. That which is clear from akusala is saddhā. When paññā is there, it knows what is right and what is wrong.

Sarah: A proximate cause of confidence that is often given is the Triple Gem that is worthy of confidence. It has to be with understanding.

Acharn: That is why the right way is satipaṭṭhāna, not sadhana-patthana or viriya-patthana. Even though there are other wholesome factors, without sati it is impossible for paññā to develop. Each factor has its own conditions and they condition each other.

Nina: You said that confidence is not just saddhā, so it is more?

Acharn: Are you sure that the truth is that there is no self?

Nina: Not sure. I am a beginner, so, not sure. I am sure only by intellectual understanding.

Acharn: When there is more understanding, one is more sure that it has to be: no self. More than hearing for the first time about no self. When one learns more, understands more, there is more confidence and one is surer, more, and more and more. Is that saddhā, it is not paññā.

Nina: So, when you say can you make seeing arise, nobody can, it makes it a little clearer that there is no self.

Acharn: Are you sure?

Nina: For a beginner only.

Acharn: The sotāpanna (who has attained the first stage of enlightenment) is more sure than an ordinary person, because of paññā. Paññā is one reality and saddhā is another reality. Without paññā there can be saddhā, no akusala. But it is not as wholesome as with more understanding.

Nina

16.2 Saturday discussion, IX, 3

Nina
Sep 2 #164379

The four Great Elements

Dear friends,

The four Great Elements (hardness or softness, heat or cold, cohesion and motion or pressure) arise with at least four other rūpas in a group, kalapa. They are called indivisible rūpas. Alberto asked whether these cannot be separated.

Acharn explained that only one of these rūpas arising in a group can impinge on the relevant sense-base and be experienced. When visible object impinges on the eye-sense the other rūpas in that group do not impinge on the eye-sense and are not experienced.

Acharn: When it is tangible object it cannot be seen. It is there when there is touching. Why are only three rūpas tangible object? The rūpa that is hardness or softness can be touched, it is sometimes hard, sometimes soft. Then there is the rūpa that is heat or cold and the rūpa that is motion or pressure. Where is the Water Element, cohesion? It holds the other rūpas in that group together, so that they cannot be apart or separated. Whenever there is touching, it just touches what is hot, or hard, or motion.

There was also a discussion on the āyatanas.

Sarah: Any rūpa is only āyatana when it appears. At the moment of touching hardness, only the hardness is experienced, only one (in a group) impinges. When hardness is experienced we know that there are at least seven other rūpas in a kalapa but these are not impinging. Hardness is the āyatana at that moment. There is the coming together of body-sense, citta and hardness.

Alan: Does it depend also on kamma which of the three great elements are experienced?

The answer is that the hardness itself must have impinged on body-sense, but heat or cold have not. It depends on kamma whether there is the experience of the hardness which has impinged. Only one rūpa at a time can impinge.

Acharn: Even while one is fast asleep are there āyatanas? How many āyatanas are there when sleeping? When we talk about āyatana at the moment of seeing, we talk about what must be there at that moment. What is meant by āyatana? At the moment of seeing, how many are there?

Alberto: Four: eye-base, visible object, mind-base, dhamma-base.

Acharn: While sleeping, how many?

Albert: Mind-base (manāyatana) and dhammāyatana.

Acharn: When we talk about objects, it is one subject, and when we talk about āyatanas it is another subject. But they are all dhammas.

We talk about dhatus, elements, or āyatanas to be conditions for the understanding of no self. They are all dhammas. They do not appear clearly yet. When paññā is there it begins to understand a little until all can be objects of no self. For example, at the moment of seeing who knows phassa cetasika (contact)? Is it there, is it āyatana? No need to classify, but they are there depending on what object citta experiences. But there must be āyatanas. Citta cannot arise without cetasika, but cetasikas are not manāyatana (the āyatana of mind), but dhammāyatana. This is just an explanation of the truth that they are not self. If we try so hard to understand this, what level of paññā is there to understand that? Can it show up at the level of intellectual understanding?

The point is not to find this out, but to understand better and better that there is no one at all.

What about the innermost reality which is citta, manāyatana? Can it appear now? Whenever it arises it experiences. It is manāyatana, it is different from cetasika. But manāyatana and dhammāyatana (cetasikas) arise together. Eye-base and visible object are āyatanas at the moment if seeing. But this does not mean that there is nothing else, there are many other things. But what is there at the moment of seeing as āyatana?

That is all, otherwise there is clinging.

Nina

16.3 Saturday Discussion IX, 4

Nina
Sep 3 #164383

The innermost is citta

Dear friends,

Alan: There is the word inside or inner used for citta. In what sense is it used?

Acharn: Is citta āyatana?

Alan: Yes.

Acharn: Is cetasika āyatana?

Alan: It is not inner āyatana.

Acharn: The difference between citta and cetasika: the innermost is citta. Sometimes there are conditions for (particular) cetasikas, sometimes not. But citta is always there.

Sarah: Alan, think of citta as the chief in experiencing. Like the king, surrounded by his ministers. There will be attendants running around.

Acharn: Is there Alan now?

Alan: Only when there is thinking. There is reality now and there is thinking now.

Acharn: What is Alan ?

Alan: Alan is a word that represents some characteristics of realities. Sound is not Alan, but it is real; it has a characteristic and we think of a characteristic. Alan is just an idea conditioned by realities. If there is no sound, no idea of Alan. Alan is just a concept, the object of thinking.

Acharn: Not real, right?

Alan: Right, not real.

Acharn: This is the beginning of understanding anattāness. The more there is understanding of seeing, hearing, smelling, tasting, touching and thinking, there will be less and less clinging to the idea of self. And now, what reality is taken for Alan?

Alan: Hardness, sound, what is seen. All realities are taken for Alan as they are experienced through the six doorways.

Acharn: Five khandhas. Who speaks now? Who is feeling now? No one.

Alan: Why is saññā one khandha?

Acharn: The Buddha spoke about the khandhas as objects of clinging, upadana khandhas. We cling to rūpa, it is so very important in life. If there is no understanding of rūpa there cannot be less clinging to rūpa as me, as my eyes. Rūpa is known in a day, but not as no self.

Th Buddha taught that even rūpa that is so dear is what arises and falls away. It appears not as it is because of the rapidity of the succession of rūpas. It appears as something permanent, so pleasant to have. That is why it is very important to understand rūpa as one khandha.

Another khandha is feeling. Why do you want to have rūpa? Because of different kinds of feeling. Feeling is very important in life. One actually clings to nothing: as soon as it is there it is gone, never to return. One clings to that which is not there any more. If there is no understanding of it, nothing can eradicate the clinging to rūpa. The five khandhas are upādāna khandhas, khandhas of clinging.

Saññā is another khandha. It remembers the pleasant feeling that is wanted again and again, on and on.

Saṅkhāra khandha are cetasikas that condition different types of citta, kusala or akusala.

So long as there is no understanding of the feeling which is there all day, it is impossible to get rid of the idea of self, or develop understanding of realities as not self. If there is no understanding of feeling when feeling is there, there is akusala, such as ignorance and also lobha, the second noble Truth (N: the cause of dukkha).

What is there now?

Alan: It is already gone.

Nina

16.4 Saturday discussion, IX, 5

Nina
Sep 4 #164388

We are like in a dream

Dear friends,

Acharn: We are like in a dream, the whole life, until hearing the truth. Life is nothing, then something, and then nothing, all the time. The flux of bhavaṅga interrupts the different doorways, one by one, until death comes, any time, by conditions. Begin again, by conditions again, on and on. Only paññā is there to see that it is so worthless to be like this, without anyone at all. Only different realities, once in saṃsāra (the cycle of birth and death). Never the same. Only different realities by conditions, to see that life is worthless, just arising and falling away all the time. (Understanding this) must be vipassanā ñāna of a high degree. To end life in saṃsāra.

Nina: We forget that seeing the next moment is a different one.

Acharn: This is intellectual understanding, not yet direct understanding with direct awareness of one reality at a time, a different one. The Buddha taught the truth, to begin to consider. There is so much ignorance that hinders understanding the truth of what is there now: a very short moment of what appears and disappears. Different ones, never the same, in each life. Where is Lodewijk now?

Nina: We do not know.

Acharn: There is never Lodewijk again. Death is like now. Exactly the same. If there is no Nina, there must be no Lodewijk. No one at all, only different realities. This is the beginning to understand the truth.

Sarah: That is the world, just seeing and visible object that appear, no one there. There never was Lodewijk, even now. Like there is no Sarah, no Nina now.

As Acharn said, if there is no understanding of rūpa, how can there ever be less clinging to rūpa, less clinging to the idea of my hand, my body, my eye-sense, myself and other people. There are just different realities, just citta, cetasika and rūpa.

Acharn: And now, what is the absolute truth? Is there the body or none at all? There is only thinking. When one thinks: "I am sitting here, this is my leg or hand", but when nothing appears, is it there? There is nothing, only what appears at that very moment. As long as it is still there, it is the idea of self. There can be the clear understanding that it is not self. Later on there can be the moment of direct experience of the arising and falling away. Even now, it begins from hearing and considering.

There can be understanding of just one reality, no attention to another reality. When only one appears to paññā, paññā can penetrate the truth of that one, it can be known that there is nothing. It appears as nothing else, only that one. That is the meaning of appearing well, stage by stage. Paññā is not me, it is conditioned. It is not there all the time, only when there are the right conditions.

One should not just "say" there is no me. Realities can appear as nothing, to right understanding which knows that it is not self.

The truth is what arises and appears, disappears. We do not mind whether that one has gone and this is the new one or the next one, different realities. So long as it is to be known as it is, as not self. This is the beginning.

Right understanding penetrates on and on, until just one reality appears to one level of paññā, before higher understanding lets go of the idea of self. It conditions the experience of the arising and falling away. There will be more confidence in the truth.

Nina

16.5 Saturday discussion X, 1

Nina
Sep 7 #164418

Reality appears well

Dear friends,

Nina: Acharn, you said that "when there is intellectual understanding, it does not know the arising and falling away of realities, but it knows the difference between intellectual understanding and direct understanding with awareness. This is the beginning." It would be helpful if you could elaborate.

Acharn: Each word of the Buddha's teachings should be studied very carefully, such as: reality appears well. There is seeing and that which is seen. We take seeing for self. Just seeing, does this reality appear well or not well? We are in darkness. Does any seeing appear well? There is no understanding of "no one, no thing". So long as it appears as something, can we say that reality appears well?

Nina: Not yet.

Acharn: This is intellectual understanding. Reality now appears from moment to moment, but no understanding of it as it is. It takes a long time. Is there any understanding of what appears; it is nothing. Seeing is seeing, it just arises and falls away, there is no one there. Appearing well means, with understanding, stage by stage. There can be the understanding of the difference between intellectual understanding and direct understanding. At that moment the characteristic of sati appears. A characteristic such as hardness one has studied appears. Everyone knows that it is hard, but it is known as something. How can any characteristic appear well, it depends on understanding. Only understanding can eliminate the idea of self. When sammā-sati (right mindfulness) arises there is a glimpse of understanding. Only for a moment. But we keep on thinking that we have arms and legs.

Citta is not cetasika. Each cetasika is different, like saññā now which remembers everything that is experienced. It is only a reality which remembers and "marks". It cannot feel, like or dislike. Without considering who can see that there is no one at all. Just one moment, can there be anything or anyone? Seeing is not known clearly now. It is only an idea that it is what experiences, but at that moment there is no understanding of it. There can only be thinking, "It is not me".

Only when it is the object of developed paññā, vipassanā ñāna, realities appear as they are, as different ones. That what appears is not the experiencing or the thinking. Seeing is not hearing. At the moment of hearing, sound has to be there, nothing else. One begins to see that the world is lost. When there is a moment of experiencing there is the world. The world of sight, of sound, seeing or hearing. Nothing is there, no shape, no form, no idea.

Alan had questions about the word suffering. Acharn had said that when you understand the cause of suffering you have less suffering.

Alan: Does this refer to the noble Truths? You said that the cause is not understanding realities as not self.

Sarah: If there is no understanding of what reality is, visible object as just that which is seen and seeing as no one, suffering and the cause of suffering cannot be understood. From the beginning you have to understand what dhamma is.

Alan: At a low level of understanding we can see in daily life that attachment conditions aversion. There will be less attachment just at the level of intellectual understanding.

Alan gave an example about unhappiness about the result of an examination.

Sarah: The cause of dukkha refers to the unsatisfactoriness of realities that arise and fall away. In your conventional example there is nothing about the understanding of dukkha, or about understanding of dhamma in the beginning. Dukkha is not just unpleasant feeling. Only understanding of conditioned realities will lead to less attachment. If there is no understanding of dhamma as anattā there will be no reduction of attachment. Attachment is still taken for "my attachment".

Sukin: When thinking, "This is happening to me, it is my attachment", attachment will not go away.

Sarah: Attachment is just a dhamma that arises and falls away, not my attachment that should be less. Less attachment for oneself, less suffering for oneself, this is more clinging. All this is the story about me, not understanding of dhamma.

Lobha is so tricky, even if it seems that there is wise reflection.

Alan: It is what you follow all day long.

Sarah: There is still more attachment thinking in that way.

Sukin: Is there suffering at the moment of attachment?

Alan: There is, but it is not understood.

Nina

16.6 Saturday discussion X, 2

Nina
Sep 8 #164430

Not a refuge of any kind

Dear friends,

Acharn (to Alan): What feeling is there at the moment of attachment?

Alan: Pleasant feeling or indifferent feeling.

Acharn: No unpleasant feeling. The suffering of all conditioned realities is that they cannot last. How can what arises and falls away instantly be object of attachment? When there is no understanding of the arising and falling away of lobha, there must be lobha. One does not see the danger. There must be life on and on because of attachment to life.

If there is no direct understanding of the arising and falling away (of realities), can anyone see them as suffering? They are not desirable. Because, actually, there is no one there. What is there: only the arising and falling away of realities, uncontrollable.

Sarah: They are unsatisfactory because of the arising and falling away, not being in anyone's control.

Jonathan: Not a refuge of any kind, of no intrinsic value.

Nina: Acharn spoke about the uselessness of life going on... We can only realize this when paññā is of the level of experiencing the arising and falling away of realities.

Sarah: There can even now be the beginning of considering that what we always hold so dear, visible object, sound, pleasant feeling, is gone completely. Even when there is not the direct understanding of the uselessness of visible object now, there can be the beginning of wise consideration. We love taste when we eat lunch, but each one is going immediately.

Nina: We can hear the words: gone immediately, but it is good to know that we do not really understand it.

Sarah: It does not matter. Understanding develops from wise consideration at this moment. If there never is wise consideration why realities now are unsatisfactory, understanding cannot develop.

One does not need to think: this is not direct understanding. That is more clinging to "my understanding".

Nina: It depends on the citta that thinks, maybe with clinging or without it. It is good to know that this is only intellectual understanding.

Sukin: This thinking is gone completely, never to arise again.

Nina

16.7 Saturday discussion, X, 3

Nina
Sep 9 #164438

Nobody can make seeing arise

Dear friends,

Alan: Can we understand kamma as a condition for seeing?

Sarah: By a higher stage of vipassanā ñāna, and now by reflection. Nobody can make seeing arise, it has its conditions. One begins to understand a little more what kamma is at this moment.

Acharn: As to your question about condition, paccaya, it does not mean that at the moment of seeing there can be the understanding of kamma, but the reality that is conditioned is there. There is no time to think about paccaya while there is the understanding of the reality of seeing. It appears; it is so clear that it is not anyone at all.

From learning about paccaya before, it develops, (and) there can be the understanding of paccaya, even though that moment has gone. This can condition the understanding of anattā when reality appears as it is.

When there is seeing, only that which experiences is there to be known as not self. There is no time to think about paccaya, but all the paccayas we learnt about are there. Without conditions how can it (a reality) arise? There can be the understanding of conditions without any words, kamma or any other condition. That is why after vipassanā ñāna there must be pariññā (N: clear comprehension arising after the very short moments of vipassanā ñāna that has to consider further and apply what was learnt at the moment of vipassanā ñāna). What is experienced is not lost, saññā begins to remember the anattāness little by little. But since atta-saññā (wrong remembrance of self) has not been eradicated, it is there.

When there is more understanding of anattāness, there is understanding of paccayas without naming them. We cannot experience paccaya together with viññāṇa, but right understanding that it is not me and that it is only conditioned (reality), is there. Pariññā applies in normal life whatever is experienced by conditions.

When touching, there is no need to say what the condition is for touching. There is understanding of that characteristic that cannot be taken for "I", because it is a moment of experiencing. When hardness is the object, it is known as not me. Usually there is an idea of the object that is experienced, such as table or chair. How can there be the understanding of no chair, no table, only a characteristic? "Only a characteristic" cannot be taken for anything, because it appears as anattā, but paccaya is there, it is there as it is.

Begin to understand that which is experienced as nothing in it, little by little. How else can what is experienced be understood as nothing, what was something before.

Even now, while talking about citta and cetasikas, it is the understanding of conascence-condition(sahajata-paccaya). When we say that they must arise together, no one can separate them. When it is the object it is just one at a time. From intellectual understanding the understanding of that object as a reality begins.

Nina

16.8 Saturday discussion X, 4

Nina
Sep 10 #164446

The understanding of conditions

Dear friends,

Acharn: The understanding of conditions follow (awareness) but we do not have to name it or call it anything. Now we understand what is there: pakatupanissaya paccaya, natural decisive support-condition (N: which includes accumulated tendencies). When we use the term sahajata-paccaya, conascence-condition, we understand immediately that it refers to conascent dhammas. Can we separate visible object, sound or taste from the four great Elements (N: arising in a group of rūpas)? But without intellectual understanding it is impossible to let go even of the idea of something. It takes time to be truthful to the truth, to understand that there is no one in it, nothing in it. Even thinking about a reality is conditioned, even the moment of direct awareness is conditioned. Each moment is life or next life, each moment is momentary death (khanika marana). It never comes again. Completely gone, like death. Never being this person any more.

Nina: As to understanding conditions without naming, you gave an example of conascence-condition, that is clear. But for kamma, this is more difficult, because kamma is in the past.

Acharn: Can anyone experience the object they like to experience? Is there always pleasant feeling? How come is there unpleasant feeling? That is the understanding of kamma-paccaya, but it is not the moment when there is direct awareness of feeling as conditioned. No one can condition feeling, that is the meaning of paccaya, condition. Seeing cannot be chosen, is that not kamma-paccaya? After seeing there is different thinking, different ideas, depending on accumulations, and that is not kamma-paccaya. Pariyatti (intellectual understanding) goes together with paṭipatti, direct understanding, all the time. It is not so that when a moment of direct awareness arises there is no more pariyatti. Developing direct awareness with understanding is not the moment of higher understanding.

Sukin: You spoke about the importance of pariyatti even when there is development of direct understanding. Does this mean that even for the sotāpanna (who has attained the first stage of enlightenment) there has to be right consideration of the Dhamma further, intellectually?

Acharn: If we do not talk about citta and cetasika, can there be moments of thinking of them and moments of direct awareness by conditions? There is seeing all day but if we do not talk and think about it there will not be better understanding.

Sukin: Thinking and considering are very important.

Acharn: Even intellectual understanding is not enough to condition better, keener, higher understanding. For example, just a moment of seeing cannot be a direct object of satipaṭṭhāna, because sampaṭicchana-citta, receiving-consciousness, and santīraṇa-citta, investigating-consciousness, have to go on, but these do not appear. What appears are only seeing, hearing or thinking. In order to know that they are different there must be the understanding what they are.

Just begin to see the characteristic which appears, there is nothing in it because it is very short. It must be through mind-door that it appears clearly. Through mind-door one at a time can be experienced, not together.

That is the beginning of understanding of what we learnt from books: about doorways, processes, realities, understanding them as not self. Each reality appears just one at a time, that moment cannot be taken for "I".

This is not enough. Reality is so much deeper and more subtle. One begins to have more confidence.

Nina

16.9 Saturday discussion X, 5

Nina
Sep 11 #164451

The Magician

Dear friends,

Acharn: I think I see you, but actually, there must be just a moment, followed by other moments which cannot see. It is so very quickly, no one can understand how it works. It is like the work of a magician how it happens like that, but citta is much quicker. The arising and falling away cannot be known, only the nimitta (the sign of it). There is the nimitta of rūpa, feeling, saññā, citta. There are many cittas in a process having different functions.

Different cetasikas arise with each citta and no one can make that (happen). There is now the reality which experiences an object. "I see", but without what arises to see, what experiences an object, how can there be the idea of "I see", or "I think"? All are different realities by conditions.

As to samanantara paccaya (N: immediacy-condition, the realities that succeed one another in a particular order), no one can make them arise in order. The paccaya of each citta conditions the paccaya of the next citta that succeeds it. The rebirth-consciousness has to follow the dying-consciousness of last life. Seeing cannot arise after the dying-consciousness. What arises after the dying-consciousness is conditioned by kamma. The same kamma produces another moment to perform the function of bhavaṅga (life-continuum). That personality keeps on until death. Death can come any time, this moment or in the evening, or the next day.

Anantara paccaya (contiguity-condition, each citta is succeeded by the next one) and samanantara-paccaya (the succession in a particular order), the next citta has to arise after this citta and not another citta. No one can change this, because there is no one at all. There is no person, this means when there is the understanding of each reality as dhamma: as what can experience and as what cannot experience. It is conditioned to arise as just to be such. Nobody can change it and that is why all dhammas are anattā.

Maeve: About what cannot be understood intellectually.

Acharn: It is there already, by conditions. You think about what has not come yet. What is real is only now, what is conditioned. We think of other things too, by conditions. There is the accumulated condition (pakatupanissaya-paccaya (natural predominance-condition), that conditions even thinking.

This is the beginning to understand the truth of each moment which will be the condition for direct awareness as anattā. The moment of understanding is the moment of understanding the anattāness of whatever is there now.

There is hardness, and there may be awareness of it or just touching. The object does not appear well because it is so short and other objects arise and follow immediately throughout life when there is no understanding. Just like a dream from life to life. What about awakening, understanding that it is not "I", or just sleep as before? No one is there, it is only thinking. No matter there is a dream or not, there is thinking.

Nina

16.10 Saturday discussion, XI, 1

Nina
Sep 13 #164485

No expectation, no choice

Dear friends,

Nina: Understanding can be classified by way of three levels: pariyatti or intellectual understanding, paṭipatti or direct understanding and pativedha or direct realization. Last time I heard that pariyatti is even necessary for enlightened people. This is a very good reminder. I look differently now at pariyatti. It is not ordinary intellectual understanding, not book knowledge, but it always refers to the present moment.

Acharn said that when we do not talk about seeing now there are no conditions to understand the reality of seeing. Acharn always refers to the present moment with many examples throughout all these sessions. We always have to understand the truth of what is there now. She gave very good examples about conditions, they are always related to the present moment. For example death, there is death at each moment, momentary death, khanika marana. We do not have to say: the present moment, but it can be understood more and more. This kind of understanding can condition later on direct understanding.

The simile of the magician I found very helpful. We look at something a magician handles, and where is that thing? It is not there any more, it is nothing. He is so fast. But citta is even faster. There is something, then nothing and then something again, all within a very short moment.

Acharn: What is there now?

Nina: Mostly thinking.

Acharn: It is time to understand thinking. Whatever appears, appears usually to ignorance. There must be the understanding of the words of the Buddha so that we can talk about what is there. No one at all. Even seeing and what is seen. This can be a reminder. There can be understanding of that which experiences from birth. Citta arises and experiences all the time, but it is not known to anyone. What is seen now can be studied, there can be a beginning to understand it as it is, little by little. Especially the reality which arises and experiences is not known. It arises and falls away in split-seconds.

No matter what is experienced, it must be always the nimitta (the sign) of reality. To learn the difference between nāmas one begins to understand: they cannot be the same and not at the same moment. Right understanding can begin to study until each moment is understood more and more. Then the reality can appear as it is, with anattāness. There is no expectation, no choice. From hearing and considering there can be a little understanding of that which appears, until it appears well, as it is, as not anything and not permanent. Little by little, from life to life.

It is not known how it is working now. All cetasikas are working, performing their function, until each one appears. So there can be more understanding from hearing and considering.

When, for example, anger arises, there is no one there. Anything which appears can be the object of considering in order to know that it cannot be taken for anyone or anything. Do you have legs, arms, face? Nothing. Only what appears is there. Each reality has gone. As soon as it has arisen it is gone. Nothing is left. What you take for something is that which is seen. The idea, the nimitta of something is there. What is seen can impinge on the eye-base and then fall away. The nimitta appears as something permanent.

Nobody can change what appears now, but right understanding can begin to understand what is so very deep, so very subtle. It is not easy to experience that, only highly developed paññā can. Paññā that developed from intellectual understanding that was sufficient to condition direct awareness, can just begin to understand the truth of a reality that appears as a reality. Not as "I" . Nothing can be taken for "I". That is only thinking.

Nina

16.11 Saturday discussion XI, 2

Nina
Sep 14 #164491

What is outside?

Dear friends,

Acharn: Just listen and paññā can arise unexpectedly, whatever level of paññā. From understanding intellectually, little by little, it can be a moment of direct understanding of a reality, by conditions. Just begin to understand the truth at any moment. One has heard a lot about the truth until it becomes one's (own) understanding.

Can you hear any sound now? Unexpectedly (and then) gone completely. Everything is like lightning, it is not known what it is yet. Whenever there is a question, "what is that", there must be "something". There is the "I" and "something". Thinking "what is that" is so natural.

Is there seeing right now? That which experiences has no shape, no form, no colour, no smell. Whenever it arises it sees. Seeing is the experience of that which has impinged on the eye-base and then it is gone. How can we take that for "I", it is gone completely. Life is a moment of experiencing an object. If there is no moment of experience there is no life. What appears now?

Azita: You said, "What appears now?" Outside there is the sound of a motorbike.

Acharn: Outside or inside, but now we are here, not outside. Where is that sound, outside or inside? What is outside? At the moment of hearing, where is it? Just a moment of hearing, nothing there, only sound and hearing. Where are they, not outside, not inside, nowhere.

Azita: I am reading from a note: "To see attachment is like seeing the space between groups of rūpa, kalapas (N: rūpas arise in groups and each group is surrounded by space), that is impossible.

Acharn: How many moments are there? A moment of seeing is not a moment of thinking. What is there in a moment? There is the nimitta (sign) of the reality of a moment. Reality is so very difficult to understand, its depth and subtlety.

Seeing just sees, many moments. It sees all the time, but the truth is not known, it is very subtle. It is gone, it just arises and falls away. There is nothing permanent, as "something" like table, chair, I or anyone.

Many things we take for "I", my throat, my shoulder. Where are they? It is only thinking. A very short moment (of experience) all the time. Sound cannot be visible object. Can sound be my sound? Or the sound of a violin? It is nothing, just a moment.

What seems to be together, like seeing and hearing, can be separated by understanding little by little. They cannot be at the same moment and they cannot be the same reality. It is ignorance to take what is no more as "something". Then there cannot be enlightenment of the truth (ariya sacca). It has to begin from intellectual understanding to condition direct awareness with understanding, not just direct awareness without understanding. Only intellectual understanding is not enough. It is so true that it can be proven, it can appear as it is. It cannot appear to ignorance, but it appears to paññā which is developed stage by stage. It is now, firmer and firmer and firmer, until there is no doubt about the truth of whatever appears, even if it is not directly known yet. One day paññā can begin with direct awareness, which is conditioned by intellectual understanding.

Nina

16.12 Saturday discussion XI, 3

Nina
Sep 15 #164497

The perfections

Dear friends,

Acharn: One day paññā can begin with direct awareness, which is conditioned by intellectual understanding. That is the meaning of the perfections of patience, energy (viriya), determination, and truthfulness. Without these it is impossible to have such understanding, (that began) from not understanding at all, not hearing the word of the Buddha. That is why the more there is understanding of the truth, the more there will be confidence in the Buddha, the Dhamma and the Sangha; it develops more and more, firmer and firmer, so that it will be known who the Buddha was. Who am I, how much ignorance; and (I am) beginning to understand, like the blind and the doctor who can cure the blind.

Azita: Why am I developing understanding? The perfections seem very far away.

Acharn: Without a moment, a moment, a moment, can we reach the goal?

Azita: I think not.

Acharn: Can it be possible, when it starts to go on little by little?

Azita: I have not much khanti pāramī (the perfection of patience), in fact none.

Acharn: The understanding of this moment is pāramī, perfection, to keep on going: listening, considering, understanding more and more, little by little. Otherwise one cannot be a savaka (a listener. N: three kinds of Bodhisatta: the person who will be the Sammā-sambuddha, the Silent Buddha and the Savaka, listener, or follower). In the past there were many savakas. From not understanding one can become someone with understanding, little by little, depending on conditions. Not only in this life but in the course of many lives. The Buddha's pāramīs were accumulated not just in one life.

Sarah: Azita, if there were no patience, would there be any listening and considering the truth of life? One sees the value of it, more than just one's normal attachment. To listen, to see the value of it, to consider wisely, that takes a lot of khanti. (For example) when it is said that it is sound that is heard, not inside or outside. One does not have to try to have khanti.

As to the kalapas, rūpas arise in groups. It is completely unknown, it is so subtle. It is there, separating each groups of rūpas. In a similar way, the attachment arising now after each moment of seeing, hearing, through each doorway, is very subtle, completely unknown. But it is there in between each moment of experience. The purpose is (knowing) how little is really understood, how great is attachment. More and more subtle kinds of attachment can be appreciated, that they are there, completely unknown.

Even now, during the Dhamma discussion, after seeing and hearing, attachment arises completely unknown, just like the space in between the kalapas (groups of rūpas). If ignorance and attachment are not known, they can never be relinquished, even a little. It does take great khanti to consider, ask questions, reflect on what is said. It has nothing to do with conventional ideas about patience.

Nina

16.13 Saturday discussion XI, 4

Nina
Sep 16 #164515

Saṅkhāra khandha, no one at all

Dear friends,

Acharn: Is there at this moment more understanding of what we are talking about, more than last time? It develops by itself, with saṅkhāra khandha, no one at all. It (reality) appears to ignorance or to paññā which begins to know its characteristic. It cannot be changed to be someone, it has to be as it is. Just as natural as usual.

How many times a day do you think about the teachings, even about one word. It is very rare. Even thinking is there, one knows, it is by conditions. How very little. That is the way it is. Because ignorance and all akusala have been accumulated from aeons and aeons. It takes a long time to be truthful. How much understanding is there of that which now appears to seeing, not as it is, until it is as it is. How much patience?

Tam: The pāramīs cannot be developed without understanding. At the moment of understanding the pāramīs are developed. In one of the Vietnamese discussions you spoke about someone who was very stingy but who could still attain enlightenment?

Acharn: If there is no understanding of the nature of stinginess, as no one, no self, can there be enlightenment?

Tam: No.

Acharn: Like Angulimala (N: who murdered many). The accumulation of paññā is there enough to condition the understanding of the truth at that moment. The asayanusaya (asaya is the accumulated kusala and akusala, and anusaya are the unwholesome latent tendencies) is the accumulation of kusala and akusala. So long as the anusaya is there, how can you eliminate (akusala) stage by stage. That is why we have to understand not only anusaya, latent tendencies, but also asaya. There is asaya as pāramī as well.

But the conditions are not right yet. No one can make it right to be a condition for such a moment of understanding. It is not known before when understanding and awareness will arise and what object they take.

When we are clinging to the idea of self there must be doubt and desire. There is natural life as usual, not self, only nāma and rūpa. One is relieved not to try or to rush to attain such knowledge.

Nina

16.14 Saturday discussion XI, 5

Nina
Sep 17 #164525

Sincerity to that very moment

Dear friends,

Acharn: From hearing, considering, sincerity to that very moment (sacca, or truthfulness), how much understanding is there now? When direct awareness does not arise yet, there is doubt, and how can it be direct understanding? The understanding of no one, no self, can condition direct awareness, any time, anywhere. The understanding of anattāness begins to develop on and on and on. What is there must be by conditions. It is by conditions (for a reality) to be or not to be there.

Sarah explains about patience: Whatever the accumulated tendencies at this moment there are, whatever ignorance or attachment is there, each one is conditioned. That is the way the pāramīs develop. Not (by) thinking: it should not be this or that.

It is a relief, letting go of the burden. The development of understanding cannot be any other way. It is a relief not to think that it should be any different. That is the wrong Path of "I". Khanti (patience) which develops accepts whatever is conditioned.

When understanding is developed there is less clinging to "my akusala", "my tendencies". Whatever arises, no matter anger or attachment, it is the way it is. Accumulated tendencies are dhammas which are anattā.

Maeve speaks about conceit, mana, and mentions that reality arises unexpectedly. Is it possible that understanding can be a cure?

Acharn: When you all the time think of something, can anything arise because of anyone? (It arises) because of its own conditions. Like seeing, seeing does not belong to anyone at all, it is a reality which is conditioned by eye-base where only visible object can impinge on. Thinking about visible object, no matter we call it cup or anything which is seen, is a reality. Something appears at the moment of seeing and that object has to impinge on the eye-base. Otherwise how can there be a moment of such a reality to arise and experience what is there? Not the sound, not the hardness. Anything which arises depends on its proper conditions. Just being annoyed or very strong anger are different by conditions.

There is no one, nothing, it has fallen away, never to return or to be found. There is the beginning to understand what is meant by suññāta (emptiness): all completely gone. No one, no I, no thing.

The word pakati is also used, natural. Hardness is hard, it cannot be changed. It is a characteristic which is conditioned, just to be hard. Odour: just to be smelled, flavour: just to be tasted. All are dhammas. This is the beginning to understand that there is no one, no thing. It is just a relief. Just gone completely.

Before being born there was nothing. Then, from moment to moment, something, in the world, in one's life. And then: gone. One can be this personality only in this life. Then everything is gone, ended, at the moment of death. Then there is a new moment, a new being, a new personality. Then one goes to the end of such conditions to be this person. Very short, very temporary. There is a condition for birth and death on and on. So that paññā can see that there is no on there. Like the fire in the forest. From here to there, there is no one, that is the way life is. Gone completely. That is the meaning of suññāta. The truth of anattā is suññāta. They are the same.

Maeve: a question about falling away being a relief. The falling away of understanding seems a loss.

Acharn: There is only one moment. If there is no previous moment, can there be this moment? The previous moment conditions the arising of the next moment. What is there in the previous moment that is passed on to the next moment? This moment now is conditioned by the previous moment. That is why one cannot change ideas one has accumulated. That is why we are all different. If there is no arising there is no falling away. Each citta conditions the arising of the next one, there is no gap. From aeons ago there are conditions to be such personality, different from others.

Sarah: In the case of Angulimala, anger accumulated from life to life conditioned anger. In his last life it was completely eradicated. In the same way, understanding that is accumulated from life to life conditions understanding to arise when hearing the right words. Even though the previous moment of understanding had fallen away it could condition understanding in that life.

Even-so for us, who are hearing, reflecting on the teachings and developing understanding, there is that tendency accumulated to make sense in this life time. Even though understanding falls away, never to return, there is still the tendency accumulated to condition arising in the future.

When one is reborn as an animal, there are no conditions for understanding during one's life. But when one is reborn again as a human the understanding from past accumulations will condition understanding to arise again. It depends on so many conditions whether it will arise. Who knows whether the next moment will be anger, attachment or understanding. The tendency is there.

Nina

16.15 Saturday discussion XI, 6

Nina
Sep 18 #164532

Where is the latent tendency?

Dear friends,

Alan: Where is the latent tendency? Attachment may be followed by aversion. Even when a moment is unwholesome, it has the latent tendency of wholesomeness in it.

Sarah: Even when citta with anger arises, the accumulated tendency of kindness is latent in the citta. For example, the citta with understanding now has still tendencies of anger, annoyance and attachment which are lying dormant. There may be understanding and instantly clinging to it as "my understanding". The tendency is there to condition understanding or wrong view at any time. Unwholesomeness is eradicated stage by stage. At the stage of the arahat all unwholesome tendencies are gone completely.

Nina: What is "appearing well" in Pāli?

Acharn: What about now? What appears now as it is? If it does not appear as it is, it does not appear well. What is seen is like something, a table or a cup. The object does not appear well as it is. What appears in a process of cittas is together with the four Great Elements (in a group of rūpas). In a kalapa (group of rūpas) there are eight indivisible rūpas (N: visible object is one of them). The four Great Elements cannot impinge on the eye-base. There is only one rūpa that can be seen. It is what appears at the moment of seeing. When paññā sees it as it is, it "appears well" to paññā. Paññā understands it and penetrates the truth of it. Even when we do not use the Pāli term, can we understand the way it is? What appears without paññā, does not appear well.

In the Pāli text it is stated that only nimitta can be the object of different vipassanā ñānas. Only Nibbāna has no nimitta, Nibbāna does not arise. Whatever appears, appears as nimitta. When it appears well, it appears as a nimitta of reality.

The subtlety of reality is now at this moment when the truth is penetrated of what arises and falls away all the time. Even when we talk about the arising and falling away of reality right now, they are not known, when there is not direct understanding of any reality yet. The nimitta of a reality can be experienced, no matter it is visible object now. It is a very short moment of what impinges on the eye-base, there are many unknown moments. How can it appear well when there is no understanding of any moment yet?

Hearing and understanding can condition a moment of direct awareness of a reality. It is by conditions. It shows its anattāness. Even now we cannot select a moment of seeing or hearing. At the moment it appears well no one can do anything, it is only by conditions. Direct awareness experiences an object more clearly than a moment without direct awareness. We begin to understand what is meant by "appearing well", little by little. At the moment of talking about seeing now, seeing may not appear well. When there are conditions for the arising of direct awareness of a reality, there will be understanding of the difference between awareness with a moment of intellectual understanding and the moment of beginning to know what is there as it is.

It is like talking about someone we have not met yet, but we know that person little by little, until the time comes that that person is there. Even-so we talk about visible object which appears but do not understand it as it is because there is no awareness yet. Only direct awareness begins to be aware of a characteristic. How many moments of seeing there are now that "see" someone or something.

Nina

16.16 Saturday discussion XII, 1

Nina
Sep 20 #164559

What is enlightenment?

Dear friends,

Acharn: If we do not understand what is meant by enlightenment, it is useless to talk about being enlightened. What is enlightenment? Why does it take such a long time?

Enlightenment is understanding the truth of what appears now. It does not appear as it is yet. Who can penetrate the truth which is so very deep? What we see is only the surface of what arises and falls away in split seconds. What appears is only the nimitta, the image of that which is there. But the truth of it is not yet understood, until we begin to understand what is the truth right now and what is meant by enlightenment. Can this moment be enlightened?

Nina: Understanding has to be developed, there were so many aeons of ignorance.

Acharn: It is not different from this moment. It depends on paññā how much understanding there is of that which is now appearing. It seems that so many things appear at once. That is impossible, each little rūpa impinges on the eye-base and that can be seen. Not a picture or anything. Otherwise there must be "something" that is there all the time. It is just a conditioned reality that arises and falls away in split-seconds. The words of the Buddha condition understanding of the truth of what is now.

Suññata (emptiness) means: From nothing there is something and then nothing again, all the time. It is not just thinking or an idea, it is the absolute truth. It can be developed and become the object of enlightenment. Only paññā is the best of all conditioned realities.

Nina: Before you came in we discussed "nothing, something, nothing".

Acharn: When the arising and falling away of a reality has not been realized yet, there must be the idea of "I", "someone" and "something" all the time. There are many levels of understanding. This moment is not the direct awareness of any reality, one at a time. Understanding will lead to the truth, little, by little, until the moment of enlightenment. But there must be precise understanding directly, now, of one object at a time.

Nina: Where comes in "nothing and something"?

Acharn: Before seeing is there seeing? Before hearing, is there hearing? Nothing. Until it is conditioned to be just that. You cannot change its characteristic, they are all anattā, no self. They just appear and disappear instantly, all the time. Now there are hundreds, thousands of realities unknown, different realities; not only one, many, many realities. We can only know one object at a time. Is this true?

Nina: Yes.

Acharn: When there is seeing, there is no sound.

Nina: We forget, we put them all together in daily life.

Acharn: Dhamma is each moment of experiencing an object, even there are conditions for more objects. But without the reality that can experience it, nothing can appear. It is this moment. It must be known as a reality that can experience it. The experiencing is not known as it is. We take it for "I" all the time: I see, I hear, I think. If it does not arise, where am I? When it is gone nothing can be taken for a permanent reality, such as the people around.

How many leaves are there of a tree? Each one has to impinge on the eye-base. It cannot be experienced as shape, form, leaf or tree. Only that which can appear to the moment of seeing (is experienced). There is no idea of "things". But we take it for something all the time. For example, what is that sound? There is the idea of something in the sound. When sound is heard, it depends on thinking whether it is the sound of music or anything else. All the time there is something there, even though just sound is heard. We live in the magical world and citta is the magician.

Nina

16.17 Saturday discussion, XII, 2

Nina
Sep 21 #164579

The Bodhisatta

Dear friends,

Sarah referred to Wilhelm's questions about the Bodhisatta and the pāramīs and about the understanding of anattā.

Sarah: Acharn was stressing: it is just like now. The understanding of the truth is not anyone who penetrates it, it is just the understanding of realities. It is hearing about what dhamma is, what the truth is. There are different nāmas and rūpas, and each one is anattā. This is the way understanding develops. It has to be the same way for the Bodhisatta and for us. It has to be hearing of the truth about realities as anattā, so that understanding can begin to develop.

It depends on conditions how much hearing there has to be before there is the wise considering and direct understanding of the truth.

Jonathan: Did the Bodhisatta hear Dhamma before he made a vow to become a Buddha in the future?

Acharn: When there is understanding is that Savaka Bodhisatta? (N: recap: a listener. There are three kinds of Bodhisatta: the person who will be the Sammā-sambuddha, the Silent Buddha and the Savaka, listener, or follower). Bodhisatta is the enlightenment of the developed paññā, right understanding. There is no one.

Sarah: Now, when there is development of right understanding, we can say that we are savaka bodhisattas. There is bodhisatta and savaka bodhisatta. In each case there has to be development of understanding of the truth, gradually, from life to life, after we have heard the truth.

Now, at the moment of understanding, is it savaka bodhisatta? Beginning to develop understanding leading to enlightenment. What do you think, does it make sense?

Wilhelm: It makes a lot of sense. The Bodhisatta vow is a strong thing, the intention to become a Buddha. In Theravāda it is the understanding of a continuation, there is some hope. It is so difficult, it takes aeons.

Sarah: It is just wishing to have pāramīs, or wishing to be a bodhisatta. Without understanding it is the wrong way, it leads to more clinging.

It is always back to this moment: understanding of the truth now. This naturally leads to the development of the pāramīs, such as determination or effort. It is not just wishing or trying to make a great resolution without understanding of reality at this moment.

Nina: As Sarah reminded me: it is still a story of myself thinking. Acharn often says: what about seeing now? What is reality now, do we understand it or do we confuse it with thinking about things? When I say, "It is difficult", it is thinking about my problem, or a story.

Sarah: It is the same when we think that we want more pāramīs, or would like to be a Bodhisatta, to be enlightened.

Sukin: Nina, the Bodhisatta did not think about becoming a Buddha. Only after the Buddha Dipankara predicted that he would become the next Buddha in the future.

Nina: It is the same with Sāriputta who listened to Assaji. He had no idea he would become enlightened. It happened by conditions when he heard just a few words. It was because of former accumulation of understanding of the present moment.

Acharn: Why do you think about bodhisatta, not about understanding of what now appears? This is on the way to be a bodhisatta.

Sarah: We are always lost in the story of lobha, dosa and moha, taking it (reality) for being something so important, forgetting about life in the world at this very moment: what is seen now, what is heard now. Dreaming about fantasies that are taken for realities. We think that if this problem is solved everything will be all right. But the accumulation of ignorance and clinging is there, so there is another story, problem or issue.

Nina: My washing, how to cope with it, something wrong with the computer. Always something coming up.

Sarah: That is life.

Nina: Acharn said that we think of all different objects but forget about citta now.

Sarah: Citta worrying about this and that, clinging to self, that is natural.

Nina

16.18 Saturday discussion, XII, 3

Nina
Sep 22 #164597

What does khandha mean?

Dear friends,

Wilhelm: What does khandha mean? This term means a group.

Nina: As Acharn said: each citta is khandha, each rūpa is khandha. It is translated as group, but we have to consider what this really means at this moment.

Acharn: Whatever arises, falls away, that is the meaning of khandha. It arises just once in saṃsāra (the cycle of birth and death). Each conditioned reality must be khandha. We have to understand that rūpa is rūpa, nāma is nāma. The Buddha taught about upādāna (clinging). (N: Upādāna khandhas, the khandhas of clinging) We cling to rūpa. It arises and falls away, and then no more. What arises falls away, each is khandha. Rūpa khandha: it is that which cannot experience. One clings very much in life to rūpa that can be seen, heard, smelt, tasted or touched. When it is pleasant, it brings pleasant feeling. Pleasant feeling is desirable. There are rūpa khandha, vedanā khandha (feeling), saññā khandha (remembrance). We want what is remembered. Paññā and sati are saṅkhāra khandha (N: all cetasikas except feeling and remembrance). Saṅkhāra khandha arises with each moment of citta. We take it for something by natural decisive support condition (N: pakatupanissaya paccaya. Because it has been accumulated).

All conditioned realities are khandha. It shows that there is no one, no permanent being. The translation (as group) can bring misunderstandings if one does not consider the Buddha's words carefully. If nothing arises can there be any khandha?

Nina: I find it so helpful that Acharn says that it is not the word that is essential, not the story or the theory, but the understanding of the reality now.

Sarah: Seeing the Buddha means understanding dhamma at this moment, not how much one is reading or in whose company one is in, be it the Buddha's, Acharn's or any one else's company. It comes back to the understanding at this very moment.

Wilhelm asked a question about meditation centres. How to deal with these?

Jonathan: It is a test of one's own development of kusala and understanding how one deals with this situation. I do not find it a problem. I do not mind if others want to express their view, regardless right or wrong. If there is an opportunity to contribute to the discussion, good, otherwise it may not be the right occasion. There is no rule.

Sarah: It helps a lot not to have expectations.

Acharn: What is the goal or the point of meditation? What is meditation?

Sarah: It is a good point to ask other people to clarify their ideas, rather than saying: "I am not interested in meditation". Can there be meditation now? What is understood at this moment? What about this moment? Why is it beneficial to sit in a particular posture? When shopping, what about meditation?

Are we talking about bhāvana (mental development)? Bhāvana is the development of understanding, not following a practice.

Acharn: It is the word of truth to know what is wrong, what is right. Before hearing the teachings it is one's own consideration.

Sukin: You think that meditation is understanding the present moment?

Acharn: Can there be any meditation without understanding, (be it) samatha or vipassanā? There are different degrees of understanding. What is meditation? Calming the mind or understanding whatever appears now? What is best, "doing" or understanding? Life exists in a moment. Bhāvana: development of tranquillity or understanding? Samatha was practised also before the Buddha's enlightenment.

Development of right understanding of what appears now leads to more understanding of the truth of this moment. It is conditioned, otherwise it cannot arise. It arises and falls away in split-seconds. It is no more, very short.

Sarah: If there never is any wise consideration of what calmness is, what attachment, mettā, kusala or akusala are, how can there be development of samatha? It has to begin with understanding, whether it is samatha or vipassanā.

Acharn: Right understanding is the understanding of reality as it is. Without the understanding of calmness it is impossible to develop it. When there is right understanding it is calm. There is no need to try to have it. To what one clings in life almost every moment? To the five khandhas. Paññā can see what one clings to: to only what is hard, soft, colour, so many things, from life to life. What is the use of clinging to that?

Sukin: We do not cling only to colour or sound, but also to colour experienced yesterday. Is this an example to clinging to saññā khandha?

Acharn: After hearing the teachings one knows that one clings to all five khandhas. Before that paññā is not enough to understand saññā as not self. There is no idea of no self at the moment of developing tranquillity. No understanding. It is useless to develop calm, at the moment of understanding there is calm already with the understanding of the truth. In the Buddha's time there were less people who had samatha and vipassanā together than those who did not have samatha.

Nina

16.19 Saturday discussion, XII, 4

Nina
Sep 23 #164601

Is there your arm or leg?

Dear friends,

Acharn: It is not easy to understand the truth of: there is no one, nothing. This is the first stage of enlightenment before arahatship, when there is not any more clinging. It has to be with understanding, otherwise there is "I" all the time.

At the moment of seeing is there your arm or leg? That which is not experienced arises and falls away all the time. Everything arises and falls away all the time. Saññā which marks and remembers is still there, so it is "I", my arms, legs, eyes. Actually, reality is only seeing and what is seen. There will be the letting go of the idea of self.

So long as all dhammas in a day are not known yet, there cannot be a stage of vipassanā ñāna of a high degree. There is nothing there when there is only a moment of seeing and visible object. Even understanding is not me. Understanding is there at the moment of considering carefully and beginning to understand little by little, but actually, there is no "I" at the moment of seeing. No "I", how can there be arms and legs?

Nina: It is all true when we think intellectually.

Acharn: Intellectual understanding is a degree of understanding. The truth cannot be changed. There is nothing but seeing and that which is seen. There is only that in the world. At that moment there is not the world of space, of trees. It appears like it is, together, but the Buddha taught about many cittas in between, citta and cetasika. All are dhammas, there is no one there.

The aim of the study is understanding one day completely that there is no one, nothing, only different conditioned realities, uncontrollable, conditioned to arise and fall away instantly. This is the absolute truth, the ariyan sacca. The four noble Truths about all realities are: dukkha, the cause of dukkha, the ceasing of dukkha and the way leading to the ceasing of dukkha. Understanding these is like climbing a very high mountain to the top. The top is letting go. There is nothing in reality, only a moment of appearing and disappearing, unknown. It is known little by little, until the moment of enlightenment of the truth. The truth is penetrated which is now covered by ignorance and attachment. When there is less ignorance and attachment realities can appear little by little at the moment of satipaṭṭhāna. Paññā arises at that moment and knows that it is different from intellectual understanding.

From understanding just one word at a time there will be more understanding of the truth of what appears in a moment. Where is Lodewijk? That person does not know you now, he has forgotten.

Sarah: You think of a dear one, no matter alive or not. There is thinking of the one who is there, thinking with attachment, sorrow or wise reflection.

Acharn: Even thinking is not you, just a moment of conditioned reality. Thinking about that person is conditioned. This is just daily life, each moment should be known, otherwise there is wrong understanding which always takes it for something, for "I" all the time.

To live alone is living with paññā, to understand that there is no one at all; only different realities, just at the moment they appear. Only when reality appears, otherwise it is gone. What we take for permanent is gone.

Sarah: Association with the wise is the moment of wise reflection.

Nina

16.20 Saturday discussion XII, 5

Nina
Sep 25 #164624

Without understanding it cannot be direct awareness

Dear friends,

Sarah: Acharn's comment (about a dear person who passed away) is opposite to what we usually hear. Usually clinging is encouraged to those who passed away. Ceremonies, rituals keep the memory alive. (There is an idea of) being together in heaven. They have completely forgotten us, they have their new life in another realm. The problem now is the clinging only. This is so helpful, so tough to hear, so precious.

Jonothan: Direct experience is meaningless without paññā.

Maeve: What is direct experience?

Jonothan: Direct experience of a reality. Only paññā can see the true nature of the presently arisen.

Sukin: I think that the problem is that one believes that after one has direct experience paññā will come. We think a lot of sati and direct experience but never about direct understanding. Actually it is all about understanding from the beginning to the end.

Acharn: Is there seeing right now? Many moments or only one? It is anattā, no one can make it arise. There are so many moments of seeing and also many moments of thinking and talking. There is no direct awareness of any reality yet. Without understanding it cannot be direct awareness. When there is intellectual understanding one begins to see the difference between sati with intellectual understanding which is not direct awareness yet (and direct awareness). Only when it arises there is no doubt what direct awareness is, because it is there with paññā. Even so short, it is there. Seeing is there, hearing is there, hardness is there. Just begin to be aware of the characteristic which is no leg, no tree. Only hardness (is known) as hardness. Paññā is so very weak in the beginning, it is only intellectual understanding. Lobha (attachment) is there after it very quickly. So long as there is lobha, the reality cannot appear well. Lobha can be less very slowly. Paññā begins to develop and it knows what moment there is direct awareness and what moment there is not.

In the beginning sati is weak and paññā is also weak. It is a very short moment and not often enough to get used to the characteristic of the reality as not self. But at this moment of understanding it is developing, there is no one there.

Nina

16.21 Saturday discussion, XII, 6

Nina
Sep 28 #164662

Saññā with diṭṭhi

Dear friends,

Nina: This life is different from past life, but we cling to the idea of accumulation. We are not this person any more after death but every moment of understanding that is accumulated now can condition the arising of understanding in the future.

Acharn: Could we remember last life, who we were? Nina: No.

Sukin: When there is attachment with conceit, mana, not atta saññā (remembrance of self), what is it?

Acharn: When we talk about about atta saññā (remembrance of self) there is saññā of something.

Sarah: There can be saññā with lobha which is not clinging to wrong view, atta saññā.

Sukin: And that saññā is also remembering something or somebody?

Acharn: Saññā with diṭṭhi (wrong view) leads to the wrong Path, to wrong understanding of self, different from common lobha. Taking whatever arises as something or someone. It is the opposite of understanding dhamma as anattā.

Jonothan: When recognizing, that is Nina, that is Alan, is that meant by atta saññā?

Sukin: No, atta must be wrong understanding.

Jonothan: So, it is a characteristic that is different from just recognizing objects.

Sarah: Saññā can be kusala or akusala, with wrong view or without.

Alan: Enlightenment is clear understanding of a reality as it is. It realizes the four noble Truths.

Sarah: It is the clear understanding of the four noble Truths, including the Truth of the unconditioned reality.

Alan: It is actually understanding the truth of life, why we are born, why we suffer. It is not just confined to the four noble Truths? That person understands the conditions for realities?

Sarah: If there is not understanding of reality even a little, there cannot be understanding of what appears well now. Without direct understanding of what appears now there can never be clear understanding of the four noble Truths at enlightenment. It has to develop.

There was a question about the Bodhisatta.

Sarah: There has to be hearing and considering what previous Buddhas taught about the four noble Truths. And that understanding has to be developed by a Bodhisatta. It is a beginning of conceptual right understanding leading to direct understanding and enlightenment. There can never be enlightenment without the firm intellectual understanding in the beginning.

Acharn: Just learn about understanding of that which can be understood. There is seeing and if you try to understand something else, there cannot be the understanding of seeing as not self. The moment of what appears should be the object of understanding as it is, not self. We can learn when there is atta diṭṭhi (wrong view of self). It is gone, no need to find out. What is appearing now?

When there is more understanding of that, it can bring about understanding of anything which appears through any doorway. When there is just thinking of what arises and falls away so rapidly, unknown, it cannot be the object of understanding. When there is something that should be an object of understanding, there is no one, nothing, no self at all. It is not just thinking or speculation. It is the moment of direct experience with right understanding. Depending on what level of understanding is there, by conditions. Otherwise it is wasting time instead of understanding.

Nina

16.22 Saturday discussion, XIII, 3

Nina
Sep 29 #164673

The truth appears only to paññā

Dear friends,

Nothing can condition the arising of sati, except intellectual understanding which has developed enough. So you know why sammā-sati does not arise and why it arises by conditions. There will be more confidence in the truth that can be realized. Many people in the Buddha's time had enlightened this truth, depending on paññā only, not on wishing or speculating. The truth appears only to paññā. At that moment nothing is there, only that which appears as object. There is nothing left after it has arisen and fallen away.

Seeing is seeing, do not take it for "I see", little by little. In a day there are uncountable moments of seeing. What about hearing and thinking, they are not known. Ignorance is there with attachment. Only when there is direct awareness realities begin to appear, until there is no self; nothing in it, because it is gone, suññāta. If it is still like now, seeing for many moments, that cannot be suññāta.

The truth of anattā begins very slowly, little by little, at the moment of direct awareness of a reality. Otherwise it is (only) intellectual understanding that there is no "I". In a moment there can be just an object and that which experiences it. No world of people and things, sun and moon, gone, lost. Only one object appears well and that means: nothing is there. That is the beginning of understanding of what is meant by loka, world, different from lokuttara. Each word is in conformity of the truth, of reality, naturally, by conditions. Deeper and deeper; it can be known and understood when it is there.

There will be more understanding of anything, not trying to control it or stop it, or wishing to have it or not have it. Lobha has to be known as it is, as the second noble Truth. That is why there are twelve rounds: pariyatti (intellectual understanding) of each of the four noble Truths, paṭipatti (direct understanding of them) and paṭivedha (direct realization) of them.

Nina

16.23 Saturday discussion, XIII, 4

Nina
Sep 30 #164683

Atta saññā (wrong remembrance of self)

Dear friends,

Acharn: There is atta saññā(wrong remembrance of self) when there is (the idea of) "I hear, I think, I understand". Even not in words, but it is there. Why do we speak about the truth of each reality? Just to understand anattāness, to understand that no one is there. We begin to listen and to carefully consider the truth so that there can be moments of understanding little by little. But it is still "I" until the arising of vipassanā ñāna. It is the beginning of anattā saññā because the object does not appear as it used to, as "something". We think about cup or hand. When it appears as hand, it does not appear well, not as the truth; it is there (many things) together, taken for something as a hand. When any reality appears there is nothing in it, there is no idea about it. Hardness is hardness as usual, but what is the difference? There is no understanding of each reality that appears now, it is not understood as anattā or suññāta. It is gone all the time.

When there is more understanding of the truth of it, it conditions moments of direct awareness and this must be with paññā. (There is) understanding of that object as we heard about it before, otherwise it cannot appear well and it cannot be paññā which experiences it as it is, as no one. When we think about the words "no one" when it does not appear yet, we cannot imagine how that could be. Without paññā it does not appear well, because there is still "something" there. Without paññā there is doubt. Wrong understanding takes it for "I have experienced that". There is no paññā, there is still "I". It is very deeply rooted, from life to life. The truth is sacca pāramī, understanding what is right and what is wrong. Lobha is there, unknown. Even when (the object) is not known as something it still clings to what appears.

Sarah: The anattā saññā that accumulates together with right understanding is very important. It is the opposite of atta-saññā like now, remembering as something or someone all the time, with wrong understanding.

Nina

17 October 2020

17.1 Saturday discussion XIII, 5

Nina
Oct 1 #164703

Strong saññā (tira saññā)

Dear friends,

Sarah: Strong saññā (tira saññā) is a condition for right awareness of realities. Through firm remembrance what is the right object there will be more familiarity with the object of right understanding: the sound that is heard, just visible object that is seen. One will become used to the right object more and more, and that is why we have these discussions. It becomes a protection against the wrong understanding, atta saññā, taking those realities for something or someone.

Without the accumulation of right understanding and right remembrance of the right object there could not be direct understanding of realities as anattā.

Nina: Acharn mentioned suññāta, she was stressing the arising and falling away of realities.

Acharn: When paññā is highly developed (it is understood that) nobody can change any reality and paññā can understand deeper and deeper. Vipassanā ñāna is the understanding of the degree that it can penetrate the truth that is hidden.

As to "appearing well", this is of different levels. When there is no direct awareness, nothing appears. When there is direct awareness it knows only one reality as object. This is not enough, until paññā develops higher and higher, stronger and stronger. At the moment of understanding anattā and suññāta, nothing is there. Otherwise there must be clinging to whatever appears. It is quite a release, being away from lobha.

Sukin: Understanding is so weak, followed by attachment as usual, a lot of akusala.

Acharn: It is better to know the truth. The Path leading to enlightenment, to know the truth must be paññā together with other conditions.

Nina: Is very deep Dhamma not too difficult for a beginner?

Alberto reminded me: It is difficult but important to start with the right reminders. Even a little of right intellectual understanding is very valuable.

Nina: I find it very good not to be afraid to explain deep Dhamma to the very beginner.

Sarah: Even when it is rejected and not appreciated one never knows when the right words will bring fruits later.

Nina

17.2 Saturday discussion XIV, 1

Nina
Oct 4 #164747

The understanding of gocara

Dear friends,

The subjects discussed:

- Upanissaya gocara: the object of understanding
- Arakkha gocara: the object that protects from akusala.
- Upanibhanda gocara: the object that is unbinding, letting go

Gocara means object. Upanissaya: nissaya is foundation or base and upanissaya is a strong base. Upanissaya is the object of understanding. Arakkha means protection, in this case protection from akusala. Upanibhanda: nibhanda is not binding, detachment.

Acharn: What appears now is the nimitta (sign) of different things and that cannot be the upanissaya gocara. But when one understands the truth that will be upanissaya gocara. It is the object the Sammāsambuddha understood, not self, not anything. The truth of it begins to show up to different levels of paññā.

When there is no understanding of the object we take it for glass or table. At the moment of seeing there is nothing. But now it is Sarah, not nothing yet. The object does not appear clearly. When the understanding of anattā has become firmer and firmer it conditions more kusala.

The object of understanding protects from the wrong method, having the wrong object, as a thing I can control. It is not understanding of the reality that appears. One may try to get rid of lobha instead of understanding it as not self.

Does anyone sees a change in life when there is the understanding of dhamma as anattā? Even understanding a little is a change from ignorance to beginning to understand. The object is the same as before, but one sees that there is nothing to cling to as much as before. The attitude changes.

What one clings to is nothing, it is all completely gone. There can be a change of attitude towards that object, even a little and not often.

It can bring the change in life from ignorance to paññā. One sees: the most valuable moment is the moment of kusala and paññā.

One has an idea of my hand, my leg, my friend, which are always there, but they are no more, completely gone. Is there any expectation? Then there is no understanding of anattā.

Sarah: When one considers sound just for an instant, it is gone, never to return. This is life at this moment. Gocara is the object of wise consideration. This is the way understanding accumulates.

Acharn: When there is understanding, there is no one; there are different realities appearing, one at a time. Hardness cannot be my leg, my arm, table or chair, only that which is hard. It cannot be anyone, it is conditioned to arise and then it falls away. That is the object of understanding, to be upanissaya gocara. We should know not only the word, but understand the reality of it. It develops little by little, also intellectual understanding develops little by little.

Nina: You said that there can be a little change in attitude when it is realized that each reality is gone, nothing left. I think that it is just for a moment. Next moment we cling again.

Acharn: Arakkha gocara is the object that protects from akusala. But there is attachment as before. That is the way to see that understanding develops gradually. There is no expectation.

Is there any arakkha gocara? Right understanding is not strong enough, it depends on conditions. That is the way to have firmer understanding as not self. There is no hurry, impossible to hasten understanding of the object right now, as it is. At the moment of understanding there is protection from akusala moments.

How many moments of arakkha gocara are there in a day? It depends on how strong the understanding of upanissaya gocara is.

Nina

17.3 Saturday discussion, XIV, 2

Nina
Oct 5 #164771

Arakkha gocara is not self

Dear friends,

Sarah: One should understand arakkha gocara as not self, and not try to do something, following wrong view and wrong practice, or taking attachment and anger for one's own attachment and anger. If there is no development of pariyatti, the dhamma that appears now cannot be a protection against wrong view and other strong akusala.

Acharn: When there is no understanding of the object we take it for a glass or a table all the time. There is no understanding that at the moment of seeing there is nothing. Now it is Sarah, not nothing yet.

When the understanding of anattā becomes firmer and firmer, it conditions more kusala.

The pāramīs are developed with understanding. There can be understanding at the moment of giving, with the idea that everyone is the same, sometimes pleasant and happy, sometimes unpleasant, everyone is just the same, as dhamma, no one there. It is upanissaya gocara that can protect at the moment of kusala.

What can protect one from having akusala? It has to be the understanding of the level of upanissaya gocara, little by little, until it conditions kusala as a pāramī, to protect from akusala, until it can be upanibandha gocara.

If upanissaya gocara is not sufficient, it needs the pāramīs and understanding of the truth of gocara as no one, no self. Without understanding there cannot be arakkha gocara nor upanibandha gocara. There can be dāna and sīla without understanding.

There cannot be pāramīs without upanissaya gocara. Upanissaya gocara conditions arakkha gocara. There can be conditions for direct awareness. One talks about sati, but where is the understanding of its nature? No one can condition awareness to understand what is there deeply down there, so very deep; it needs many conditions. Upanissaya gocara is there, otherwise there can never be upanibandha, but before that arakkha gocara is needed. There is so much akusala, how could there be upanibandha?

Sarah: Sound is heard, it depends on upanissaya gocara whether it is object of understanding or of ignorance and attachment.

Acharn: Even this understanding cannot arise without upanissaya gocara. It depends whether it is of a slight degree or firmer, only sati of the level of satipaṭṭhāna can know. It is the nimitta of reality, not "I" any more. Reality has to be understood more and more clearly in order to have less attachment to the idea of self, āsavas (intoxicants) arise, even while talking. Only paññā can begin to eliminate them. Without direct awareness reality cannot appear well.

Nina

17.4 Saturday discussion, XIV, 3

Nina
Oct 6 #164779

The five khandhas as no one

Dear friends,

Acharn: The development is very difficult because it has to be so natural, there has to be understanding what is there: wrong view, attachment? Paññā has to understand the five khandhas as no one, to be upanissaya gocara. They are all anattā. When they show up as anattā it is the way of having less attachment.

Sarah: Seeing, hearing, just dhammas arising by conditions.

Nina: It is so good that Acharn reminds us all the time of the intoxicants, āsavas, arising after a moment of seeing or hearing, by conditions.

Alan: Sarah, can you explain the words upanissaya gocara and arakkha gocara?

Sarah: Gocara means object, what is experienced, another word for ārammaṇa. In the context of upanissaya gocara, it refers to the object that can be object of understanding, the object that can only be explained by the Buddha. Visible object is usually object of ignorance and attachment. But when one has heard the Dhamma, it can be object of understanding, upanissaya gocara. Nissaya means support and upa is strong or decisive. It is the object which is the strong support for understanding at that moment. It refers to pariyatti understanding. We can hear the word seeing and it can be meaningless. There is ignorance, not upanissaya gocara. Only at the moment of understanding it is upanissaya gocara. This is understanding that has to accumulate; we can become more familiar with those realities so that understanding will become a protection from wrong view and other akusala and lead to the three gocaras (upanissaya gocara, arakkha gocara and upanibandha gocara) which have to be supported by the pāramīs, the perfections. The pāramīs are a protection that develops with understanding. Understanding, no matter intellectual understanding or direct understanding, has to accumulate in this way.

Acharn: The object is not far away, it depends on understanding. The absolute truth is no one, no self. It is very hard to experience it as it is. Since there is a great amount of ignorance for years and years and attachment, the great master, how can there be moments of understanding of the truth? It has to develop little by little, from moment to moment, with the pāramīs of viriya (energy or effort), sacca (truthfulness), khanti (patience) and adiṭṭhāna (determination). No one can do anything, it is not in anyone's control, but paññā is there.

Nina

17.5 Saturday discussion XIV, 4

Nina
Oct 7 #164789

Appearing well

Dear friends,

If there is not enough understanding (of all realities that appear) it is impossible to get rid of the idea of self, even reality appears well to vipassanā ñāna, vipassanā ñāna cannot let go of the whole idea of "I". There are different levels of khanti, patience, and vipassanā ñāna is the beginning of khanti. When vipassanā ñāna is strong, it experiences all objects in daily life; there is no choice. It depends on conditions only. The anattāness shows itself more and more; all are dhammas, not self.

As to the expression "appearing well", no one can imagine how well it is. Seeing with ignorance and seeing with understanding must be quite different. Reality appears well to different levels of paññā. Everything has to be known perfectly, completely, in order to eradicate the idea of "I".

Seeing cannot be taken for "I", he, she. It is only a reality which arises just to see, and then it is gone. At the moment of thinking, saññā remembers and marks the object and vitakka (thinking) touches the object. The ten cittas (five pairs of sense-cognitions, seeing etc.) do not have vitakka. The other cittas need more then seven cetasikas(the universals) by conditions. This is the beginning of developing understanding of the second vipassanā ñāna (direct understanding of conditions).

Paññā can begin to develop when there is firm confidence of the truth, until it is upanibandha gocara, direct understanding of the truth of no one. Everything is gone, it is no more.

Nina

17.6 Saturday discussion XIV, 5

Nina
Oct 8 #164797

Understanding of anattā becomes firmer

Dear friends,

Acharn: The absolute truth of any reality does not show up yet so long as there is only intellectual understanding, but this will lead to direct awareness little by little. It is not enough in the beginning, it takes a long time. There should be no expectation, it depends on conditions. This indicates that paññā becomes stronger little by little, to letting go wanting, clinging to what has not come yet, until it arises unexpectedly. Nobody can do anything; there are only realities, absolute realities by conditions. That is letting go, little by little, from the very beginning. The understanding of anattā becomes firmer little by little. The clearer appearance is upanissaya gocara and upanibandha gocara with arakkha gocara.

Sarah: Even when upanissaya gocara is weak, it is known that it is upanissaya gocara, no matter what words we use.

Nina: It is only visible object, it is only sound, but it is not yet upanissaya gocara.

Sarah: It is just sound that is heard now. Are we just repeating the words or is there some understanding, even at the beginning? If there is no understanding I do not think we would be here at all. There would be no point in hearing and considering more. There must be understanding that it is the truth taught by the Buddha and that it is correct, that it leads to more understanding. That is upanissaya gocara.

Even from the beginning patience (khanti) develops with understanding and leads to less expectation about it whether understanding will be weak or strong and there will be more contentment. That is the benefit of upanissaya gocara. More contentment with whatever is conditioned at this moment.

Nina: We do not try to change anything.

Sarah: That is a real hindrance. It does not matter what reality arises, but it is a hindrance if one tries to change it, tries to select an object.

Acharn: Is there khanti now?

Nina: A little.

Acharn: It is not the word. It is understanding the difficulty of experiencing the truth. Develop it against the current of akusala. The pāramī of khanti together with the pāramī of viriya. Listen and listen, consider and consider, not "I".

Sarah: That is a very good example of arakkha gocara. How the right intellectual understanding leads to the development of the pāramīs such as khanti. These are the protection from following the wrong way, selecting an object, from strong akusala. Understanding has to develop with khanti pāramī from the very beginning.

Acharn: Are you afraid of akusala?

Nina: It has to be known, that is the only task.

Acharn: When paññā is there, there is no fear.

Question: Arakkha gocara is conditioned by upanissaya gocara?

Acharn: Gocara is the object when there is a moment of paññā. It knows what is upanissaya gocara. Paññā knows that it is nothing, just a moment that is conditioned, no "I". It protects from clinging to it, from wanting to have kusala. It depends on conditions.

When the conditions for akusala are so strong, no one can stop conditioning more and more akusala. It depends on the arising of upanissaya gocara to protect until there can be conditions for direct awareness to begin to understand even akusala at that moment. No matter how strong akusala is and how long there is akusala, there are still conditions for the arising of upanibandha gocara. There is no choice, no one can do anything. Whatever the level of accumulated understanding is, no matter it is strong or not, paññā can understand it as no one, no self.

Nina

17.7 Saturday discussion, XIV, 6

Nina
Oct 9 #164810

Ten perfections

Dear friends,

Acharn: Even at the beginning of upanibandha gocara paññā is so weak, compared to the accumulation of akusala. There are ten perfections, pāramīs, and it depends on conditions at what moment a particular pāramī arises. Why is there dāna? Usually people do not give, but what conditions the moment of giving? With or without paññā? Not everyone understands the moment of giving as not self, because there is no upanissaya gocara. But when upanissaya gocara is there, it is strong enough to condition the arising of kusala more than akusala. When there are moments of akusala in one's life all day, can there be moments of upanibandha gocara? When there is not upacaya gocara nothing can protect from akusala.

Even when there are many moments of kusala in a day, it depends on upacaya gocara whether it is enough to understand that object as not self. One has to see the danger of akusala, otherwise there are conditions for akusala all day. When there is akusala there is no arakkha gocara. But when it is there based on the understanding of not self, it can condition any level of kusala, until the moment of upanibandha gocara.

We can understand what moment there is satipaṭṭhāna and what moment there is not, but is this enough to condition the moment of upanibandha? Without the pāramīs? Can anyone condition direct awareness with understanding when one is all day full of akusala? One does not think about the pāramīs but one thinks just about direct understanding, and this is impossible.

One can have understanding of one's great amount of akusala, it is there now. What can condition upanibandha? Study, hearing and considering the teachings is the way leading to understanding. It depends on one's accumulations to understand clearly or roughly, to understand very little or to understand keenly. It depends on conditions which have to be also the protection from all akusala, from conceit, wrong view, stinginess, and aversion. Those who have strong wrong view do not listen to the teachings.

Sarah: No one can overestimate arakkha gocara, protection. It is much greater than we think. There have to be much more khanti pāramī, viriya pāramī, all the different pāramīs.

Acharn: One should see the danger of akusala and the benefit of kusala. The best is paññā that understands the truth.

Nina

17.8 Saturday dsicussion XV, 1

Nina
Oct 19 #164946

Ten instances of talk

Dear friends,

There are ten instances of talk, done by the good friend in Dhamma, dasa (ten) kathavatthuni (footnote 12 in Visuddhimagga I, 49): On wanting little, contentment, seclusion, aloofness from contact, strenuousness, virtue, concentration, understanding, deliverance, knowledge and vision of deliverance (M i, 145, and III, 113).

The discussion was mainly on citta and here it became clear that it pertains to the citta with understanding at this moment.

Then follows the transcription by Alberto:

Nina: I have a question about satipaṭṭhāna and thinking about realities. You often reminded us that the difference should be known between the moment there is sati and the moment there is not.

Acharn: What is the object of satipaṭṭhāna? When there is no understanding of this moment as it is there is no condition for satipaṭṭhāna. We learn from the very beginning, at the level of pariyatti, that there is seeing and that which is seen. At that moment no other object can appear. That which is seen cannot be anyone. It impinged on the eye-base. We think that we see many things, but only one reality impinges on the eye-base.

Nāma arises just to experience an object. It does not appear like that yet, even it is there all day. There cannot be any moment without that which arises and experiences, for a living person who has not died yet. It is there but it cannot be easily known. Actually at this moment of seeing it is there. It experiences what appears. This will lead to satipaṭṭhāna. Without understanding this it would be impossible. The understanding of no self has to be firm enough.

If we had not read about the processes of citta it seems that there is nothing in between seeing and hearing. What can be known is what appears. We cannot know the cittas before and after seeing. From knowing this there is a little letting go of misunderstanding of whatever is now appearing.

The beginning is very little at a time before there can be direct awareness of realities by itself, unexpectedly. It has not arisen before. No one can choose the time, the place, the object for it to arise. This indicates the anattāness of everything.

Hearing that there is no one, nothing at all, and considering condition a moment of direct awareness. Paññā may not be keen enough to understand (realities) directly. It is just the time of developing understanding of what is there by conditions. Conditions to let go of the idea of self. No one can do anything.

When paññā is keen enough, it does not matter whether or not there is direct awareness.

Nina

17.9 Saturday discussion XV, 2

Nina
Oct 20 #164958

Food for paññā

Dear friends,

Acharn: If there is not direct awareness, also that is "not me". One may think: "I feel sad if there is no direct awareness today, how long will I be", but it does not matter. Sāriputta could directly understand the truth (when he listened to Assaji) because of the (accumulated) paññā. It was sufficient to let go of clinging to the idea of self.

Sarah: That is the whole point. Sound that is heard now is just sound. It just depends on conditions whether understanding now is intellectual understanding or direct understanding. It is anattā and it does not matter. It is conditioned.

Sukin: Why satipaṭṭhāna and not samadhi-paṭṭhāna or viriya-paṭṭhāna?

Acharn: Right awareness is just a moment, different from what you take for sati in different languages. Not forgetting to understand this moment. There is, for example, hardness now, it is touched. When there is no hearing about the truth, one does not know that there is nothing, only hardness which is the object which is there as the object of touching. One has no idea about this when there is no understanding of it.

But when there is understanding from hearing, considering, (understanding) is not there all the time, only some time when there are conditions for it to arise. We do not know how long it (understanding) has been developed. The moment it arises it means that there must be conditions to understand that with direct awareness of that object.

It seems that when we think (of an object) we follow (that object). When we think of that which is seen, thinking follows that which is seen, it does not follow other things. After seeing it thinks and follows it closer and closer, to be sati, but in truth it is there together, in the same way as seeing and hearing which seem to be together.

When sammā-sati is there it seems it is there at the same time as the experiencing of that object, but in reality they arise in different processes. Even now, how many processes (of cittas arising and falling away), and how many processes there are in between seeing and hearing, they seem together.

So, this is just the way to understand and let go. Leave it to saṅkhāra khandha (the conditioned cetasikas apart from feeling and remembrance and including sobhaṇa cetasikas) and dhammas. It is not the (right) way to think, "I can do, I can try".

There is seeing now, why is there not direct awareness? Because there is not enough understanding as no one, no self. There is attachment, unknown as āsava.

Nina: It is very helpful that you always say again and again: There is no one who can do anything. A very good reminder.

Acharn: Without hearing and considering there cannot be food for paññā to develop. That is why we listen and listen and listen, and there is understanding little by little, until there can be conditions for direct awareness, unknown, unexpectedly, as anattā. It shows the anattāness of more understanding as no self, no one, little by little, from moment to moment.

Nina

17.10 Saturday discussion XV, 3

Nina
Oct 22 #164984

A trap of lobha

Dear friends,

Sarah: It is a trap of lobha when there is clinging to the idea that there should be more understanding, instead of being content with whatever understanding there is now or with whatever appears now. When one does not see the trap of lobha, there is clinging and trying to find another way (of development). That is a hindrance to the development of satipaṭṭhāna. It can come in any time.

The contentment with whatever appears now and the development of understanding of reality now is very important. It is the opposite of trying to do, to find a way to have more understanding.

Ann: We heard definitions but did not understand what appears now.

Sarah: It is attachment to wanting it to be different from this moment.

Acharn: Even at each level of vipassanā ñāna there is (the understanding of) "no one". The truth of impermanence, dukkha and anattā can be known clearly. Understanding knows little by little that there is "no me". The clinging to the wrong view of self is the first to be eradicated and in the beginning other forms of attachment are not eradicated. Even the "non-returner", the anāgāmī, (who has attained the third stage of enlightenment) has different levels of attachment. They have to be known, otherwise they cannot be eradicated.

When there is not yet the paññā of the sotāpanna (who has attained the first stage of enlightenment), the very subtle lobha cannot be known. After developing more understanding of no self, the idea of self becomes less until the magga-citta (path-consciousness) of the sotāpanna arises and the idea of self is eradicated forever, absolutely. But there is still lobha; lobha is attached to everything except lokuttara dhammas (N: Nibbāna and the lokuttara cittas that experience it).

Also in the development of insight, after vipassanā ñāna has fallen away there can be lobha. It has to be known, otherwise it cannot be eradicated.

Tam: You just mentioned that subtle lobha has to be known. What about people who develop samatha? They have to know very subtle lobha?

Acharn: What is anattā?

Tam: All dhammas. So they know subtle lobha but not anattā, right?

Acharn: When there is understanding at the level of the sotāpanna, there is no more lobha that takes realities for "I" or something permanent, but there is lobha for other things.

Sukin: The sotāpanna understands the āsavas, but those who develop samatha can never understand āsavas.

Ann: The sotāpanna has no more the āsava of wrong view.

Sarah: The āsava of wrong view, diṭṭhāsava, no longer arises for the sotāpanna. Subtle attachment to sense objects (kāmāsava), to becoming (bhavāsava), and ignorance (avijjāsava) are most of the time unknown. They are only eradicated by the arahat. It is still a long way to go before these are eradicated.

Acharn: Is this kathavattu we are talking about?

Sarah: When one is understanding more the danger of different degrees of attachment and seeing the value of understanding, there is more contentment. So, it is kathavattu. Upanissaya gocara understands different realities now, what appears now, sound that is heard now. Without hearing about different realities and about the development of upanissaya gocara, there can never be understanding of those realities. That is why we discuss.

Acharn: Is there upanibandha gocara now? There is no understanding of it. It has to be the beginning. If it is not the beginning, how can it grow? So, it is there as beginning.

When you do not have akusala as before it is arakkha gocara (protection), so that it protects against lack of direct awareness and there is direct awareness.

Sukin: Do you think there is arakkha gocara when there is not satipaṭṭhāna?

Acharn: Yes, there cannot be always satipaṭṭhāna. There are different levels of kusala. There are moments of direct awareness and moments of kusala without it. If there is no direct awareness, how can there be conditions for direct awareness?

Sarah: Here the contentment and the development of all perfections (pāramīs) comes in, conditioned by understanding. They have to support and nurture that understanding to condition direct understanding and its development.

Acharn: Is there "you" now? The understanding that there is "no me" can little by little condition moments of direct awareness.

Sukin: (That is) when firm intellectual understanding of "no me" is already a protection?

Acharn: Any moment of kusala is arakkha to be kusala, not to be akusala.

Nina

17.11 Saturday discussion XVI, 2

Nina
Oct 26 #165042

The four āsavas

Dear friends,

Sarah: As understanding develops, khanti, patience, develops with it. Understanding becomes firmer and firmer, one knows that it (khanti) is conditioned. It cannot be any other way. Without that understanding it can never develop.

Acharn: So now is there viriya or khanti? No need (to know) so long as there is no understanding of nāma which experiences and rūpa which does not experiences anything. Otherwise the self is there.

The point of talking about viriya and khanti is that nothing can be taken for self. It appears as "something" all the time.

Azita: Among the four āsavas (intoxicants) which are kāmāsava (the āsava of clinging to sense objects), the āsava of clinging to existence (bhavāsava), the āsava of wrong view (diṭṭhāsava) and the āsava of ignorance (avijjāsava), kāmāsava arises more often.

Acharn: When there is nothing, there is no world. Can there be the world, even there are citta, cetasika and rūpa? It is impossible to stop the way it is. There must be the reality which cannot understand anything.

When nothing appears and then just one reality, who knows there is attachment to that reality already, because of ignorance. Attachment to a very tiny piece of rūpa and that is kāmāsava.

Nina: I do not understand bhāvāsava, the āsava of existence or becoming.

Acharn: Is there you? That is bhava, being. "I" see, "I" think. Āsava arises because there is still the latent tendency, anusaya. It is unknown all the time, because there is ignorance all the time. Can anyone stop it? How can the "I" stop it, because there is no "I". There is so much defilement in a day. Is there any idea of "I am"?

Nina: Yes.

Acharn: Without the āsava of wrong view, diṭṭhi and the āsava of avijjā can there be such thinking? When one does not hear the teachings, how can one know the difference between seeing and thinking, as different moments?

The Buddha taught the truth of realities, even though they cannot be known, like receiving-consciousness, sampaṭicchana-citta, investigating-consciousness, santīraṇa-citta, determining-consciousness, votthapana-citta. Āsava is so subtle, it is not known. Even liking, when we wake up it is not known.

Nina

17.12 Saturday discussion XVI, 3

Nina
Oct 27 #165056

Understand the truth of it, little by little

Dear friends,

Nina: Acharn, you said when there is understanding of "no me", this can condition direct awareness. I think that it depends on the level of understanding of "no me". It can condition theoretical understanding, superficial understanding.

Acharn: When there is the idea of "I" very firmly, can there be moments of understanding as not self?

Nina: No.

Acharn: That is why we have to think of each word, over and over again, to understand the truth of it, little by little. It has to begin, not all at once. For example, when talking about bhavaṅga, is there bhavaṅga? Understanding of bhavaṅga is the moment when it does not appear. bhavaṅga has no object of this world.(N: It experiences the same object as the rebirth-consciousness) But can it be known? Nina: It can be known, but not yet.

Acharn: It cannot appear to ignorance.

From hearing (the teachings) we know that seeing is not thinking, and that seeing is not hearing. Why are they different from each other? If there is just seeing all the time, there are no conditions for the arising of hearing. After it (seeing) has arisen it must fall away.

Before there can be hearing because of different conditions, there have to be ear-base, sound and the impingement of sound on the ear-base. Contact (phassa cetasika) is a condition of the arising of one reality. There must be a moment which is not seeing or hearing, but in between. This is the understanding of bhavaṅga. Otherwise seeing sees all the time, no moment of hearing to arise. There are not yet conditions for hearing after seeing, there has to be bhavaṅga citta. That is intellectual understanding. If one has not heard the words (of the teachings), there will never be understanding of the teachings.

Nina

17.13 Saturday discussion XVI, 4

Nina
Oct 28 #165064

Each word of the Buddha can be understood

Dear friends,

Acharn: There is seeing right now, but no understanding. There are not enough conditions to experience the arising and falling away of realities, or the nature which can experience and the nature which cannot experience anything. Or to experience the difference between sati and intellectual understanding. We should not merely understand the word, but the characteristic of that object, the object of direct awareness. It has to be with understanding.

Now when hardness appears, there is not enough understanding, to understand it as anattā, unexpectedly, otherwise there is an idea of "I can do, I can practise". Each word of the Buddha can be understood stage by stage, until it appears well.

There are different names and different degrees of understanding. There are different stages of insight and different pariññās. Whatever appears is to be known, it is to be studied little by little, until there is firm confidence in the truth of reality. When understanding becomes firmer there is no way to go wrong, to go to a meditation centre. There is just letting go by (the understanding of) anattāness. If one hears the word anattā without understanding, that it is this moment, how can it eliminate the idea of self?

Azita: Can you talk more about bhāvāsava, the intoxicant of clinging to being, to existence? I always thought it was clinging to life, but you said something about "I" and "me".

Acharn: We should come back to the beginning: what is life, what is real? What is nimitta (the sign of realities that arise and fall away very fast). How can there be a nimitta if there is no reality. Why does it not appear as it is? Because of the rapidity of the arising and falling away of realities. It is so fast that it covers up the truth; there is no time to understand anything without the Buddha's teachings

Sarah: There can be clinging to living, clinging to seeing. There can be an idea of "I am seeing", but without wrong view. Thus, there are different kinds of attachment.

Nina

17.14 Saturday discussion, XVI, 5

Nina
Oct 29 #165068

Clinging to being

Dear friends,

Sukin: Usually we cling to sense objects and also to the experiencing of them. Is clinging to the experiencing bhāvāsava (the intoxicant of clinging to being)?

Acharn: Do you want to understand the difference? Can there be at this moment, when one is not clinging to diṭṭhi (wrong view), an idea of self? Even when you do not think: "I, I, I" at any moment of seeing, hearing or thinking, there is "I" because the āsava is there, unknown. Even when we do not speak out, it is there.

Sukin: Diṭṭhi can arise even without an idea of "I"? We can begin to understand the difference.

Acharn: When we feel very fresh, happy, is there kāmāsava (the intoxicant of clinging to sense objects)? Or bhāvāsava, diṭṭhāsava, avijjāsava (intoxicant of ignorance)? They cannot be the same. Not "I" would like to know that, but whatever can be known in daily life can be known by paññā, not by ignorance. Ignorance can appear as not understanding this or wanting to be that. Without ignorance there cannot be any akusala.

It is not just thinking. While listening, it is the understanding which understands: there is no one. Then it is gone, no more.

Sarah: What about now, one just enjoys clinging, just enjoys living. Even when there are many moments of diṭṭhāsava, we do not know. We enjoy living right now for a moment. As Acharn said, there is no point in working out what is what. There is not necessarily wrong view at the moment of clinging.

Kāmāsava is common but what about avijjā at almost every moment? It is completely unknown.

Azita: I never thought about bhāvāsava (the intoxicant of clinging to existence). Maybe it is a little clearer intellectually. It made me think how difficult the Path really is, because we want result.

Sarah: This is khanti, this is viriya, this is bhava (becoming, existence), diṭṭhāsava, that is "I". We want to work it out, to catch it, to be aware, it comes in so quickly.

Sukin: Dhamma often ends up enjoying more attachment than thinking.

Sarah: This is catching the snake in the wrong way. We think it is Dhamma study which must be useful, but there is a lot of clinging while trying to catch different realities, trying to know bhavaṅga or bhāvāsava. Just understand what appears very naturally. We can see not only diṭṭhāsava, but much stronger degrees of diṭṭhi arise so commonly, even during Dhamma discussion.

Nina

17.15 Saturday discussion XVI, 6

Nina
Oct 30 #165077

All are saṅkhārakkhandha

Dear friends,

Lukas had problems with forgetfulness and he discussed this with Acharn.

Acharn: Intellectual understanding is not enough so that it is a condition for direct understanding for that moment, unexpectedly. That is the way for understanding anattā.

Lukas: Forgetfulness is a concept, and a concept is not dhamma.

Acharn: Should we not forget what has gone? Understanding has to be now. One would like to remember this and that and take it for "I will remember".

Remember that this moment is the only reality that can be understood more and more, only when it appears. 0therwise it is gone.

If you forget that paññā can only understand now what appears, not by me, but by conditions, that is the worst forgetfulness. This is the only way to eliminate desire and attachment to the self, because all are conditioned. When paññā arises it indicates the anattāness of it. Whatever arises is gone now and it is useless to think about it.

There is no one who can do anything, understanding works its way. All are saṅkhārakkhandha (the khandha of formations, all cetasikas except feeling and saññā). No thought about me, where, what and how. Whatever is there is conditioned, to be understood.

Forgetting about anything is all right if one does not forget about the truth of this moment that is to be known little by little. There is very thick and strong kilesa (defilements) to be known, from aeons and aeons ago. How can it be eradicated so soon? Impossible. That is the way to understand the truth which will eliminate the idea of self from time to time, until paññā is strong enough. Strong enough from understanding the reality when it appears well, as it is, not as nimitta (the sign) of people and things.

Each moment is so valuable when there is even more a little understanding, or even any kind of kusala with or without understanding but based on understanding. If there is no kusala, there is akusala.

Sarah: All dhammas are anattā. It is not anyone who is aware or who is not careless. He (the Buddha) just points to the benefit of developing understanding. It has to develop very naturally. When there is forgetfulness it is another dhamma that arises and passes. No fear of anything, fear of having a lot of lobha, fear of being careless. Reality appears and is gone.

As Acharn mentioned, there is thinking lots of time. We say we are forgetful when it is not the object we would like to think about, but it just depends on what saññā is marking and what vitakka (thinking cetasika) leads the citta to what is thought about.

We usually talk about the story of lobha, not the object we would like to think about. Even for whom we say conventionally that he has lost memory, saññā is marking (the object).

Everyone would like to have understanding all the time, to be enlightened. The understanding has to understand the truth of this moment as it is. It just shows the strong clinging to self if we would like it to be different from how it is.

It is helpful you brought up the questions for everyone.

Lukas: What is the proper way of living, the proper way to study and understand dhamma, to listen and understand the meaning of the word?

Acharn: So now, live to understand Dhamma.

Lukas: Dhamma is reality and it also means the word.

Acharn: Whatever arises must be conditioned. No one can understand what will be there next. Why do we live, what for? To understand the truth which can be understood.

18

November 2020

18.1 Saturday discussion XVII, 1

Nina
Nov 1 #165091

What is dhamma?

Dear friends,

What is dhamma? It is not the word, but whatever appears. It appears now, to be known as not self. The words of the Buddha state that what is seen is no one and no thing. Only that which impinges on the eye-base. Even while talking there is seeing. Visible object impinges again and again but there is no understanding of seeing. It is all gone and what is left is the memory. A little more understanding of "no one" is very helpful.

The sound has gone, there is no one. There are conditions to let go attachment, aversion or whatever appears.

Nina: This is more difficult when it concerns myself. I am talking now, I am thinking now. There is the idea of "I, I, I".

Acharn: Are you thinking of that now: "I, I, I"? Sometimes when a reality like anger appears (it can be known) anger is anger. One can study it, and not try not to have it. But from hearing again and again one can consider it and understand it as dhamma, no one, little by little.

Whatever arises is by conditions, for a very short moment and then gone completely. Understand one word at a time, like dhamma. The Buddha could not become enlightened if there was no understanding of that which appears. It appears to be object of attachment, aversion or right understanding.

If there is no understanding there must be the self, trying and trying to understand this. Can seeing be "I", can hearing be "I"? Seeing cannot be anything at all, it has arisen. No one can make it arise and it is gone. That can be directly experienced but not (by understanding) at the level of listening.

Whatever is there in life can be object of understanding, from hearing and considering the truth. Seeing is a reality. How can there be a moment of seeing? There are many conditions for its arising.

Nina: You helped us a lot to understand the shortness of the moment. It is nothing, gone already when we consider that moment. By saying this again and again it helps to understand a little better how short it is.

Acharn: So, can there be "I"?

Nina: No.

Acharn: Hearing the truth of what appears conditions more understanding of no self. One can see one's own misunderstanding of whatever appears and know that there is only one way. By listening carefully one understands better and better, until there is the moment of direct understanding of a reality.

Nina

18.2 Saturday discussion, XVII, 2

Nina
Nov 2 #165099

Upanissaya gocara is not an ordinary object

Dear friends,

Acharn: Upanissaya gocara is not an ordinary object, but the truth of the object which has been understood little by little. (Sarah: upanissaya gocara refers to the object resort (gocara) of right intellectual understanding. Upanissaya means literally upa (strong) nissaya (support). In other words the object taught by the Buddha to be understood).

Acharn: Taste is not smell, they are all different by conditions. There is not yet understanding of each reality, that is why they appear as "something". It is very simple but very deep to understand. Simple, because the truth is as it is. No change. It is not different from that very moment. Only that and then gone.

That is the way to study the teachings. Beginning to understand the words more clearly until the truth appears as no self. From intellectual understanding to direct understanding, by conditions. Understanding by conditions, direct awareness by conditions, all levels by conditions. That is the way of letting go understanding as something. The darkest reality is not understanding the truth of what appears now. What is a moment?

Sarah: (returns to my point about sense of self as regards "myself" and other beings): There is a sense of other beings and things out there. It does no have to be in words like it is someone, it is a chair...

Nina: It is deep rooted, not in words. Now I see you and Jonothan, it is deep rooted.

Jonothan: This does not necessarily imply a sense of self, this is the way thinking goes. It conceptualizes. We should not assume it is wrong view, it can be conceit, māna, or attachment.

A situation is not important, it is the nature of the mental state that is to be known. The only way to overcome wrong view is understanding what is appearing at the present moment. That is the condition for letting go the idea of self. Letting go the idea of self is the end of the development of understanding. This cannot be soon, there will always be an idea of self until the time of enlightenment.

Nina: Very good you remind us that when thinking of people there is not necessarily wrong view. It may just be thinking of a concept on account of sense impressions. You warn us against that idea.

Jonothan: When Acharn speaks about a sense of self she is not referring to wrong view all the time. It can be (just) clinging or conceit.

Acharn: What is meant by self, or what is self? Self is a thing or "I". Or whatever is there: something. When I touch the body there is "something" so long as it does not appear well. The Pāli term attā includes: whatever is there as something. Is "I" something? Is a glass "something"?

Seeing cannot be "I see", it is a reality which sees. Each reality has its own characteristic. We can use different words like "I" or self, or thing, he, she, table or chair. All are "something". There is something what we take for "I". The best way to understand is the Pāli term "attā". It is "something" including he, she, table, chair. So long as it is "something" it is wrong. It cannot be taken for anything. It seems that it is there all the time, so it is a "thing". The truth is: it is anattā, no thing. Attā includes everything which is taken for a "thing".

Nina

18.3 Saturday discussion XVII, 3

Nina
Nov 3 #165105

Attā, something

Dear friends,

The Pāli term attā includes everything that is taken for a thing as a whole, not as it is. Even sound itself is not just a sound; many processes experience that very shortly. All together come to be nimitta (sign), nimitta of different sounds. We live in the world of not understanding what comes together and appears as something, no matter we call it dead body or living body, as "I". It is something there, not you. The hardness is hardness, no matter where, smell is smell, no matter where. Smell is not to be taken for the smell of flowers, smell is just smell. When you take it for something, it is the meaning of attā. No matter in the sense of I, you, dog, cat. It is attā, something. Different by appearance, (experienced) through different doorways.

Tan Than: Paññā helps to see that there is nothing? How towards vipassanā ñāna?

Acharn: These are so many words. Better talk about each word, to have more understanding as it is.

Tam: Direct understanding.

Acharn: One word: understanding and direct understanding. Is there "I" now?

Tam: There is not "I" now.

Acharn: What is that which is not "I"? Only one word at a time. Actually, there is no understanding of the truth which is so very deep, such as no "I" at all. So what is there now? Which is not "I"? Just one word: what is there now?

Tam: Seeing.

Acharn: Is there direct understanding of seeing? Or is there just hearing the word seeing? There is seeing, there is the idea of "I understand seeing". What is the truth of that seeing? This is the way to understand the teachings of the Buddha which are so very deep. Only one moment, just one word. When we talk about seeing, what is seeing? Otherwise there cannot be understanding of seeing. How does seeing arise?

Tam: Because of conditions.

Acharn: What conditions seeing?

Tan: Object, eyes and light.

Acharn: There is a lot of thinking whether there is direct understanding or not yet. There must be talking about seeing in order to know: right understanding knows it as intellectual understanding, not yet direct awareness.

Tam: What is direct awareness?

Acharn: Can there be the understanding of seeing as it is? The understanding of "no I". What is the difference between intellectual understanding and direct understanding?

Tam: Intellectual understanding understands: I see, with "I" in there.

Acharn: We are talking about what seeing is, to understand the direct understanding of seeing.

Even if you don't say it, there is seeing. There are conditions for seeing and seeing appears right now. It sees, but the characteristic of seeing does not appear. We just know that there is seeing when something is there to be seen. What about the understanding of seeing? No understanding of it. "I see", is that the understanding of seeing? It sees, it is not thinking. No direct understanding of any object.

Nina

18.4 Saturday discussion XVII, 4

Nina
Nov 4 #165118

The function of the brain

Dear friends,

Acharn: If there is no direct awareness, can there be direct understanding of what appears? It is gone. How can there be such ignorance of seeing right now? From aeons and aeons ago.

Tam: Seeing is done by the function of the brain.

Sarah: It seems like the brain has to do so many things, it is difficult to understand it. What is the reality at that moment when it seems that there is the brain doing all these things? What is the reality now?

Tam: Thinking about concepts, this is an object.

Sarah: Thus, thinking about different concepts, stories and ideas about the brain, the brain being so busy. This has nothing to do with the understanding of seeing. It is not intellectual understanding or direct understanding of seeing. At this moment of seeing it is just the reality of seeing itself, seeing at this moment, then gone instantly. No time for any thought about the brain. Thinking of brain and processes will not help.

If there is no beginning of understanding there can never be direct understanding of seeing. In the beginning there should be firm understanding that seeing is a reality, and this has nothing to do with brain and processes. Very simple and very deep, as Acharn mentioned. It is very subtle.

Seeing is not someone, not something, not a person, not a brain. That is the meaning of anattā.

I think that you know that there are two kinds of reality: nāma which can experience an object and rūpa which cannot experience anything. Seeing is a nāma which arises and sees the object. Not someone or something which sees.

Jonothan: Seeing is a kind of experience, it experiences visible object. Hearing is the experience of sound. Tasting is the experience of taste and so on.

Any kind of experience is a mental process. Though it relies on the various bases, eye-base etc., the actual experience must be a citta, a moment of consciousness. If we think that the experiences are a function of the brain, that is going to be an obstacle to direct understanding of the actual moment of seeing which is a moment of consciousness, not a function of the brain. People are misled by the fact that science can measure brain activity whenever there is seeing.

According to the Buddha's teaching seeing must be a mental process. Dhamma is quite basic, the Buddha spoke about things that are to be understood. He spoke about seeing, visible object and feeling that arises associated with that contact, about hearing and sound. He was emphasizing the importance of seeing those realities as they are.

Nina

18.5 Saturday discussion XVII, 5

Nina
Nov 5 #165131

The world of nimitta

Dear friends,

I was wondering about the meaning of the words, used by Acharn, "the world of nimitta" and I was not sure whether this is the same as the world of concepts.

Sarah gave additional explanations of Acharn's words: "we live in the world of nimitta".

Since realities arise and fall away, succeeding each other very quickly, a sign or nimitta is experienced of a particular reality. One unit of a nāma or a rūpa cannot be experienced since it has gone immediately. Just the nimitta or sign of it remains.

Sarah: We can say we live in the world of nimitta or in the world of concepts. We can refer to the idea of a whole that is a concept or nimitta or refer to either concepts or nimitta as the shadow of realities. It can seem confusing. I think that when there is understanding of realities such as seeing, (or rather of the nimitta of the characteristic of a reality), it does not matter whether we refer to nimitta or concepts as being the shadow of realities, or whether we refer to the whole as being nimitta or a concept. The point is whatever words are used, it is referring to the understanding of realities and to the understanding of the nimitta of realities. This is different from the idea of the whole, the dream world or fantasy world.

We know that it is the nimitta of reality that has to be known, because realities arise and fall away so fast and through the mind-door there can only be nimitta anyway, even at the moment of vipassanā ñāna. After a reality appears there is thinking of the idea of a whole. Whether we refer to the nimitta or to the concept at different moments is not important. The point is to understand that it is reality that arises and falls away and that there has to be nimitta of reality that is understood. When the nimitta of reality is understood there is not any idea of a whole, or fantasy thinking. Otherwise we get stuck on the terms and the labels, wondering why are we using this term, not that term and we forget the understanding of the nimitta of the reality now.

Nina: Thank you, that is clear now.

Azita: Acharn, you reminded us that we should consider each word. How is that done? One word again and again?

Acharn: What is seen?

Azita: We are told: visible object.

Acharn: If we do not talk about it can there be any moment of just visible object?

Azita: No.

Acharn: See, that is why: just one word, visible object, to remind about one's own understanding which is enough to understand what is appearing as no thing, no one at all. This will be to let go the idea of self. Not by "me" but by knowing the way to let go the idea of self. Otherwise, "let go, let go", it is "I", no understanding. So, there must be ignorance there, always there. Just one word from now on: visible object. That which is seen does not appear as it is.

Azita: I can remind myself during the day that it is just visible object, not me, but I often wonder: is that "me" talking?

Acharn: It is not "me", (it is) the understanding of what is thought about. Not me who thinks, not me, not me. No matter it is thinking or reminding. It is not only the word. Anyone can understand the word but not the meaning or the reality represented by that word. Use the word object, that which can be seen, only a reality. The other realities cannot appear as that which is seen. When this is true, and only when conditions are ready, there can be just thinking about that and later on not just thinking but understanding directly.

Nina

18.6 Saturday discussion XVII, 6.

Nina
11/06/20 #165152

Not moving away

Dear friends,

Acharn: What is the characteristic of awareness? "I know what I am doing, I am aware that I am sitting". That is not the understanding of the characteristic of sati. What knows what one is doing is not wholesome, not kusala. But sati is wholesome. There is a moment of seeing, follow that object. Does it go away from that object? Follow that which sees, which hears, which is hard or soft. But that is so far away. It has to be just right. There are seeing and hearing now, who can separate them?

While we are talking there are thinking, sound, hearing and seeing. Only paññā can separate (N: and distinguish) the different moments. Even though the reality appears as nimitta, paññā knows the truth, depending on the level of paññā.

Azita: You said that paññā does not go away from the object.

Acharn: What is meant by moving away? When there is seeing and thinking about the chair, it seems that there is instantly moving away from seeing, from understanding it as it is. Only seeing sees.

Each word should be studied carefully, to understand the truth that is so very deep. Sati can be translated into different languages, but its characteristic is: not moving away, not away from seeing right now. Seeing and hearing seem together, they cannot be separated when there is no understanding. When there is understanding of the truth (it is known that) seeing cannot be hearing. (It arises) in a process of cittas that experience that object through through that doorway. There is only one moment of seeing, the other cittas (in that process) do not see. We can understand how the nimitta (appears) so very rapidly, when there are so many things seen when one opens one's eyes. How deep, how subtle it is. But it can be studied to be known, little by little, "no one" can do that. Confidence, saddhā, sees little by little the benefit of knowing the truth. It is now at the moment of understanding, listening, thinking carefully, wisely. It can be known directly. Only one (reality) at a time, by conditions only, unexpectedly. No need to think about it or to wait for it.

Sarah: Considering is anattā too, but if there is any idea of repeating: "seeing sees visible object", to remind oneself, there may be some moments of considering. But there may also be sīlabbata parāmāsa, wrong ideas, trying to consider. That is the opposite of wholesome consciousness with understanding naturally, by conditions. Wrong practice can come in any time.

Azita: When I remind myself is there some degree of understanding? Wrong practice is difficult to know.

Sarah: Different moments. Only understanding can know that there are moments of trying, doing anything. Like talking now about seeing. If there is any trying to understand or trying to consider, it is not the same as understanding the reality when there are conditions, naturally, as anattā.

Azita: Reminders are important, the self slips in any time, probably quite often.

Sarah: Self would love understanding, catching realities. The trap is the wrong Path.

Nina

18.7 Saturday discussion, XVIII, 2

Nina
11/09/20 #165184

Fantasy

Dear friends,

Sarah: If there is the idea that there should not be thinking of a car and no attachment, it is not the right object of sati and paññā. There is the wrong idea that there should be thinking of another object. Thinking is conditioned, attachment is conditioned, it cannot be any other way. There is no understanding of what is conditioned right now.

Acharn: There can be understanding of any moment as it is. Only the magga-citta (N: the Path-consciousness which is lokuttara) of the sotāpanna eradicates wrong practice.

Sarah: It can come in so easily, even when we hear about protection and about the right object. There may be some idea that a car is not the right object, that it should be something else. The right object is what is conditioned at this moment.

Acharn: Even that is "not me". Even that moment is conditioned.

Sarah: It is conditioned, it is just dhamma. It is very natural. That is the right object, when it is the object of understanding. Expectation that there will be more right considering is clinging to the self. Who knows what will arise next moment. Any reality can arise by conditions, any reality can be object of understanding.

Alan: Can you explain more about living in a fantasy world?

Sarah: Life carries on the same, but occasionally understanding can dart in and understand the truth at this moment. So, then there can be a beginning of understanding of what is real and what is fantasy. But most of the day there is living in fantasy, as usual. It is best having no expectation and beginning to understand a little, a little, not thinking: what will be the next moment, what is the right object or how can there be more understanding in a day. That will be a disappointment.

Alan: Can you explain what you mean by fantasy?

Sarah: When there is no understanding of realities, we are dreaming about what is seen, heard, what is taken for real. Fantasy is like a dream. There is dreaming at night time, but this is a dream or fantasy in day time. These are just ideas: cars on the road, people outside the window, friends seen on the screen. That is not understanding the truth of this moment: just seeing, just visible object that is seen at this moment.

Alan: We are under the ocean. When there is awareness our head is above the ocean, for a few seconds.

Sarah: A glimmer of light, taking a breath above the ocean. Most of the time there is the world of concepts, of attachment and ignorance. Acharn even refers to moments of kusala (that can be fantasy). Even at the moment of mettā or generosity, when there is no understanding of realities, there is fantasy. The Buddha said that anything other than direct understanding of realities or the path of satipaṭṭhāna is in this sense the wrong path. Only the understanding of reality now is being away from fantasy, moving out of saṃsāra.

Jonothan: When there is no awareness there is likely to be some fantazising. The sotāpanna who has no more wrong view still thinks of concepts but it would not be correct to call that fantasy. The sotāpanna does not have awareness all the time but still thinks in concepts of people.

Sarah: When there are ignorance and attachment, it is fantasy. We can still use terms but with more understanding of what realities are.

Alan: I like the comment that the Abhidhamma is an explanation of the Dhamma. Many times we are talking about conventional things, it is talking fantasy and not understanding realities that are behind that fantasy.

Sarah: We can read suttas in the same way and forget that there are just dhammas arising and falling away. It has to come back to this moment: the understanding now of what appears, of what is the reality now. It is the only way to understand what is fantasy.

Nina

18.8 Saturday discussion, XVIII, 3

Nina
11/10/20 #165188

The ocean

Dear friends,

Acharn asked Alan what the ocean is.

N: By ocean is meant the four floods or oghas: clinging to sense objects (kāmogha), cling to being or existence (bhavogha), clinging to wrong view (diṭṭhogha) and ignorance (avijjogha).

Acharn: We do not understand what is ocean now: no understanding of no self, ignorance, wrong understanding of the truth.

Alan: Ignorance covers up the truth of realities as they are.

Acharn: Is there ocean now? What is this moment which is ocean?

Sarah: They are the four floods. The same qualities as the four intoxicants, āsavas.

Acharn: We do not understand what is ocean. No understanding of no self, avijjogha (flood of ignorance). Like the ocean, so great and so deep. If the Buddha did not teach, can we find out? It appears not as it is, it appears as something. Seeing is ocean, what is seen is ocean, because of not understanding the truth of it; it arises and falls away in split-seconds. All kinds of realities that are not known are like the ocean. The truth is there down deeply. It is very subtle and paññā is the only reality that can penetrate the truth, little by little. It can go deeply down, little by little, until the moment of enlightenment, unexpectedly, by conditions.

Alan: This is an example how to read the teachings: all about the present moment. We read about the ocean, like in the book, but actually it is the present moment.

Acharn: We have ignorance of that which appears now. There must be the object of ignorance, otherwise we cannot find of what there has to be letting go. We should consider very carefully and this leads to more understanding of no self. Otherwise we read the Tipiṭaka like any book and understand the Pāli term, but it represents reality, deeper and deeper. Even the word anattā. It has to be every moment, otherwise there cannot be a sotāpanna (N: who realizes the first stage of enlightenment).

It has to be this moment, is there right understanding? What about now? Whatever the Buddha taught is this moment. This will lead from intellectual understanding to direct understanding, little by little. It begins to appear well. The truth is now, there is clinging to every moment and to everything. That is the great ocean.

Not understanding is also an ocean. Not understanding and wrong understanding. Liking a car is the flood of clinging to sense objects, kāmogha. Not just the car, even the moment of seeing is kāmogha. Each word should be studied carefully: the term, the meaning and the truth. Only developed paññā can study more carefully, because of that level of paññā (that has been reached). It is not enough so long as it is not all (realities) in daily life. Not by anyone, but by conditions. It needs viriya (energy or effort) and khanti (patience).

Nina

18.9 Saturday discussion, XVIII, 4

Nina
11/11/20 #165193

Viriya

Dear friends,

Sarah had a question about viriya and khanti. (N: khanti is actually viriya cetasika.)

Sarah: When reading about viriya as indriya and bala, power, is that viriya referring to khanti, patience? (N: the five indriyas or spiritual faculties, indriyas, are: confidence, energy, mindfulness, concentration and wisdom. When indriyas are more developed they become balas, powers, unshakable by their opposites.)
Acharn: We do not need any word. Even that degree of understanding is not enough. The higher degrees are much keener and stronger. It takes time, from life to life, not a few moments, depending on the accumulation of each individual. When we stretch out our hand, viriya is there, but that kind of viriya is not patience, khanti.
Sarah: Viriya as indriya must refer to satipaṭṭhāna.
Acharn: It must be referring to satipaṭṭhāna from the very beginning, and it must refer to khanti with satipaṭṭhāna.
Acharn: People think that it is so very difficult and they are not interested. It is so very deep, how can one understand it in this life, impossible. So, they do not have khanti, to know that it is so difficult but that it can be directly experienced. What is there now as the Buddha has enlightened? Each word is so true, but it takes viriya and khanti from life to life, and to understand that viriya can arise with

citta. Even when one opens one's eyes there must be viriya. But it is not viriya with the indriya or bala of sati. There is a great difference between each one, depending on understanding.

It is very difficult, it takes not just one life but aeons and aeons. This is the way of letting go of attachment and ignorance. This is the way to pay respect to the teachings of the Buddha and to the Buddha himself. No one can understand the virtues of the Buddha, only someone who understands his word, how deep it is, how true it is.

Tam: Saddhā has viriya as well?

Acharn: Which citta arises with saddhā, how many cittas with viriya? One may think: sometimes I have viriya, at other times not. That is thinking with ignorance. What is viriya, what is its nature. It can be opened up (become clearer) when there is understanding, little by little, stage by stage. Understanding the difference between pariyatti (intellectual understanding), paṭipatti (direct understanding) and paṭivedha (direct realization (by vipassanā ñāna and enlightenment).

The world does not appear well now. There can be the understanding of the truth of it. We live in darkness, we are in the ocean, trying to go to the other side of the ocean. Without the pāramīs it is impossible. The perfection of truthfulness, sacca pāramī, and the perfection of energy, viriya pāramī, are beneficial. Otherwise there cannot be understanding of what is appearing now. The truth is this moment of conditioned realities, arising and falling away, unknown. There is no darkness when there is light. It is the light of paññā.

Sarah (to Tam): Which kinds of citta viriya arises with?

Tam: Seven cetasikas arise with all cittas.

Sarah: Is viriya one of them?

Tam: No.

Sarah: It is not one of the universals. Viriya arises with all cittas, except sixteen. It does not arise with the sense cognitions of seeing, hearing, etc. Saddhā cannot arise with with akusala citta, it cannot condition akusala viriya. That is why Acharn mentioned that one has to understand more the different realities and when they arise. Then one can begin to answer one's own questions.

At the moment of kusala citta now, many cetasikas arise, at least nineteen, and they all condition each other. Saddhā is there, kusala viriya is there, sati is there. Usually when people read about viriya, they think of energy or effort. They have the idea: I make an effort with kusala viriya. That is wrong thinking and akusala viriya, because there is the idea of "I" who can do something. Or when making an effort while cooking there is most of the time akusala. Cittas are arising with lobha, attachment. There is akusala viriya most of the time.

Nina

18.10 Saturday discussion, XVIII, 5

Nina
11/12/20 #165204

Viriya and saddhā

Dear friends,

Tambach: In the case of viriya, usually people think of making an effort.

Sarah: When we think of the development of viriya at the moment of satipaṭṭhāna, when it is strong enough to be an indriya, usually we do not consider that it refers to great patience. Patience enough to understand reality as it is, just a dhamma, and no clinging. Khanti is developed in vipassanā ñāna, and then it is khanti ñāna. We are just talking about effort and energy and forgetting about patience, when it is developed strong enough to be indriya and bala (power). The quality of viriya is quite different from how we used to think of it.

Tam had a question about saddhā which is translated as faith. Belief as it is used in conventional language, like belief in God, is not saddhā.

Sarah explained that it does not arise with lobha, only with sobhaṇa citta. It purifies the citta.

Azita had a question about āsavas and oghas which are the same cetasikas. Jonothan explained that oghas, floods, are stronger than āsavas.

Acharn: What arises more and is bigger and bigger than the ocean? The truth is understanding realities as not self. We are talking about seeing and this is not the same as a moment ago. Ignorance cannot understand that because of the rapidity of the succession of cittas that arise and fall away.

One has to understand where is the ignorance, the attachment, the hindrance, different kinds of akusala as the Buddha taught. Āsava is not the same as nīvaraṇa, hindrance.(N: hindrances are coarse defilements: sensuous desire, illwill, sloth and torpor, restlessness and worry, doubt)

Can we say they are all the same? Impossible. Characteristics cannot be changed. Their degrees are different.

Understanding each word of the Buddha can be a condition for direct awareness. No matter it is āsava, but the characteristic is: no one there at all. Let go what is there. Not "I". Its own characteristic appears to what experiences it as not self, no me.

Nina

18.11 Saturday discussion, XVIII, 6

Nina
11/13/20 #165209

The bonds yoke one to existence

Dear friends,

Jonothan: There are the intoxicants, the floods, the bonds (yogas). The bonds yoke one to existence.

Sarah: The flood of ignorance is very great ignorance, the flood of attachment is very great attachment. They are not just āsavas, intoxicants.

Azita: Acharn I appreciate it very much that you say that there is no one. Only paññā can unyoke.

Acharn: What is the function of sati?

Azita: Sati is aware.

Acharn: Of what?

Azita: Of kusala.

Acharn: People who have no understanding of the truth of realities think: I am aware that I am drinking, eating. Is that sati?

Azita: No.

Acharn: Can sati arise with akusala?

Azita: No.

Acharn: What is the function of sati?

Azita: Sati must also be aware of akusala. Not at the moment of akusala, but sati has to be aware of all realities.

Acharn: Does it protect citta at that moment? But it is different from the moment of understanding. It protects one from misunderstanding. That is why one knows that all dhammas are anattā. There are the wholesome cetasikas of saddhā (confidence), hiri (shame of akusala), ottappa (fear of blame of akusala), sati, sati which is not yet satipaṭṭhāna. They arise to protect from akusala. Whenever they arise, akusala cetasikas cannot arise. No matter they arise with or without paññā.

It is very subtle. Without the enlightenment of the Buddha we would not know. The Buddha could see the subtlety of dhammas like āsavas, anusaya (latent tendency), kilesa (defilement), nīvaraṇa (hindrance). Without paññā can there be a condition for direct awareness? Even intellectual understanding which is of the level of pariyatti has to be very skilful to understand the real meaning of not self, its characteristic, function, manifestation, when it is there as object. It is not only just paññā which protects from attachment and other akusala. Even each cetasika has different levels too. Kāmāsava (intoxicant of clinging to sense objects) is very, very subtle. It is different from liking something so much, wanting to have it.

All kusala protects, but they have different functions. The function of just protecting is of sati. Viriya cetasika is not sati. Kusala has to be kusala, but kusala (dhammas) are of different types. At the moment of kusala, who knows sati is there?

Sarah: We read that the function of sati is heedfulness, guarding against unwholesome states that arise. Guarding and being heedful is the same as protection.

Azita: The answers become deeper and deeper as understanding grows. It is getting very dark.

Acharn: Only paññā can understand what is darkness, getting darker and darker because of no understanding. Without understanding it is not as dark. The reality does not appear well.

The nāma, the experience, has no shape or form. Citta just arises to experience. Citta cannot be cetasika. At the moment of enlightenment there is perfect understanding, no doubt about what is now appearing. Is there doubt now? When there is no paññā it is "I" who thinks. Even (when there is) a very simple question about now.

Sarah: It is very dark.

Acharn: Only paññā understands the truth. It knows that there is no one, and no one, on and on. It just experiences the characteristic. The characteristic as "no one" appears at the moment of vipassanā ñāna. That is khanti pāramī.

Seeing now is there, and the experience of what is seen. That cannot be understood when there is no hearing again and again. From now on we understand the characteristic of seeing as that which sees. There is no one. There can be more understanding of the different levels of no self.

Nina

18.12 Saturday discussion, XIX, 1

Nina
11/16/20 #165245

There is "something" all the time

Dear friends,

Acharn: We talked many times about anattā, but what appears now? There is "something" all the time. That which is seen is not a cup, it is only that which can be seen.

Usually when I finish the talk before lunchtime, everyone comes in. "O, that person is coming", is the thought. Only paññā can know how much understanding there is. There is no doubt about the word "no one" if there is no reality which can be experienced. The moment of seeing is different from the moment of hearing, but there are not enough conditions to know exactly what appears. You can talk about no Nina, no Sujin, but the intellectual understanding is not enough yet, it needs more khanti, patience.

When we use the word viriya, it is viriya cetasika that arises with many cittas. We cannot lift our hand without viriya.

Nina: It will take a long time before we understand what you are saying just now. We do not consider enough and there has to be khanti.

There was a question related to a text about viriya, that it is consolidating the other (accompanying) cetasikas.

Acharn: We just think and talk for two hours. Is there khanti? It is viriya each moment, but when it is more and more in order to reach the goal, attain realisation, is it khanti? It cannot be just one moment of viriya. It takes more time from life to life, so that is khanti. Sometimes we have the intention to do something, but we do not follow up, that is not khanti. Some people read Tipiṭaka and find that that is enough. There is no khanti to see the danger of saṃsāra and understand better and better the truth of no one, no self. Like now, they see that there is no one, no self, no thing, but (do they realize) what is meant? There is "something" there.

Is there khanti on and on, until there is very strong understanding, firmer and firmer? We use the word "appear well" without any understanding of what is there now. Does it appear well? (It develops) from intellectual understanding to condition direct awareness and understanding, which can condition the moment of vipassanā ñāna. Without the teaching of the Buddha no one knows when it does not appear well. The understanding of it has many degrees, that is why different words are used: viriya and khanti.

How long will it take? Can we find khanti without viriya? Not giving up, keeping on, that is viriya which performs the function of khanti. At this moment there are seeing and visible object which are different (from each other). How long does it take just to understand nāma, as that which experiences. As soon as we hear the word "nāma", the experiencer, it is not so that there can be full understanding of that. There is khanti to understand, with viriya arising with each moment.

When we think of just one word "appearing well", who knows without paññā whether it appears well or not? How well is it? There are different degrees of understanding. Hardness appears, does it appear well? It is gone. When there is more and more understanding, direct understanding, it begins to understand the object which appears, little by little. Otherwise we might have doubt about it. The object appears clearer and clearer.

It takes viriya on and on to be khanti. Never give up. Khanti for what? To understand what is there as it is. When there is no understanding it cannot be a perfection.

Nina

18.13 Saturday discussion XIX, 3

Nina
11/18/20 #165270

Lobha is there all the time, to hinder

Dear friends,

Acharn: In the beginning the development of understanding is not easy at all, because lobha is there all the time, to hinder, or to change the right way into the wrong way, or to try to make it faster.

Alan: In the beginning everybody goes wrong, the idea of self is there naturally.

Sarah mentioned the text of the Visuddhimagga about the chariot wheel that touches the ground at one point as it goes along.

Sarah: So, our life, pleasure and pain in life, are just at this very moment. We forget that life is just this moment. There are just seeing now, touching, hardness. Whatever arose a moment ago, was thought about a moment ago, is completely gone. Everyone can understand that life is at the present moment, but the point is: what is appearing now.

The conventional idea about mindfulness has nothing to do with understanding realities now.

Some people in the group who had asked Sarah to give a lecture, found that they were leading a good life since they did not kill and were generally kind. She explained to them that what one takes for wholesome or pure is clinging to oneself.

Through the development of understanding one realizes how little kusala there is in a day. Most of the time there are ignorance and attachment. What one takes for wholeome or pure is clinging to oneself.

Alan was wondering about the benefit of advancement in modern technology and science.

Acharn: Ignorance is ignorance, attachment is attachment. In the past or today there are seeing, hearing, smelling, tasting, experiencing tangible object and thinking. There is no one there at all. Thinking of being more advanced is just thinking. Only a story.

Sarah: There is no point in comparing... We know that the goal is the development of understanding and this has nothing to do with modern technology or science. It comes back to what is the reality at this moment. Seeing now is not different from seeing 2500 years ago. Life is at this moment, otherwise there are just arguments about which one is better or more advanced.

It is difficult to understand dhamma as anattā, not in anyone's control. People like to control life. There can be a beginning to understand seeing now which is not in anyone's control. It just arises by conditions.

Nina

18.14 Saturday discussion XIX. 4

Nina
11/19/20 #165278

Is there now dukkha?

Dear friends,

Acharn: Is there now dukkha?

Alan: Yes, but it is not understood.

Acharn: Is understanding also dukkha? The truth can be known. Letting go little by little ignorance and the idea of self, attachment. Is this the way to enlightenment?

Alan: Yes.

Acharn: Is there any other way? Is there advancing now?

Alan: A tiny bit of advancing, a little bit more understanding of the present moment.

Acharn: The first truth, "This is dukkha", not everyone knows. What arises falls away, never to return. Is it dukkha? There is attachment to that. The benefit in life is understanding the truth. There will be more confidence, saddhā.

Alan: Yes, for sure.

Acharn: The understanding of this moment is paññā pāramī and it leads to other pāramīs because there is less attachment, aversion and ignorance by conditions.

What about thinking of the truth instead of thinking about the advance of science. Where is the world, the crisis of the world? It is here, each moment of the arising and falling away of the absolute truth. There can be a moment of thinking of letting go of attachment and ignorance. When there is no condition for paññā there is no thinking about that. Even this is conditioned.

What about seeing now? Not anyone. Wrong understanding that someone is there is accumulated each moment. Understanding of the absolute truth conditions more respect to the Buddha, the Dhamma and the Sangha. There can be conditions for listening and reflecting wisely on the Buddha's words which are not easy to understand. Attachment hinders understanding of the arising and falling away of realities. It pays attention to the next reality, knowing that it is not the same one as a moment ago.

There is no one at all, no matter we hear harsh words or experience undesirable objects, there is no one there. Be kind, generous, forgiving, more and more with understanding.

Sarah to Zofia: You are a doctor, do you have any comments about the discussion on the advancement of modern science and Dhamma?

Zofia understands that science and the Dhamma have completely different goals. They are incomparable.

Sarah: Some people think that the world is now more advanced and that the Buddha's teachings are out of date. But what is real now is just the same as at the Buddha's time. The development of understanding has nothing to do with advance in technology, engineering. That is just the world of concepts, not the understanding of Dhamma.

Nina

18.15 Saturday discussion, XIX, 5

Nina
11/20/20 #165286

Impermanence is dukkha

Dear friends,

Nina: I find it very helpful that Acharn said that we are only this person in this life. No more in the next life.

Acharn: It takes time for everyone to think carefully of what is heard, before there can be understanding. Is seeing advanced now? It takes time to understand what is seeing, what is meant by advancement. There is the idea to think in terms of science, as one has accumulated. But it is only thinking, no matter what is thought about. It can just think of the idea that is conditioned by saññā (remembrance) and the object that is experienced is taken for "something".

What about the understanding of the absolute truth of this moment? Seeing has conditions to arise. It sees and is gone completely, never to arise again. Is this true or not? Impermanence is dukkha, it is the arising and falling away of each reality. No one can change the truth at all. Is there advancement of thinking, of seeing? Seeing is only seeing, it does not think. Even the word advancement, what is the truth? It is only thinking about different ideas which are heard. It is gone, it cannot last. There is the impermanence of everything: it has conditions to arise and fall away, that is all. Who can change this truth?

Everyone is going to die. Can the scientist change this, to understand the way not to die? Impossible. What is meant by ignorance, what by wisdom?

Who can condition right understanding? Only the words of the Buddha. Enlightenment is so great, not just learning or understanding. The absolute truth is each moment, now. It is what appears now. It shows that no one is there.

Seeing just sees, never to arise again. Is it beneficial to cling to what is no more? The four noble Truths have to be experienced by paññā, not only by thinking, that is not enough. It is not enough to eradicate the accumulated idea of self in saṃsāra. How can anyone take it (the accumulation) away from citta? Only paññā can learn to understand the truth little by little, to understand the truth as the truth, as no one. This is forgotten. Even hearing now is "I". There is not enough understanding.

Paññā develops little by little, so that there is more confidence. The sotāpanna is more confident than the person who has not attained enlightenment yet. Completely gone, nothing at all, that is the meaning of anattā.

Those who listen to the teachings begin to let go, little by little, until it conditions direct awareness with understanding. It is based on the intellectual understanding of that moment as it is, clearer and clearer. It takes a long time. The perfection of patience, khanti pāramī, does not give up the development of understanding to be great enough to experience directly the truth, right now. What we are talking about will lead to direct awareness of what is there now. Otherwise we just talk about seeing, hearing, without direct understanding of any reality now. Paññā is not developed to that degree yet. The pāramīs are the only way to let go the idea of self, to eradicate wrong understanding completely.

It needs considering carefully what is heard, to condition more confidence in the truth, not going away from this moment... One day there must be conditions, by hearing again and again, for a better understanding of the difference between intellectual understanding and direct understanding. It is so natural and confirms the truth that no one can make it arise.

Nina

18.16 Saturday discussion XX, 1

Nina
11/22/20 #165316

One moment of experiencing an object

Dear friends,

Acharn: Realities arise and fall away in split-seconds. We see a glass. Each visible object is together with hardness, softness (and other rūpas of the four great elements) but those do not impinge on the eye-sense. Visible object impinges (on the eye-sense), kamma produces seeing. Everything appears together, but in reality there is just one moment of experiencing an object. Whatever appears is the nimitta, the image, of that reality which arises and falls away continuously, to form up the idea of "something" there. Only one reality cannot be experienced. What is now appearing is only an image of what arises and falls away countless times. Since that nimitta can be known as different from other nimittas there can be understanding of that characteristic which is different from other realities. It is real but the moments of the arising and falling away cannot be known yet.

Just nimittas are experienced, the nimittas of the five khandhas: rūpa nimitta, vedanā (feeling) nimitta, saññā nimitta, saṅkhāra nimitta, viññāna nimitta. What appears is the image of different realities. So many appear and disappear, but the image is there to be known. It cannot be anything or anyone, it has its own characteristic, no matter it has fallen way. The next one is similar but not the same. That is why the object does not appear clearly. It appears a little more clearly when paññā develops to the different degrees of understanding.

For example, we are talking about seeing as not me, but what is seen now? It is gone, but the image is there to be known.

Nina: A question about the different levels of anattā.

Acharn: We are talking about seeing, about the intellectual understanding only. It cannot be taken for anyone, without conditions there cannot be the arising of seeing. Can there be understanding as not me? It arises because of conditions. The truth of it does not appear yet. We are talking about seeing while it is gone all the time. Without intellectual understanding there are no conditions to understand seeing at the moment of seeing only. Seeing is not hearing. There is (the idea of) someone all the time until one reality is considered carefully: it has conditions to arise and to appear.

When we are talking about seeing there are so many things arising. Even while talking many realities arise and fall away, unknown. There is no understanding of the moment of seeing. Seeing of what? Of what impinges on the eye-base. Who can do that, who can control it, it is gone.

When anger arises there is an idea of: I do not like it, I can stop it. But understand: it is gone completely. We live in the world of ignorance, in darkness, not understanding what is there as it is.

Whatever appears we take it as "something" there. There is the idea of something we do not know yet. From hearing and considering there can be conditions for thinking about it (reality), and even thinking is not self. Can anyone stop thinking about it? It is the beginning of intellectual understanding of that characteristic as only a reality, different from other realities, like hardness is not seeing. When hardness appears, it is true, nothing is there. Hardness appears, it has to be just hardness. There are not enough conditions yet to understand it more and more clearly, to understand the moment of its arising and falling away. It appears as nimitta, depending on understanding.

Nina

18.17 Saturday discussion XX, 2

Nina
11/23/20 #165322

Understanding will let go clinging

Dear friends,

Acharn: At this moment there are so many realities, not just one, but all of them fall away instantly, all the time. Understanding will let go clinging little by little, and this is intellectual understanding. Its function is to understand, little by little, having heard about the truth. But it is not yet the direct experiencing (of the truth). There must be doubt about what is not considered as it is, as no one.

Seeing cannot be anything else, it just arises to see, it is not anyone. Without the eye-base there cannot be any seeing. The object has to impinge on it to be experienced. It is so subtle, so intricate. There has to be hearing the truth of it again and again. When there is more understanding what is heard there will be more confidence.

One cannot choose the reality which appears because it is gone completely. There is not only the chief of experiencing (N: citta), but also other realities that experience that object, different cetasikas. There is saññā (remembrance) of everything that is now appearing. There is attachment to whatever is there, because of ignorance, not understanding the arising and falling away of realities, only once in saṃsāra. This has to be considered in order to understand that there is no one at all.

It is very natural: (it concerns) what is now appearing: Seeing, hearing, thinking, visible object which is seen, it is now. How deep it is, how subtle it is. Attā (self) is there. The way is longer and longer with akusala, with wrong understanding.

So now, no "I", but that is only thinking. What about seeing now? There cannot be precise understanding of what is nāma, the experience, and that which is rūpa, in the beginning this is impossible. There is the beginning of understanding (the distinction between) awareness at the level of intellectual understanding and the direct awareness of what is now appearing. It shows its anattāness. There is not enough (paññā) to understand it, and it is not "I" at all. Each word (of the teachings) is about the understanding of anattā. Consider it until there is a beginning to understand the meaning of it. It is not as clear as vipassanā ñāna yet.

Nina

18.18 Saturday discussion XX, 3

Nina
11/24/20 #165333

All pāramīs (come) from understanding

Dear friends,

Acharn: Paññā begins to develop to understand the characteristic (of reality), not just the word. It needs the pāramīs: khanti pāramī, sacca pāramī (truthfulness), nekkhamma pāramī (renunciation), adiṭṭhāna pāramī (determination). All pāramīs (come) from understanding, it cannot be any other way. Just one moment is not enough.

Nina: We tend to forget that the pāramīs are the only way to let go of self. We have discussed how beneficial are viriya and khanti, determination and evenmindedness. They help not to become disheartened when there is a long way to go.

Acharn: That is why one should listen more. All is "me". There are not enough conditions to even think of the truth. For example, when hardness appears, to think: "It is not me, it is just hardness." It appears for such a short time, because other objects are there, now, all the time.

Sukin: We usually think of other things with attachment and ignorance.

Acharn: There are not enough conditions. Thinking is anattā. It needs great khanti and viriya. It is impossible to let go the idea of "I will think, I will try."

The understanding of anattāness is the way to let go the wrong understanding. If there is concern about oneself, it hinders.

Akusala is all around. Paññā develops in the midst of akusala, at the moment of seeing or hearing. That is why it takes a long time.

Sacca pāramī is not afraid of whatever arises, even of akusala. Whatever is there, there is no doubt about the nature of no one, until there can be conditions for vipassanā ñāna.

No need to try to know an object because it is there, it is known directly.

Tam: How to experience one object at a time?

Acharn: What are there between seeing and hearing? We think of a cup. How many moments?

Tam: Uncountable. A million moments of seeing.

Acharn: That is why all appear as nimitta.

Nina

18.19 Saturday discussion, XX,4

Nina
11/25/20 #165337

Dhammāyatana

Dear friends,

Sarah: The development of the pāramīs has to be very natural, not trying to have them or wishing to have them. The clinging to the self comes in all the time, making life difficult.

Alberto asks for more explanation of dhammāyatana. (N: āyatana means the coming together, the meeting of different realities.)

Acharn: What is āyatana? They are different realities. Citta and cetasika are indivisible, āyatana is their meeting. When there is seeing there are different āyatanas: the experience is manāyatana, there is rūpāyatana (N: eye-sense and visible object), there are cetasikas which are dhammāyatana. When there is āyatana, they are together.

Is there āyatana now? Not the word, but the truth. Is there cakkāyatana (eye-sense)? Only at the moment of seeing, together with the other āyatanas, at the meeting moment.

Alberto: Are there at the moment of thinking manāyatana and dhammāyatana?

Sarah: When subtle rūpas like masculinity and femininity are objects of understanding (for highly developed understanding) they are āyatanas when they are objects of understanding.

Your question was, when a mental object such as lobha is the object of understanding, whether it can be āyatana. It does not matter, because at that moment it is the object of experience.

It is āyatana at the moment of being experienced, like subtle rūpa, otherwise subtle rūpa could not be āyatana. When cetasika or subtle rūpa is the object of understanding, it is āyatana. The reason is not that it has fallen away already, like lobha, but it can be object of understanding.

Nibbāna can be dhammāyatana. Visible object experienced through the mind-door can be dhammāyatana.

It is the coming together of different realities, no matter they have fallen away. Like heart-base, it is āyatana (N: when it is experienced by highly developed paññā).

Nina

18.20 Saturday discussion, XX, 5

Nina
11/26/20 #165354

Ārammaṇa

Dear friends,

Acharn: We have to distinguish whether we are talking about ārammaṇa (object) or āyatana. As to ārammaṇa, we talk about what is experienced as object of experience. No matter what is experienced, it is ārammaṇa. When we talk about āyatana, what are there (N: associating, meeting) at that very moment?

What is meant by the characteristic of mind-door? It is beyond imagination, beyond thinking. Until it appears. Then there is no doubt what is meant by mind-door, different from the sense-door.

Develop understanding of what is there, from hearing, considering, until there is more and more understanding, firmer and firmer. There are not only different sense-doors, but also mind-door in between each doorway. The Dhamma is very subtle and deep; it can be known that this moment is arising and falling away so rapidly, as Buddha taught.

Nina

18.21 Saturday discussion, XXI, 1

Nina
11/27/20 #165369

What is touched now?

Dear friends,

Alberto: Even the pāramīs can be taken for self.

Acharn: When there is not yet the understanding of the arising and falling away of realities, there must be the idea of permanence until right understanding from hearing and considering is accumulated with patience and viriya.

Each word of the teachings is very subtle, like "appearing well".

Icaro likes to hear more about suññāta (emptiness).

Acharn: What is meant by anattā, and what by suññāta.

Icaro: Anattā means no self, suññāta means emptiness.

Acharn asked Icaro several questions about what rūpa is, what touching is.

Acharn: What is touching, is there touching?

Icaro: I touch my cheek, it is a physical perception. Touching is only a word.

Acharn: If it is only a word, it is not true. (Transcription by Sarah) What is touched now? Not a chin or a cheek, but just hardness. It's thinking which imagines chins and cheeks and bodies and selves. Touching is a citta which experiences hardness. No self is there to experience anything, just touching or body-consciousness which experiences hardness for an instant and then is gone never to return. The hardness is a rūpa which also arises for an instant and when it impinges on body-sense it's experienced by that citta. After having arisen it's also gone, never to arise again. That's why it's suññāta. (End of transcription)

Acharn: Is seeing real? Seeing just sees, it is a reality. Is seeing real or not real?

Icaro: Not real. The only real thing is the "I".

Acharn: Is there "I" now? What is there at this moment?

Can we say: there is seeing, there is thinking, but no "I"? Because seeing sees, hearing hears, no "I". Without the ear-base and sound, there cannot be hearing. There are conditions to condition whatever appears now. What is real has its own characteristic. Smell cannot be sound, sound cannot be smell. Whatever falls away, never to arise again is the meaning of anattā.

No one there. Each reality has its own condition. Without the eye there cannot be seeing, without the ear, there cannot be hearing. That is why there is no "I".

Even right now, what is there falls away completely. Where is the "I"? Wrong understanding takes it for "something". Something is in Pāli "attā". Anattā is not anything. It is better to understand each word, clearer and clearer.

Seeing is not permanent. It is gone. The rapidity of the arising and falling away is not known, it looks as if it is permanent. There is seeing all day, but actually, it arises only once in saṃsāra. To understand anattā, what is there? Not something as a glass or a table, a person or an animal. It is that which can be seen. Seeing cannot be anything, it cannot belong to anything, because it is gone. That is the meaning of anattā. What is there is not permanent. Is there your cheek? It is gone forever, no "I" at all. Not under anyone's control is another word for anattā. The absolute truth cannot be changed. What is the world? If nothing arises, can there be the world?

19

December 2020

19.1 Saturday discussion XXI, 2

Nina
12/01/20 #165439

Patience develops

Dear friends,

There was a discussion about ārammaṇa (object) and āyatana, which are different classifications. Sarah explained that āyatana is always about the association or meeting of different dhammas. They always refer to paramattha dhammas only. Ārammana is any object which is experienced, including concepts.

Alberto: There is āyatana at any moment.

Sarah: What is there right now?

Alberto: We can talk about the word, but it is there now.

Betty: On politics. Betty finds that we are so involved in stories and that we need a trigger that keeps us on track.

Sarah: That is something to do, no matter a trigger or a schedule. There are just dhammas that are anattā... By listening more and more, there will be less attachment to the wrong idea of something to be there, to be done, to a choice or selection that can be made.

Jonathan: It has to be accepted that understanding and awareness will be very occasional. The trigger is always an internal one, not an outside one.

Sarah: Patience develops with right understanding, to overcome the idea of "I can do something."

There was a discussion with Icaro about paññā.

Sarah: Can it last, can it arise every moment? At the moment of touching, can there be paññā? Seeing, hearing and touching experience their objects, paññā cannot arise with those cittas... In the beginning it has to be intellectual understanding that has to develop, in order that it can condition direct understanding. At the moment of wise consideration paññā must be there. Paññā never lasts, it falls away instantly.

Alan: Can we say: appearing well is another word for understanding?

Sarah: It refers to paññā that has been developed, for example, at the moment of satipaṭṭhāna, when it is direct understanding.

Alan: So, it is another word for direct understanding?

Sarah: It begins to appear well, more and more well.

Alan: I read in the beginning of the "Visuddhimagga" that if someone does not understand about conditions he cannot develop the Path. There would always be the idea of self developing. It is so important to know what is understood by conditions.

Sarah: There will always be the idea of "I" doing "something". Who can determine what touching touches now, what hearing will hear now... Understanding leads to more acceptance of conditions. Whatever arises cannot be any other way. It depends on the meeting or association of dhammas and the conditional nature of each moment.

Nina

19.2 Saturday discussion XXI, 4

Nina
12/03/20 #165477

The eye-door covers up the mind-door

Dear friends,

Azita had a question about sense-door and mind-door. It was said that the eye-door covers up the mind-door.

Sarah explained that the moment of experiencing tangible object is very brief and all ideas about my cheek that is soft are just thinking. Countless mind-door processes follow upon the brief moment of the experience through the body sense. It is the same with seeing. We think that we see people, that seeing lasts, but actually seeing visible object is very brief and it is followed by so many mind-door processes, thinking of something, a person, an idea.

Sarah: When it is said that the eye-door covers up the mind-door, it is because of ignorance and wrong view. It is because of the idea that there is something there, but just a moment of seeing is so brief. As understanding develops the mind-door becomes more apparent. There is so much more thinking than there is seeing.

Azita: For the development of jhāna there has to be the knowledge that the sense-door is dangerous?

Sarah: Like now, seeing experiences visible object so briefly. There is attachment instantly and then thinking about the stories, the dreams, the ideas. There is more and more disturbance in life because of seeing, hearing and bodily experiences. Understanding the danger of that attachment and how it is the opposite of calmness there is a condition for less and less clinging. There has to be the understanding of the danger of attachment and the nature of calm, the nature of kusala and akusala. Without the understanding of this it is impossible for calm to develop.

Nina: Sacca pāramī, the perfection of truthfulness, is important. You may say, I see the danger of seeing and hearing, but that may not be true. We all like seeing and hearing and want to to go on living. We are not sincere.

Sarah: We enjoy clinging so much. Better to develop understanding and be sincere. Nina: That is why Acharn emphasizes so much sacca pāramī.

Azita: If there is development of samatha, is there also the development of the pāramīs at that time?

Nina: Only if there is no self involved; there has to be right understanding of realities, otherwise there is no pāramī.

Sarah explained that calm arises with all kinds of kusala. Samatha that arises with the development of satipaṭṭhāna is "higher calm". It develops naturally with the understanding of realities. It is higher than samatha without the understanding of dhammas as anattā because it is part of the Path.

Nina

19.3 Saturday discussion XXI, 5

Nina
12/04/20 #165482

Jhāna is dukkha

Dear friends,

Tadao asked a question in relation to viparināma dukkha, dukkha because of change. Why is desire the cause of dukkha?

Sarah: When clinging is eradicated there will be no more life in saṃsāra, no more dukkha. Clinging is the condition for going on in saṃsāra, or the arising of dukkha again, again and again, lifetime after lifetime.

Even paññā or jhāna is dukkha, it is not permanent, not satisfactory, worth clinging to.

Tadao: Is it possible to see the four noble Truths in just this moment?

Sarah: I think that understanding begins to develop and will be firmer and firmer. Sacca ñāna is the firm intellectual understanding, the beginning of understanding of the four noble Truths. It begins to understand that what is arisen now is dukkha and that the cause of dukkha is attachment. That the only way (to its ceasing) is the development of understanding, not "I" doing anything. Whatever is conditioned is unsatisfactory and Nibbāna is the dhamma that is not dukkha. This is the beginning of understanding of the four noble Truths until it is the direct understanding of realities and then it is kicca ñāna, a deeper understanding of the four noble Truths, leading to kata ñāna when it is vipassanā ñāna. The commentary to the sutta "Setting in motion the wheel of Dhamma" explains these three levels.

Nina: Understanding the four noble Truths is just at this moment, not just words. Everyone can say that.

Tadao: Some people are more inclined to understand what appears through the eyedoor, others what appears through the ear-door?

Sarah: It depends on the accumulated tendencies.

Nina: this shows how anattā it is. It all depends on conditions.

Sarah: If there is any expectation, one goes wrong.

Tam Bach asked why the heart-base is not an inner āyatana.

Sarah: The Buddha taught what appears and what is apparent... We can think on and on and forget what appears at this moment.

Sarah explained that all subtle rūpas are included in dhammāyatana.

Nina

19.4 Saturday discussion XXII, 1

Nina
12/06/20 #165507

Four nāma-khandhas are taken for self

Dear friends,

The four nāma-khandhas are taken for self, even right now. Feeling, saññā (remembrance) and saṅkhāra khandha (fifty cetasikas) are not known. Like now, are there enough conditions (to know the truth)? It takes years and years, a long time, to let go the idea of self. The words of the Buddha in the Vinaya, the Suttanta and the Abhidhamma are all about now. Seeing, hearing, thinking, like, dislike, hardness, softness, sound, all day, they are nothing, completely gone. Khanika marana (momentary death) from moment to moment; unknown until the Buddha had enlightened.

Sarah: You mentioned that pleasant feeling and unpleasant feeling which are dukkha are a condition for more mettā to all human beings. Just the fact that any feeling is dukkha conditions more mettā. Someone had a question about this.

Acharn: Is the point of the question to have more mettā or to have less attachment to mettā?

Sarah: There should be less attachment, that is a condition for more mettā.

Acharn: Mettā is like any reality. It is conditioned to arise and fall away like other realities. All saṅkhāra dhammas are impermanent, dukkha and anattā. If there is more understanding and less clinging it indicates that paññā has developed to the degree that it can understand any reality as just dukkha, arising and falling away. It does not belong to anyone. Even mettā is there, and it is gone, but no understanding of the five khandhas. When there is a moment of meeting anyone, what is there, what kind of feeling? It is paññā which understands what is there. Can there be kindness, no matter what happens? It is not the matter of trying to understand and have more mettā. Understand that it is just a reality. Paññā begins to condition more and more kusala. All beings are the same. Is there kindness or is there no thought about the welfare of others as usual, or no thought about that person?

When we hear that all beings are the same it can condition moments of thinking of what is the same; they like pleasant objects and dislike unpleasant objects. What is the best one can do at such a moment? It is time to understand the truth. Is there kindness or is there not paying attention to the other's welfare? It has nothing to do with this or that person. They are exactly the same. Everything goes on as usual, but understanding begins to understand that which is not self. When there is no understanding of "I", one clings to the idea of "I". One has mettā, but actually, there is no one there. One realizes that only hardness is there and this is from understanding that all beings are the same. I and others may be in different situations. There is no selection, no trouble.

Nina: Mettā, because all beings are the same. I find that point a bit difficult.

Acharn: What is difficult?

Nina: All beings are the same.

Acharn: Are they not?

Nina: Citta, cetasika and rūpa.

Acharn: It does not belong to anyone at all. No he, she, I. Only a reality which is different from other realities. Mettā is different from lobha. Mettā is kindness, friendliness. One begins to understand that characteristic, any time, by conditions. No selection, thinking that I would like to study this situation, whether I have mettā or not. One has to understand reality as reality, they are all real. That is the only way to let go. Understanding can grow little by little. The understanding of the truth is that there is no one. It (reality) just arises and falls away in split-second, why bother? It is gone. It is very difficult to let go of the idea of self; It has to be by paññā only, performing its function of no attachment, less clinging.

Jonothan: When Acharn says that all beings are the same, it means that all beings are to be regarded equally, without favouritism, like or dislike. Mettā is towards all equally.

Sarah: Pleasant and unpleasant feeling are common to everyone, conditioned dhammas. There is not this or that person, they are just conditioned dhammas. What arises is just dhamma, not belonging to anyone. That is a condition to have more mettā. Without understanding we think that this person is a good person, that person is a bad person. There is not this special person or that special person. It is a very deep topic. It all comes back to the understanding of dhamma as anattā. The less favouritism or thinking of "that person" there is, the more conditions there are for mettā to anyone one can be friendly to.

Nina

19.5 Saturday discussion, XXII, 2

Nina
12/07/20 #165525

No being in this world

Dear friends,

Tadao: We are trying to understand citta, cetasika and rūpa, no being in this world. Why should we develop mettā which requires beings as object? Why is mettā emphasized in Buddhism?

Acharn: Not only mettā but all kinds of kusala (are emphasized). What about understanding, what about compassion, karuṇā? When we talk about citta and cetasika, it does not mean only the word; they experience. We are so used to the word citta but do not understand that it is now, it is experiencing. When there is seeing, there is experiencing. We use the word citta all the time, but we forget its characteristic now. (We should know) not only the word citta, but its nature of experiencing now, any time, any moment in this life, (but) unknown.

Is there mettā now, what is there now to be known? It depends on one's accumulations for anything to arise.

One may have mettā and understand it as not self. No choice. It depends on whether there is understanding of different realities.

Tadao: No self, that means, no beings.

Jonothan: Sometimes we use the term being as shorthand for citta, cetasika and rūpa. When we say that mettā has beings as object, that means that the object is someone else's citta, cetasika and rūpa, apart from ourselves. The purpose is to see that all conditioned dhammas are not self. What we take for being is just a conditioned reality. There is no contradiction or conflict. When talking about mettā that has a being as object, there is a reference to the citta, cetasika and rūpa of others.

Tadao: The "Divine Abidings"(brahma vihāras) are necessary, but we are looking for sati and paññā which understand realities as they are.

Jonothan: We know what the conditions for the development of understanding are. The first one is hearing the Dhamma. The development of the Brahmavihāras can be done by people who have not heard any Dhamma.

The hearing of the Dhamma is independent on whatever level of mettā and karuṇā may have been developed already.

Tadao: Why is it necessary to develop mettā for a better understanding of reality? I think mettā is a very good quality, a very important quality for everyone, but is it necessary to develop mettā?

Jonothan: It will develop, regardless it is necessary or not. If one thinks that mettā is necessary for understanding to develop that is a mistaken perception. The Buddha never said that there have to be the development of the Brahmavihāras for the development of understanding. As Acharn explained: understand what is appearing at the present moment.

Sarah: When there is no understanding of the nature of reality, can there be understanding whether there is mettā or not? We know that there are so many different realities. Mettā is not the moment of karuṇā or upekkhā. When there is the understanding of mettā as not self, there can be the understanding of the characteristic of mettā when it is there. Mettā is the characteristic of adosa. When there is no being how can it be such? When a being is there, is there thinking with mettā, dosa or attachment? We have to understand the truth of each reality as it is, instead of saying she, he or I have mettā.

What is mettā? Otherwise we (just) think that there is mettā. What about so much attachment?

Tadao: Mettā is difficult to experience.

Sarah: Citta now, is it easy to experience? It depends on understanding, not just the word. Its characteristic is there. There is seeing now, hearing, thinking, every moment is different. There is not yet the understanding of the nature of citta as not self. It is there in thought, but what about the moment it is there? That is why it needs more development of understanding, to be sure, confident in the truth.

Nina

19.6 Saturday discussion, XXII, 3

Nina
12/08/20 #165527

No self to be lost

Dear friends,

Acharn: Without the pāramīs it is impossible to let go clinging to the idea of self. If there is still the "I" who tries so much to understand (reality), it is wrong. It is easy to go wrong because of ignorance and clinging.

Tadao: There is fear of reality which is no self.

Acharn: It takes a long time to understand the truth (even) at the level of intellectual understanding.

Sarah: When there is understanding of dhamma there is less fear of losing self. One lives more easily, no self to be lost. Even right now there is just seeing, hearing, thinking and attachment. Different realities arising and falling away. What one is afraid of does not exist. As understanding develops, the pāramīs which include mettā develop with the understanding. When there is less clinging to oneself and one's own importance, it supports the development of understanding. Relinquishing the idea of self conditions more kusala.

Tadao: There are not many moments of mettā.

Sarah: Feeling ashamed, minding that there is not as much mettā as one would like is clinging to oneself. Just a passing dhamma, not my clinging.

Maeve spoke about taking realities for people and things. If she would not see Acharn any more she would miss her.

Acharn: I am glad to see you, no one can stop that kind of feeling by conditions. But there is no doubt about the characteristic which is rūpa or nāma. We may not meet again, we do not know the next moment. We should understand the truth of khanika marana, the death of each moment, but there can be less fear of whatever will come. It is just that moment of thought and then it is gone.

There can be more understanding of the truth of no one, nothing. All are conditioned realities. There can be less clinging and less akusala because of understanding anicca (impermanence), dukkha and anattā. No one at all. Even one moment is so very worth while, so precious, when it will condition understanding the truth little by little.

We are talking about different cetasikas but there is no direct understanding of what is there... Without intellectual understanding it is impossible to have direct awareness and understanding.

Nina

19.7 Saturday discussion, XXII, 4

Nina
12/09/20 #165535

Three kinds of bodhisatta

Dear friends,

Acharn: Paññā develops on and on with more confidence that no one can do anything. Otherwise there must be a moment with intention, even just a little bit. If this is known there will be less intention to be this or that. Be patient.

Not "I" but understanding conditions such patience, each life, little by little.

When it is time to understand even just a little more, there is a relief from ignorance, stage by stage, little by little. Relief from fear of anything, of death. Patience is there to protect one from akusala. When there is such understanding with the perfections, pāramīs, it is of a savaka bodhisatta. There are three kinds of bodhisatta: the bodhisatta who will be the Sammā-sambuddha, the bodhisatta who will be a Pacceka Buddha (silent Buddha, who realized the truth by himself but who does not proclaim it to the world), and the bodhisatta who will be a savaka Buddha (who will attain enlightenment as a true listener, who developed right understanding).

Tadao: What is the goal of (the state of) savaka bodhisatta?

Acharn: There is no hindrance to become an arahat, by conditions.

Tadao: The goal is understanding?

Acharn: Without understanding there cannot be any pāramī.

Tadao: It has to be with patience.

Acharn: Khanti pāramī. Patience not to like rūpa with ignorance all the time. Understanding what is kusala, what is akusala and kusala with paññā that is going to be a condition for enlightenment. It is so easy to say that seeing sees, but that is not enough, because seeing is not self. So, what is its nature: that which arises, otherwise it cannot see. There can be more kusala, thinking with mettā, just wanting to share. No one can change the characteristic of reality. Understanding understands it, it has conditions for more kusala.

Tadao: When I pass away, who is going to continue with sati and paññā? You often say that there is no Tadao.

Acharn: Who was there a moment ago? This moment is not a moment ago. There must be that which arises by conditions: anantara paccaya (contiguity condition) of each citta and cetasika. Who can stop anantara paccaya from what is now? As soon as it (citta) has gone completely, it conditions the next moment by anantara paccaya. The only citta that does not condition the next moment is the citta arising at the pariNibbāna of the arahat. No doubt how it (citta) can continue. But it is not the same one.

Tadao: That is a very hard point to understand.

Acharn: That is why the Buddha said after his enlightenment: (the dhamma is) very subtle, very difficult to understand. But since there can be a person who understands, he taught for the sake of all those who see the benefit of the truth. Khanti pāramī and adiṭṭhāna pāramī (determination) condition the moments to hear again and again, by conditions.

Sarah: Tadao, you said earlier that we listen and we think, but even the listening and the thinking are not "I", they are just different cittas that arise by conditions and fall away. In reality there is no "I" who can do anything. It is the same with the accumulation of sati and paññā, they accumulate by different conditions, by upanissaya paccaya (strong dependence condition), anantara paccaya. No I who can listen, no I who can think, no I who can make sati develop.

Acharn: There are different moments for everyone and everything. Even listening, or the moment of enlightenment, no selection. It all depends on conditions.

Maeve: We cannot know what the conditions are, they are complex, unknown.

Acharn: That is why there can be conditions for more confidence in anattāness, in all aspects. From understanding the truth of khanika marana, the death of each moment, there will be less fear of whatever will come. It is just that moment of thought and then it is gone. Another moment is conditioned instantly, so, how can anyone do anything. There can be a moment of understanding the truth of no one, nothing, all are conditioned realities. There can be less clinging, less dosa, less akusala because of the understanding of anicca, dukkha and anattā. Each moment of understanding is so very worth while, because it will condition other moments of understanding the truth.

Nina

19.8 Saturday discussion XXIII, 2

Nina
12/14/20 #165582

Truthfulnes

Dear friends,

Sarah (to Acharn): A very important point you make is that there is a little paññā at a time, a little consideration of what is appearing now. Of course there is a lot of attachment as usual. It is precious to have a little paññā, a little wise consideration on and on. This is the importance of khanti pāramī, the perfection of patience. No clinging to have more, or trying to find a short cut, trying to make it arise by focussing on something. Just being contented that it develops by conditions naturally.

Acharn: There should be letting go from the beginning of hearing the truth. There can be more and more understanding of the difference between intellectual understanding and direct understanding.

Tadao: We are full of the idea of self.

Sarah (to Tadao): Sacca pāramī, the perfection of truthfulness, has to develop. Develop understanding of what is appearing now. Truthfulness of what life is at this moment. It has to be developed with understanding of realities as not self from the beginning. It cannot be the perfection of truthfulness without understanding of nāma as nāma and rūpa as rūpa.

Tadao: There should be devotion to the Buddha, the Dhamma and the Sangha.

Sarah: What do you mean by devotion? Some people are very devoted but they have no understanding at all. Sacca, truthfulness, refers to the truth of what is conditioned at this very moment. Not taking wrong understanding for right understanding. The truth is that there is no arm, just softness that is touched. It is truthfulness that is developed with right understanding. It has nothing to do with common ideas about devotion and sincerity. Be truthful to this moment.

Tadao: Why is it so important to develop mettā?

Sarah: We think of people a lot, usually with attachment. Thinking with mettā when one has the other people's welfare at heart is precious. In the deepest sense even those moments of mettā are dukkha. They arise and fall away and can be object of clinging. They are anattā, they just arise by conditions, but still a moment of kusala is better than a moment of akusala. They support the development of understanding. When one is totally carried away, thinking of one's own needs and problems, there is not much support for understanding.

Tadao: I do not understand why mettā is so highly regarded. I do not think of anybody, I have no opportunity to develop mettā.

Sarah: What about now, you are talking to people now. It is a good opportunity to understand mettā now when it arises. It is the basis for the other brahma-vihāras (divine abidings). Mettā has to be there to support the joy in someone else's good fortune, and compassion when others suffer difficulties. It is adosa cetasika when other people are the object. Mettā is there.

Nina

19.9 Saturday discussion, XXIII, 3

Nina
12/15/20 #165607

The truth of reality conditions more mettā

Dear friends,

Acharn: Understanding the truth of reality conditions more mettā. Understand that mettā is a wholesome reality, and no one can make it arise. Understanding of the truth will bring more mettā while one thinks of the others who do not have enough understanding to see the danger of attachment and wrong understanding which takes realities for "I". When there is more understanding it conditions more wholesomeness as "not me." It is so very precious.

Tadao: Yes, anattā is very important. I think of anattā all the time.

Acharn: Who is thinking? There is no understanding that actually, in the absolute sense, there is "no me". Patience is needed to understand that there is no one there at all. Without conditions it cannot arise.

Azita: A question about saññā. If saññā arises and falls away, we do not remember in a next life anything of this life or of a former life. Why do we remember the Dhamma? How does it work?

Acharn: Who remembers? Saññā marks and remembers. Can it arise without conditions? It depends on conditions. Now we think:

"Does saññā remember this and this". But saññā remembers what is appearing, together with the citta that experiences it, and that will bring more understanding of no one, no self. Saññā is saññā, vitakka is vitakka cetasika. Saññā remembers but it cannot perform the function of vitakka, thinking about what is remembered. At the moment of thinking there must be saññā as well, but saññā is not vitakka.

Azita: When listening to Dhamma, saññā marks and vitakka thinks about what is marked. If we hear the Dhamma again, we have an interest in what has been heard.

Sarah: When we hear the Dhamma, paññā accumulates when it arises, little by little. Because of that accumulated paññā, the hearing makes some sense and there is the interest to hear and consider more. In another life the paññā that has been accumulated conditions more understanding to develop when there are the right conditions. In the same way kusala saññā that arises with paññā, marking and remembering the right object also accumulates so that what has been understood is not forgotten. But if one remembers just names, details, terms without any understanding, they will be forgotten.

When there is the habit of being kind, that tendency accumulates, when there is the habit of being angry or fearful, that tendency accumulates. In the same way, when there is kusala saññā with understanding, it accumulates.

Nina

19.10 Saturday discussion XXIII 4

Nina
12/16/20 #165624

Paññā is difficult

Dear friends,

Alan: The development of paññā is difficult, because it is natural to have attachment after seeing. When we talk about mettā, we cannot have it at will. To develop mettā seems to be an impossible task.

Sarah: Usually, when we have an idea to develop mettā, we are clinging to "I", wanting to have mettā again instead of understanding it as a conditioned dhamma that just arises naturally, when there are conditions.

When there is mettā, the citta is calm, it is like a holiday from being obsessed as usual, from clinging as usual, from being disturbed. It is a kind of letting go. The more understanding there is, the more wholesome states develop naturally. But it depends on conditions whether there will be attachment or mettā. Each reality is conditioned and anattā. Otherwise there is no letting go, just thinking about "I".

Q: Do people have more mettā in a country like Thailand ?

Sarah: It is like making generalizations. We do not even know for ourselves whether there is mettā or attachment. How can we judge other people? We just think of a story that these people have a lot of mettā. It is just a conventional idea, not understanding Dhamma.

Nina

19.11 Saturday discussion, XXIII, 5

Nina
12/17/20 #165638

Remorse about something that happened

Dear friends,

Tadao: Had a question about remorse. He has remorse about something that happened in his life.

Sarah: It is all gone. There is just thinking about it again and again.

Tadao: I do not want to remember it just before my death.

Sarah: No one can control what kind of thought arises now, or before death or in a next life.

Tadao: There is no way to avoid unpleasant feeling when thinking of death.

Sarah: Understand how useless it is, (thinking of) just a dhamma that is past. There is death at each moment now. Why waste time with remorse and worry about what happened. It is conditioned, but understanding that they are dhammas which are not self is helpful. It has to be that way by conditions, like thinking now. It cannot be any other way.

Tadao: The best way is the understanding of non-self.

Sarah: The understanding of dhamma that has to be that way by conditions. No one can stop akusala from arising, or fear from arising. Whatever arises is by conditions. When accumulated tendencies are so strong, it has to be like that.

Tadao: I am afraid of my defilements. Without aversion about people, my life would be much easier.

Sarah: Each moment of thinking, of accumulated tendency is conditioned. Each moment of aversion, of fear, is conditioned, it can arise unexpectedly any time.

Tadao: Wrong view has to be eradicated.

Sarah: The Buddha spoke about living alone, not in any secluded place, without company. It is living alone without attachment. So it comes back to the understanding.

Acharn: What about "I" who is thinking? It is by conditions that one thinks of such or such object. When will there be listening to the teachings to understand the truth. It is so very difficult to understand it, even if it is now appearing.

Seeing now, thinking now, no one is there at all. They are different kinds of reality. They fall away in split-seconds, never to return again. Understanding can condition letting go of wrong understanding of self. It depends on whether one can understand the benefit of the truth of no self, no one at all.

There is touching hardness, and one reality at a time appears. It depends on conditions to directly understand what is there. Even hardness is not known as no thing in it, no finger, table or chair. What about Sāriputta's paññā? It did not show up until hearing the words of Asajji. The paññā that had been accumulated for so long could understand those words to the degree of direct experience. The accumulation of paññā was enough to condition that moment. There was no doubt about the experience of hardness and about hardness as that which is experienced. Hearing again and again can condition direct experience of such objects as not "I". Only that which appears now can be known, no matter it is pleasant or unpleasant. With understanding one lives more easily.

Nina

19.12 Saturday discussion XXIV, 1

Nina
12/20/20 #165700

Worldly beings are like mad people

Dear friends,

Sarah: The Buddha said that all worldly beings are like mad people because of not understanding the truth of life. One thinks: What should I do in this or that situation, controlling life.

Alan: The arahat is described as sane. So much thinking is useless, thinking that a self can control things or has responsibility to do things.

Sarah: Even when one thinks what the most useful way is to help others it seems beneficial, but behind it there is the idea of what should "I" do. It is not the understanding of reality now as anattā.

Acharn: Is seeing dying now?

Alan: Each moment is dying.

Acharn: Are you afraid?

Alan: I am not afraid of that. But the opportunity for hearing Dhamma is extremely rare. In my next life it probably won't happen. It is so rare to hear the right words. Not having access to the Dhamma means a lot of trouble.

Acharn: Are you afraid to die?

Alan: I am not quite ready to die. When there is right understanding one is free from fear of death.

Acharn: Everyone is afraid of Covid so long as there is the idea of self. Only paññā can understand that moment as it is.

Alan: There is not "somebody" who has Covid.

Acharn: It takes time to consider how much ignorance there is of each moment that appears as some "thing" all the time.

Alan: It is very easy to think that you have awareness when you do not have awareness.

Acharn: Different degrees of sati should be understood as indriya, as bala (strength), sammā-sati, sati of satipaṭṭhāna.

Nina

19.13 Saturday discussion, XXIV, 2

Nina
12/21/20 #165705

Different levels of sati

Dear friends,

Huong asked about different levels of sati.

Acharn: Is there sati now? Is sati there as not self?

Huong: Yes.

Acharn: How do you know? What is its object? The reality of sati does not appear as no "I". Then it is useless to talk about it. We are talking about seeing. Seeing is not self, it is that which sees. This is the beginning to understand why it is so deep, so subtle. There is no one that can be self or permanent? Little by little just one word can be understood as it is.

We have heard a lot about sati, but when it is there does it appear as object of understanding? If it does not appear how can there be the understanding of it as "no one there"?

It is conditioned to arise unexpectedly when there is enough development of understanding. Understanding grows little by little. Sati is not paññā, it cannot perform the function of understanding. Paññā cannot arise without sati.

Sati does not appear yet, there is not enough understanding to let go the idea of self. One has to learn the truth that nothing can be taken for self.

Sati arises by conditions and it falls away instantly, never to return. How can there be understanding of what is gone, there can only be understanding of what is there now and it can be known little by little. It seems that it is still there but it is gone. Nothing is there.

Pariyatti (intellectual understanding) has to be very clear and firm, otherwise it cannot condition direct awareness. Then there is no doubt about the characteristic of sati. It has to arise with paññā which is conditioned by intellectual understanding. What appears now is actually gone. It is ignorance to cling to what is no more, what is never the same. It looks as if it is the same.

Huong: We always forget about realities, the "I" is always there.

Acharn: Listen again to have stronger understanding. Firm understanding of the truth, little by little, by conditions.

Sarah: Sati has to arise with kusala moments, not yet as faculty (indriya), that is only at the moment of satipaṭṭhāna, when there is direct understanding and direct awareness of realities. Or when it is bala, strong and powerful, at a higher level. Sammā-sati usually refers to sati as path-factor.

When there is right considering of the nature of seeing now as anattā, sati is there with those kusala moments. It is like a precursor or the way that leads to the Path, to sammā-sati of the Path.

Nina

19.14 Saturday discussion XXIV, 3

Nina
12/23/20 #165746

This moment is Abhidhamma

Dear friends,

Lukas: Studying dhamma is very hard.

Acharn: This moment is Abhidhamma, right? No one, that is Abhidhamma. What is not taken for anything at all. There may be no understanding of the truth of that which is conditioned to arise. Just to arise and then fall away.

Lukas: I lack motivation, I need more effort to better understand.

Acharn: Does effort belong to anyone?

Lukas: No, it does not.

Acharn: Can it be wrong effort?

Lukas: There are right effort and wrong effort, mostly wrong effort.

Acharn: How can there be right effort? What is the difference between right effort and wrong effort? Wrong effort arises with wrong understanding.

Lukas: When there is the idea of "I" and me, there is wrong effort.

Acharn: Can there be right effort?

Lukas: Only with right understanding.

Acharn: It is by conditions.

Lukas: What kind of condition?

Acharn: Understanding that there is no one there. Understanding arises because of conditions, only very shortly, then it is completely gone, never to return. Can anyone make effort arise? That is the beginning of understanding, but not firm understanding yet.

Actually, there are different realities, no "I" or self at all. This is why we learn the teachings of the Buddha. There is effort, but no one can condition the arising of effort. With ignorance it is wrong effort. When there is understanding it begins to be right effort, little by little. There are viriya pāramī and khanti pāramī. Right effort arises only with paññā. When there is effort with kusala but without paññā, it cannot be a pāramī, perfection.

There can be a little more understanding about no self. No self is not just the word, but the truth of whatever appears now. No one can make it arise without conditions. Is there effort now? When it does not appear as object of understanding there must be the idea of "my effort" all the time.

Lukas: I do not understand and this is like madness and suffering.

Acharn: So long as reality does not appear as object of understanding, there cannot be understanding of the truth of no self. Even paññā is nobody. It arises and performs its function of understanding. Hearing about the truth of reality now can bring about the understanding whether there is right or wrong understanding. When there is wrong understanding paññā knows that it is wrong. It conditions wrong speech and wrong deeds because of ignorance of what is right or wrong. In a day all are dhammas, different by conditions.

Nina

19.15 Saturday discussion, XXIV, 4

Nina
12/24/20 #165759

Anattāness is there, every moment

Dear friends,

Acharn: There is not enough considering of what is "me". Is there "I"? No "I", not anything until it appears as it is by understanding, little by little. Letting go the idea of self, little by little. Each moment is unknown until hearing the teachings and considering wisely what the truth is and what is not. What is true now?

Lukas: There is a moment now.

Acharn: What is that moment? What is there now that is not conditioned? You know the Buddha as what?

Lukas: The Buddha is enlightened.

Acharn: When there is no understanding of his words, can you know the Buddha?

Lukas: Whatever arises has to fall away and all is anattā.

Acharn: Why did he teach for forty-five years?

Lukas: For people to understand Dhamma. That is quite clear to me.

Acharn: Keep on learning, studying so that paññā can develop little by little, to understand reality as not me, not "I". We are talking about seeing, which is not thinking, not hearing. What conditions such a moment of experiencing? What is there which is seen, by conditions only? What has not been there before can be there by conditions. Each moment of understanding is a moment of letting go. To understand the arising and falling away by conditions. Can we change that? Can we change the way it is?

Lukas: No. I wish I could, but it is impossible. I am trying my whole life.

Acharn: Why do you want to change?

Nina: I think that Lukas is very lucky to be able to come here. I know that Lukas understands so many things Acharn explains about conditioned reality as not self and that it cannot be changed. So many people are unable to listen to Acharn. I like to encourage Lukas. The dialogue between Acharn and Lukas is very useful to all of us. Do not underestimate it, Lukas. Lukas, you understand so much already, I can notice this from your words.

Acharn: When we talk about seeing, where is seeing now? Without the eye-base, how can there be seeing right now? When nothing impinges on the eye-base how can seeing see? Seeing sees what is impinging, not a table. How could that be a table? A moment of seeing is not taking it for some "thing".

Anattāness is there, every moment. Not attā. One or two moments of understanding is not enough. Listen again and again. There can be different degrees of understanding: pariyatti (intellectual understanding), paṭipatti (direct understanding) and pativedha (direct realisation of the truth).

When the arising and falling away of seeing is not directly experienced, it is always some "thing". There should not only be thinking about seeing. When sati is strong enough it is not only an indriya, but it can also be a bala, a power. There should be no expectation about this, it is the result of understanding from moment to moment so that there is more and more detachment, letting go the idea of self. It appears by conditions and then there will be more confidence in anattā.

Nina

19.16 Saturday discussion XXV, 1

Nina
12/27/20 #165814

The less idea of "I", the easier life is

Dear friends,

Acharn: Only one reality is the object of understanding as it is. It appears so shortly, no one knows that it is not there any more. It is just the way it is, there is no one there. One moment of understanding is very precious, it is a condition for understanding of no one, no thing.

Even now, what is there as "I"? It has been accumulated for aeons with ignorance. Understanding cleans up a little of misunderstanding. We have to understand the very fine line between the "I" and the thinking, and the "I" and the seeing, to understand the truth that there is actually no one at all.

Sarah: When you mention "the fine line", even then "I" can come in any time.

Acharn: So long as there are conditions for no understanding. Only understanding is the opposite.

Sarah: It can clean up just a little bit.

Acharn: Life is easy without trouble to try so much what is impossible.

Sarah: The less idea of "I", the easier life is.

Acharn: There can be a beginning to understand conditions. What is there is only by conditions. It is beneficial to talk about what is now appearing. Only different colours are seen, there is no one there, it is gone. What is not there is gone.

Sukin: Thinking is not awareness, but can there be thinking with understanding about what has fallen away?

Sarah: Thinking is there, it has to be known. Otherwise it is "I".

Sukin: It takes time to get closer and closer to the moment that there is a level of understanding, thinking about the Dhamma.

Acharn: Can there be a beginning to even think about it, not directly experiencing yet? There has to be conditions to think about what is heard too, otherwise how can it (understanding) develop? But there is not always hearing about what appears now. Even when there is not hearing (about the Dhamma) there are conditions for thinking and beginning to have a little less attachment, from time to time. Very, very little, but it is there.

Sukin: Is there any thinking about the reality?

Acharn: You want to think, or is it by conditions?

Sukin: By conditions.

Acharn: Try to understand that all dhammas (in our life) must be conditioned. There is no one at all, that is the absolute truth. Be patient to understand the truth. It is quite a relief. Paññā does not belong to anyone. It has to go on and on and on until there is no self at all. That can be realized. That moment is abhisamaya (enlightenment). By conditions when there is the opportunity to hear the right words, to consider (the Dhamma) from life to life.

Sukin: Can you say more about abhisamaya?

Acharn: It is the enlightenment of the four noble Truths. It is the greatest moment in saṃsāra. How far it is, how great it is.

Sukin: Is even intellectual understanding for us abhisamaya?

Acharn: Without understanding it is impossible. Each moment is very important, very precious.

Sarah: Only by understanding little by little, on and on.

Acharn: Magga-citta (path-consciousness which is lokuttara citta) is only once in saṃsāra. It can let go wrong understanding.

Sukin: You were referring to relief. Is that from ignorance and wrong view? When there is kusala, there is no akusala. Is that also a relief?

Acharn: When there is more understanding of conditioned realities it is quite a relief.

Nina

19.17 Saturday discussion, XXV, 2

Nina
12/28/20 #165821

Dhamma is to understand, not just to listen

Dear friends,

Sarah: When there is understanding, there is no restlessness, no disturbance by clinging, wanting, wishing, misunderstanding, that is a relief. At that moment the citta is calm, not agitated, disturbed by wanting, trying to see something different, trying to think in a special way.

Acharn: (Understanding is) very little at a time.

Nina: Acharn often says that there is no one there. I think of Jonothan's reminder that it is natural to think of other people. We need to think of other people in daily life, otherwise we cannot lead our daily life. But at the same time we should not forget the absolute truth. There is no contradiction.

Acharn: Otherwise there is not the understanding of no self, no "I". The reality is there, seeing is still there, no one, no self at all, not even in thought. When one reality appears, it is the absolute truth that nobody can change.

Because of the rapidity of the arising and falling away of realities, they all appear together and this conditions the idea of "some thing" all the time. So, it is not the actual experience of the truth by vipassanā ñāna, that is so clear, not as usual, not as before, because it begins to eradicate the idea of self. Nothing is there, only that reality (that appears). It needs more application of the clear understanding, the comprehension of the truth, to condition higher (stages of) understanding of vipassanā ñāna, before there can be eradication of other defilements stage by stage. The defilements are so very, very dirty.

(N: the pariññā, clear comprehension, arising after a moment of vipassanā ñāna, has to apply the knowledge gained at such a moment in daily life)

Since there is no "I", how can there be my leg? Dhamma is to understand. Not just to listen.

Jonothan: When one does not understand the reality appearing at the present moment, citta will be akusala. Three kinds of akusala are mentioned mostly: attachment, conceit and wrong view. Each of these has a different characteristic.

Acharn: It is not the word, it has its own characteristic.

Jonothan: Right, I think we understand the characteristic of attachment quite well, and even conceit. But the characteristic of wrong view is more difficult to understand.

Acharn: When there is anger, it is still my anger. There is no understanding of the characteristic which is not self.

Jonothan: Only understanding of realities can gradually eliminate the idea of self.

Acharn: Where is that particular anger now? Never again.

Jonothan: The tendency is latent.

Acharn: There can be less attachment to the idea of self which has been accumulated from life to life. There can be less attachment to what appears now from understanding a little more, a little more. When understanding is there, it is different from other moments.

Nina

19.18 Saturday discussion XXV, 3

Nina
12/29/20 #165843

Being without akusala is the best

Dear friends,

Jonothan: When I cling to my arms and legs, could it be conceit, or attachment, or wrong view? It depends on the moment.

Acharn: Even now, it does not appear, but the thought (of the "I") is still there. Until there is more and more understanding that only one reality can be object of experiencing and then it can be object of understanding. Now there is seeing, but no understanding of it yet. When there is a little more understanding: seeing is seeing, just very shortly, how can that be someone? Just one moment cannot be someone.

It is not controllable, because no one can make it (appear). That will bring about a little detachment.

Being without akusala is the best, but it takes more time, from one stage to another stage of paññā, until the stage of the sotāpanna. And then to the following stages of enlightenment: of the once-returner, of the no returner and of the arahat, depending on the accumulations.

Paññā cannot eliminate wrong view right now. Paññā has to go deep down to what has been accumulated as anusaya (latent tendency). This moment of understanding is gone, but it is there (as an accumulated condition), deep down, to clean up very little of the dirt of akusala. This is what the Buddha said: it is very subtle, very deep. It is not only this moment but it goes deeply down to the accumulations of aeons and aeons ago. Each moment is gone, but the accumulation is there.

It is beneficial to understand the subtlety of defilements, instead of trying so much in order to gain knowledge. What is there now? It depends on conditions.

Jonothan: Whatever is appearing at the present moment.

Acharn: Little by little. But it is so very precious because it can go down deeply to clean up the (unwholesome) accumulation of citta.

Nina

19.19 Saturday discussion XXV, 4

Nina
12/30/20 #165848

Satipaṭṭhāna

Dear friends,

Azita: Many people talk about satipaṭṭhāna. That is sati with paññā which knows an object?

Acharn: What is now appearing?

Azita: The heart-base.

Acharn: Without that which experiences it, can it appear?

Azita: No, there must be citta arising which experiences it.

Acharn: Citta is so common that it is not known as no self. That cannot be satipaṭṭhāna, because there is no paññā that understands (the object) as no thing. When we are touching something hard, is it not some thing? It is always some thing, even we do not call it (that way). When experiencing hardness there is no satipaṭṭhāna. It is satipaṭṭhāna when there is paññā, but when there is no paññā it cannot be satipaṭṭhāna because of not understanding.

Hardness appears but there is no understanding. When there is listening and studying the word of the teaching, it (hardness) is (realized as) a reality because it has its own characteristic, it is conditioned, that is the way it is. There are realities that can experience and that cannot experience. There cannot be understanding of this if one has not heard about it. That which experiences just arises by conditions, it is no one. This is the beginning of understanding. There can be the moment which understands that which is no "I".

When one opens one's eyes, is there any idea of no "I", no thing? Not at all, because the "I" is there very deeply, as āsava (intoxicant, very subtle defilement). It is unknown but it is "I" already. Whatever is there must be the "I" who sees, who experiences and that is not satipaṭṭhāna. Until paññā knows different realities as not self and understands that they are conditioned to arise, otherwise they could not arise at all.

Nina

19.20 Saturday discussion, XXV, 5

Nina
12/31/20 #165872

Begin and begin again and again

Dear friends,

Acharn explains that when intellectual understanding is not sufficient yet there cannot be satipaṭṭhāna.

Acharn: When satipaṭṭhāna arises, there is no doubt what is meant by anattā, no doubt about conditions, no doubt about: not "I" who can make it arise. But it is so short, just to be aware directly. Directly means when that reality appears. For example, there is seeing of visible object. Is there satipaṭṭhāna? No. Even one knows and learns about no "I" who sees, and that seeing which sees is there, and that only what impinges on the eye-base is what can be seen. The other realities cannot be seen, because they do not impinge on the eye-base. This is learning about the words, about the truth of what is there. It is not yet the understanding of no self. It is still "I" who learns, "I" who hears, "I" who understands. It is not reality, it is not dhamma. We need more intellectual understanding. When it unexpectedly becomes strong enough it can be understood: no "I", it is only a moment of experiencing.

It takes a long, long time, which means that it is the nature of anattā. No one can condition it. Every moment is anattā but no one talks about it as anattā.

Sati of satipaṭṭhāna is not sati of the level of listening, thinking, considering only. But hearing again and again shows the anattāness, no one can make it arise. Whenever it arises the understanding of anattā begins.

The Buddha taught: it is now, this moment can be known. There has to be understanding at the level of intellectual understanding, strong enough, clear enough. That is why the meaning of pariyatti is not just hearing the word of the Buddha, but firmer understanding, more confidence in anattā. No one, no self, that conditions direct awareness. The understanding of no self begins to develop, so very little.

What is there is there very shortly and no more. Nothing can be taken for permanent and for self. Begin and begin again and again. It is not easy, but it (the truth) can be studied, can be known.

Nina

20
January 2021

20.1 Saturday discussion XXVI, 1

Nina
Jan 3 #165928

Nothing to something to nothing

Dear friends,

Acharn: There is nothing, then something very shortly and then nothing again. Something happens and then it is gone completely.

Nina: People often wonder about the words: nothing, something and nothing.

Acharn: Before seeing, is there seeing? Before hearing, is there hearing? How do they come from nothing? And after hearing nothing again. It cannot arise again, only once in saṃsāra. In the teachings of the Buddha each word is about what appears now. Letting go the idea of self and permanence. It cannot be changed. It is dhamma, no one at all. Seeing, hearing, thinking, they all seem to be together, and at the same time, but they are quite far apart and never at the same time.

When it is there, just once in saṃsāra. Are you Nina? No Nina in next life. Is there Nina in this life? Only different realities. No one, no thing.

Nina: We still cling, we have to hear the truth a lot.

Acharn: Because there is no direct understanding of one reality at a time. Now there are so many things, but learn to understand that they are different, they cannot be at the same moment. When seeing is the object (that is experienced) the cetanā and the other accompanying cetasikas cannot be the object, even they are there.

How fast citta arises and falls away to form up the idea of something with different shape and form, from moment to moment. Actually it is just a dream, no one there. It is like reading a book. There are many people in that book, from page to page, but actually, there is no one at all. Dreaming, thinking about what is not there. While one is reading about a particular person, nothing is permanent.

Even thinking about Lodewijk, without paramattha dhammas how can there be such thought?

Jonothan: You say that what we see we take for a permanent thing. Many times we see people and things, but there is not thinking whether they are permanent.

Acharn: When you think of people, what is there?

Jonothan: While we are talking to each other there are a lot of faces on the screen, but no idea of permanence.

Acharn: Who knows that what is seen cannot be any shape or form, because before it becomes shape and form many realities are arising and falling away in split-seconds.

Jonothan: There are lots of objects I do not pay attention to. I can see my computer screen but I do not give any importance to it as a thing.

Acharn: But is that which is seen a thing?

Nina

20.2 Saturday discussion, XXVI, 2

Nina
Jan 4 #165938

What is seen?

Dear friends,

Acharn: But is that which is seen a thing?

Jonothan: I am not sure what you mean: is it a thing? Can we talk about the ear-door for a moment?

Acharn: We do not talk about any doorway yet. We talk about many realities in order to know what is meant by reality. So what is reality? We learn a lot about what seeing sees, but it does not appear.

Jonothan: But it does not mean that the concept we have involves an idea of self. It means an idea of permanence or persons.

Acharn: Does what is seen now arise and fall away? For example, I see you.

Jonothan: Things are not seen as they truly are.

Acharn: It is not easy to understand the truth that what is seen cannot be anything at all. The Buddha taught what is there which is seen. What impinges on the eye-base is what is seen, no matter it is white, black or blue. It falls away so rapidly, how can it be a pencil? One can understand one's own ignorance by considering what is (meant by) no one, no thing. Only when there is paññā with the pāramī viriya which conditions the development, can there be letting go.

No one knows that there is no letting go of anything when paññā does not directly experience the truth. In order to let go it has to be anattā. The moment of understanding lets go, but no one knows. The saṅkhāra khandha (the fifty cetasikas which are saṅkhāra khandha) are performing their functions. At the moment of understanding where is the anusaya, latent tendency? Anusaya is there at the moment of seeing, at the moment there is citta. What is aeons and aeons ago passes on to this moment, all anusaya is there now. (N: Anusaya is accumulated in each citta, it lies dormant in each citta.)

The moment of letting go is at the moment of understanding, but what about other moments when there is no understanding? So, it works its way, all cetasikas work their way. There is no one there at all.

Jonothan: Can you elaborate on: what is seen cannot be anything? What appears to be seen are people and things. Saying that people and things are not anything is not the true meaning of anattā.

Acharn: Is seeing very short?

Jonothan: Momentary, we are told. Extremely short.

Acharn: That which is seen is short as well? So, it cannot be the same (object) for the next moment of seeing.

Jonothan: Correct.

Acharn: So, nothing is permanent.

Jonothan: That is just by thinking.

Acharn: Thinking arises and falls away, thinking cannot see. There is seeing for a moment, who knows how short it is. There is nothing, then seeing arises and then nothing again. It cannot arise again, it cannot be taken for anything.

Jonothan: That is correct, but it is not directly known.

Acharn: How can there be something? (There should be) understanding of what really is the object of seeing, as it is.

Jonothan: Only when there are moments of awareness and understanding.

Acharn: There is just a moment of seeing, but it is the nimitta (sign) of seeing. Seeing can only see what impinges on the eye-base. The whole body cannot impinge. What is there? When there is no seeing it cannot appear. Hardness is there, but when there is no touching it is not there. Life is so short like this. It cannot be taken for permanent or "I". It is so short. That is why ordinary people cannot see the truth. Just hearing is not enough. But one should understand now what we are talking about.

Jonothan: You say: nothing can be taken for permanent, which is correct. But in normal daily life, to what extent do we take things that are seen, heard, tasted, in the course of a day as being permanent or "I"?

Acharn: When can understanding develop?

Jonothan: It can, gradually, by conditions.

Acharn: (It depends on whether we take) seeing and what is seen as something. Letting go the idea of something. Letting go has to be from the very beginning.

Jonothan: Understanding can condition some moments of letting go.

Acharn: No one can hope to have it. A moment of right understanding can let go. There was wrong understanding for a long time, not seeing realities as they are. The way to let go is not trying to do anything different.

Nina

20.3 Saturday discussion, XXVI, 3

Nina
Jan 5 #165954

Dhamma means: no thing

Dear friends,

It is not "I" who can try, who can understand. The moment of understanding is there to clean up the akusala which is there enormously, no one can fathom. Each moment there is more.

How can there be the understanding that there is no self, only dhammas? Why did the Buddha use the term dhamma? Dhamma means: no thing.

Jonothan: Only when dhammas are seen with awareness and understanding there may be an appreciation of no one there.

Acharn: Paññā knows how much understanding there is. When we read from the book and consider it, the intellectual understanding can condition understanding of what is appearing now. It is so short, it is another higher level of paññā, paṭipatti (direct understanding). The arising and falling away of different realities can be realised, only one at a time.

The world of ignorance is not understanding whatever appears. Beginning to understand the teaching of the Buddha, to understand the truth, can lead to enlightenment of the truth.

When hardness does not appear there is the idea of something that is hard. There is an idea of legs and arms.

Jonothan: There is the idea of some thing, but there may not be the idea of permanence.

Acharn: Its arising and falling away does not appear.

Jonothan: Correct.

Acharn: That is not enough but it will lead to more understanding. To letting go of wrong understanding. To understanding that actually there is no one. The truth should be understood from the very beginning: dhamma cannot be taken for anything because it is conditioned.

Something is there, for how long? It will take time to consider and have firm understanding of no "I".

Jonothan: If I want to walk from this room into the next room, I have to open the door, I cannot walk through. There is some thing, but it does not necessarily imply an idea of self or permanence. There is hardness.

Acharn: What walks through the door ? Forget about that. Try to know that there is not self, only each moment of the five khandhas.

Jonathan: Even the sotāpanna has an idea to open the door to walk into the next room.

Acharn: Is there understanding of a permanent I, a real I? There are only dhammas by conditions.

Jonothan: The idea of an underlying self depends on the individual. There is not necessarily wrong view. No one can let go strong attachment. Paññā which is conditioned can let go of it.

Acharn: Who wants to open the door?

Jonothan: It depends on the moment. Sometimes there might be strong attachment, sometimes not, depending on the thoughts that are conditioned.

Acharn: Paññā is not enough to understand one reality at that moment. What can understand that as not self?

Jonothan: Only paññā. There could be ignorance or wrong view as well.

Acharn: Can there be understanding of a reality at that moment?

Jonothan: When understanding is developed it can.

Acharn: That is why we consider about it, to have conditions for right awareness, more confidence in "not me".

Nina

20.4 Saturday discussion, XXVI,5

Nina
Jan 7 #166001

Lastingness

Dear friends,

Sarah: As soon as there is the idea of something there, such as my arms, Nina, or Lodewijk, there is the idea of lastingness.

Sukin: You do not have to label, there is always something around.

Sarah: Something instantly, that is why the anusaya is so deeply engrained and the āsava of diṭṭhi comes in so quickly, long before any idea of my arm.

Jonothan: It depends whether at that moment the characteristic of wrong view is appearing.

Sarah: That is the point of the āsavas. They are not apparent, not known at all. Usually when gross wrong view arises, there is the idea that there is a self. The more paññā grows, the more subtle kinds of diṭṭhi appear and can be known. What is understood now is just the tip of the iceberg.

Even now, while looking at the screen, there is something there, and there is the idea of permanence instantly, quickly, and then gone. There is an idea of people, colours, shape. It is very subtle, the idea of someone or something.

Sukin: Very often it is ignorance and attachment, not necessarily wrong understanding.

Sarah: Walking through the door, looking at the screen, only paññā can tell what reality is there. The more paññā develops the more there is understanding of the more subtle degrees of ignorance. When people first study the Dhamma, they think that there is not much attachment, ignorance and wrong view. But when understanding develops it is more apparent that there is far more ignorance than one can imagine.

Sukin: Acharn, you mentioned the latent tendency of wrong view of taking for permanent what is not permanent.

Acharn: Not seeing as it is, as not I, this is the beginning to let go. We should study very carefully and have more confidence in "not me". Otherwise we study with anusaya all the time. If there is no me, what is me now. Where is me? Nothing at all. Seeing is not me, not I who sees. Everything is as it is, not I. This is the beginning to let go wrong understanding and the idea of self.

Sarah: You asked before whether there can be understanding of anusaya. Understanding can only understand what appears, what arises and is the object of citta. Anusaya are unwholesome cetasikas that do not arise, but they are carried on from one citta to the next moment, until they are eradicated. They cannot be object of understanding, they have not arisen. Without the anusaya, lobha now, diṭṭhi now could not arise

Acharn: Khun Tam, when you see something, do you like it?

Tam: Yes.

Acharn: Only at that moment. Later on we can hate it. When there is sometimes like or dislike, there must be the accumulation for that to arise. So long as it arises there is anusaya. When there is dislike there must be accumulation of that level to condition its arising.

Nina

20.5 Saturday discussion XXVI, 6

Nina
Jan 8 #166024

Being tired

Dear friends,

Alberto had a question about the meaning of being tired, being tired of seeing, of visible object.

Sarah spoke about different meanings of being tired, depending on the context.

Sarah: people say they are tired of living, of hearing, these are just different kinds of dosa with unpleasant feeling. When one is physically tired there is painful bodily feeling accompanying vipākacitta just for a moment. Then it is followed by countless cittas that think with dosa. This is different from when Acharn referred to it that the best is being tired of ignorance. When there is paññā it understands how unhelpful all the countless moments of ignorance are. This is quite different from just being tired of seeing. Usually when we talk about being tired, it is dosa. Tired of doing the cooking, of hearing.

Sukin: When referring to paññā of that high level why not (being tired of) any reality?

Sarah: It can be any reality: not understanding the truth, time to develop understanding.

Nina

20.6 Saturday discussion XXVII, 1

Nina
Jan 10 #166049

Wholesomeness

Dear friends,

Dialogue with Lukas about wholesomeness.

Acharn: Would you like to have wholesomeness or understanding.

Lukas: I would like both.

Acharn: Is there you? The more there is understanding of dhamma, the less there is the idea of self. There is self all the time. Seeing is me, everything is me. Akusala dhammas are anattā, no one, no self.

What is there now? It is just what arises and performs its function. Otherwise there must be wholesomeness as "I" and no understanding of what is now. Can there be wholesomeness so long as there is an idea of self? Or more and more akusala? The only way is understanding, not me. Otherwise it is: "I" understand, "I think, "I" have more wholesomeness. What is this moment? Dhamma is now. It seems that one understands dhamma, (but it is) only the word. What about the nature of what is now appearing, there is no one there at all.

There should be the development of understanding of dhamma as not self, up to the moment of enlightenment. Otherwise there is not the right purpose of listening to the teachings: to have more kusala or to understand that from life to life there are all dhammas, even right now. Any moment can be taken for self. Otherwise there is only thinking of the words of the teachings.

We talk more about the present moment, even that seeing is nāma that experiences the present object. Any moment there is "I" who sees. There can be the understanding of the depth, the subtlety of dhamma that arises and falls away right now. But paññā is not enough. That is why hearing more, considering more each word, each reality is the only way. Dhamma is so close, not far away. Understanding dhamma is understanding what appears now. No one develops, it is the understanding of each moment. Conditions accumulate, little by little.

When there is the development of understanding, there is no need to think of other kinds of kusala. It depends on conditions how much one understands from the book. When there are conditions for akusala this can be object of study. No one can make it arise, it is already conditioned. No need to go anywhere, to any place, trying to be "something". Even that is done by the self. No understanding of the nature of it as conditioned.

Lukas: As you always say to us, understanding is anattā.

Acharn: Paññā begins to understand how subtle it is. So many things are unknown, but we do not have enlightened the truth of each reality. From hearing, considering little by little, one hears the truth of "no me". One can understand how much understanding one has developed. Otherwise it is not enough, never enough, until time comes by conditions. What has been conditioned right then. No need to do anything, but the understanding from hearing begins to develop, little by little. Not by anyone, but by conditions.

More confidence in the truth conditions more viriya and khanti (patience), more aditthāna, determination. They lead to understanding more and more, little by little. The most difficult is: not by anyone.

From morning upto now, how many moments of akusala arose? That is why we can see the great benefit of understanding, that reality which is conditioned by hearing, considering.

Lukas: There is no understanding, but ignorance. This is also to be understood as anattā?

Acharn: One thinks: I understand dhamma. How much understanding is there now? It is not strong enough yet. There is attachment to whatever is there. When we dream and then wake up there can be understanding that it is only a dream. It is only memory of thinking. At the moment of waking up one understands that it is not true. The absolute truth cannot be changed. Only paññā can have understanding of it, little by little. Saṅkhāra dhammas, conditioned dhammas, there cannot be anyone at all. They are all dhammas.

Nina

20.7 Saturday discussion XXVII, 2

Nina
Jan 11 #166075

Saṅkhāra dhammas, conditioned dhammas

Dear friends,

Acharn: Saṅkhāra dhammas, conditioned dhammas, there cannot be anyone at all. They are all dhammas. Otherwise one cannot understand the present moment, understanding is developed by conditions, from moment to moment. This is the confidence of dhamma. Otherwise we are saying "dhamma", what dhamma? Just the word but not the confidence of the truth of each reality that is conditioned. Right now we are talking, but what conditions seeing? Seeing is there all the time, while thinking or doing anything. Realities cannot be understood clearly when they are together. Intellectual understanding will condition direct understanding to have more confidence in "no one there at all". From this moment it can develop. Seeing is not that which is seen. How fast life goes on from moment to moment.

Lukas: When I am understanding is it māna, conceit, or diṭṭhi, wrong view?

Acharn: Do you have to think, "I am understanding"?

Lukas: I have a feeling that it is me who understands.

Acharn: How do you know it is you? It is not known, but from learning we know that it is āsava. That is why it is as if there is seeing all the time. Three moments after seeing (N: in the process of cittas) there are diṭṭhāsava (intoxicant of wrong view) and avijjāsava (intoxicant of ignorance). This is the way of dhamma, no one can change it.

Lukas: There is a difference between wrong view and conceit.

Acharn: If there is no hearing about these two how can one know the difference? After a few moments of seeing there is no māna, but there is the āsava of diṭṭhi.

Lukas: Why is it not māna?

Acharn: In a day is there any moment you understand māna? Which moment is diṭṭhi? Does māna arise all the time? Not as āsava. At the moment of waking up it is so pleasant. The "I" is there. Diṭṭhāsava comes in unknown. The most precious moment is the moment of understanding the truth, from hearing, which can be a condition for direct understanding.

Lukas: Every moment can be understood as anattā.

Acharn: We can understand just one word, for example: letting go. How can there be understanding? Only this moment.

Nina

20.8 Saturday discussion XXVII, 3

Nina
Jan 12 #166101

What did the Buddha enlighten?

Dear friends,

What did the Buddha enlighten? The four noble Truths. What are they? There should be understanding of just one word, more clearly and more clearly. It cannot be anything, just what arises and falls away, only once in saṃsāra. One can let go the idea of self, little by little, from hearing.

Sarah: Is any citta which arises now a khandha? What about now, any citta, seeing or hearing. Is any citta a khandha?

Tam: No.

Sarah: Yes. Any conditioned reality is a khandha, any citta is a khandha, any cetasika is a khandha, any rūpa is a khandha. When it arises it is a khandha. What is the absolute reality which is not a khandha? Nibbāna.

Sarah: Nina, do you have anything you want to bring up today?

Nina: I was so impressed by the dialogue between Acharn and Jonothan. Jonothan went on asking what is "something"? He said that in daily life people do not think so much : "This is impermanent". Then Acharn brought him back to the present moment: realities arising and falling away at this moment. Acharn also spoke about what is impinging on the eye-sense. Seeing experiences visible object. You have to hear this many times before it really sinks in. Acharn explained that the very tiny rūpa that impinges on the eye-sense is not a whole body. I have heard this before but suddenly it can make more sense. Hearing again the same thing is always helpful, I noticed.

Acharn: And that is paññā. It can understand the subtlety of rūpa and nāma. As to letting go, if one just understands that seeing is not self, that it arises and falls away, that is not enough. Hearing again and again can condition direct awareness of just one characteristic which appears, to understand what is meant by: it cannot experience, it is that which is seen. That which is seen is no one, there is nothing in it, and that is the higher understanding of the truth. But when there is not enough paññā at a higher level, it can know that it is not direct awareness yet. Paññā can know everything as it is of any level, any degree. That is why one can see the depth, the subtlety of dhamma as Buddha said after his enlightenment: all dhammas are anattā. It is so very subtle, very profound. So, we learn to understand that which arises and falls away, letting go the idea of self from moment to moment, unknown from life to life. Do you have any arms and legs when they do not appear? There is (just) thinking that they are there. What arises and falls away so rapidly covers up the truth.

Nina

20.9 Saturday discussion XXVII, 4

Nina
Jan 13 #166116

How to live our life?

Dear friends,

Sarah: Coming back to Lukas question how to live our life.

When one asks oneself how should I live, what should I do, it is not the understanding of dhamma. It is just an idea that I can choose how to live. No one can select that there will be kusala citta or akusala citta. When paññā begins to understand dhamma as anattā, it does not mind what the object is: seeing, hearing, anger, strong lobha.

Understanding leads to more wholesomeness but not by expectation to have it. It depends on the accumulation whether strong anger will arise. In whatever way life unfolds, there are just dhammas.

It is the confidence that life is just at this moment. At the very beginning there has to be the understanding of dhammas as anattā.

Nina

20.10 Saturday discussion, XXVII, 5

Nina
Jan 14 #166134

The right beginning

Dear friends,

Acharn: The beginning has to be the right beginning, otherwise it will not lead to more understanding. Lobha is very tricky, only paññā can know it. We talked many times about hardness and the experience of hardness, and it is now. In the beginning paññā is so weak, it is not vipassanā ñāna yet.

Nina: It is good to remember this, otherwise we may be impatient. We have no arms and legs and we do not understand this yet. We have to be more patient.

Acharn: Understand again and again and again. There is the experience of hardness almost all the time, but it is not yet the moment of understanding. This comes from listening again, and considering wisely. Actually, there is nothing and paññā will begin to let go, until understanding the precious moment of "no I", no thing. Otherwise it is the object of clinging, because of ignorance. This is the profundity and subtlety of dhamma. The arising and falling away is this moment. Where is that which has fallen away? Can that be taken for "I"? It is gone completely, never to arise again. Letting go, it is not as heavy as before by trying so hard to experience this or that. The meaning of letting go: when it is there it is different from other moments.

Nina

20.11 Saturday discussion XXVII, 6

Nina
Jan 15 #166147

Nimitta and anubyancana

Dear friends,

Sukin asked about knowing the image and details, nimitta and anubyancana.

Acharn: Do you see anything now?

Sukin: A laptop, pictures.

Acharn: And more details about just one reality, one characteristic?

Sukin: Do you mean one characteristic like Nina's face?

Acharn: What about her face and her shawl?

Sukin: You see something and then you think about more details.

Acharn: If there is no nimitta can there be details?

Sarah: We are usually lost in the fantasy world, thinking about details.

Sukin: It seems, looking at the blue scarf that there is a concept of something.

Sarah: When you describe it and think about the blue shawl there is a concept about what has been seen.

Acharn: Just the words rūpa and nāma are only words. When rūpa does not appear as that which cannot experience, we should know: it is just to be seen. That which is seen, no thinking in it. We begin to learn that we live in the world of signs or nimittas. When you are thinking Tadao is wearing a hat, Nina a shawl, it is thinking about different images. There have to be visible object, nimitta and details of different visible objects in order to be thinking of different signs and details: this is Tadao, this is Nina.

Sarah: If saññā did not arise and mark visible object would there be any thinking about Tadao or Nina?

Sukin: We do not confuse one with the other.

Sarah: Each moment of visible object is not the same. Saññā marks each reality that is experienced. Because of different nimittas of what is seen there can be thinking about Tadao and Nina.

Acharn: Is there understanding of what is seen now? What is seen is just what is seen, nothing in it, no one in it, no shape, no form. How much ignorance is there.

Sukin: There is less understanding than we realise.

Acharn: So we understand what is meant by the perfection of patience, of viriya, of truthfulness, determination. All pāramīs go together to let go ignorance, attachment and all akusala, stage by stage.

Sarah: When we just try to work things out we forget all about just understanding this moment of thinking we find so important. It just comes back to this moment. That is more precious than working out the story.

Nina

20.12 Saturday discussion, XXVIII, 1

Nina
Jan 17 #166185

Always "I" who sees, hears, thinks

Dear friends,

Acharn: It is always "I" who sees, hears, thinks. They just arise to see right now, hear right now. When there is not the understanding of the truth, it is "something" all the time. Life is just what arises and falls away. Confidence in the truth will condition awareness of just one reality at a time, when time comes. Intellectual understanding is not clear yet, it is not vipassanā ñāna yet.

Nina: We live in the world of nimitta.

Acharn: Is that not right? Now I see Khun Nina. Saññā is saññā, it cannot be anything else. It marks the object. Visible object is what can be seen but one takes it for a person or a being. Can that which is seen be your friend?

Jonothan: We live in a world of concepts, but Nina wants to ask: how to understand the world of nimitta as different from the world of concepts?

Acharn: Can there be concept without nimitta? We talk about "something" all the time: children, chair. Is that not nimitta of what is real? It arises and falls away so very rapidly. What is seen is only what impinges on the eye-base. No one at all. And seeing is there, just to arise and see. Not the table, not a concept, only that which appears to seeing. How fast, how little, how very short. That which is seen is nothing, no one in it. Before it can be taken as a concept, there must be nimitta. Just the nimitta of one reality. Without the mark, shape and form can there be the idea of concept?

Just close your eyes, everything is gone. When you open your eyes, how fast it is to see Sarah and Jonothan. Without seeing how can shape and form be known? Seeing does not know anything. No shape and form, only that which is seen. This is the subtlety, the deep truth. All realities arise and fall away, from nothing to something and then nothing. If there is no deeper and deeper understanding, there is no letting go. The moments of understanding are very precious, they lead to letting go. One may try so hard to go somewhere to meditate. It is not the understanding of this moment. If this moment is not known, what about the next moment? Letting go the idea of self, very, very little. This is the only way. The eightfold Path is so subtle, the noble Truths are very, very subtle. The way to let go is very subtle because it has to begin now.

Nina

20.13 Saturday discussion XXVIII, 2

Nina
Jan 19 #166222

Continuity, santati

Dear friends,

Jonothan asked about continuity, santati.

Acharn: What arises and falls away is followed by the next reality, by conditions, anantara paccaya, contiguity-condition. Also by absence-condition, natthi-paccaya. It has to be gone completely, otherwise the next reality cannot arise.

Nina: I had not understood what Acharn had said about nimitta, we live in the world of nimitta.

Sarah: I do not think it matters whether we live in the world of nimitta or of concepts. Seeing just sees visible object, no shape or anything. Because of the rapid succession (of realities) the nimitta of visible object appears. There is thinking about this or that because of the nimitta that thinks of different ideas. When we say that we live in the world of nimitta there is thinking of different people and different things. So it is implied like a shorthand that now there is the nimitta of so many realities appearing as condition for the thinking of different objects.

Nina: Acharn spoke about nimitta of concept if there is no direct awareness?

Acharn: Nobody can change the concept not to be concept. When there is no hearing of the truth everything is permanent, like a chair, a body. But in reality nothing is there, only what appears to the eye, the nose, the tongue, the body-sense. We keep on thinking about what is not seeing. It is like a dream. In a dream there is no actual seeing, only saññā is there, marking and remembering. When there is not a dream there are actually seeing and hearing. In a dream there is no experience through the sense-doors, only through the mind-door.

Each word of the Buddha is helpful to condition understanding of the truth as it is. Otherwise we have the idea of "I" all the time. A moment of understanding is very precious. We talk about visible object and it seems everyone understands that. But it is actually the plant in the pot, all the time. Without intellectual understanding and confidence it is impossible to have higher understanding, understanding with direct awareness. Whatever is there is like a test for paññā. To understand what is there is not far away, it is now.

Maeve: It is impossible to develop paññā without patience.

Acharn: Patience is not me, no one there.

Nina

20.14 Saturday discussion XXVIII, 3

Nina
Jan 20 #166236

The role of chanda

Dear friends,

Jonothan asked about the roles of chanda (taking an interest in the object) and lobha. Can their roles be distinguished when pursuing anything that requires skill?

Acharn: Lobha appears but does its characteristic appear, depending on conditions? Do you have chanda to sing?

Jonothan: Sometimes.

Acharn: It takes a long time and it is hard to understand each different one (of lobha and chanda) when they do not appear clearly. What can be known is the different nature of citta and cetasika. Paññā can know that citta is the chief in experiencing an object. There is seeing and we cannot have a clear understanding of it yet. We just know that it is there. It is that which is conditioned just to see. Without awareness it is impossible to understand the difference between seeing and thinking. Is paññā strong enough to understand clearer and clearer from hearing and considering the different levels of understanding, so that it can let go clinging and ignorance, and the inclination to select any object?

Some people like breath as object, that is clinging and no understanding of anattā. Citta is anattā, cetasika is anattā, everything is anattā, no one, nothing, no control. That which appears can be object of understanding. Even a cetasika like dosa. Who does not know dosa when it is there. What about lobha? When we like something very much it is there. But when it is not as strong, who knows it? Lobha can be object, even when it is very slight. Otherwise paññā cannot eradicate it and there must be the wrong understanding of self.

In every day life there can be moments of understanding the difference between intellectual understanding and direct understanding and awareness as not self, stage by stage, by anattāness. There is more confidence in anattā and that is the letting go.

Sarah: At any moment of lobha there is an interest (chanda) in the object. At any moment of dosa there is an interest (chanda) in the object. During my early morning swim many moments of lobha and dosa continued because of interest in the object. At the moment of moha and doubt there is no interest. Evenso during the moments of ahetuka cittas no interest in the object. With all sobhana cittas, with kindness, generosity, there is chanda, an interest in the object.

Nina

20.15 Saturday discussion, XXVIII, 4

Nina
Jan 21 #166254

Thīna and middha

Dear friends,

Nina: Thīna and middha, torpor and languor, can arise with cittas that are sasankhārika, cittas that lack strength. It seems that thīna refers to torpor of citta and middha refers to torpor of cetasikas.

Acharn: You waste time, not understanding this moment. What about the understanding of what is now? There must be forgetfulness when there is not direct understanding. What is there can be object of understanding. That is much better than keeping on thinking about what is not there. For example, is there thīna and middha now? Do they appear as they are or (does one think of) just the word?

One can understand the truth of seeing and what is seen, right now. There can be understanding of what is seen only. Letting go the idea of someone or something in it. What about phassa, contact, it does not appear and therefore, how could there be the understanding of it as not self? The difference should be known between intellectual understanding and the understanding of the nature (of reality) that appears all the time.

Hajji, do you understand nāma and rūpa?

Hajji: No, there is so much ignorance.

Acharn: What is the point of listening to an explanation about nāma and rūpa which are not self?

No one knows until paññā develops enough to know the difference between nimitta and concept. Do you have arms?

Hajji: No.

Acharn: Can there be a little more letting go if there is not thinking about other things but attention to the characteristic of that which is conditioned to appear and then gone. No regret. Is there viriya now?

Hajji: There has to be.

Acharn: Is it known? When it is stronger there will be more confidence and it can condition naturally, when time comes, any moment of understanding of what is there. It is not far away. Just to understand intellectually is not enough to let go the idea of things and beings. At the moment of touching, what can be the object of understanding?

Are you patient now? It is easy to say: no me, but even we say it, it is still me.

Nina

20.16 Saturday discussion XXVIII, 5

Nina
Jan 22 #166278

What is seen is only that which is seen

Dear friends,

Acharn: What is seen is only that which is seen before it is "something", otherwise it cannot be directly understood as it is gone. When there is right understanding with direct awareness of that particular object there can be letting go. So, there can be understanding of the arising of the next reality, but there are many processes in between. It can be understood, it is there, its characteristic shows its anattāness.

Azita: It can be understood, but when there is not that understanding yet there must be some belief or confidence that this will happen. I do not know it is confidence or clinging to what I hear.

Acharn: It does not matter, they are gone. Paññā develops little by little, to understand whether that is again object of clinging. Later on it can be object of understanding, when there are conditions.

Azita: There is not enough development of paññā.

Acharn: Understand that it is gone. Letting go little by little, so very little, because the accumulation of ignorance and defilements is so much. It blinds, everything appears not as it is but as something permanent. That is why it takes time for the bodhisatta to become the Sammāsambuddho or (for us) to become a savaka bodhisatta. Everything has to be anattā, it occurs unexpectedly. Otherwise there cannot be the elimination of the idea of "I can do". When there is (understanding and akusala arises), there will be no more the idea of "I do, I let go". It is not me, this is the best to know.

One understands the fine line between paññā and attachment to have paññā. What is there can be known from hearing and considering, by conditions. Even if there is very strong attachment paññā can see it as no me, only a conditioned moment and then gone. It cannot stay for long. It is just like a dream. What is there in a dream? It is not there when one wakes up to understand the truth.

Nina

20.17 Saturday discussion, XXIX, 2

Nina
Jan 27 #166382

The truth is very subtle

Dear friends,

Acharn: There is no one who sees, hears or thinks. One can begin to remember that they are not self. How can paññā penetrate the truth?

It appears but there is no understanding. The study of the truth will lead to understanding. The truth is very subtle, no one can understand it, only when paññā develops from hearing up to the moment of direct awareness. It is the beginning of understanding the subtlety. Touching now appears. One may just try to understand other things which are not appearing.

There were questions about visible object.

Jonothan: When we talk about characteristics of realities, colour is not part of characteristics. Visible object appears as different colours by thinking.

Sarah: If we try to work out what visible object is, there is just the story of visible object, not the understanding of the reality as it is now.

Jonothan: The characteristic is the unique quality of a reality, different from all other realities.

Tam: Can akusala arise in a dream? I see myself fighting in a dream.

Sarah: There are mostly akusala cittas when dreaming. What about now? There is akusala, trying to remember one's past dreams. What about thinking at this moment? Kusala or akusala? They are all gone.

One gets lost in the story, no understanding of dhamma at this moment. What does it matter what the dream was last night, it is all gone anyway.

Each visible object is different, but it is just visible object that is seen. It is not easy to understand absolute reality, because we live in the world of concepts. It is not just understanding only the word.

Nina

20.18 Saturday discussion, XXIX, 3

Nina
Jan 28 #166395

What is visible object?

Dear friends,

Acharn: Colour is there. Only at the moment of seeing. When there is seeing, we do not think about shape and form. It is so fast, no one can say anything about it. We think about colour, about the word visible object, but it is not like the moment it is there with right understanding. We live in the world of ignorance, not understanding the truth. There is the moment of letting go of trying to think about this or that instead of understanding what appears. What is seen now is seen as something, all the time. When it appears there is no need to say that it is eye-door or ear-door because the doorway does not appear. The point is to understand that nothing is permanent. It is gone as soon as it is there. There is no condition for that level of understanding yet. Just be aware little by little of what appears now.

Nina

20.19 Saturday discussion, XXX, 1

Nina
Jan 31 #166464

Nekkhamma, renunciation

Dear friends,

Acharn: We should not mind about the word or term. What is now appearing?

To understand what is appearing now is the moment of letting go. Letting go thinking of the world, people and things. We do not mind the word, but the truth. Because of ignorance we always think of something there. Study the teachings to let go. To let go the idea of something permanent.

Sarah: Letting go refers to the development of the Path. Nekkhamma pāramī, the perfection of renunciation, is letting go the idea of self, someone, something, anyone who can do anything. At any moment of kusala there is nekkhamma, but it is not nekkamma that is letting go the idea of self. In the Buddha's teachings it always refers to the Path.

Acharn: We keep on talking about words. What about reality? What about the understanding of what is appearing now? It is very difficult to experience the truth of reality. There is the idea of something all the time. It is just that level of understanding, paññā is not enough yet. We keep on listening carefully to really understand how much ignorance has been accumulated. What about saññā, remembrance, now? Should it be known as not self? If there is no letting go how can there be less attachment to the "I"?

There can be intellectual understanding of the meaning of the word "direct awareness". It must be different from learning about the word. If there is no understanding of the truth of realities right now, there are no conditions for direct awareness. It is not a matter of just thinking about it, dreaming of it, but understanding little by little. That is the right way, the Path.

Actually there is nothing, realities just appear and disappear. There is no self, no one, nothing. Only different realities that are conditioned, arising and falling away all the time. It is impossible to make them different from the way they are. It is impossible to understand the truth without hearing, considering and letting go.

Nina

21 February 2021

21.1 Saturday discussion XXX, 2

Nina
Feb 2 #166489

Decisive support-condition

Dear friends,

Acharn: Each moment of kusala is nekkhamma. When it arises with paññā it is a perfection. We should see the danger of what is no more as something permanent, as I, from life to life.

There was a discussion with Alberto about decisive support-condition of object, ārammanuppanissaya paccaya. What about the rūpa, can it be ārammanuppanissaya paccaya? Only for lobha-mūla-citta, not for kusala citta. This is because of attachment, we are so attached to that rūpa.

Acharn: Do you like to have moha and dosa? No one likes to have them. kāyaviññāṇa with painful feeling, no one likes to have it. It cannot be ārammanuppanissaya paccaya.

At this moment can there be understanding of the object that appears? Does one know whether it is ārammanuppanissaya paccaya, adhipati paccaya of object, object predominance-condition?

When there is no understanding that all dhammas are conditioned, there are no conditions for letting go. There can be a little more letting go. It is not the moment of thinking about the term but the understanding that whatever is there is conditioned.

Sarah: If visible object had not already impinged on the eye-sense, there could not be seeing.

Acharn: Why does one have attachment very often? Anantarūpanissaya paccaya, strong condition for the next reality. There is always attachment to a pleasant object.

When there is attachment to an object it is ārammaṇa paccaya, but when the object is very special there is anantarūpanissaya paccaya.

What conditions attachment? Ignorance. So long as there is ignorance, there must be attachment and other akusala. Anantarūpanissaya paccaya, it is the strong condition for the arising of the next reality. It is like anantara paccaya, but it refers to the strength.

The point of studying details is not to remember terms. Whatever arises in life is due to many complex conditions. We have to understand that it cannot be any other way. People may be put off by complicated terms and details.

Nina

21.2 Saturday discussion, XXX, 3

Nina
Feb 3 #166496

Life is conditioned right now

Dear friends,

Sarah: To understand life is conditioned right now. Seeing now is anattā.

Acharn: Just to know that there is no one there. Paccaya, condition, means no one. Paccayupanna, conditioned, means no one. Just understand the truth of each word. People are different. This can condition more compassion.

Answer to Maeve:

They are all gone. Thinking is thinking, memory is memory. The understanding of what appears is the best. To understand the truth of what is shorter than we could expect. Otherwise it could not condition shape and form. Understanding is the best cure for everything.

Paññā is here, ready to understand that moment and let go. Let go the burden. Understand the truth: it is gone, it is not me. There are only different realities in life, unexpectedly. Whatever comes or arises is there by conditions, just for a moment and then gone. That is why we can endure everything, pleasant or unpleasant.

Nina

21.3 Saturday discussion XXX, 4

Nina
Feb 5 #166519

Live to understand the truth

Dear friends,

Acharn: When there is understanding it begins to develop, so be confident in the truth. This moment is not the previous moment, nothing can stay. The self has been accumulated so long, so much, but the understanding of the truth is there. You do not mind that there is the idea of self, because there are conditions for such thought.

What about this moment? Seeing is not thinking. The idea of self is only that which arises to see. This life is conditioned by previous accumulations and this life will condition the next life. We cannot know what will be in the next life.

Accumulate more understanding from hearing and considering, we do not know what will happen in the next life. The understanding is there.

Before hearing the teachings there was no expectation to come to listen to the word of truth. But by conditions it just arises to hear on and on.

Develop the wholesome conditions and the understanding of no self. So that one day, no matter in what situation, there can be the arising of the truth and that moment is understanding. There is no ignorance like before. One should be brave enough to know that actually there is no me.

We cling to different realities because of ignorance. There can be more understanding of no one, no legs, no arms, no eyes. Only one reality appears as it is, as no one there at all. At this moment there are only citta, cetasika and rūpa. Different ones, they never arise again. Just live to understand the truth of this moment. It can be known.

At the moment of touching, no one is there, no person. There are only hardness and that which experiences it. When there is hearing there are only sound and that which experiences it. Just be alone, no one there, only thinking of people and things. There can be more confidence in anattā. What can be taken for "I" is gone.

Nina

21.4 Saturday discussion XXXI, 1

Nina
Feb 8 #166558

What is ageing?

Dear friends,

The Buddha taught by his enlightenment the absolute truth, of no one and nothing. It has its own characteristic that can lead to direct understanding. There can be confidence about the truth by hearing, considering wisely, on and on. No expectation. There can be the understanding of anattāness of what appears by conditions. Thinking, pleasant feeling, unpleasant feeling, all are no one.

Tadao: I want to know what ageing is, is it only rūpa or also nāma?

Acharn: We have to know just one reality at a time.

Tadao: Ageing, getting older.

Acharn: What arises, falls away. Can it change? Is the Sun old? Today it is older than yesterday.

Tadao: Is ageing a concept or a reality?

Sarah: It is the wrong approach. Understanding develops and works its way.

Sukin: Is ageing just a conventional observation?

Acharn: Is seeing right now old? Visible object?

Sukin: It is another rūpa. The moment of its arising is not the same as the moment of its falling away.

Acharn: It is only paññatti, concept.

Nina

21.5 Saturday discussion XXXI,2

Nina
Feb 9 #166569

When will death come?

Dear friends,

Jonothan: Ageing is an inevitable aspect of life, it is getting a moment closer to death.

Acharn: Who knows when death will come? It is only thinking.

What is the actual meaning of ageing?

Sarah: Azita was speaking about bhava, becoming, and bhāvāsava, a very subtle clinging to existence. Bhava in the Dependent origination teaches us how clinging conditions bhava, becoming. Clinging that is strong enough to condition kamma that brings result by way of becoming, birth.

Clinging now conditions kamma now that can bring result.

When we read that ignorance conditions saṅkhāra, it refers to kamma of the past. Clinging now conditions kamma that can bring result.

Nina

21.6 Saturday discussion

Nina
Feb 16 #166661

Bahu-sutta, heard a lot

Acharn: Letting go little by little the idea of self, even intellectually. This is the understanding of the fourth noble Truth. All four Truths are subtle, because it is the natural way. Paññā develops, no one to let go the idea of self. Can we see the little ant's eyes? But it sees. What about hardness? Exactly like ours, or whatever now is hard.

Sarah: Each moment of seeing is just seeing, no matter an ant's or a human's. What is seen is just that which is seen.

Nina: I find it such a good reminder that we just cling to the story of realities instead of understanding of what appears now.

Sarah: There is so much attachment to the story of realities. There is no one who can try to do anything, to have sati. The understanding of saṅkhāra dhammas (conditioned dhammas) develops on and on.

Azita: If we do not hear these words often, life time after life time, there is no development of understanding. We cannot develop understanding by ourselves. We must have heard these words in the past.

Acharn: That is the meaning of bahu-sutta (heard a lot). It refers to the one who hears more and understands more. When there is development of understanding from a long time ago and then there is hearing again, there is understanding.

Azita: We have to continue to listen.

Acharn: Bahu-sutta. It depends on understanding, developed a long time ago, then one heard it again and understood. It has developed to that degree. That is why someone can attain enlightenment very soon, whereas others have to listen more and more.

All are dhammas, anattā, depending on conditions. Understanding is most important, from hearing and considering. For example, in reference to the understanding of kalapas (spaces in between groups of rūpas). The ant's kalapas and our kalapas are exactly the same. At a moment of realizing the truth it has to be like that. It is not as we used to take it for something, shape and form. It is not that all realities appear together as something, all the time.

Nina

21.7 Saturday discussion XXX, 6

Nina
Feb 16 #166674

Hearing more in the future?

Dear friends,

Azita: Listening becomes like an accumulation. Is that a condition for hearing more in the future?

Acharn: Yes. Everything is not self, but it is saṅkhārakkhandha, the accumulation of fifty cetasikas.

Sarah: When you say that listening leads to understanding, it refers to listening with understanding. Not to the number of hours we have the audio playing. Even five minutes of understanding is more precious than listening two hours without understanding.

Jonothan: I think that understanding accumulates more than listening as such. That is the condition for hearing again in a future life. Any understanding arising in this life time is kamma patha which can bring as result hearing dhamma in a future life.

Acharn: What about this life? There must be the first time (of listening with understanding) up until now. When one is interested to understand the truth, it conditions a next moment of hearing again. When you hear for the first time and you see the value of understanding, that can condition discussion on dhamma today. If there is no interest in what appears now, there are no conditions for listening. Can we have anything at will? There must be conditions. The most important is that there is no one, only different dhammas. Each cetasika is different and it has many different degrees, by accumulation. Tomorrow is not like today, by accumulations. Otherwise how could there be enlightenment? Abhisamaya: samaya means moment and abhisamaya is moment of enlightenment. With understanding, not without understanding.

Nina

21.8 Saturday discussion XXX, 7

Nina
Feb 17 #166681

Dhammas are very subtle

Dear friends,

One can come to understand the difference between nimitta of reality and nimitta we take for a concept.

What is the difference between a small ant and us? Any difference? The rūpa is the rūpa, the kalapa (group of rūpas) is the kalapa. When it is directly experienced what about it? It has to be just like that. The seeing is the same, hardness is hardness. What is there? Not a table. This is just the way to condition letting go the idea of self, from hearing and considering, to have less attachment to the idea of self. No I, only saṅkhāra khandha and paññā which is the best of all dhammas because it can understand. It can understand even the words about realities on and on until the moment of direct experience. If it is not true it cannot be known or realized by enlightenment.

Azita: At the last session we have been talking about arms and legs. When I listen again and hear: "no arms and legs", I see that it just takes paññā. I have arms and legs.

Acharn: And gone completely.

Azita: It is hard to grasp

Acharn: That is why dhammas are very subtle. These are the Buddha's words after his enlightenment. How long it takes to realize the truth, stage by stage. Confidence in intellectual understanding will condition direct awareness. It can be known only when it is directly experienced with paññā from the very beginning, before it can appear as it is.

Nina

21.9 Saturday discussion, XXX, 7a

Nina
Feb 17 #166682

Reality is there to be understood

Dear friends,

Acharn: Abhisamaya, enlightenment. This was never before in Saṃsāra. It has to be the understanding that can eradicate ignorance with the idea of self and attachment to the idea of self. No one there, that is the right way to understand the truth. One should read the texts with the understanding of no one.

We are sitting right now, what about understanding? Of what? It depends on conditions.

Azita: Does kukkucca, regret, arise when there is a missed opportunity for kusala, or when there is akusala, or does it cover any type of regret? For example, I regret it not to bring up my children in the right way.

Acharn: We have not done what should be done.

Azita: The means it pertains to anything, not just to kusala and akusala?

Acharn: Is it kusala to regret?

Azita: It is akusala.

Acharn: One may just learn about the words, but when time comes, what about the understanding? We can talk about situations, but what about the moment it is there? About the understanding. Without understanding the truth as no self, it is like a story. It should not be the story in the book, but it is now, this moment.

Seeing, thinking, regretting, any reality is there to be understood. Actually, it is conditioned by many conditions. We just learn the words in the book, but when time comes, it is from intellectual understanding as the foundation for the moment of understanding the truth. Without that it is impossible to know what is meant by direct awareness and intellectual awareness.

One can understand the difference between nimitta (sign) of realities and nimtta we take for a concept.

Nina

21.10 Saturday discussion XXX, 8

Nina
Feb 18 #166694

No arms and legs

Dear friends,

Jonothan tries to understand what it means to have no arms and legs.

Jonothan: Do we need to distinguish just thinking about arms and legs or taking them for something real, something that exists. The latter is wrong view, but just thinking about arms, legs, face, body, table, chair, is not necessarily accompanied by wrong view.

Acharn: Even now, do you have arms and legs if you do not think about them? It seems that they are there all the time. The truth is the truth, it never changes.

Nina: In the same way, if you do not think of your money, you do not have it.

Acharn: There is thinking of subjects all the time as "some thing", as "I", as something that belongs to me. Because the idea of "I" is there.

Jonothan: The Buddha taught the understanding of whatever appears at the present moment. Any thought that money is not real is not necessarily understanding of the presently arisen reality.

Azita: Dhammas have a characteristic and manifestation. What is the difference?

Jonothan: Every dhamma is said to have a characteristic, a function, a manifestation and a proximate cause.

Sarah: People find it difficult to understand that patience is a characteristic of viriya. The way viriya manifests is enduring whatever appears now. That is an aspect of patience. Its proximate cause the understanding that conditions kusala patience. The more understanding there is, the more enduring there is of whatever is conditioned. No matter there is seeing, hearing, jealousy, energy, they are conditioned as they are, they are anattā.

That is why understanding conditions more patience, more letting go the idea of : "I can make it different, I shall understand this reality better than another reality".

Sarah: More understanding conditions more patience and more confidence in what is true. They all condition each other.

Azita: Cetasikas are interconnected, and sometimes similar. It is difficult to know them, because there is no direct understanding. Without understanding there is such a big tangle, not knowing one reality from another.

Nina

21.11 Saturday discussion, XXX, 9

Nina
Feb 19 #166705

All our thoughts are concepts

Dear friends,

Jonothan: No self is a characteristic of conditioned reality. We cannot think of no self in an abstract way.

Acharn: But usually in a day does anyone think of no arms, no legs?

Jonothan: All our thoughts are concepts.

Acharn: When we use the word leg, there is an idea of "some thing".

Jonothan: We may think of table or chair.

Acharn: That is the same as thinking of arms and legs.

Jonothan: This is not about understanding of the present reality.

Acharn: It is. Understanding what we usually take for I, the body, citta, cetasika, feeling are mine all the time.

At the moment of thinking about arms and legs, who is arms and legs? I or me.

The sotāpanna can think of concepts, but the truth is realized through enlightenment. There is "no one" and "nothing" as before. Different realities are directly experienced.

Before hearing the teachings everyone says: I have arms and legs. After listening, there is no "I", so, no arms and legs. There is the understanding of no "I". No arms and legs.

Jonothan: The idea of self is without foundation or basis. The idea of arms, legs, table, is because of what has been seen.

Acharn: That is not the understanding of citta, cetasika and rūpa,

Jonothan: It does not mean it is wrong view.

Acharn: For the person who is not enlightened yet it is wrong understanding.

Nina

21.12 Saturday discussion, XXXI, 2

Nina
Feb 22 #166738

Everything is gone now

Dear friends,

Sarah: People may be dreaming, fantasizing, that if they were in the forest there would be less dosa. That is forgetting about this moment of seeing, right now. It is wrong understanding to cling to the idea of another time, place or occasion.

Jonothan: People think that some situations are better than others, but that is a mistake. They think that if there is more calm, more dhamma friends, it would be better for developing understanding. One does not appreciate that it is the understanding of what appears at the present moment, regardless of the situation that is important.

Sarah: They do not understand that seeing now is dhamma, hearing now is dhamma. One cannot control life and make it different, that is the greatest hindrance.

Azita: Samma-sankappa is translated as right intention, but it is also defined as initial application. Why not translate it as right thinking?

Sarah: Vitakka is not intention. It is just the understanding of the tanslator to translate it as intention.

Azita: The more I listen, the more I realize how difficult it all is.

Sarah: There is no point in getting disturbed by different translations, according to the understanding of the translator. One has to consider for oneself what the different terms mean. As Acharn said to Hajji, it is all about understanding, not trying to work out the best definition. That is not the understanding of what appears right now. There is the trap of lobha, again an again.

Maeve: there is Acharn's helpful question: what is something. There are still visible object, sound or hardness. They have arisen, but they are misunderstood. When one takes them for something, it makes it impossible to understand them.

Acharn: Before hearing the words of truth from the Buddha there is something in one's life. No matter there is seeing or thinking, everything is gone now, unknown all the time. This is the absolute truth. There is the idea of something when it is not the moment of directly experiencing the truth right now. It is something all the time. The absolute truth is that nothing lasts. It is gone all the time. But the idea of a thing is there all the time.

Nina

21.13 Saturday discussion XXXI, 5

Nina
Feb 23 #166742

Sīlabbata parāmāsa, wrong practice

Dear friends,

Acharn: The absolute truth is that there is nothing now, because what is there is gone. It seems that there is always a "thing", a self, or "some thing", but actually there is nothing, no "I". From nothing, there is something, there is seeing, and then no more seeing. That can be directly experienced, but not by wanting or trying. There is no control, no one by conditions, anattā. We learn to understand anattā and then there will be more confidence when we hear about how reality is conditioned to arise.

It seems that there is seeing all the time, but actually, there are different realities in between. "Some thing" is there when there is no understanding of that which arises and falls away by conditions. "By conditions" means more understanding of anattā and this is the way to realize the truth. The Path is the fourth noble Truth. There is no other way.

When it is not the right way there is sīlabbata parāmāsa, wrong practice. Only paññā can know that it is not right.

The way is letting go from the very beginning. Paññā leading to enlightenment is very deep and subtle, because it is now at this moment of understanding, developing on and on.

Nina

21.14 Saturday discussion XXXI, 7

Nina
Feb 25 #166763

Each moment is unexpected

Dear friends,

Acharn: One should letting go just a little until there can be understanding of the difference between direct awareness and just thinking.

Alan: Whatever appears is unexpected, that is anattāness.

Acharn: Are you expecting anything now? What about the four noble Truths. Can they be as you expect?

Alan: No.

Acharn: It means the anattāness of everything, Not as anyone expects. Hearing is unexpected. Did you think of hearing before it arose?

Alan: What is unexpected? Anattāness is unexpected. Each moment is unexpected.

Acharn: There should be no expectation of the arising of vipassanā ñāna. Sāriputta never expected to see Assaji and become enlightened. This was by conditions, unexpected.

Nina

21.15 Saturday discussion, XXXI, 8

Nina
Feb 26 #166774

What is dukkha ariya sacca?

Dear friends,

Alan: The Path is learning little by little that reality is unexpected. I understood that if you understand the cause of suffering you will have less of it and if you don't you will have more. Is that the understanding of the four noble Truths?

Jonothan: That is giving a certain meaning of suffering. The deepest meaning of dukkha is that all conditioned dhammas arise and fall away. In that sense there is not more or less suffering. It is just an aspect of life in saṃsāra which is there for everyone, for the worldling like us and for the enlightened one who sees suffering more clearly than we do. Unsatisfactoriness is more apparent to the enlightened being. We can just think about it.

Alan: Attachment is a condition for aversion. Understanding this helps to have less aversion?

Jonothan: The Path to the cessation of dukkha is not having less akusala. It is having more understanding of the true nature of the present reality. The unsatisfactoriness is directly seen by paññā. It is the development of awareness and understanding of what is appearing at the present moment.

Acharn: What is dukkha ariya sacca (the noble truth of dukkha)? It does not mean only what you do not like, unpleasant feeling. It means: that which arises has to fall away instantly, never to return. It is not just thinking, but paññā which begins to experience the truth. It is very little in the beginning, from hearing and understanding. Sammāsati is there, otherwise it is not awareness and understanding an object as nothing, no legs, no head. What we cling to is it worth clinging to?

Nina

22

March 2021

22.1 Saturday discussion, XXXII, 2

Nina
Mar 1 #166799

Understanding is not anyone

Dear friends,

Acharn: The Buddha taught the conditions for whatever arises, such as seeing, hearing, smelling, tasting, touching. It is the truth of what is there very temporary. There is no Sarah, no Jonothan, no seeing, no hearing. One just has to understand the truth and understanding is not anyone.

Even just hardness now is not known as it is, it appears as "some thing" all the time. It cannot be taken for anything, such as a chair, a table. Paññā develops to be more confident in the truth. Paññā develops until reality appears, not like now, but as it (really) is.

We are talking about the absolute truth that can be known, that can be directly experienced. Without firm confidence in the truth it is impossible to understand what is now appearing, to let go the idea of "I" or "some thing".

Jonothan: Can we say: when we see a tree, a flower, it is also a moment of truth?

Acharn: That is not absolute truth, only sammutti (conventional idea). There is a concept, paññatti, because of the very quick arising and falling away of realities. What is now appearing has to impinge on the eye-sense. Different realities cannot all at once impinge on the eye-sense before it can be any shape and form.

Sarah: Thinking is real but its content is a concept. Paññatti is a concept.

Nina

22.2 Saturday discussion XXXII, 3

Nina
Mar 2 #166808

Conventional truth, sammutti sacca

Dear friends,

Sarah: What is seen, visible object, is an ultimate reality. Flower or tree is just conventional truth, sammutti sacca. They are concepts, paññatti, that are thought about.

Acharn: At the moment of touching, is there a tree or a table? Is a flower also hard? There must be solidity, the element of earth. There are so many cittas before there can be the idea of flower. Thinking about it is not a moment of direct experience which is another level of understanding. At the moment of experiencing hardness, we never thought how minute it is. No table, no chair is touched. (If this is not realised) there cannot be the elimination of the idea of self.

Sarah: The only realities in daily life are citta, cetasika and rūpa. Seeing is a citta, hearing is a citta, thinking now is a citta. Cetasikas are mental factors that accompany cittas. Mettā, anger or paññā are cetasikas. Rūpa is the reality that does not experience anything. Rūpas are visible object, that which is seen now, or hardness, that which is touched now. Cittas arise and fall away seventeen times faster than rūpa. What we take for life are just citta, cetasika and rūpa. Everything else is just an idea, a fantasy of what is experienced.

Acharn: There can be understanding of what the Buddha taught at different levels until there can be the moment of enlightenment of the truth just as the Buddha had enlightened the truth.

Jonothan: There is eye-consciousness experiencing visible object followed by many moments of thinking about the visible object that has been experienced. By thinking in this way there is the idea of people and things. The moment of seeing is just a moment of eye-consciousness experiencing visible object. Those moments are not apparent to us, and there is no point in looking for seeing and visible object, hearing and sound. That is an idea of being able to create conditions for understanding.

Nina

22.3 Saturday discussion, XXXII, 4

Nina
Mar 3 #166812

Who can control life?

Dear friends,

Acharn: It is only because of the Buddha's teachings that the truth of life can be known. The idea of self is so very deeply rooted. We have considered a lot about the realities in life now in order to have confidence that this is the truth and nothing else. There is no one who can do anything or who can control life.

Nina: "No control" can be experienced without thinking? There is no control of what will arise next.

Sarah: If there is no understanding of seeing which sees and has arisen by conditions, there cannot be any understanding of no control. It is just thinking of an idea. Without understanding of reality now nothing can be understood of reality as not being controlled. It is thinking of the story of no control.

Nina: No control of the arising of seeing now, that is thinking of a story. Is that right?

Jonothan: I think it is like knowing impermanence. We all know what impermanence means. We know that everything is impermanent, that this moment is impermanent, but it is not the impermanence the Buddha spoke of as a characteristic of conditioned dhamma. Only when conditioned dhammas are the object of understanding, impermanence of conditioned dhammas becomes apparent. It is the same about "no control" which is an aspect of not self.

If we talk about no control as not knowing what will happen the next moment, it is useful but it is not the understanding of the uncontrollability of realities.

Nina: That is clear now. I wonder whether at the first stage of understanding, which is pariyatti, intellectual understanding, there is already a beginning of direct experience? How can there ever be direct experience if there is only thinking?

Sarah: As regards everything in life being impermanent or uncontrollable, it has to be right understanding of reality now, such as visible object at this moment which appears. Otherwise there is just a conventional idea that dhammas are impermanent or that one not always gets what one wants. It is not understanding of the Buddha's teachings about realities now which are anattā. This is the beginning of pariyatti.

Acharn: There are many realities around now but can there be the understanding of what is there? It is like a whole, a tree, table or chair. We can begin to understand different realities. For example, we are talking about Khun Vicai. Who knows him? But if we talk a little more about him we acquire an idea about him. Like, when we talk more about seeing we have some idea about it. We acquire some idea about hardness, about thinking. We have to understand the characteristic of just one reality at a time. Even-so, the more we know different characteristics of Khun Vicai, his eyes, his ears, we can find him very quickly. We can know him when we see him.

It is like seeing now, hearing now, thinking now. We have no idea what they are like, until there is a moment of understanding. We are talking about the phenomena of body and mind until they are known one by one. Seeing is not hearing, not thinking. Without the word of truth there is no understanding of realities as not self.

Nina

22.4 Saturday discussion XXXII, 5

Nina
Mar 4 #166820

Pariyatti, paṭipatti and paṭivedha

Dear friends,

There can be clear understanding of seeing and what is experienced by seeing. It appears well, one by one, and very fast. No "I", there are different realities. Just understanding, no expectation, letting go the idea of self. There can be more and more understanding of each reality, such as chanda, interest. Chanda to listen to the truth or to talk about the truth. To have more understanding of realities as "no one" is quite a relief, a relief that there is no one, only different realities. Saṃsāra keeps on by conditions. It is now, no matter it is understanding of the level of pariyatti, of paṭipatti or of paṭivedha. Paññā understands correctly what level it is.

There is nothing in visible object, only different colours.

Sarah: When Acharn mentions pariyatti, paṭipatti and paṭivedha, these are stages of understanding. Pariyatti is right understanding, but at the level of thinking. Now, when we talk about seeing, it is not the direct level of the understanding of seeing, but it is the right intellectual understanding that it is just seeing that sees. Without reflecting wisely about different realities there is no condition for higher understanding, direct understanding of realities, which is paṭipatti. Some people translate this word as practice and they say that there must be practice first before there can be intellectual understanding. That is the wrong way round. There must be intellectual understanding of dhamma as anattā, by conditions, before there can be direct understanding of realities as in satipaṭṭhāna. This understanding is not practice, no one can practise or can do anything.

Paṭipatti is the momentary, direct understanding of the reality appearing now, about which we heard before or which we considered before. There should not be selection, focussing or desire to be aware. And only this paṭipatti or satipaṭṭhāna will lead to the realization of the truth in vipassanā ñāna and enlightenment. These are the levels of understanding of pariyatti, paṭipatti and paṭivedha.

Nina

22.5 Saturday discussion XXXII, 6

Nina
Mar 5 #166838

Realities "pop up"

Dear friends,

Sarah: Acharn was using the expression "popping up" for realities that appear. Usually ignorance, attachment and aversion "pop up" all the time after seeing or hearing. Wise reflection on the Dhamma is a condition that understanding can pop up from time to time, not because anyone is trying to have it.

Acharn also spoke about chanda which is often translated as desire and this is quite misleading. Chanda is the reality that takes an interest in the object and this is not only with lobha, but also with kusala citta. When there is wise reflection on Dhamma there has to be wholesome chanda. Chanda is one of the iddhipādas, factors leading to enlightenment.

Another word Acharn mentioned was Saṃsāra, the cycle of birth and death, but each moment of life is saṃsāra, every moment now is saṃsāra.

Sundara stressed that not the word is important but the understanding.

The word paṭipatti was discussed. Tina suggested that it is direct experience.

Jonothan elaborated: There is an experience all the time. Seeing is an experience. What is special about paṭipatti? What makes it different from just this moment of experience? It is experience with understanding.

Sarah: One thinks, for example, that there can be direct experience of the body or of breath. This is not the direct experience of a reality, it is thinking of a concept, an idea about reality. There has to be pariyatti, intellectual understanding first. If one thinks that one touches an arm or the body it is not right understanding of a reality.

Jonothan: When touching an arm, only hardness, softness or temperature is experienced. The idea that what is touched is an arm is just thinking.

Sarah: One has to consider what is real. If there is no understanding of what is real now realities cannot be directly understood.

Nina

22.6 Saturday discussion, XXXIII, 1

Nina
Mar 7 #166866

The meaning of popping up

Dear friends,

Discussing the meaning of popping up, used by Acharn.

Acharn: Popping up: it appears suddenly, it shows the truth of it. Now nothing pops up: seeing, hearing, like, dislike. It is conditioned to go on rapidly, as it is. When it is clear, by conditions, it pops up, to be known. It is nothing, then something and then nothing again. When it pops up, by conditions, there is no doubt about the reality at that moment. This is the fine line between the meaning of different words.

We talked before about the object experienced through a sense-door and then through the mind-door. Seeing sees in the eye-door process, and the citta before and after seeing does not see but experiences visible object, but not through the mind-door yet. No one can understand the fine line between the sense-door and mind-door, but it is there: the citta which experiences an object through the sense-door is different from the citta which experiences the object through the mind-door. That is why we have to consider more and more to understand the fine line between different realities.

Is it true, does it appear as it is, or not yet? We have to consider again and again and again, until paññā develops to understand the difference between intellectual understanding and paṭipatti, direct understanding, more and more, so that there will be conditions for pativedha, direct realization of the truth. No one knows when it will pop up, depending on conditions.

Understanding develops so little at a time. In a day there are many moments of forgetfulness of what appears. Understanding is not enough to become direct understanding. We have to hear again and again and, for example, at the moment of touching there can be non-forgetfulness. It is direct understanding, but understanding is not enough. It is the beginning of direct understanding which knows the arising and falling away of a reality. Paññā understands more and more and it is not forgetful that there is a reality. It just begins. It is like you have something to plant but you do not put it into the soil yet.

At that very moment of understanding, it develops by saṅkhāra khandha that arises, performs its function from moment to moment. Paññā is accumulated to condition moments of understanding later on. If there is no letting go, and one is trying so hard, it hinders the development of paññā to directly understand what is appearing now.

Nina

22.7 Saturday discussion XXXIII, 2

Nina
Mar 8 #166896

What is the meaning of a good friend?

Dear friends,

Alan: What is the meaning of a good friend?
Acharn: What is a friend?
Alan: Someone who is helpful to you.
Acharn: Who is your good friend?
Alan: The best friend is the understanding of the teachings. The Buddha is the best friend.
Acharn: And those who follow the Buddha.
Alan: We think of people, but it is association with the wise words. If you do not come across a good friend, it is so rare to find.
Acharn: Who knows who is a good friend?
Alan: It has to be paññā, it is not somebody.
Sarah: If we do not know realities and talk about a good friend it is just a concept. When we talk about that person as a good friend it is just citta, cetasika and rūpa.
Azita: You do not know when you will meet a good friend, when understanding will arise.
Tadao: What is ānussati, reflection: Buddhanussati, Dhammānussati, Sanghānussati. I hardly contemplate the Buddha, the Dhamma and the Sangha.
Acharn: Now we are reflecting on Dhamma, we do not have to say: Dhammānussati. When you are reflecting on what life is now, it is already dhammānussati. It is only through the understanding of the Dhamma that there can be a beginning of a little understanding of the virtues of the Buddha.
Sarah: It is not a matter of going somewhere and paying respect to the Triple Gem. One can begin to understand what is meant by Sangha, those who enlightened the truth so that it is possible for us to hear about the truth.

Jonothan: A lot of confidence is based on it that others have become enlightened by following the Buddha's Path.

Acharn: There is the understanding of absolute realities, and at that moment do you ever think of the virtues of the Buddha? At any moment of understanding do not forget who brings about this understanding to the whole universe. Any moment when citta is full of gratitude we come to understand what was hidden. It appears clearer and clearer, little by little. By whom? That is the moment of thinking of the Buddha. It is not something to perform but it is the moment of understanding, never forgetting the virtues of the One who has enlightened, who brought the light to the world. That is Buddhānussati. It depends on conditions how much in a day there is Buddhanussati, or not at all. When one sees the value of understanding the truth, understanding the nature of realities right now, by way of bodhipakkhiyadhamma, the factors pertaining to enlightenment, one can think of the excellent qualities of bodhipakkhiyadhamma. No one there at all and that is dhammānussati.

Nina

22.8 Saturday discussion XXXIV, 1

Nina
Mar 14 #166951

The Buddha's virtues

Dear friends,

Acharn: There must be sati while thinking of the Buddha's virtues and great compassion, so that we can understand what is appearing. At that moment, sati is aware of the virtues and the great compassion of the Buddha. That is Buddhānussati. The word of the Buddha is just for understanding, otherwise it is useless, no matter we talk about the truth of the reality at that moment. Even now, there can be more confidence in enlightenment and his words, and then thinking of his great wisdom, compassion and purity. It is sati that does not think of other things besides the truth of his words.

Sarah: when we think of the gocaras, of arakkha gocara (the object that is a protection against akusala) this is also Buddhānussati. All the teachings lead to the appreciation of the Buddha's qualities, appreciation of the Dhamma. It is always this moment.

Nina

22.9 Saturday discussion XXXIV, 2

Nina
Mar 15 #166966

Nāma rūpa pariccheda ñāna

Dear friends,

Acharn: There should be understanding of what is nāma and what is rūpa, but not just by words.

Nina: I find it difficult to know a reality as nāma, not rūpa.

Acharn: The object of experience is usually rūpa. Who considers the nature of that which experiences now? It is not "I". No one. This is the point to understand the truth in life. There are conditions for the arising of what can experience and what cannot experience, and then gone completely. The whole life is like this. When death comes, all is gone completely. The absolute truth is that nothing is left, even this moment.

There can be a beginning to understand the nature which is not self. No matter we call it sama-lobha (ordinary lobha) or visama-lobha (extraordinary, very strong lobha), it is there to be known as not self. Otherwise there cannot be clear comprehension of nāma and rūpa. Nāma rūpa pariccheda ñāna (direct understanding of the different characteristics of nāma and rūpa, the first stage of vipassanā ñāna). Insight knowledge begins and develops, having more confidence in the truth of no-self. We just understand the words, but what about the experience now. There is no one.

It (nāma) is now experiencing whatever appears, as no one, but the idea of something is always there because of ignorance. Paññā is working its way at the moment of understanding of what experiences and of that which is experienced. They just arise, performing different functions and they fall away, never to return. Otherwise there cannot be less clinging to that as "some thing" with different levels of attachment and akusala. Each word, carefully thought about, leads to understanding the truth more, and to the eradication of anusaya (latent tendency).

Nina

22.10 Saturday discussion, XXXIV, 3

Nina
Mar 16 #166982

Different levels of anusaya (latent tendency)

Dear friends,

Sarah: If there were not the accumulation of the ordinary lobha, again and again, there would not be conditions for the strong lobha that causes harm and disturbance to oneself and others. It accumulates on and on, so, it has to be understood as well. It is just dhamma, not my disturbance. It is helpful to appreciate the different levels of anusaya (latent tendency) that condition the subtle or low level of lobha. The low level of lobha conditions very strong lobha in life, often unexpectedly.

Slight lobha is difficult to know, but it is not a matter of trying to find it or to catch it. Gradually as understanding develops lesser kinds of lobha are understood. Even now when hearing the discussion or when we see our friends, there are so many moments of ordinary lobha.

There was a discussion with Harji about nimitta (the sign of reality).

Sarah: What is important is awareness of visible object or hardness now, awareness of the characteristic of what appears at this moment. No need to think of how many visible objects have arisen and fallen away. The reality of visible object has gone. There is awareness of the nimitta (sign) of that visible object which appears now. At the moment of awareness there is no thinking whether there is nimitta, or how many visible objects there were. The point is the understanding of what appears at this moment. Visible object must have gone already.

When there is understanding and awareness of visible object, it is just understanding and awareness of a characteristic of that reality, the sign of the reality itself. We get closer and closer to the understanding of the nimitta of the reality, which is the opposite of an idea about visible object, right now while we are talking about it.

The main thing is the understanding of what appears, instead of getting lost in the whole story, trying to work out all the details, rather than understanding of what appears.

Nina

22.11 Saturday Discussion XXXIV, 4

Nina
Mar 18 #166998

The best miracle

Dear friends,

There was a discussion about the difference between a Sammā-sambuddha and a Pacceka Buddha, silent Buddha, who has realized the four noble Truths but does not proclaim Dhamma to the world. The Buddha could perform miracles, but teaching Dhamma is the best miracle.

Acharn: What the Buddha taught, each word can be directly experienced. That is the most wonderful miracle. Just one word will bring about the understanding of the truth, and it can lead to the end, the eradication of anusayas, latent tendencies, the cause of all akusala. That is the most precious miracle.

The Pacceka Buddha understands the same, experiences the four noble Truths, depending on accumulations.

People may experience the four noble Truths, but the understanding is according to their accumulations. For example, the understanding of Sāriputta, Moggallana, Anuruddha, or, when there is no Buddha, of the Pacceka Buddha (it is according to their accumulations). What about just one word from the Buddha, it depends on the listener to understand it. The words are the same but the paññā is different. Even right now, there are so many people around, it (the understanding) depends on accumulations.

As to each word taught by the Buddha, it depends on how it is considered and considered again, to understand it deeper and deeper, to understand the truth of what is now appearing. It is so deep that paññā can go down deeper and deeper, little by little, to experience what the Buddha said. This is so true to the Savaka (listener or follower) who has experienced the truth. So, there is more confidence when there is more understanding of the teachings, of the factors leading to enlightenment (bodhi pakkhiya dhammas), the khandhas, etc. But it has to be by paññā.

Nina

22.12 Saturday discussion XXXIV, 5

Nina
Mar 19 #167004

Nāma, as no one at all

Dear friends,

Nina: Acharn, you spoke about nāma, as no one at all, different from rūpa.

Acharn: It is not just the word, but the truth, the nature, the characteristic of that as it is. We say many times: "this is nāma", but what is nāma does not appear as nāma. We can say "this is lobha", but lobha does not appear as nāma. What is meant by nāma? It is just conditioned to arise and experience. No one can stop its arising, no one can stop anything to arise, because all dhammas are anattā. There can be more understanding, more confidence in the fact that no one directly experiences what is there. Direct understanding pops up... no words, no one at all. At the moment of understanding the arising of that which experiences and that which is experienced no word is needed. It is like the moment of tasting something, no word is needed indicating whether it is sweet or sour, but it is there, experienced beyond words. So as to the understanding of nāma, when it appears, it arises and experiences. It has no shape, no form, no colour, nothing in it. It experiences in processes, mind-door process and sense-door process. After seeing, paññā cannot arise instantly. There is the appearance of the object through the sense-door, bhavaṅga-cittas in between and then the object is experienced through the mind-door. There is a fine line between mind-door and sense-door. What appears is the same but in truth what is experienced through a sense-door must be different from what is experienced through the mind-door. Who knows without the word of the Buddha? What appears has to be as it is, no one can change the way it is.

Nina

22.13 Saturday discussion XXXV, 1

Nina
Mar 21 #167015

Appears well

Dear friends,

Nina: Acharn, you said that there is ignorance and attachment to the objects that follow so rapidly, taking realities for permanent. Could you elaborate?

Acharn: Does sampaṭicchana-citta, receiving consciousness, appear? We can understand the rapidity of the arising and falling away of realities. Everything arises and falls away in split-seconds. It has to be this moment from understanding the processes of the different doorways.

Like seeing now, how fast it is. Because that characteristic of of seeing cannot be experienced. Is cakkhu pasada rūpa, eye-sense, very tiny? How little it is. Visible object that impinges on it has to be very tiny too. It cannot be the table or the flower. It conditions the process of experiencing that which appears now. Just imagine how tiny it is. It cannot be taken for table and chair.

Even at the moment of touching there must be the reality of softness or hardness. We have to understand how tiny the body-sense is.

When a reality appears through one doorway we usually take it for something. The idea of self can be eliminated little by little, depending on it when paññā develops more and very naturally, to be vipassanā ñāna and higher stages of vipassanā ñāna. That is the meaning of the subtlety, the profoundness of what the Buddha taught. All dhammas are very subtle, very difficult to understand, but they can be understood. There can be more understanding stage by stage, from hearing, until one understands directly: this is the Path, the only Way, not just thinking about realities. Reality now can be directly experienced but not with understanding when there is no hearing the truth about it. And after that it depends on conditions: is it enough for direct awareness and understanding of that to begin to develop little by little?

What about just a moment. When we talk about a moment, so many things are seen, but in truth just one moment of seeing cannot be anything, like we used to take it when there is seeing. Can that be the object of studying, considering wisely? To understand the truth that is not like the world which appears to ignorance. Otherwise how can we understand what is meant by vipassanā ñāna, or bhāvanā, or intellectual understanding and the development of understanding until the object appears well. Well means: not as something, but as it is.

Nina

22.14 Saturday discussion XXXV, 2

Nina
Mar 22 #167026

Do you know the Buddha?

Dear friends,

Acharn: Develop understanding of no one and nothing. As soon as it is not as object it is gone forever in saṃsāra. What is there now, seeing, and it is gone completely in saṃsāra. Is it worth to cling to it? It is no more, just gone.

That which is seen can be seen only, and then it is gone, just one moment. Everything is gone.

Azita: When the Dhamma is seen, the Buddha is also known. The Buddha is known, when the Dhamma is known.

Acharn: Do you know the Buddha?

Azita: Only by reading about him.

Acharn: Do you understand all his teachings?

Azita: Not all, no.

Acharn: When there is more understanding you begin to see the great wisdom of the Buddha. Only his words bring us closer and closer to know him, knowing what is meant by enlightenment, because he showed the Path leading to understanding of what is there now, little by little, until the truth can be directly experienced as he taught.

What about nāma and rūpa? We heard the definitions of them, but now at this moment is there no touching? There are hardness, seeing, they are all absolute truth, absolute dhammas, but there is no understanding of them, one by one. Now they are together, but from hearing again and again there can be the understanding of no self, before there can be the actual moment of direct understanding and direct awareness. By conditions, and there should be no expectation. It brings more confidence in the truth of no one, just dhamma as it is. The more understanding there is, the more one begins to see and know the Buddha, his great wisdom, his virtue and compassion.

Azita referred to a Thai saying that if you know a lot you realize that you do not know much.

Acharn: Now we know how little we understand the teaching. It is just intellectual understanding and without paññā how can we know that it is not enough. It is just only talking about what has not been seen. Like nāma and rūpa now. They are there now, but no understanding. The more we know the more we understand that we just know very little, not enough. When there is no understanding one thinks that one knows enough.

What about the meaning of profoundness or subtlety of the reality? If we just talk about table and just think "I is not me", is that subtle, is that profound? The Path is very profound because it is the moment of understanding. From moment to moment we are clinging to the idea of self and this is only intellectual understanding, not yet understanding directly, precisely of what is now appearing. It has to depend on conditions. Even one tries so hard, no one can make sati and paññā arise.

Nina

22.15 Saturday discussion, XXXV, 3

Nina
Mar 23 #167038

Hiri, shame of akusala

Dear friends,

Acharn: Each word of the Buddha is about what is there now. For example, hiri, shame of akusala, may arise at the moment of not understanding the truth and knowing that it should be the object of understanding, not by oneself but by the words of the Buddha, clearer and clearer, little by little. And that is hiri. One sees the danger of not understanding the truth of this moment. One may not understand anything in life, and what about next life? There will be more and more ignorance which is a great danger because it brings more akusala.

Paññā which develops can know more and more about the understanding of truth, and it knows what level (of understanding) there is and it knows that no one can make it to be more than that. Only paññā can understand and let go and bring about the moment of appearing well of what is there, not as what we take for something, for people and things.

Sarah: As regards the subtlety of what is heard and understood, this depends on the wise considering or understanding now. Like Nina said, sometimes there is a new emphasis on "no one", but actually, from the beginning Acharn was stressing that the Buddha has always said that what is seen is just visible object, what is heard is just sound. But it may not have been apparent what is being referred to: just dhamma that it is seen, no one at all. It may make more sense now, but that has always been the message.

It is the same when we read the Buddha's teaching, about the point Azita mentions and Sundara refers to, that who sees the Dhamma sees the Buddha. In the beginning one might have thought of the Buddha as a person, but with understanding it is clear that there never was a Buddha or is a Buddha, but those qualities we refer to as Buddha can be understood more and more as understanding develops.

Nina

22.16 Saturday discussion, XXXV, 4

Nina
Mar 25 #167049

Shame of akusala

Dear friends,

Sarah had a question about hiri, shame of akusala, and ottappa, seeing the danger of akusala. She asked whether ottappa refers to understanding of the danger.

Acharn: Can a moment of kusala arise without hiri? There is shame about being ignorant of akusala. It is not yet seeing the danger of what arises and falls away. It is not the exact moment which appears as it is. There can be just talking about the arising and falling away of seeing and hearing.

At the moment of understanding of what appears well, as just arising and falling away so very fast, is that seeing the danger?

Sarah: It is dangerous but it is not really understood. We know that it falls away instantly, but there is clinging immediately, so, it is dangerous.

Acharn: Only wrong view, diṭṭhi, and doubt are eradicated at the first stage of enlightenment. But how strong lobha is. Even when it seen clearly and there is no wrong understanding any more. How much clinging has been accumulated will be understood more and more.

Acharn mentions different stages of vipassanā, and there has to be knowledge of dissolution (bhaṅga ñāna), which is the fifth stage of vipassanā ñāna before there can be higher stages, such as the sixth stage, knowledge of terror (bhaya ñāna) and the seventh stage, knowledge of danger (ādinava ñāna) before the eighth stage, knowledge of dispassion (nibbida ñāna) can arise (See Survey of Paramattha Dhammas, the stages of vipassanā).

Acharn: It is not thinking, it is understanding. The truth is when it appears. Paññā is so great at that moment, much more than thinking. Otherwise (when they do not appear) the accumulated latent tendencies, anusayas, cannot be eradicated.

There can be more confidence in no one and nothing. The proof of that is when it appears. Paññā is so great at that moment, it is more than intellectual understanding. It is developed with sati, direct awareness, until time comes by conditions for reality to appear well, as it is. So it can be right now. Begin to know it is just daily life. But paññā is not strong enough, until it begins to develop on and on, and the object appears, depending on how much understanding is there.

Citta, what is meant by it? Citta experiences one object at a time. The Buddha taught that even one moment of citta or one object which is the object of a citta cannot be known. The Buddha taught about the process of seeing. Seeing now is very subtle, hearing, sound, everything, because they arise and fall away in split-seconds. Citta arises and falls away faster than rūpa. All can be known by way of nimitta, (the sign, that is) the succession of that which can be known. Just one characteristic at a time (can be experienced). When it is clear, just one object is there, no other objects.

Nina

22.17 Saturday discussion, XXXV, 5

Nina Mar 26 #167053

Touching fire

Dear friends,

Acharn: Is akusala good, wholesome? What is not wholesome is dangerous, depending on the degree of akusala. Sama-lobha (ordinary lobha) is so natural, like now. That is why it is not easy to understand lobha, because it is always there, in any situation. For example, someone who just wanted to study Abhidhamma, studied it and took examination. To get what? Is that not lobha? Each word should bring detachment, letting go the idea of self. When understanding is not strong enough he can (still) have some understanding, such as knowing what fire is like. But when we do not touch it yet how can we know that it is so dangerous? The heat is so little and it touches lightly (when just near the fire), but there is not enough understanding of its danger. Before there can be the (actual) touching of fire, it is so far away. It is now arising and falling away, but it is far away from understanding. What appears does not appear as it is, it does not appear well.

We begin to see where we are now: we are in darkness of ignorance, not understanding the truth of whatever is there. Is that not dangerous? We are not understanding what is akusala, and we think not of the value of understanding the truth. Is it not dangerous to be born again and again? Who knows in what plane and what would happen, like in this life no one knows what would be the next moment, kusala or akusala. Is it not dangerous? It is like living in a house on fire, not finding the way out. Not understanding the cause of the fire. Ignorance, not understanding the truth. We cling to nothing, because it (the object of clinging) has gone immediately, as soon as it is appearing.

As to the two cetasikas of hiri and ottappa, they are shame of not understanding the truth and not seeing the danger of not understanding the truth.

There may be no chanda (interest) to listen to the Dhamma, but how can there be more understanding without chanda? All dhammas were unknown until the Buddha taught each of them as it is, as not self. We can begin to have confidence in the truth which has been accumulated little by little. It conditions seeing the benefit of the precious moment of understanding. Without this moment of understanding how can there be more understanding and firm understanding later on?

Nina

22.18 Saturday discussion, XXXVI, 1

Nina
Mar 28 #167075

Nimitta (sign of a reality)

Dear friends,

Harji had a question about nimitta (sign of a reality).

Sarah: There were countless visible objects so it is the sign of visible object that is experienced. It is the understanding of the characteristic of visible object that appears. When there is direct understanding of a characteristic of reality, that characteristic appears. In truth it is the nimitta of that reality.

Nina: I still find nimitta a difficult subject. I just understand it in theory.

Jonothan: Only the nimitta, the after-image, can be experienced. Also the thinking about what has been seen comes in very quickly. The idea of people and things comes in so quickly. When there is understanding of reality, reality cannot be found in people and things, in trying to see it in people and things there is a concept, which is different. What the Buddha said has to be considered very carefully.

Acharn: If you do not think of the term what is now appearing? We do not call it anything yet, but what is there now? It is very hard to say, it arises and falls away instantly. We think of a table or a chair. The absolute reality is seeing and that which is seen. What is seen is only that which is now appearing. How can seeing arise without the object which is seen? Studying dhamma is studying what is there now in truth, in the absolute truth. We take it for a chair, but where is it? When there is seeing, is there any chair? We learn to understand each moment as it is. When we talk about a table, it is a "thing" but what is there can be experienced, through one doorway at a time. If there is no understanding of the absolute truth, of what is there now, there cannot be the understanding of dhamma.

What is the absolute truth of seeing, hearing, smelling, tasting, touching and thinking? There are only six doors from day to day, from life to life. Different moments, not all at the same time, like seeing cannot be hearing, no matter in what life. Seeing has conditions to arise but it does not see a table. Is there anything on the table? That is not the truth, because then there would be something there.

Understand the truth of not self until there can be the understanding of dhamma, of anattā, that is uncontrollable. There can be more confidence in dhamma as not self.

Nina

22.19 Saturday discussion, XXXVI, 2

Nina
Mar 30 #167093

Nimitta and concept

Dear friends,

There was a discussion about nimitta and concept.

Acharn: Do we have to use the word concept? What is meant by concept? Without that which experiences, can there be any concept?

That is why we have to hear the teachings on and on. One day the understanding of no one and nothing can be at the moment of touching, and then there is awareness and understanding of that particular object, not any other, until one is used to the characteristic of no self. There is more and more letting go, until the reality appears well, as it is, not as nimitta of things, but it has to be nimitta of a characteristic of reality.

Sarah: It has to be understanding of the reality itself, otherwise one takes just the word and it becomes the object of clinging. There has to be awareness of the reality itself, then there is no doubt what is a reality and what a concept.

Trying to catch it and work it out is the opposite of letting go. Understand what appears now, no matter it is confusion, doubt, seeing, anything. Otherwise there will be more clinging in the name of dhamma.

The main point is: just understanding of the reality that appears. Otherwise someone may have the idea that when working out the story of nimitta, there will be more understanding.

Nina

22.20 Saturday discussion XXXVI, 3

Nina
Mar 31 #167101

Can there be anyone moving?

Dear friends,

Azita: Can anyone say and do what he wants?

Acharn: Is there no dhamma? Can there be anyone moving, thinking, talking at will? There is a reality, cetanā cetasika. I can say: I see Khun Azita, and then there is understanding of what is there. I have to say whom I see. I see Khun Azita but I understand what Azita is. That is why the Buddha can talk to Ānanda, to Sāriputta etc. But there is the understanding of the truth at that moment: no one, no thing, only paramattha dhammas together. We have to understand words so that it can be understood whom we mean: Khun Azita, Khun Jonothan, Khun Sarah.

There are different levels of understanding, depending on conditions. Is understanding ready to understand quicker and quicker? Or understand what is just there once and then gone? One may not be used yet to understand that characteristic as not self. It depends on how much paññā develops.

Realities may pop up (appear suddenly), but there may not be enough letting go more, to see that it is so useless. What about the arising and falling away not only once but all the time in this life, and not only in this life but also in the next life. No one, just the way dhamma is. Seeing that arises to see and then no more. Just experiencing that, what for? To see only what arises and falls away. Each moment is conditioned.

When we say: I can see, it may be with or without understanding. "I" is not me, but I have to use the word "I", he, she. But there is the understanding that it is a reality which has been conditioned to arise and see, and fall away instantly. It all depends on understanding, on what level of understanding there is, how much paññā there is and how sharp, to let go the idea of self, and at what stage of paññā. But the arising and falling away at this moment does not appear as no one and nothing.

What about the arising and falling away of seeing, can anyone make it that way? It depends on understanding, no matter what word you use: I, he, she, table or tree. The understanding is there, to know what it is. Does phassa (contact) pop up? It arises, but paññā is not yet of that degree (to understand it). There is nothing, then something and then nothing. Each moment is gone.

Nina

23

April 2021

23.1 Saturday discussion XXXVI, 4

Nina
Apr 1 #167122

The danger of saṃsāra

Dear friends,

Acharn: Seeing now, there are uncountable moments. That which is seen are so many things, they have to impinge on the eye-base. Seeing arises and falls away and then there are other cittas that experience the same object. They are so short, before there can be the idea of something there with different shape and form. And this is life, no one at all, before there is shame (hiri) of clinging to that which is nothing. It is not that level of shame yet until the truth is realized more and more, enough to condition even thinking: "But what is the use of being born, no matter in what plane, as what?"

There is just arising and falling away, all the time. Then there is the end of this life which is the end of this personality.

What is the use of having everything in a day, gone at night, then waking up, having something more in a day and then gone at night, falling fast sleep. The same thing will be next life.

Harji: I see more the uselessness of dhamma. What is the use of what arises and falls away.

Acharn: Otherwise how could there be seeing and understanding the danger of saṃsāra.

Azita: This is a slightly different answer to my question: "Can anyone say and do what he wants?".

But it is a very good comment you are making. What people say is a sound, a reality, just sound. Or what they are doing, and I am thinking that that is not good, it is just visible object that occurs. A whole lot of thinking of what I hear, I see.

If I do not hear what is the reality that arises and falls away, I am making judgement about people and this is not helpful.

Sarah: Anyone can say anything, anyone can have his own idea. One has his own point, but what is the truth now? The understanding has to be of what appears now.

Azita: Just hearing sound, seeing visible object. Develop paññā, know it is just a reality.

Sarah: Each person has his own way of thinking. The more understanding, the more hiri and ottappa (shame and fear of the consequences of akusala), the more mettā. The more understanding the more compassion when we see what is not right.

Nina

23.2 Saturday discussion, XXXVI, 5

Nina
Apr 2 #167136

Kalapas

Dear friends,

Sundara mentioned that there must be, in the case of body-sense, thousands of kalapas (groups of rūpa) with body-sense, kāya pasada rūpa, since body-sense is all over the body.

Acharn: Can we talk about what number of kalapas? When talking about the body, the hand, the foot, whenever hardness or softness appears, there must be the kalapa with kāyappasāda (body-sense) on which hardness can impinge. Otherwise kāyaviññāṇa (body-consciousness) cannot arise. We cannot count kalapas and we have no idea about the whole body when there is just that which experiences hardness. So, how tiny that hardness is, and the kāya pasada rūpa, the body-sense which arises with the other rūpas in that group, the four primary rūpas and others, is very tiny.

There is only the world of nimitta (sign), and each process cannot be known. It is impossible, because they arise and fall away so rapidly. What can be known is only the nimitta, because only one process cannot be the object of understanding, according to the way cittas have to arise in (a particular) order in a process. So there has to be firm understanding about dhamma, each one, so very tiny, so very fast. Otherwise citta cannot be the magician making to appear what is seen and touched as people and things.

As we read in the commentary to Khandhavagga § 95, Foam:

> "Consciousness is like a magical illusion (māyā) in the sense that it is insubstantial and cannot be grasped. Consciousness is even more transient and fleeting than a magical illusion. For it gives the impression that a person comes and goes, stands and sits, with the same mind, but the mind is different in each of these activities. Consciousness deceives the multitude like a magical illusion."

Nina

23.3 Saturday talk, XXXVII, 1

Nina
Apr 5 #167189

Against the stream of common thought

Dear friends,

Alan mentioned that the Buddha, after his enlightenment, said that what he taught is against the stream of common thought. He wondered how to deal with this.

Acharn: People have different interests. The truth cannot be wrong. It depends on how much understanding there is of the truth as it is. No one can do anything, even about one's own accumulation. As one cannot change one's own accumulation how can one change someone else's?

It depends on how much one can see the value of understanding which can condition more kusala, up to the complete eradication of all akusala that has been accumulated.

What one can do is just talk about the words of the Buddha, about the absolute truth, whatever is there. One can begin to understand what is the absolute truth. Is there a self? Yesterday I did this and that, I ate this and that. What about now? Where is the "I" who ate yesterday. Today the "I" is gone. It depends (on conditions) who would like to understand better, until there can be clear comprehension, and one can penetrate the absolute truth, just as that which is now appearing.

The anattāness becomes clearer. Even right now anattāness is each moment. But it does not reveal itself. (The change) from a moment of seeing to thinking is so very rapid. There is no attention, no chanda (interest) to understand that. That is why we keep on talking about the truth that is hidden. It is now, this moment, but it is hidden.

Nina

23.4 Saturday discussion XXXVII, 2

Nina Apr 6 #167217

The uselessness of dhamma

Dear friends,

Alan: Because of lack of understanding the reality is hidden.

Nina: On the Dutch Dhamma evening one of the subjects was death. People always talk about stories, their relatives and dear ones they lost. It is difficult to explain the real meaning of death, each moment. To bring them back to reality. Like Alan said, it is against the stream of common thought.

Jonothan: People are concerned about those aspects you mention and not interested in the reality, and this is just a moment of citta, consciousness.

Nina: How can we help? We cannot always help.

Sarah: As Acharn said: they each have their own interest. They just want to talk about different stories.

Nina: Last time there was a discussion about pain. Acharn asked: "Where is it?" She had asked before: "Where are you now?" She explained that it is nowhere, in no place. In the absolute sense there is no place. She had said that there is no Vietnam, no Thailand. It is the same for painful feeling, there is no place . It is so difficult, because pain can be acute, my arm is so painful.

Jonothan: Pain is real, but the idea of a place is just thinking.

Sarah: Even for us there are long stories all the time. A long story about my arm hurting. There could be more understanding and compassion for those who often get lost in stories.

Nina: Acharn stressed a lot the uselessness of dhamma. What is the use of being born again and again, seeing and hearing. In the evening we go to sleep and everything is lost. A good reminder. I usually do not think of the uselessness of life.

Sarah: Usually we think of the body, my arm, we take it for my body. What is experienced is just the hardness. Unpleasant feeling is just a moment of experiencing unpleasant feeling. What is taken for the body is so important to us. What we find so important, my body, is just fantasy, because there is no body. Just different nāmas and rūpas.

Nina

23.5 Saturday discussion XXXVII, 3

Nina
Apr 8 #167251

Life is very short

Dear friends,

Acharn: Life is very short, only one moment. It is different all the time. Paññā can realize it as it is. Otherwise there cannot be any moment to let go the idea of self, little by little, gradually, until the end, no more (self) at all, absolutely eradicated.

Touching now, hardness cannot be anything else. It appears, while the other objects do not appear. But there is not enough understanding. One keeps on thinking of something else all the time. It takes a long time to be used to the real characteristic of hardness as just hardness, even though hardness appears and is then gone. Saññā marks and remembers wrongly all the time, because there is no direct experience of the arising and falling away (of realities).

There can be more direct awareness when there is direct awareness with understanding, not without understanding. Understanding is so very weak because of ignorance, and wrong understanding has been accumulated for so long, aeons and aeons. So, it cannot be clear at the beginning, but later on it is a little clearer. This is the way to understand the great wisdom of the Buddha who showed the Path leading to the eradication of ignorance. It has to be understanding of what is appearing now, little by little until there is more confidence in the truth.

For example, there is hardness now at the moment of touching, but there are (also) seeing and thinking. These are different moments, but they arise and fall away so very rapidly, impossible to experience just one characteristic in a moment. When there is more understanding there will be less ignorance and wrong understanding, little by little. There can be more confidence that whatever is appearing is conditioned and then no more, never to arise again. Life is just like this, from moment to moment. Next life is the same: seeing, hearing, enjoying oneself and then no more.

Nina

23.6 Saturday discussion XXXVII, 4

Nina
Apr 9 #167262

Not "I" who is aware

Dear friends,

Acharn: The world appears as it is to right understanding, stage by stage, unexpectedly. Now saṅkhārakkhandha (the khandha of fifty cetasikas) and paññā are performing their functions. Not "I" who is aware, who understands. They are all different realities that arise together and fall away together. I listened to the voice or the story just a moment ago, and it is gone. So the "I" who was listening is gone and there is no "I". Then there is another moment of hearing, seeing or thinking. Actually, when they are gone how can there be "I". When there is seeing right now there is the idea of "I" again, or when hearing, "I" again.

Right now there is a reality appearing but it is gone, and others follow instantly, all the time. How can there be no thought about shape and form because of the arising and falling away so rapidly as different colours, to be eyebrow, to be ear, to be hair, so very quickly, beyond imagination. Paññā has to be great enough to really penetrate the truth as the Buddha taught, as he had enlightened. And he taught others to understand little by little, to open up, to reveal the truth of the arising and falling away of realities, one day, we do not know long it will take. But that is the way to let go, depending on conditions.

Each word of the Buddha brings about the understanding of letting go the idea of self at the end. There is no other way. One can see that even a short moment of kusala is so very precious, because we live among akusala from moment to moment. After seeing there is ignorance, the āsava (intoxicant, very subtle akusala) of ignorance. After hearing, there is again ignorance and the āsava of diṭṭhi. The accumulation of clinging to sense objects is there, by conditions. This is life, anattā. That is why learning to understand anattā means letting go atta (self). The understanding of anattā has to go on and on, because paññā understands that it is not enough to eradicate akusala, there are so many kinds of akusala. But what has to be eradicated first is wrong understanding.

Nina

23.7 Saturday discussion XXXVII, 4

Nina
Apr 11 #167273

Clinging to what is next?

Dear friends,

Some short notes: Sarah was having a cold in Thailand and Acharn reminded her that painful bodily feeling is just a moment. It accompanies vipākacitta. Shortly afterwards in the process of cittas, kusala cittas or akusala cittas arise. When there is unhappy feeling it arises with dosa-mūla-citta, citta rooted in aversion. We think about a long story, about painful feeling. Sarah said: my pain, my arm, or we focus our attention to be aware, try to be aware (with an idea of self).

It was stressed that one should not try to be aware. We cling to what? To that which is gone.

Another subject discussed: people have sorrow about the loss of dear ones. Clinging causes sorrow. Sarah said that the only remedy against clinging is understanding right now.

Sarah: Seeing, hearing are gone immediately. Different realities that arise and fall away are not someone. The only way of letting go clinging to my dear one is the understanding of death at this moment. Whatever arises is gone.

Acharn often says that when there is right understanding there is no clinging to the next reality.

Sarah: Seeing and instantly clinging arises to what is next, to what I can experience next. Now we have everything we wish for, seeing now, hearing now, pleasant feeling at this moment. Clinging leads us astray all the time from just understanding with detachment.

Nina: Clinging to what is next?

Sarah: Thinking about what is seen now. Clinging to another reality, wanting to experience another visible object, another sound, another hardness. Other than what appears right now.

Alberto had a question about the four kinds of patisambhida, analytical knowledge: of attha, result, of dhamma, cause, of nirutti, the right word to explain the truth, and of patibhana, the knowledge which has the first three as object. Acharn brought all this back to the present moment. Today one was born, that is result. Or seeing now is result. The condition for birth or for a reality like seeing, that is dhamma patisambhida, cause. Nirutti: the use of the right word to make someone understand the meaning. This is not just knowing the words used in a translation. Not just a word but the nature of a reality has to be understood. Keen understanding of result and cause can condition letting go the idea of self. Each word of the Buddha will lead to more understanding.

Patisambhida of patibhana; this has as object the first three patisambhidas. Right understanding of the first three patisambhidas. They all pertain to our life now. They are not theory.

Nina

23.8 Saturday discussion XXXVIII, 1

Nina
Apr 12 #167285

Begin again, begin again

Dear friends,

Acharn said: "Seeing, it is there. Begin to understand is as that which experiences. No 'I' who sees."

Acharn explained that there can be a beginning of developing understanding, even it is not clear in the beginning. She said: "Begin again, begin again. When it is gone there is a moment of akusala... When we talk about seeing, seeing is now." She explained that attachment and ignorance cover up the truth. When there is more understanding only just one reality can appear clearly, well enough. She gave an example: when there are many people it is impossible to know them all, just know them one by one. Even-so as regards knowing many realities. She said: " It begins to understand this one is not that one... The understanding of anattāness begins to be firm, and there will be more confidence about anattā which means: nothing, no "I"... There are different realities and they can, one by one, be object of understanding. When there is no paññā there is no understanding of each different one that arises and falls away. It appears with the sign, the mark, the nimitta as something there... We live in the world of nimitta when there is no understanding... What appears is nimitta of that which arises and falls away in split-seconds. How can seeing be anyone? Because it is gone."

Sarah to David: she explained that there are two kinds of reality. We think: "I see", but there is seeing and that which is seen. She said: "We think that which is seen is my arm. It is just what is visible."

Nina

23.9 Saturday discussion, XXXVIII, 2

Nina
Apr 13 #167315

The greatest kind of wholesomeness

Dear friends,

Jonothan explained that the greatest kind of wholesomeness is the understanding of the present reality. He said that it is not important whether there is kindness or anger What matters is the understanding of the reality at that moment. All realities are conditioned and there is more unwholesomeness accumulated than unwholesomeness.

Jonothan: "There is as much kindness and wholesomeness as conditions would allow, because for each of us there has been over lifetimes the accumulation of different mental states, wholesome and unwholesome, and that makes us as we are today."

He said that it is not a matter of changing the present moment.

David asked how he could apply it in his daily life. Sarah explained that this is strong clinging to the self. She said: "What is the I that can apply? Is seeing I, is hearing I, is touching I? Or is it just thinking about an idea that it I?"

She said that this causes a lot of disturbance. That is why the Buddha talked about realities that experience and realities that do not experience.

Acharn: "Does anyone would like to be kind? Life goes on by accumulated conditions.

Seeing now is not just as seeing a moment ago. Is the idea of 'I see' right or wrong? Seeing is gone, never to return. Sound is gone, hearing is gone. Everything is there just for a short moment. How can that belong to anything? Can it be something, it is no more."

She explained that the Buddha said after his enlightenment that dhamma is so subtle, very difficult, but that it can be understood.

Acharn: "We have to understand what is there in a moment. There is seeing, no one makes it arise, it has arisen already... What has gone can it belong to anyone? That is the way to let go ignorance and all troubles in life, because of understanding that whatever is there is conditioned. Without the eye can there be seeing?" She said that one cannot try to have seeing. Who made the eyes? The arising and falling away of dhammas is so rapid that no one can experience it. Is it enough to know that seeing is not hearing? All unwholesomeness, all unpleasant situations come from ignorance."

Nina

23.10 Saturday discussion, XXXVIII, 3

Nina
Apr 14 #167331

Atta is something

Dear friends,

Acharn: It does not matter what is there for a very short moment. It cannot bring about regret or sadness as before, because it is not there any more. But as there are still conditions for the arising of such or such reality, nobody can stop it and one can begin to understand is as no one, no self, anattā.

Atta is something, it lasts very short, it is very minute, very tiny. How can it be something like a table, a chair, flowers. In truth, there are not my hands, my head. Touch it, it is hard, hot or cold. It is anattā, no one, there are only absolute realities. Just experience hardness, there is body-sense all over the body.

One day when death comes, we forget about this life, just as we forgot about last life. There is continuation of arising and falling away by conditions. So long as there are still conditions life has to go on. The arising and falling away each moment is birth and death. The moment of death and the next moment of birth is like now.

Jonothan: One may wish to be useful to others and develop more wholesome states, but it is not the highest goal. Before the Buddha's enlightenment people developed wholesomeness to a very high degree, to the level of jhāna, but there was no enlightenment. One was born again, there was no eradication of accumulated tendencies and there was still wrong understanding and ignorance.

Understand the true nature (of realities), what we take for people and things are just conditioned dhammas. If there is just kindness it is temporary, it cannot eradicate unwholesomeness. The understanding that is developed is helping to eradicate unwholesome tendencies.

Sarah: One thinks that different situations like bringing up one's child, driving a car, are different from now, but one gradually learns that life is just in a moment. There is death at this moment: seeing, hearing, thinking, they fall away instantly. In conventional sense it is true: cooking, looking after a child are different from discussing (dhamma), but there are just different moments: seeing, hearing, smelling, tasting, touching, thinking, no matter now or alone in one's flat. Life comes back to his moment, always right now life is just this very moment and then gone instantly.

David: this exercise is easy when doing things that do not require strong concentration like cooking.

Jonothan: We all have similar thoughts when learning about the teachings. When learning more what is real at the present moment there is no reason why those thoughts do not come to mind. Even when playing chess, there are lots of thoughts going on. Whatever interests us comes to mind, unbidden.

Jonothan explained that before we heard the Dhamma we thought of life in terms of situations, but after considering what we have heard we begin to understand that hearing and thinking are the same regardless of the conventional situation. He said that thinking that there has to be a special situation for the development of understanding is an obstacle.

Nina

23.11 Saturday discussion XXXVIII, 4

Nina
Apr 16 #167361

Sacca ñāna and pariyatti

Dear friends,

Alan: I would like to know the difference between sacca ñāna and pariyatti. There are the three levels of understanding: pariyatti, paṭipatti and pativedha, and also sacca ñāna, kicca ñāna and kata ñāna.

Sarah: Alan refers to the different levels of understanding the four noble truths, beginning with the unsatisfactoriness of each reality. Sacca ñāna is the intellectual right understanding which considers the truth as taught by the Buddha. Sacca ñāna is pariyatti which is firm. One does not try to focus on something, going to a special place, wishing for a different situation.

Acharn: What is sacca ñāna? The understanding of the four noble Truths that is so keen with confidence. One does not think: It is I, me, I can do that to condition that.

The first noble Truth is dukkha ariya sacca. Whatever arises has to fall away, no matter in the past, present or future. What is there after death? The arising of the first moment of this life.

This is sacca ñāna: listening, considering very firmly, understanding the truth. Just hearing some words about reality, is that enough? Not enough, so, it cannot be sacca ñāna of the first noble Truth. Life is dukkha, true nor not, firmly understood or not?

Acharn explained that the arising and falling away of realities is dukkha, arising and falling away right now. She said: "What is the use of 'no one at all?' (That) there are only conditioned realities arising and falling away."

Nina

23.12 Saturday discussion XXXVIII, 5

Nina
Apr 19 #167394

Paññā is not sharp enough

Dear friends,

Alan: How does the intellectual understanding of the third noble Truth (Nibbāna) help to understand reality?

Acharn: How can there be conditions for seeing?

Alan: Because of previous moments of seeing?

Acharn: Can there be the end of attachment and ignorance because of more understanding? Not just from learning, hearsay and considering, but when reality appears directly it is the beginning of studying to have more letting go of that reality. It has to pertain to all realities of daily life.

Lobha is there. When it is unknown how can it be eradicated. We can understand that there is no "I" but reality does not appear as it is, even to direct awareness. So long as attachment is not known in daily life there cannot be higher understanding, it is only intellectual understanding. Even it is there it depends on how great, how sharp paññā is to let go.

It depends on the accumulations how many stages of insight can arise. Attachment appears, but paññā is not sharp enough, it may be just the first stage of insight, nāma-rūpa paricheda ñāna, knowing the difference between nāma and rūpa. There is more considering in daily life while one applies the knowledge gained from vipassanā. That is why there must be pariññā, full comprehension: ñata pariññā (full comprehension of what has been understood), tirana pariññā (full investigating comprehension) and pahana-pariñña (full overcoming comprehension).

(Nina: Acharn has explained before that the moment of insight is very brief but what has been realised is not forgotten. It must be applied in daily life. There are several stages of insight and after attaining each stage of insight there has to be the application in daily life of what has been realised at that moment. Pariññā is the application.)

Jonothan: The understanding of conditions is the key. The understanding of conditioned realities helps the understanding of the four noble Truths, it helps reflection on the third noble truth, on the unconditioned reality.

Acharn: What is sacca ñāna?

Alan: The firm intellectual understanding.

Acharn: No choice, no selection. This is understanding more about anattā. Until atta (self) is gone completely.

Nina

23.13 Saturday discussion XXXVIII, 6

Nina
Apr 20 #167399

Wise considering

Dear friends,

Acharn: When fast asleep, is there anything?

Alan: There is no object of the world.

Acharn: No one, no thing, no whole. When fast asleep, there is no understading. But when there is understanding there has to be one object at a time. But now there are so many things. When they are together it is not clear, it does not appear well.

Sukin: Can we say that sacca ñāna and pariyatti are the same?

Acharn: What about now?

Sarah: It is the wise considering that gradually leads to direct understanding. There is less trying to work it out, to apply it or less wondering how it happens. We should not get lost in terms.

Acharn: Ñata pariññā (full comprehension of what has been understood), understands clearly each reality as it is. Nāma cannot be rūpa. Tirana pariññā ((full investigating comprehension) means: it is not enough. Impermanence, dukkha, it can let go the idea of self. Vipassanā ñāna is so short to let go the idea of self. Without the application, tirana pariññā, it is impossible to understand the truth of the arising and falling away of realities.

It has to be so natural, more understanding of anattāness. Begin to see the master, lobha. Otherwise it is there unknown all the time. Even right now, a few moments after seeing.

Sarah (to David): As understanding develops no one can try or apply. It is understanding very naturally, no matter the situation. It is a great relief, no thinking of doing anything, like one needs to be a good person first.

Jonothan: Letting go does not mean no decision making in daily life. No need to stop thinking. In the Dhamma there are no "shoulds". One acts naturally as one does now, by conditions. But the understanding of the true nature of the present moment begins to develop.

David: said that he worries about the consequences of his actions.

Alberto: You think that you need special concentration, otherwise you lose the game (when playing chess). That is life: sometimes gain, sometimes loss, no matter we concentrate or not.

We think of different situations in our life. The present moment is always now, no thinking of another moment that has not come yet. We keep on thinking about tomorrow and yesterday, we forget about now. Life goes on as before, no expectation of a better life. It is just by conditions. That is a good reminder for more understanding in the future.

Nina

23.14 Saturday discussion XXXIX, 1

Nina
10:46am #167402

Can there be my arms, my legs?

Dear friends,

Acharn to Sarah's cousin Andy:

What is your interest in Buddhism?

Do you like to experience the truth of whatever is now appearing? What is there now, is it very interesting?

Andy: Yes.

Acharn: It is there now, and then gone forever. Hearing now is not a moment of seeing. Nobody arranged that, but it is there by conditions. Without eye-base and what impinges on it can there be seeing right now? Each moment is anattā, not under anyone's control. There is the idea of "I see".

Is it possible for seeing, hearing or thinking to be at the same moment?

The truth that is directly experienced is called enlightenment. Paññā begins to understand at this moment. Everything is gone as soon as it is there. There is only memory of legs, arms. When there is no thinking can there be my arms, my legs? At the moment of seeing is there any idea of leg, arm, chair? When nothing is understood at that moment how can there be the letting go of the idea of self? There is the idea of I see, I hear, I think, all day long. But in truth there are different realities, conditioned to arise and then fall away instantly.

Nina

23.15 Saturday discussion XXXIX, 2

Nina
Apr 22 #167407

Is what is heard true?

Dear friends,

Acharn (to Andy): Is what is heard true? Can it be directly experienced? If it is not possible, it is useless, it is only an idea or thought about it. There can be moments of understanding more and more deeply, and letting go what one takes for "something". Is there what is seen now? It is there, unknown.

Sarah: The truth of life we do not have to call anything, like the Buddha's truth or give it a particular name. Understanding what life is at this moment is the way to gradually know that what we take for true is actually fantasy, a dreamworld.

Now there are seeing, hearing, smelling, tasting or touching but we think of a self that sees, hears, smells, tastes, or touches. These are just different moments of consciousness. There is just one moment of consciousness at a time, arising and falling away. There is no one who experiences.

Jonothan: When talking about life, what can be directly known as being true? We can talk about other aspects of life, such as how the world began, but that is not the same as directly knowing for oneself the truth about life at this moment.

Sarah: Does one really have an interest to understand what life is now? Or is one happy to just carry on in ignorance, life after life? The truth is that there are two kinds of reality: the reality that experiences an object and the reality that does not experience anything.

Nina

23.16 Saturday discussion, XXXIX, 3

Nina
Apr 23 #167420

Against the stream of common thought

Dear friends,

Jonothan (to Andy): You mentioned mindfulness as the basis how you became interested in the Buddha's teachings.

Mindfulness in the Buddha's teachings is a mental factor, sometimes translated as awareness. Mental factors (accompanying consciousness) can be wholesome, unwholesome (or neither). They are wholesome or unwholesome by nature, not because of a situation. Wholesome means not harmful to oneself or others. Mindfulness is not alertness of what is going on, it performs its function together with understanding of what appears at the present moment.

Nina: I understand that you must be overwhelmed by all the new things, Andy. Also for me, what I learn here is something new every time. For example: "there is seeing now while we talk about seeing". We forget to consider what is real now. We often hear: "It is gone" and after all the explanations we begin to understand more that this moment is so short.

The present moment, what is it?

When we hear about it for the first time it does not have so much meaning to us, but we have to hear about it again and again. A few moments of listening is not enough. There can be a little understanding at a time. It is gone, it is gone but it is not really there. It is accumulated. Accumulation means that a moment of consciousness with understanding conditions a next moment of understanding and this again conditions a next moment. Little by little there will be more understanding. I learn something new in these sessions what I did not realize before. We learn and then we forget again. Before we really understand it takes a while.

Alan: It takes a long time before it sinks in, it is not easy. It is "against the stream of common thought" as the Buddha said after his enlightenment. We have to be patient to listen a lot.

What is touched? Deep in our mind it is the computer or chair that is touched, but actually the reality is just hard or soft. That is rūpa, a physical phenomenon that is impermanent. In our mind it lasts a long time, but hardness does not last. This is a very different way of thinking, and it takes a long time to understand it. Without the Buddha's teaching it is impossible to understand the present moment precisely.

Nina

23.17 Saturday discussion XXXXI, 4

Nina
Apr 25 #167442

What are the realties?

Dear friends,

Sarah explains that there are two kind of realities: a reality that experiences something, which is called nāma, and a reality that does not experience anything. Seeing experiences what is seen, hearing experiences what is heard. The reality that does not experience anything is called rūpa. At the moment of touching it seems that a table or a chair is touched, but actually what is experienced through the body-sense is softness, hardness, cold or motion.

Sarah: The chair is just an idea in the mind... We learn the difference between what are the realities in life and what is just an idea or concept... When we wake up in the morning after a dream we know that that is just imagined. Actually in daytime it is just the same. There is thinking of different fantasies, but they are taken for being real.

Jonothan reacted to what was said before about mindfulness in connection with spirituality.

Jonothan: To me Buddhism does not have any spirituality. No things to believe, it is all about verifying for oneself the truth of the present moment.

Mindfulness in the Buddha's teaching plays an essential part in understanding the present moment. It is a mental factor, not a formal practice to be undertaken.

Acharn: Why are you interested in Buddhism? The Buddha taught the truth about everything. Consider his words, whether they are true or not. There is no one, but what is there now? What is meant by "one" in "no one"? Person, table, chair? How could these be experienced as "some thing" if there is no seeing of that which can impinge on the eye-base... Each day there is seeing and thinking of what is seen. What is the truth of each moment as it is? There is no understanding of the truth of not "I". Not "me'. (When there is seeing), it is only a reality which can experience an object. Then gone completely, never to arise again. Just listen to the truth. No matter how we call it.

Nina

23.18 Saturday discussion XXXIX, 5

Nina
Apr 27 #167502

Life and death

Dear friends,

Acharn: Follow the Way of that which cannot be understood by oneself. From hearing and considering there can be conditions for understanding it. Each moment which arises is gone. It is a momentary death of what has arisen. Death is at each moment because reality is not there any more. This is the way of letting go wrong understanding. Clinging takes what is already gone as something that is there all the time, as something permanent. Before it appears it is not there and when it is there it is conditioned. No one can make it arise.

Only just a moment of reality that impinges on the eye, can it be something? Can it be the table at the moment of touching? What is touched? It is so tiny. It is only that which is hard, not a table, and then gone. The arising and falling away of a reality is so rapid, it appears as a sign, an image of something.

Sarah: Today is the funeral of Prince Philip, so we are thinking about life and death. It is so helpful to reflect that there is death of consciousness at this moment. Every moment is gone, never to return.

Jotika: Is there anything we can do?

Sarah: Can you make seeing arise?

Jotika: No.

Sarah: Can you make hearing arise? Actually there is no "I" who makes whatever is there to arise.

Why do you like to do something so much? Now there is seeing, hearing, thinking. Each reality is arising by conditions and it has to be the way it is by conditions.

Jotika: I think there is a way to have more peace.

Sarah: When wishing so much to have peace, we can see that attachment is the second noble Truth. The cause of all difficulties in life is strong clinging to "I". There is a wish to be able to control situations.

The Buddha's teaching is the development of detachment. Acceptance, understanding what is conditioned rather than trying to change it.

Jotika: It is the idea of self.

Sarah: The fantasy of "I" that can do something. Pleasant feeling or unpleasant feeling cannot be changed, they have already arisen by conditions. The purpose of the Path is not changing of what is conditioned or make calm arise, but just understanding of what is conditioned at this moment. This is the letting go of the strong clinging to the self that can control life.

Nina: Conditions is the coming together of different phenomena. The more we understand that it is impossible to make them arise, the clearer it becomes that nothing can be done. Then you will be less overwhelmed.

Nina

24
Pāli Glossary

Compiled by Jonothan Abbott and Sarah Procter Abbott

abhiñña supernormal power

adhimokkha determination (a cetasika)

adhipati paccaya predominance condition

adosa non-aversion or kindness(a cetasika)

ahetuka rootless (citta)

ahetuka diṭṭhi the wrong view of no cause for what arises

ahirika shamelessness(a cetasika)

ākāsānañcāyatana sphere of boundless space, the subject of the first arūpa jhāna-citta

ākiñcaññāyatana sphere of nothingness, the subject of the third arūpal jhāna-citta

akusala unwholesome

alobha non-attachment or generosity (a cetasika)

amoha understanding(a cetasika)

anāgāmī non-returner, the noble person who has realized the third stage of enlightenment

anantara paccaya proximity condition

anattā non self

anicca impermanent

anottappa recklessness or disregard of unwholesomeness(a cetasika)

anuloma adaptation (citta) arising before jhāna or before enlightenment

anupādisesa nibbāna final nibbāna, khandha parinibbāna at the death of an arahat

anusaya latent tendency

āpo dhātu element of water

appaṇā (samādhi) absorption (concentration)

arahat noble person who has attained the fourth stage of enlightenment

ārammaṇa the object of consciousness

ariya noble, the person who has attained enlightenment

arūpa-brahma-bhūmi plane of existence of immaterial beings. Birth as a result of attaining arūpa jhāna

arūpavacara belonging to the immaterial plane of consciousness, arūpa-jhāna-citta

arūpa-jhāna immaterial absorption

asankhārika strong (cittas) spontaneously arisen, not induced by others

āsava cankers, influxes of intoxicants, group of defilements

asobhana not beautiful, not accompanied by beautiful roots.

asūbha foul

asura demon, being of one of the unhappy planes of existence.

ātāpī heedful, with awareness

atīta bhavaṅga past life-continuum, arising and falling away shortly before a process of citta experiencing an object through one of the sense-doors starts

āvajjana adverting of consciousness to the object which has impinged on one of the six doors

avijjā ignorance

avyākata dhammas (realities) which are not kusala or akusala

ayoniso manasikāra unwise attention to an object

āyūhana kamma at birth which brings results during a lifetime.

bhāvanā mental development, the development of calm, samatha, and the development of insight, vipassanā.

bhāvanā-māya-paññā understanding based on mental development

bhavaṅga citta life-continuum citta which does not arise within a process but in between processes

bhavaṅga calana vibrating bhavaṅga, arising shortly before a sense-cognition process starts

bhavaṅgupaccheda arrest bhavaṅga, last bhavaṅga-citta before a process starts. The bhavaṅgupaccheda which arises before a mind-door process is the mind-door of that process.

bhikkhu monk

bhikkhunī nun

bhūmi plane of existence

brahma-vihāra one of the four "divine abidings". which are loving kindness, compassion, sympathetic joy and equanimity

cakkhu eye

cakkhu-dvāra eye-door

cakkhuppasāda rūpa eye-sense

cakkhuviññāṇa seeing-consciousness

cetanā intention or volition (a cetasika)

cetasika mental factor arising with consciousness

chanda interest (a cetasika)

citta consciousness, the chief reality which experiences an object

citta-kammaññatā wieldiness of citta (a cetasika)

citta-lahutā lightness of citta (a cetasika)

citta-mudutā pliancy of citta (a cetasika)

citta-passaddhi tranquility of citta (a cetasika)

citta-pāguññatā proficiency of citta (a cetasika)

citta-ujukatā uprightness of citta (a cetasika)

cuti-citta death consciousness

dāna generosity, giving

dassana kicca function of seeing.

dhamma reality, the natural law, the Teaching of The Buddha

dhammārammaṇa any object which can only be experienced through the mind-door

dhātu element, any reality

diṭṭhi wrong view

diṭṭhigata sampayutta accompanied by wrong view

domanassa unpleasant feeling

dosa aversion or ill-will (a cetasika)

dosa-mūla-citta citta rooted in aversion

dukkha vedanā painful feeling or unpleasant feeling.

dvāra doorway through which an object is experienced, the five sense-doors or the mind-door

dvi-pañca-viññāṇa the five pairs of sense-cognitions, which are seeing, hearing, smelling, tasting and bodily experience

ekaggatā cetasika one-pointedness which makes citta focus on one object.

ghāṇa-dhātu nose element

ghāṇappasāda rūpa nose-sense

ghandha odour

gantha bond, a group of defilements

ghāyana kicca function of smelling

gotrabhū change of lineage citta before jhāna or enlightenment is attained

hadaya-vatthu heart-base

hasituppāda citta smiling-consciousness of the arahat

hetu root

hiri Moral shame (a cetasika)

indriya faculty, leader

issā jealousy, envy (a cetasika)

jāti birth, class (of cittas)

javana impulsion (function of cittas) which "run through"the object

jhāna absorption, burning, developed in samatha or vipassanā

jhāyati it burns

jivhā tongue

jivhāppasāda rūpa tongue base

jīvitindriya life-faculty, (a cetasika or a rūpa)

kalyāṇa mitta good friend

kāma bhūmi sensuous plane of existence

kāmāvacara citta sense-sphere cconsciousness

kamma intention or volition; deed motivated by volition.

kammaṭṭhāna object of samatha bhāvanā

kamma-patha course of action, which is wholesome or unwholesome

karuṇā compassion (a cetasika)

kasiṇa disk, as meditation subject in the development of calm, samatha

kāya collection, body of rūpas or mental body, the cetasikas.

kāya-dhātu body-sense element

kāya-kammaññatā wieldiness of cetasikas (a cetasika)

kāya-lahutā lightness of cetasikas (a cetasika)

kāya-mudutā pliancy of cetasikas (a cetasika)

kāya-pāguññatā proficiency of cetasikas (a cetasika)

kāya-passaddhi tranquility of cetasikas (a cetasika)

kāyappasāda rūpa body-sense

kāya-ujukatā uprightness of cetasikas (a cetasika)

kāyaviññāṇa body consciousness

kāya-viññatti bodily intimation (a rūpa)

khandha one of a group, any conditioned reality, i.e. any rūpa, vedanā, saññā, saṇkhāra or viññāna

kiriya citta inoperative citta which is not kusala, akusala or vipāka

kukkucca Regret, worry (a cetasika)

lakkhaṇa characteristic

lobha attachment (a cetasika)

lobha-mūla-citta citta rooted in attachment

lokiya citta mundane citta

lokuttara citta supramundane citta which experiences nibbāna

lokuttara dhamma nibbāna and a citta or cetasika which experiences nibbāna

macchariya stinginess (a cetasika)

magga path, Eightfold Path

magga-citta path-consciousness, lokuttara citta which experiences nibbāna and eradicates defilements

mahā-bhūta rūpa the rūpa which is one of the four great elements of earth or solidity, water or cohesion, fire or temperature and wind or motion

māna conceit (a cetasika)

manasikāra attention (a cetasika)

mano consciousness, citta

mano-dhātu mind-element. The five-sense-door adverting-consciousness and the two types of receiving consciousness

mano-dvārāvajjana-citta mind-door adverting consciousness

mano-dvāra-vīthi-citta citta arising in a a mind-door process

manoviññāṇa dhātu mind-consciousness element. All cittas other than the sense-cognitions (seeing, etc.) and mind-element cittas

mettā loving kindness

middha torpor (a cetasika)

moha ignorance (a cetasika)

moha-mūla-citta citta rooted in ignorance

muditā sympathetic joy (a cetasika)

nāma any reality which can experience an object

natthika diṭṭhi wrong view that there is no result of kamma

n'eva-saññā-n'āsaññāyatana sphere of neither perception nor non-perception, the object of the fourth immaterial jhāna

nibbāna the unconditioned reality which is freedom from dukkha

nimitta mental image or sign

nirodha-samāpatti attainment of cessation of consciousness

nīvaraṇa hindrance, defilement

ñāṇa wisdom, understanding

oja nutriment (a rūpa)

oḷārika rūpa gross rūpa. Any sense-object or sense-base

ottappa blameless (a cetasika)

paccaya condition

pakatūpanissaya paccaya natural decisive support condition

pāṇātipāta killing

pañcadvārāvajjana citta five sense-door adverting-consciousness

(dvi-)pañca-viññāṇa citta sense-consciousness (seeing, etc.) There are five pairs

paññā wisdom or understanding

paññatti concept which makes known

paramattha dhamma absolute, ultimate reality

pāramī perfection, 10 pāramī

parikamma citta preparatory consciousness

pariyatti intellectual right understanding of reality

pasāda-rūpa sense-base (eye-sense, ear-sense, nose-sense, tongue-sense, body-sense)

paṭibhāga nimitta counterpart image acquired in the development of calm, samatha

paṭicca samuppāda dependent origination

paṭigha aversion, ill-will, dosa (a cetasika)

Pātimokkha rules for monks

paṭipatti direct understanding of reality, lit. reaching the particular (object)

paṭisandhi citta rebirth consciousness

phala-citta fruit-consciousness which experiences nibbāna as a result of magga citta

phassa contact (a cetasika)

phoṭṭhabbārammaṇa tangible object, experienced through body sense (hardness/softness, heat/cold or motion)

phusana kicca function of experiencing tangible object

pīti joy, (a cetasika)

puthujjana worldling, ordinary person

rasa taste

rūpa physical reality which cannot experience anything.

rūpa-bhūmi plane of beings where birth was the result of rūpa-jhāna, fine-material jhāna

rūpa-brahma-bhūmi fine material plane of existence

rūpa-jhāna fine material absorption

rūpa-khandha any rūpa, one of group of physical phenomena

rūpāvacara citta consciousness of the fine-material sphere, rūpa-jhāna-citta.

sabhāva nature, characteristic of reality

sadda sound

saddhā faith or confidence in wholesomeness

sahetuka accompanied by roots

sakadāgāmī once-returner, noble person who has attained the second stage of enlightenment

samādhi concentration or one-pointedness

samatha calm

sampaṭicchana-citta receiving-consciousness

sampayutta associated with

saṃsāra cycle of births and deaths

saṅkhāra dhamma conditioned reality

saṅkhārakkhandha all cetasikas other than vedanā (feeling) and saññā (memory)

saññā perception or memory

santīraṇa-citta investigating-consciousness

sasaṅkhārika induced by oneself or someone else, weak (citta)

sassatavāda diṭṭhi eternalist view

sati awareness (a cetasika)

satipaṭṭhāna awareness of a reality. It can be the cetasika sati or the object of mindfulness

sa-upādi-sesa nibbāna arahatship with the khandhas or "groups of existing" remaining

sīla morality, behaviour of cittas

sīlabbatupādāna wrong practice which is clinging to certain rules (rites and rituals)

sobhaṇa beautiful, accompanied by beautiful roots

somanassa pleasant feeling.

sota-dhātu element of ear.

sota-dvāra-vīthi ear-door process

sotāpanna noble person who has attained the first stage of enlightenment

sota viññāṇa hearing-consciousness

sukha-vedanā pleasant feeling

tadālambana/tadārammaṇa retention or registering, last citta of a complete process.

Tathāgata "Thus-gone", The Buddha

tatramajjhattatā equanimity or even-mindedness (a cetasika)

tejo dhātu element of fire or heat.

thīna sloth (a cetasika)

uddhacca restlessness (a cetasika)

upacāra access or proximity (concentration)

upādā rūpa derived rūpa, any rūpa other than the four great elements

upādāna clinging

upādānakkhandha any khandha which is the object of clinging.

upekkhā indifferent feeling or equanimity

vacī-viññatti speech intimation (a rūpa)

vatthu base, physical base of citta.

vāyo dhātu element of wind or motion.

vedanā feeling (a cetasika)

vicāra sustained thought.

vicikicchā doubt (a cetasika)

vinaya discipline for monks

viññāṇa consciousness

viññāṇa khandha aggregate of consciousness, any citta

viññāṇañcāyatana sphere of boundless consciousness, subject for the second stage of immaterial jhāna

vipāka citta (and cetasikas) which are the result of kamma.

vipallāsa perversion

vipassanā insight, wisdom which sees realities as they are.

vippayutta unaccompanied by.

viriya energy, effort, patience (a cetasika)

vitakka striking, directs the citta to the object (a cetasika)

vīthicitta citta arising in a process

vīthi-vimutti-citta process freed citta, citta which does not arise within a process.

voṭṭhapana determining consciousness

vyāpāda ill-will

yoniso manasikāra wise attention

25

Books by Nina van Gorkom

- *The Buddha's Path.* An Introduction to the doctrine of Theravada Buddhism for those who have no previous knowledge. The four noble Truths - suffering - the origin of suffering - the cessation of suffering - and the way leading to the end of suffering - are explained as a philosophy and a practical guide which can be followed in today's world.

- *Buddhism in Daily Life.* A general introduction to the main ideas of Theravada Buddhism.The purpose of this book is to help the reader gain insight into the Buddhist scriptures and the way in which the teachings can be used to benefit both ourselves and others in everyday life.

- *Abhidhamma in Daily Life* is an exposition of absolute realities in detail. Abhidhamma means higher doctrine and the book's purpose is to encourage the right application of Buddhism in order to eradicate wrong view and eventually all defilements.

- *Cetasikas.* Cetasika means 'belonging to the mind'. It is a mental factor which accompanies consciousness (citta) and experiences an object. There are 52 cetasikas. This book gives an outline of each of these 52 cetasikas and shows the relationship they have with each other.

- *The Buddhist Teaching on Physical Phenomena.* A general introduction to physical phenomena and the way they are related to each other and to mental phenomena. The purpose of this book is to show that the study of both mental phenomena and physical phenomena is indispensable for the development of the eightfold Path.

- *The Conditionality of Life.* This book is an introduction to the seventh book of the Abhidhamma, that deals with the conditionality of life. It explains the deep underlying motives for all actions through body, speech and mind and shows that these are dependent on conditions and cannot be controlled by a 'self'. This book is suitable for those who have already made a study of the Buddha's teachings.

- *Letters on Vipassanā.* This book consists of a compilation of letters on the Dhamma to Sarah Abbott, Alan Weller, Robert Kirkpatrick and other friends. The material used are tapes of Khun Sujin's lectures and conversations with her on the development of right understanding. She encourages people to develop the understanding of the present moment, since that is the way to the ultimate goal, namely, the eradication of the clinging to the concept of self and of all other defilements.

- *A Survey of Paramattha Dhammas* by Sujin Boriharnwanaket, translated by Nina van Gorkom. A Survey of Paramattha Dhammas is a guide to the development of the Buddha's path of wisdom, covering all aspects of human life and human behaviour, good and bad. This study explains that right understanding is indispensable for mental development, the development of calm as well as the development of insight.

- *The Perfections Leading to Enlightenment* by Sujin Boriharnwanaket, translated by Nina van Gorkom. The Perfections is a study of the ten good qualities: generosity, morality, renunciation, wisdom, energy, patience, truthfulness, determination, loving-kindness, and equanimity.

- *An Introduction to the Buddhist scriptures* with the aim to encourage the reader to study the texts themselves. In that way they can verify that the Buddha's words were directed to the practice of what he taught, in particular to the development of right understanding of all phenomena of life.

- *Understanding Realities Now: Nina's Travelogues.* Compilation of articles discussing the development of insight, the understanding of the present moment in daily life. It contains over 60 quotes from the original scriptures and commentaries.

- *Buddhism: Learning to understand life.* The purpose of this book is to help the reader gain insight into how Buddhism works to understand life. It is not mere theory, but it is to be applied right now, at this moment. The Buddha taught that all mental phenomena and physical phenomena which naturally appear in our daily life can be objects of mindfulness and right understanding. Available on Amazon Kindle only.

www.ingramcontent.com/pod-product-compliance
Lightning Source LLC
Chambersburg PA
CBHW031425160426
43195CB00010BB/610
9781897633427